Shakespeare's First Reader

MATERIAL TEXTS

Series Editors

Roger Chartier   Leah Price

Joseph Farrell   Peter Stallybrass

Anthony Grafton   Michael F. Suarez, S.J.

A complete list of books in the series is available from the publisher.

Shakespeare's First Reader

The Paper Trails of Richard Stonley

Jason Scott-Warren

PENN

UNIVERSITY OF PENNSYLVANIA PRESS

PHILADELPHIA

Published by
University of Pennsylvania Press
Philadelphia, Pennsylvania 19104-4112
www.upenn.edu/pennpress

Printed in the United States of America on acid-free paper
10 9 8 7 6 5 4 3 2 1

A catalogue record for this book is available from the Library of Congress
ISBN 978-0-8122-5145-6

Contents

Guiseppe Arcimboldo (copy after?), *The Librarian,* c. 1566? Slott, Skokloster, Sweden.

Preface

The painting by Arcimboldo known as *The Librarian,* which survives today in several copies, depicts a man who is made out of books. A crudely piled heap of large volumes roughs out the shape of a body, its bent arm made out of two hefty folios; gold-tooled bindings hint at a luxurious jerkin. Perched perilously atop this assemblage, a leaning tower of smaller volumes serves for a head, with a number of jaunty little books doing duty as nose, cheeks, and mouth. Higher still, an open book, its brilliantly white pages fanning out with luxurious abandon, evokes a shock of white hair. The fine details of the illusion are provided by a variety of appendages and add-ons: the painting is full of ribbons, clasps, and textile bookmarks that double as fingers, earlobes, nostrils, and flying locks. The spectacles are fashioned from the keys of book chests, while the beard is a duster made of animal fur. A black curtain draped over the whole thing becomes a stylish cloak, adding a touch of courtly refinement to this singularly odd-looking character.

The painting is a visual joke, a strained and perhaps a silly conceit. One's eye struggles to put the image together, to blur the stubborn rectilinearity of the books into the subtle contours of a human body, before giving up and enjoying the objects simply for what they are. It may have been a joke at somebody's expense, if the painting was, as has been suggested, a portrait of a particular person. More generally, the visual gag seems to be the literalization of a metaphor ("that man knows so much that he's practically made of books"), or just of a hunch that too much reading can make you a bit strange.[1] One recent commentary suggests that *The Librarian* may have been inspired by verses in Sebastian Brandt's *Das Narrenschiff* (*The Ship of Fools*) of 1494 that satirize "an ignorant dilettante for whom books are objects of desire rather than objects of study." This is the man who owns innumerable books but understands none of them, and who keeps them spotlessly clean (with his animal-fur duster) while scarcely turning the pages.[2] In this reading, the beauty of the books becomes rather barbed, since it suggests that they are designed for display rather than use. Tricked out in ribbons and bows, our bookman is an icon of superficiality.

Despite or perhaps because of that possibility, Arcimboldo's grotesque image has accompanied me during my research for this book, as a stand-in for my subject, the Elizabethan Exchequer clerk Richard Stonley, the first person known to have bought a printed book written by William Shakespeare, for whom no portrait is known to survive. This book reconstructs the life of Stonley through his library, exploring the intersections between his experience and the texts that he accumulated across the course of a long life that ended in his conviction for embezzlement on a massive scale and subsequent incarceration in the Fleet Prison. Since Stonley did not do anything so seemingly straightforward as telling us what he thought about the books that he owned, my task has been to put flesh on the bare bones of a pile of books—or to blur my vision to give them a human shape.

In the process I have been forced to question some of the values that Arcimboldo's painting may enshrine, according to which some interactions with books are "superficial" while others are "deep." Historians of reading have in recent years been getting more interested in "book use" and the wealth of things people do with books that do not involve an intellectual engagement with their content. They have increasingly paid attention to doodles in the margins, to evidence of ownership and transmission, and to all of the ritual and totemic ways in which the codex could be deployed. They have begun to attend to forms of "non-reading," the strategies by which people evade the written material that is foisted on them.[3] At the same time, anthropologists and cultural historians have taught us that the "superficial"—the outer layers, which according to our usual throwaway modes of thinking are to be unwrapped and discarded—demands our careful attention.[4] Arcimboldo's librarian, who wears his books like clothes, needs to be reconsidered in the light of this work.

In *Shakespeare's First Reader*, I challenge the tidy distinction between reading and book use, arguing that even the most fleeting encounter with a text (hearing it discussed, seeing it in a shop window) counts as a reading. To grasp this point, we need to think of the book as an object that comes swathed in layers of wrapping. A preface like the one you are now reading is just one of the many coverings that you have to peel off before you can fully engage with the content, content that will already have been intimated by the title, the cover image, the dust-jacket blurb, and many other physical and verbal cues. But, as the great theorist of the paratext Gérard Genette understood, any book radiates outward far beyond its physical body, not least via the channels of the publishing industry, in such phenomena as ads, reviews, and author interviews. Not all paratexts are contained in the book itself; in Genette's terms, we have to reckon with "epitexts" as well as "peritexts."[5] Books are interpreted by innumerable individuals who never turn their pages; they are read first and foremost not by readers but by the culture. This is not to deny that for some books, novels above all, a cover-to-cover, immersive reading is the point. But most of our textual engagements are not like that—few people would read a cookbook, for example, from beginning to end.[6] We need to admit our more fleeting engagements into our definition of reading in order to understand this central aspect of human culture.

One of the most underexplored aspects of our engagement with any book is the simple question of where we put it. What shelf does it sit on, and what sits alongside it? Which room does it live in, and what does that tell us about our choreography of the spaces that we inhabit? How does it connect up with its locale? *The Librarian* is full of clasps and ties and flying loose ends; Arcimboldo's mannequin is strung together from the material linkages that were part of the furniture of the early modern book. Like bookbindings, these appendages tied a book to itself, but (like bookbindings) they also served to tie the book outward, to its wider environment. *Shakespeare's First Reader* turns these material mechanisms of attachment into a metaphor for thinking about how books work to link people, places, and things. "Reading" is partly a matter of how we use objects to put our worlds together, and sometimes to pull them apart again too.

A Note on Conventions

I have modernized the use of *i/j* and *u/v* in all direct quotations from English sources, and have silently expanded contractions wherever possible. All dates are new style.

References to Stonley's journals (Folger Shakespeare Library, MS V.a.459, 460, and 461) are given in abbreviated form by volume and folio, thus: "459/ 60r." References to unlocated books in Stonley's library supply details of the earliest surviving edition and provide a reference to the numbering adopted by the *Private Libraries in Renaissance England* project (http://plre.folger.edu). Stonley's inventory is identified by *PLRE* as "Ad4," and so "Ad4.1" indicates the first item in the inventory, a copy of Holinshed's *Chronicles*. Stonley's journals can be consulted online via the Folger Shakespeare Library's digital image collection, LUNA.

Material Readers

When, in George Eliot's *The Mill on the Floss*, Maggie Tulliver confronts the stark consequences of her father's bankruptcy, the superiority of her nature shines through in her dismay at the sale of the family's books:

> Her eyes had immediately glanced from him to the place where the bookcase had hung; there was nothing now but the oblong unfaded space on the wall, and below it the small table with the Bible and the few other books.
>
> "Oh Tom," she burst out, clasping her hands, "where are the books? I thought my uncle Glegg said he would buy them—didn't he?—are those all they've left us?"
>
> "I suppose so," said Tom, with a sort of desperate indifference. "Why should they buy many books when they bought so little furniture?"
>
> "Oh but, Tom," said Maggie, her eyes filling with tears, as she rushed up to the table to see what books had been rescued. "Our dear old *Pilgrim's Progress* that you coloured with your little paints; and that picture of Pilgrim with a mantle on, looking just like a turtle—O dear!" Maggie went on, half sobbing as she turned over the few books. "I thought we should never part with that while we lived—everything is going away from us—the end of our lives will have nothing in it like the beginning!"[1]

While Maggie's mother worries only about her initialed silver teapot with its stand (334), her "chany" (china) with "the tulips on the cups, and the roses, as anybody might go and look at 'em for pleasure" (328), not to mention her sugar tongs, Maggie's attention moves to the gap in the fabric of the room where the bookshelf used to be. But Maggie resembles her mother insofar as her reaction to the loss of her favorite things is unabashedly sentimental. Although the family retains its Holy Bible (a book that will prove to be immensely significant as the plot unfolds), Maggie laments the loss of the pleasurable Christian allegory of Bunyan's *Pilgrim's Progress*, a volume made more precious by her brother's coloring and by an illustration that makes the hero look like a turtle. Books here stand for religion and literacy, for the possibility of wisdom and goodness, but for much more besides: shared experience, shared jokes, and a tangible link back to childhoods that are receding all too rapidly. In Maggie's concluding sob, the disappearance of individual "things" is subsumed into a much larger loss—"every*thing* is going away from us—the end of our lives will have no*thing* in it like the beginning!" Her words suggest the power of objects to hold our memories and to secure our identities, providing anchors amid the flux of experience. As she loses her grip on things, Maggie is cut adrift.

Thanks to their physical resilience, books are potent carriers of personal associations and memories. Although their spines fade and their pages yellow with time, they have a tendency to endure on the shelves, serving as visible reminders of the circumstances in which they were first bought and read. Philip Larkin's poem "Love Songs in Age" conjures up a widow's music books—"One bleached from lying in a sunny place, / One marked in circles by a vase of water, / One mended, when a tidy fit had seized her, / And coloured, by her daughter." Opened again after many years, the books and the songs they contain allow "the unfailing sense of being young" to "spread out like a spring-woken tree."[2] Marcel Proust speculates that "there are perhaps no days of our childhood we lived so fully as those . . . we spent with a favourite book." But this retrospective sense of plenitude derives not from the text but from all the things that seemed at the time to distract us from it: "The game for which a friend would come to fetch us at the most interesting passage; the troublesome bee or sun ray that forced us to lift our eyes from the page or to change position; the provisions for the afternoon snack that we had been made to take along and that we left beside us on the bench without touching, while above our head the sun was diminishing in force in the blue sky; the dinner we had to return home for, and during which we thought only of going up immediately afterward to finish the interrupted chapter."[3] Such seemingly extraneous things stay with us, so that now, "if we still happen today to leaf through those books of another time, it is for no other reason than that they are the only calendars we have kept of days that have vanished, and we hope to see reflected on their pages the dwellings and the ponds which no longer exist."⁴ Like a taste or a scent, a book can bring the past flooding back.

Books decay over time, of course, and countless numbers have been lost. But they put up a dogged (or dog-eared) resistance to change that allows them to bear witness to distant times. James Joyce's story "Araby" begins with a boy's recollection of coming to live in a new house: "Air, musty from having been long enclosed, hung in all the rooms and the waste room behind the kitchen was littered with old useless papers. Among these I found a few papercovered books, the pages of which were curled and damp: *The Abbot* by Walter Scott, *The Devout Communicant* and *The Memoirs of Vidocq*. I liked the last best because its leaves were yellow."⁵ In the dank air, a flash of color— which is at once a visible color and the literary color of books that continue to communicate long after the worlds that gave them birth have passed away. This power of the book as witness has been pushed to an extreme by the photographer Yuri Dojc, in a project entitled *Last Folio*. Dojc was making portraits of Holocaust survivors when he was taken to see an abandoned school in Bardejov, on the border between Poland and Ukraine. The school was a time capsule: everything remained where it was left on the day in 1942 when the Jewish students were taken away to the camps. On seeing the building, his collaborator Katya Krausova recalls, Dojc became fascinated by the books. "The disintegrating tomes, the beautiful decaying spines, all the crumbling pages are mesmerizing. They speak volumes about those who never came back to read the texts, to explain, to teach, to learn from them."⁶ The felicitous wordplay of "speaking volumes" captures the miracle of Dojc's photographs, in which the brooding presences of Hebrew books become powerfully eloquent. They tell of loss and the evisceration of human lives, but they also come to seem like Holocaust survivors, things of flesh and bone rather than paper and cloth, guarding unspeakable memories.

The histories that lie buried in books are often traceless; purely personal associations that leave no physical mark. But books become more palpable "calendars . . . of the days that have vanished" when they are annotated by their owners. An act as seemingly straightforward as writing one's name and the date on a flyleaf makes the book part of a skeletal autobiography—why that book, for that person, at that time? A gift inscription marks a particular occasion and a particular relationship, and makes us wonder still more about the title in question—why *that* book, passing between those people, at that time? If the book is the gift of its author, it is known in the trade as an "association copy," but any kind of inscription creates an association that can reveal something important about the lives of those who made it. One of the most familiar kinds of annotated book in the West was the family Bible that was turned into a repository for lists of births, marriages, and deaths. This usage, which materializes Proust's sense of the book as a repository of past times, presumably evolved partly because Bibles were once prefaced with calendars marking out the red-letter days of each month.[7] It was eminently practical; if a family had no other books, it would have a Bible, and the durability of the volume would help to protect precious information. But it also had a powerful symbolic role, bringing together the human and the divine, and framing the family in the sight of God. When, in *The Mill on the Floss*, Mr. Tulliver asks his son, Tom, to write a declaration of abiding hatred for "the man as had helped to ruin him" in the family Bible, forcing Tom to sign his name beneath it, it is a terrible perversion of the traditional use of the Good Book.[8] This attempt to make the end of the Tullivers' lives have something in it like the beginning takes root in one of the few objects that escapes the sale of the family's property.

At the points where the lives of people and of books overlap, books can come to seem strange objects. John Milton offered one of the most eloquent accounts of that strangeness, writing against prepublication press censorship in *Areopagitica* (1644): "Books are not absolutely dead things, but doe contain a potencie of life in them to be as active as that soule was whose progeny they are; nay they do preserve as in a violl the purest efficacie and extraction of that living intellect that bred them." A book distils its writer's rationality, producing a quintessence of wit like the elixirs and waters that were manufactured in early modern households or sold by apothecaries for use as medicines, perfumes, or ingredients in cookery. The effect of the elixir is revealed in the next sentence to be nothing short of magical: "I know they are as lively, and as vigorously productive, as those fabulous Dragons teeth; and being sown up and down, may chance to spring up armed men." Writing in the thick of civil war, Milton draws on the myth of Cadmus to demonstrate the proximity of the pen and the sword, and the way that printed polemic fuels needless conflict. But the most remarkable twist in this skein of metaphors comes when the radical Protestant reaches across to the Catholic culture he reviles and turns the book into a sort of relic: "A good Booke is the pretious life-blood of a master spirit, imbalm'd and treasur'd up on purpose to a life beyond life."[9] This is one of the best accounts we have of the mysteriousness of the book as an object and the sense of desecration that can attend on its destruction.

If the book is the blood of a spirit, it occupies a privileged middle ground between the flesh and the soul; it shares the betwixt-and-between nature of man. This in part explains why the book can stand in for its writer, or can continue to be its writer after the writer is dead. On this account, the book is numinous and set apart from other material things. But if we are to understand the power of ink on paper, we also need to put the book back into the world of material things, albeit a world imagined as full not of absolutely dead things but of objects that might be conceived of as alive. This is the thought experiment urged on us by Jane Bennett in *Vibrant Matter*, a study that challenges us to reconceive our relationship with "stuff."[10] Instead of seeing humans as set on some lofty plane of being, a giddy height from which they manipulate the world and mold it to their will, Bennett suggests, we need to understand ourselves as material things among material things. Agency, or "vibrancy," is not a human or an animal privilege: humans do things, but so do storms and asteroids and bags of potato chips. Things do what they do both on their own and as part of larger systems, chains of object agency; so to think about the vibrancy of the book means thinking about structures of publishing, institutions of education, and the paper industry, to name just a few of the systems in which the book is embedded. For an example, we might ponder the development of the daily newspaper in the nineteenth century, which was dependent not just upon the invention of the mechanized steam press (replacing the manual labor of presswork) but also upon the replacement of rag paper with paper made from wood pulp (which was far more abundant). The reengineering of paper allowed the newspaper to happen. But the acidity of the new paper meant that it began to discolor and crumble after a few decades, making nineteenth-century materials a headache for conservators in libraries around the world.[11] Materiality bites, all the time, in ways that we frequently try to hide from our own view.

In coming to terms with the ontology of the book, we can also benefit from the work of the anthropologist Tim Ingold, who believes that we are prone to think far too abstractly about the world we inhabit.[12] In his account, material things may appear to be contained and self-sufficient, but they are actually always in dynamic relationships with their environments. Humans invest heavily in the idea of stasis—they create closed environments that put a brake on change—but what appears to be stasis is really flux. Books readily bear out this claim. Designed to preserve text, they sit on the bookshelves, achieving the feats of endurance that I described earlier. But their endurance is also change: as they persist, they gather dust, bleach in the light, dry out, feed worms. They start to look dated; more subtly but just as ineluctably their texts date, thanks to the shifting meanings of words, the volatility of intellectual currencies, the rise and fall of authorial reputations. While they are changed by the world, books also change the world, effecting revolutions of thought and perception or (more locally) transforming their owners, turning them into magicians who sell their souls or dukes who neglect their dukedoms. Even when a book appears to be doing nothing, to be simply part of the furniture, it remains intricately entangled in the world.

If we want to think about the materiality of the book, we need to attend to the circuits in which it moves. A desire to understand wider ecosystems is increasingly important to historians of reading, who often start from particular volumes preserved in libraries and seek to move out to understand the circumstances of reading, the when, where, and how. One of the seminal contributions to this field, the celebrated article by Lisa Jardine and Anthony Grafton entitled "How Gabriel Harvey Read His Livy," is important precisely because it stops us thinking about reading as a private, subjective act, enclosed (as it were) within the cranium, and re-embeds it in time and space.[13] When Gabriel Harvey read, he read as a professional reader, with other people, in particular historical circumstances, for clearly defined ends. Crucially, he had furniture (at least several very large tables to facilitate constant cross-referencing; at most a book wheel, an ingenious device that allowed the scholar to access multiple folio volumes at once). This account of Harvey's reading might transform our sense of our own reading, whether we are journalists or political aides scanning the latest government documents, or idlers flicking through the newspapers over coffee at the weekend. Reading always needs furniture, though that furniture may be a bed rather than a book wheel. Even if we are playing the modern, private, subjective reader, we have to be plugged into a particular set of circumstances for that style of reading to be possible.[14] Understanding what reading might have meant in different periods requires us to parse the changing relationship between texts and environments.

When she laments the loss of her Bunyan, what Maggie Tulliver misses above all is its record of a social interaction, the childhood jokes and games that anchor her life in a shared past. The book is remembered through its material features—funny pictures colored in with a child's paints—rather than through its text alone. It is a particular copy of *The Pilgrim's Progress*, not just any copy, that matters to her. We might think of this as a "material mattering," in which the book as a whole, in both its content and its physical appearance, signifies. Work in book history has drawn attention to the many ways in which (as D. F. McKenzie put it) "forms effect meaning," or in which (for Jerome McGann) bibliographic codes help to frame our interpretation of a text.[15] Yet for those of us brought up on modern reading, with its associations of privacy and intimacy, mediated by the relatively disposable paperback or e-book, it is still hard to put the physical book and the text together. In *Dreaming by the Book,* Elaine Scarry distinguishes the written arts from other forms, like music and painting, that work with sensuous materials: "Verbal art, especially narrative, is almost bereft of any sensuous content. Its visual features, as has often been observed, consist of monotonous small black marks on a white page. It has *no* acoustical features. Its tactile features are limited to the weight of its pages, their smooth surfaces, and their exquisitely thin edges. The attributes that it has that are directly apprehensible by perception are, then, meager in number."[16] For Scarry, there is nothing to see or hear in a book, which is above all a vehicle for the imagination. There is plenty to argue with here. Those with an interest in type design might baulk at the claim that the small black marks on the page are monotonous, and those who have explored the way in which the brain processes text, and who ascribe a significant role to subvocalization, will wonder at the idea that text has "*no* acoustical features."[17] Still, the passage makes sense in context, where it serves Scarry's larger point about the contrast between the sensuousness of the world we imagine when reading and the restrictedness of the medium that provokes that imagining. A similar point is made from a very different perspective when the textual critic Randall McLeod confesses that "I can't READ a book and LOOK at it at the same time." To start to see a book in its physical detail, McLeod has to abandon "The Missionary Position of Reading," turning it upside down and using an optical collator to compare the typesetting in two supposedly identical copies from the same edition.[18] For both Scarry and McLeod, the book performs a disappearing act when we read; it becomes a kind of non-object. Removed from society into a sphere of privacy, it represents an honorable exception to the things in the world. We might turn that idea inside out and say that a book is a paradigmatic object, in that centuries of refinement to the human and material hardware of reading have rendered it invisible. For the literate, the process of textual engagement is so fluent that it seems to lack a material substrate (we feel a jolt when a typo brings us back down to earth).[19] Books thus share in the subservience that Daniel Miller ascribes to material culture in general, a subservience that makes "objects" seem secondary to "subjects" when in fact the two terms are inextricable.[20]

Shakespeare's First Reader has its origins in my fascination with the strange material and immaterial nature of books as they appeared in early modern account books and household inventories. I had been immersing myself in these documentary sources partly because they offered interesting information about what people were reading (all those titles long forgotten, many of them now lost for good) but also because they set reading matter so provocatively alongside all the other matter in the world: the food and clothing, business and pleasure that go to make up a life. Reading these lists proved a disorientating experience, since it forced me to wonder how we could put the heterogenous worlds of the account book or the inventory back together again. I was aware that book historians had used these kinds of source to compile library catalogues, separating the bibliographical materials out from the flotsam and jetsam of everyday life, and releasing them into a higher sphere of intellectual or literary history. Comparably, when social historians explore such documents, they save the books until last; reading becomes the cultural icing on the economic cake, offering an insight into the "hobbies and pastimes" of the distant past.[21] For Renata Ago, books and paintings can be categorised as "immaterial things," luxuries that float free of the world of material necessity (the original Italian text puts it slightly differently, but equally starkly, distinguishing "i beni dello spirito" from "i beni del corpo").[22] There is in all this a rage to separate and classify, to draw lines between different areas of culture so as to render the diversity of the account book manageable and meaningful. My own impulse runs counter to this. I want to blur the lines, to recombine body and soul in order to fully understand the textual cultures of the past. I want to use these dusty documents as a way of plugging the book back into its social and physical ecosystems, and so of coming closer to understanding what reading is.

In this I have been emboldened by early modern writers who delight in thinking across the boundary between books and things (with a pronounced emphasis on clothing and foodstuffs). John Lyly's *Euphues* (1578) opens with an epistle "To the Gentleman Readers" that compares a book to a flower in the hair of a gentlewoman, which will end up on the floor, or to a cherry that overripens; or to a fashionable garment that is "but a dayes wearing," as a book is an hour's reading. Sir Philip Sidney famously called his unpublished *Arcadia* "but a trifle, and that triflinglie handled," and urged his sister to look in it for "no better stuffe, then, as in an Haberdashers shoppe, glasses, or feathers."[23] John Heywood and Sir John Harington both wrote poems comparing books with cheese, largely on the grounds that both provoked spectacularly subjective judgments of taste.²⁴ The metaphor of the book as food was played out on a much larger scale in a masque performed in 1635 at the Museum Minervae, a newly established academy in Covent Garden for the sons of peers and gentlemen. Welcoming a party of royal visitors—Prince Charles, his brother James, and his sister Mary—the masque initially presented a table full of books. But the young royals were expected not to read the books but to eat them; opening them up revealed a banquet, made up of food that punned on the names of celebrated authors. Suetonius contained "a history of sweete meates," Aulus Gellius "nourishing strong gelly," Levinus Lemnius "Dried cand[i]ed Lemons."²⁵ Friar Bacon needed the least verbal wrenching to fit in. This was a mode of learning that supposedly used "sense" to "extract the sweetest quintessence" of learning.²⁶

The comparisons surveyed in the previous paragraph may strike us as somewhat bathetic, focusing on the way that literary texts might fall into materiality rather than allowing that there are genuine comparisons to be made between texts and things. The lame jokes that underpin the *Corona Minervae*'s book banquet look like precursors of those made on eighteenth- and nineteenth-century "dummy spines"—fake books such as those that lined Dickens's walls, bearing titles like *History of a Short Chancery Suit* (in twenty-one volumes) or *Cat's Lives* (nine volumes). One of the dummy spines on the library staircase at Chatsworth promised its reader *Pygmalion: By Lord Bacon*.²⁷ These examples are cited by Leah Price, who links them up with other groan-inducing puns on books and food:

> I lost my *Bacon* t'other day—could anything be harder?
> My cook had taken it by stealth—I found it in the *Larder*.²⁸

Price moves from bad jokes like this to critique the recent swerve in literary studies toward the consideration of the material book, offering a withering account of "the literary-critical profession on its trek from the abstract to the concrete."²⁹ The turn to "book history" is inevitably deflationary, as critics start to privilege "the mundane over the ideal, the local over the transcendent, the concrete over the abstract." High theory once made literary studies something of a master discipline; now an oxymoronic "thing theory" threatens "to drag ideas into the marketplace, the mind down to the level of the body." "A dogged or even mulish taste for the mundane, the contingent, and the simpleminded finds its only aesthetic outlet in puns," as ideas of the marginal and the stereotypical are upstaged by real margins or real stereotypes.³⁰ By replacing ideas with things, the new materialism turns its practitioners into dummies.

The witty survey that Price offers here prefaces a book about the representations of the material book in Victorian fiction, and hers is not the only attack on thing theory that paves the way for a new, improved contribution to thing theory.[31] Still, it is worth emphasizing that the "trek from the abstract to the concrete" in literary studies and across the humanities has been anything but mundane. With its roots in the cultural turn of the 1990s, the material turn has produced a rich interdisciplinary ferment, sparking new conversations between critics, historians, anthropologists, museum curators, and (more recently) scientists. Studies in this area have not merely transformed our understanding of the past; they have challenged our sense of our own being-in-the-world, speaking to the most intimate of our everyday actions and transactions.

Among the most significant contributions to the material outpouring for early modernists are Juliet Fleming's *Graffiti and the Writing Arts of Early Modern England* and Ann Rosalind Jones and Peter Stallybrass's *Renaissance Clothing and the Materials of Memory*.[32] Both books propose that, far from experiencing the material as bathetic, writers in the past were much more at home with it than we have subsequently become. Jones and Stallybrass propose a genealogy of the transition to modernity, grounded in the (Protestant, imperialist, capitalist) subject's desire to imagine himself or herself as set over and above the world of objects, which have to be imagined as exchangeable and disposable in order to serve as vehicles of monetary accumulation in the marketplace.[33] Shaping the modern subject required the creation of the category of the "fetish" and the "fetishist," the person who is excessively and improperly invested in material things—invested in a way that makes investment of the capitalist variety impossible. The result of this intellectual dispensation is the world described by Daniel Miller, in which "either we desperately want to escape being material, or we spend our lives trying to accumulate more material, or, most bizarrely, most of the people I live amongst in London want to do both of these things simultaneously."[34] Dependency and disavowal are the stuff of modern life.

While it is hardly free from anxieties about the material (often based on Christian or Platonic versions of object disavowal), early modern literature is vehement in its determination to think through things. The metaphysical conceit is just one of many modes of metaphorical thinking that saturate the writing of the period. John Lyly's attempt to think through the material is not confined to a few metaphors in a prefatory epistle; the "Euphuistic" style is characterized in part by its relentless similitudes, which attempt to understand human affairs with reference to all of the bizarre phenomena in the Plinian book of nature. The Sidney who talks of his prose masterpiece as glass or feathers in the haberdasher's shop is the same Sidney who imagines poetic inspiration as a shower of rain falling onto a sunburnt brain (in the first sonnet of *Astrophil and Stella*), and who describes tragedy as the genre that "openeth the greatest woundes, and showeth forth the *Ulcers* that are covered with *Tissue*" (in the *Defence of Poesie*).[35] Early modern literature, like many other literatures, reminds us that the material is all we have; we can populate the cosmos with all manner of numinous entities, but if they are not made manifest in some this-worldly form, they will not register.[36] Or, to put the point more strongly, for those who are thoroughgoing materialists, we might say that the world offers us a range of materialities, some obvious (the stone that hurts me when I kick it), others so subtle and complex that we struggle to think of them as material (things such as consciousness, language, personal identity, and perhaps also, by extension, books). We need to be alert to the forms of alchemy that mediate between the former and the latter, for example by transforming an agglomeration of ink on paper into a cultural monument or a treasured possession. Reading literary texts is often a process of learning to care about the material, and to see that it is material; you cannot understand a detective story, or a novel, or *Hamlet* unless you keep an eye on the movement of things. It is in this sense a process of curation, in its etymological sense of *caring*. The material turn does nothing if it does not invite us to care more about things in the world, in part as a possible route out of the environmental impasse to which capitalism has now brought us.[37]

This book represents one such act of curation, applied to a single sixteenth-century life that left its primary trace in the form of account books and inventories. Richard Stonley was an Exchequer clerk under Mary Tudor and Elizabeth I, and he is (in historical terms) a minnow; only in 2016 did he acquire his own entry in the *Dictionary of National Biography*, the work of the historian Felicity Heal.[38] He was born, around 1520, in the Warwickshire village of Bishop's Itchington, where his father owned about sixty acres of land at his death in 1547.[39] Much of the village has now disappeared beneath the fields, partly as a result of another event that took place in 1547 in the nearby chapel of Chadshunt, where a "Picture and Ymage of [Saint] Chadde [was] broken downe and burnte," and lucrative offerings to the shrine ceased.[40] While Chad was falling, Stonley was on the make and heading for

London. We know nothing about his education, but by the late 1540s he had attached himself to William Petre, a secretary of state, who between 1535 and 1538 had been one of the overseers of the dissolution of numerous ancient monasteries, abbeys, and chantries in England and Wales. As a reward for his faithful service, Petre had been granted one of the Essex lands formerly owned by Barking Abbey, the manor of "Gyng Abbess" or "Yenge atte Stone," familiarly known as Ingatestone.[41] The stone in question was a "sarsen stone" boulder deposited by a glacier; Petre might have been charmed by its fittingness with his own name (the Latin "petrus" means rock), and that of his new servant.[42] In November 1549 Stonley was given a hundred pounds "in ready money" by Petre, "to be by hym delyveryd over to my Ladie"; thereafter he seems to have served Petre in a variety of offices.[43] It was presumably thanks to Petre that Stonley was installed, in 1554, in a job for life, as a teller in the Exchequer of Receipt. His relationship with his patron remained close, in the most literal sense; the property he acquired on Aldersgate Street, in the suburbs of London, was a stone's throw from Petre House. In the early 1550s Stonley married a widow, Anne Donne, who brought with her three sons, two of whom would go on to achieve positions of eminence, Daniel as an ecclesiastical lawyer and William as a physician.[44] If his Exchequer position brought Stonley into regular contact with courtiers, involving him in the financing of the political nation, his marriage brought him city connections, since Anne hailed from a family of Drapers, the Branches, who were based in the parish of St. Mary Abchurch. In 1557 he secured a grant of arms and in 1579 acquired a country estate at Doddinghurst in Essex, just down the road from Ingatestone and close to Branche family lands at Margaret Roding.[45] He sat in the parliament of 1571 for Newton in Lancashire, a place with which he had no obvious connection, and in 1574 was made a governor of the newly founded free school at Lewisham in Kent.[46]

To his contemporaries, Stonley might have registered as a "new man," a social mushroom who sprang up overnight and went from complete obscurity to the heights of wealth and significance. His job, a secure bureaucratic position with a guaranteed income, was the kind of post that many men spent their lives dreaming of. As well as benefiting from the fees that went with it, Stonley seems to have used some of the vast sums that passed through his hands to engage in moneylending and land speculation.[47] He accumulated property not just in Essex and London but also in Berkshire, Buckinghamshire, Kent, Oxfordshire, and Sussex. Such investments required a considerable outlay in legal fees, repairs to the fabric of buildings, and travel to visit tenants, not to mention the purchase of more material goods to bolster an ever-expanding status. One of the key sources for this study is a series of account books that show us a material world being assembled through ordinary and extraordinary expenditure. Besides his lands, Stonley invested in books, acquiring a library of perhaps around five hundred titles—not an enormous collection to rival those of contemporaries such as John Dee and Matthew Parker, or of still more ambitious 'universal' collectors like Hernando Colón, but likely among the largest English collections of its day.[48] The journals allow us to see him buying books from day to day, often hot off the presses. Shakespeare's poem *Venus and Adonis*, the author's first published work, was one.

All of these goods would later be dispersed. In his old age Stonley was convicted of having embezzled a spectacular sum of money—just under £13,000—from the Exchequer, and was incarcerated in the Fleet. For him, these events spelled the collapse of the social role that he had sustained for more than four decades; for us, they are the amber in which an Elizabethan fly was caught. The other key source for my book is an inventory that shows the contents of his London townhouse being priced up for sale, and in the process documents the book collecting in which Stonley had been engaged for several decades. His was an extraordinary library. Like many in the period it was very heterogeneous: the bulk was made up of religious works, including fifteen Bibles or part-Bibles (roughly 38 percent of the whole), alongside substantial holdings in classical and modern literature (11 percent), history and geography (9 percent), moral/political philosophy (8 percent), and law (8 percent). But the collection was startlingly new in its inclusion of so much vernacular literature (55 percent of the books were in English, where in other contemporary libraries the figure is less than 10 percent).[49] Still, in this document the books are not allowed to steal the show; like the account books, the inventory sets them alongside the flux of material culture, a wealth of domestic furnishings in a house that was stuffed with stuff. Book historians long ago separated out Stonley's booklist from his inventory so that it could become an object of independent analysis. My book brings the two back together, exploring the role of the material text in the life of an Elizabethan household.[50]

Stonley probably died in prison. His life must have ended in a howl to echo that of Maggie Tulliver—in his final years, everything was going away from him. It is not true that we have no first-person expressions of pain from his pen (our knowledge of his date of birth comes from a document of 1585 in which he complains that "I am now in case to begge in my old Dayes . . . being now lxv yeres olde").[51] But we do not have the benefit of a nineteenth-century novelist to provide a three-dimensional, psychologically nuanced rendering of the loss Stonley suffered. His books are comparably recalcitrant; of the two dozen volumes known to survive today, dispersed in libraries across the world, only one bears readerly annotations in his hand, and those are fleeting. To understand his life and his reading will therefore require a more roundabout method; indeed, it will require us to follow a series of paper trails. For the notion of the paper trail, I am indebted to the work of the late Lisa Jardine, who throughout her career delighted in the construction of resonant and moving historical narratives based on links and connections that had all of the delicacy and fragility of the archival documents on which they were based. Jardine showed a generation of scholars how to bring together an interest in literature with an understanding of pragmatic transactions and power relations, by pursuing social and political life into its minutest capillaries, where so much of the action is.[52] Inspired by this approach, my chapters move paratactically through the evidence, exploring the relationships that surround the archival and bibliographical record and reconstructing the processes underpinning apparently innocuous textual phenomena. As a scholarly genre, the paper trail foregrounds the materials—the books and documents—from which an argument is constructed, often ranging them in the order in which they were first encountered, with all of their gaps and occlusions (the conceptual equivalent of torn-out pages or missing volumes) open to view. This is a mode that, while it appears crudely empiricist, demands imagination, as it forces us to abandon our comfort zones in the already known and to listen for stories hidden in the interstices.

In this book, what the paper trail discloses is a network or circuit that brings texts, people, and objects into a dynamic set of relationships. I am indebted to Bruno Latour, as recently remediated by Rita Felski, for a methodology that feels adequate to the concatenations of people, places, and things that are the focus of my interest. Drawing on the actor-network theory adumbrated by Latour in such studies as *Reassembling the Social*, Felski's *The Limits of Critique* imagines a literary criticism focused not around the unmasking and demystifying of texts but instead on *attachments*—the ways in which works of literature connect up with readers, affective regimes, and many kinds of institution, figuring as "nonhuman agents" that take their place in wider assemblages.[53] By adopting a "flat ontology" in which people, objects, and texts are equal players, Felski hopes that we shall find a way to acknowledge the power of texts, their ability to "make friends" (like people in a social network) and to reconfigure the circuitry of the world.[54] While my book does not respond to all of the challenges of Felski's manifesto, it profits from the fecundity of the notion of attachment as a way of thinking simultaneously about chains of objects, interpersonal relationships, affective investments in texts, and the things that people do to books when they cut and paste their contents.[55] The idea of attachment offers a powerful counterweight to the "detachment" that we sometimes believe we enjoy in relation to the world of things.

My study sets out from Stonley's purchase of *Venus and Adonis* on 12 June 1593, asking why it is so difficult to treat this as anything more than a literary-historical trifle, and unmasking the "trifling" as a category precisely designed to trivialize the presence of poetry, and other goods, in the market. To challenge the logic of the trifling, I begin to limn a mode of material reading that works through the attachments between *Venus* and the other items entered into Stonley's accounts on that day, including buttons, fashionable leggings, and another printed book, John Eliot's *Survay of France.* Disrupting our standard narratives of literary history simply by dint of his age, Stonley also forces us to reframe Shakespeare in relation to transnational literary cultures and to transnational trade. At the end of this paper trail, I show how the practice of commonplacing—probably the dominant mode of reading in the period—aligned reading with account keeping, turning texts into marketable wares.

Chapter 2, "Accounting for the Self," turns to a larger consideration of the journals within which Stonley's purchase of *Venus and Adonis* is embedded, exploring the nuances of their material form in relation to the rhetoric of bookkeeping, understood as a mode of specifically financial self-knowledge and self-discipline, a way of ruling in and regulating the self. Following a material trail that leads from the implements of Stonley's writing to the turnspits in his kitchens and the clocks on his walls, set in relation to representations of social disruption in the text of the daily entries, I adumbrate a notion of the account book as a way of ordering the world, a medium for materializing the subject as a disciplined and ordered object. The journals present us with "life in a box": as the self acquires property, it is produced as a property that can, at least notionally, be filed away alongside other objects in the household.

Chapter 3, "On Aldersgate Street," turns to the other key source for the life and library of Richard Stonley, the inventory produced when the contents of his house were sold off upon his imprisonment in 1597. This chapter begins where the last leaves off, with the self-as-object and the propensity of early modern mock inventories (whether they are offered in Shakespearean plays or popular broadsides) to include people in their lists of property. Again what is at stake is status or "estate," the material constitution of the self through its props and properties. With this in mind, the chapter explores the circumstances in which the inventory was compiled, with attention to its many gaps and occlusions, before taking us on a tour of the book-strewn household that it describes. Focusing on the anomalous presence in Stonley's bedchamber of an item described as "xj printes for pastery," I read his house as a textscape, in which visual and print cultures were densely intertwined. But if the house, through its pictures and its books, provided a series of windows onto the world, it was also a mirror, reflecting the aging of its owner in the fading of fabrics and the yellowing of paper. Finally, in its proliferation of books and boxes, the house modeled the self as a container and the book as a thing. Exploring his penchant for the ostentatiously commodified products of a new generation of "polygraphs," I suggest that Stonley was a new kind of reader, a product of the press in the first great age of vernacular publishing.

My fourth chapter, "People of the Book," focuses on the small number of books that survive from Stonley's library. Here I unpick the process by which Stonley took possession of his books, through rituals of inscribing and witnessing that were ubiquitous in book culture but are thinly understood today. Whereas we expect reading to point inward, to the self, Stonley's books direct us outward, to networks and connections: family members who patronized the same bookbinders, members of the book trade centered around Paul's Churchyard, and Catholic associates, who may or may not have been coreligionists, and who were on occasion persecuted for possessing the wrong kinds of books. I suggest that the layering of Catholic, Protestant, and "crossover" texts in the library that Stonley amassed points us in the direction of his layered and multiform religious identity. I go on to explore how the ownership of books might be understood as shared or devolved within the family, lingering in particular on a remarkable *Sammelband* signed by Anne Stonley as well as by her husband.

Chapter 5 follows paper trails that are also "Paper Travels," exploring the power of the book to cross physical borders and to facilitate the crossing of mental borders. The chapter offers a diptych, attending to two books that ought not to have been in Stonley's library—the first Giles Fletcher's *Of the*

Russe Common Wealth, which had been banned, the second a copy of the *Oeuvres* of Hélisenne de Crenne (the pen name of Marguerite Briet), which is not known otherwise to have circulated in early modern England. I read the first in relation to Stonley's family networks, which thanks to the recent expansion of English trade stretched as far as Moscow. Following a remarkable paper trail that leads us to a story of early modern technology transfer and tangled financial exchange, I show how the translation of materials between London and Moscow destabilized the distinction between civilization and barbarity, and threatened the supremacy of Elizabeth I, who was accused by the tsar of being subject to "boors and merchaunts" who sought not her honor but "there own proffit of marchandize." Hélisenne's *Oeuvres* have at their heart the story of a woman "completely ablaze with erotic fire," who speaks of her violent passions in a remarkably vivid first-person account. This is a tale of sexual errancy that prompts romance wanderings and ends up celebrating the mobile medium of print; it is one of a number of books in Stonley's library that became best sellers thanks to their pioneering of a new kind of urban realism in the vernacular. While we can only imagine how Hélisenne's narrative might have been read in Stonley's household, it is easy to see how it destabilizes an early modern literary history that continues to be divided on anachronistic national lines.

Chapter 6, exploring the purchase by Stonley on 8 May 1594 of "A Booke in Commendacion of the Ladye Branche," carries us still further into his familial networks. Venturing into the bowels of a rancorous family dispute, articulated via churchyard scoldings and accusations of witchcraft, it uncovers the print agency of Stonley's close relative Robert Nicolson, a merchant-reader whose procedures, for all their distinctiveness, were all about splicing himself into networks of family history and family property. Whether or not Stonley knew his younger relation, Nicolson's practices of reading and writing confirm that the material book was a key site for the cementing of familial and interpersonal relationships in this period.

Chapter 7, "Meet the Chillesters," carries our story forward to the events that led to Stonley's decline and fall in the 1580s and 1590s. The chapter is based on a curious coincidence—that Stonley owned two books by authors with the highly unusual surname Chillester. The first was a translation of a French mirror for princes, published in 1571, the second a pioneering anthology of poetry and prose fiction, published a decade later. Digging into these publications, I open up a fantastically seamy paper trail that links literary piracy with counterfeiting, lynching, murder, and extortion, and that leads directly to the door of Thomas Lichfield, the government informer who was pursuing Stonley for his peculation in a public office. The web of hidden agencies that underpins his reading matter thus turns out to be the trap in which Stonley was caught.

Finally, in Chapter 8, "Reading in the Fleet," I explore the motley community that surrounded Stonley in prison, where the networks of London life were crushed together into a universe of debt. Having begun to reconstruct the community of the Fleet, I pursue that community into the two books that we know he bought during his time there, the first a commentary on the biblical book of Proverbs, the second Deloney's work of rags-to-riches prose fiction, *Jack of Newberie*. To read in the universe of debt was, I show, to encounter a hall of mirrors in which the material underpinnings of early modern social life were repeatedly exposed to view. As his personhood dissolved, a few last books remained to remind Stonley of what he had lost.

As this summary suggests, *Shakespeare's First Reader* begins by exploring the key sources for Stonley's life and adopts a more biographical (or bio-bibliographical) mode of working as it proceeds, with familial and social networks coming to the fore. My shaping of the material is constrained by the fact that all of the key sources date from the end of Stonley's life; so this is a story focused on decline and fall, and on the 1580s and 1590s, rather than a more distributed narrative. My hope is that, as well as making its own methodological innovations, the book will encourage further exploration of a neglected body of materials: there are many more stories lying in wait here.

To begin, we need (of course) to go shopping.

Chapter 1

Shopping for Shakespeare

"With the Venus & Adhonay per Shakespere"

Our first paper trail starts in the Folger Shakespeare Library in Washington, D.C. Among its voluminous collections of sixteenth- and seventeenth-century books, there survive three volumes of manuscript journals that offer a detailed record of a life lived in the 1580s and 1590s. The volumes are somewhat erratic in their coverage, the first spanning a period from 15 June 1581 to 31 December 1582 in one hundred leaves, the second running from 14 May 1593 to 24 May 1594 in ninety-two leaves, and the last starting on 31 March 1597 and ending on 18 May 1598 in seventy-seven leaves. These small books are packed with text, penned in a crabbed hand that presents a challenge to the most accomplished readers of Elizabethan script. As one learns to decipher the entries, a daily round comes into view; we catch glimpses of the working, eating, and praying, the sociability and domesticity, the law-mongering and sermon-gadding, along with fragments of news and gossip. Names recur, limning a set of family relationships, daily meetings and partings, payments to servants, business partnerships. Records of purchases—of everyday items and more luxurious goods, of food and clothing and furniture, from shops scattered across London—abound, as do payments for services, since these are fundamentally account books, records of daily expenditure. In among the welter of names and dates and places, the eye alights on the titles of books nestling like gems among the variegated stuffs in the late Tudor shopping basket.

So much for the accumulation, the atoms of substance that come together in the ongoing process of forming a life. The process of dispersal is also represented, to some extent, in the journals, the last of which was written in the Fleet Prison. Not much gets bought or sold within the walls of the

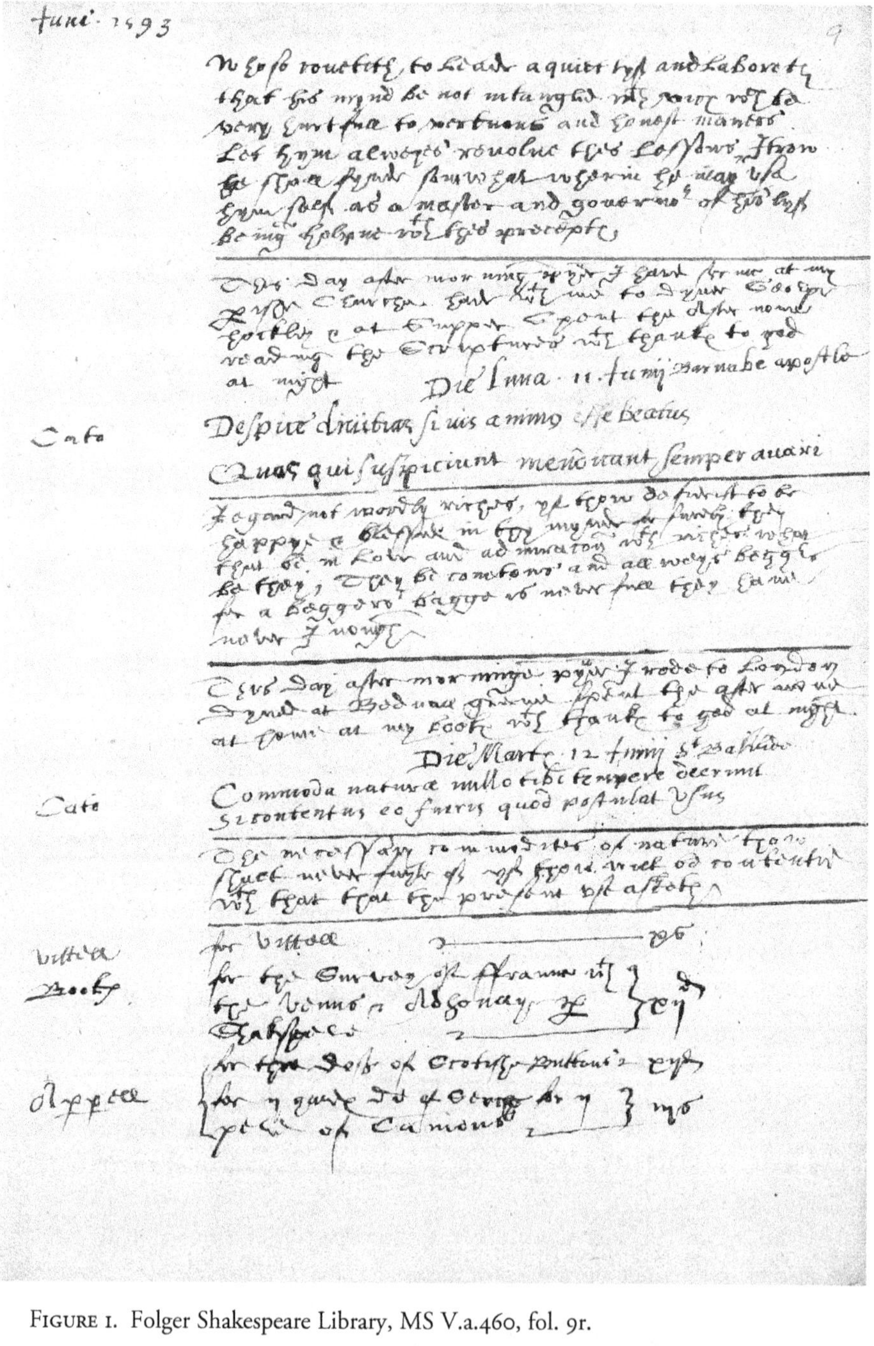

Figure 1. Folger Shakespeare Library, MS V.a.460, fol. 9r.

debtor's prison, but it is here that we get a clue to the identity of the journals' compiler, as a second writing hand—that of a prison warder signing off receipts for rental payments—appears on the page:

Received of Master Stonely for one weekes Chambre rent ended the sixt of maye 1598 xvs

Thomas Phillips   (3/75v)

"Master Stonely." The name is that of an elderly Exchequer clerk—a teller in Her Majesty's Exchequer of Receipt, to give him his full title—who had recently been sent to the Fleet for his failure to repay the huge sum (just under £13,000) that he had allegedly embezzled from the royal finances. The case against Stonley is laid out in full in an Exchequer Memoranda Roll, a lengthy document penned on parchment in an unflappable court hand and now housed in the National Archives at Kew, and in a series of shorter documents identifying debtors who are to be chased and landholdings that are to be sold to recoup the Queen's losses. The centerpiece of this legal outpouring is a huge list of household furnishings, headed "An Inventory of the goodes of Richard Stonley Esquier remayninge in his howse in the parishe of St Botolphe without Aldersgate in the Suburbs of the Cittie of london." Drawn up in 1597, the list offers a room-by-room sale catalogue of personal property, taking us inside a London townhouse at the very moment that it is being broken up forever. Like the journals, the inventory pours forth a cornucopia of material things—beds and bedclothes, chairs and tables, chests and pictures. But now the books are unavoidable—more than four hundred entries, evidence of a life that was crammed full of print.

From the point of view of literary history, Stonley has hitherto been the merest of footnotes. Interest in the man and his accounts has been confined almost exclusively to a single entry, a record of expenditure for 12 June 1593 (Figure 1):

vittell	for vittell ——————————————	x s
Bookes	for the Survey of Fraunce with the Venus & Adhonay per Shakspere ————————————	} xij d
Apparell	{ for thre dosen of Scotishe Buttons —— for ij yardes dimidium of Serge for ij pere of Canions ———————	xij d } iij s

vittell $\left\{\begin{array}{l}\text{for vittell} \rule{5cm}{0.4pt} \text{vjd}\\ \text{To Margery for vittell} \rule{3cm}{0.4pt} \text{ixs xjd}^1\end{array}\right.$

This is the earliest reference we have to the purchase of Shakespeare's first foray into print. *Venus and Adonis*, a cheekily erotic poem describing the flailing efforts of the goddess of love to woo a beautiful but utterly uninterested boy, had been licensed for publication by the archbishop of Canterbury on 18 April. Now, not quite two months later, it was on sale in the London bookshops, where it could be snapped up by anyone with sixpence to spare.[2] The work was destined to be a best seller, going through at least sixteen editions by 1636 and putting Shakespeare on the map of literary culture some years before his plays began to make a serious impact.[3] Stonley's journal entry, scratched in tiny, rapid letters, with plentiful use of contractions, puts him at the head of this torrent of popularity and gives him a claim to be considered Shakespeare's first reader.

Of course, the idea that we can identify "Shakespeare's first reader" is a simplification. Even if Stonley may have been Shakespeare's first reader in print, a work like *Venus* might well have been circulated in handwritten copies, distributed by the author (like his "sugred sonnets") among his "private friends."[4] Even if it wasn't, it is likely that Shakespeare made some sort of presentation copy of his poem for its dedicatee, the Earl of Southampton. If Southampton can be considered Shakespeare's patron, he would have a strong claim to be considered the work's first reader.[5] Publishers are readers too: so we might want to identify Richard Field, whose name (unlike that of the author) is privileged to appear on the title page, as another earlier reader of the poem.[6] (We could push this line of thought still further and say that the author is always the first reader of her or his own works). Then, of course, Stonley is not Shakespeare's first reader at all, but Shakespeare's first buyer—we have no evidence that he read *Venus and Adonis*, nor do we know what he made of it if he did. Finally, he is merely the first documented buyer, because there were probably others before him. The journal entry, itself a chance survival, was made by a professional accountant, someone for whom the writing of financial records was second nature. Bureaucrats are of course likely to be overrepresented in the archives. We might suspect them to be the sort of people who know the cost of everything and the value of nothing.

So much for the idea of identifying Shakespeare's first reader. But the category is in any case of no self-evident interest. Literary history does not follow the rules of *The Guinness Book of Records*. The *second* identifiable reader of *Venus and Adonis* was a soldier-turned-millenarian prophet named William Reynolds, who read the poem through the lens of his paranoid delusions and who seems to have believed that its narrative of attempted female rape was a coded commentary on his personal relationship with Queen Elizabeth I.[7] This fact has little bearing on critical interpretation of the poem. "So many men, so many minds," ran the proverb; doubtless a thousand crack-brained readings were fomenting in the grimy taverns of plague-stricken London. Perhaps reading is a kind of lunacy, a wildly subjective thing, unless it is trained by a literary education or brought within the confines of an interpretative community that will establish the rules of the game.[8] But in Stonley's case we do not even have the benefit of this ungovernable subjectivity—we have no subjectivity at all. Stonley's reading, if it ever happened, has succumbed to the fate of most reading, vanishing without trace. All we have is the bare record, the bleached bones of history. And something that we might roughly equate to a modern shopping list, the costing up of random bits of stuff. In the circumstances it is hardly surprising that nobody has known what to do with this archival gleaning.

The scholarly prehistory of our anecdote appears to confirm its insignificance. The Stonley journal entry first resurfaced on 7 May 1794, when the antiquary Francis Douce sent a rather formal, third-person note to the Shakespearean editor George Steevens at Hampstead Heath. The letter begins elsewhere, begging leave to inform Steevens about "a print of Uliespiegle by Hondius after Lucas Van Leyden, probably an imaginary portrait."[9] It then moves on to offer information that bears on Edmund Malone's recent efforts to establish the date of *Venus*'s first publication. "In a manuscript diary which has lately passed through Mr D's [i.e., Douce's] hands there is the following entry upon the *12th June 1593*." A transcription is immediately followed by an apology: "Mr Douce hopes that the opportunity which has offered of communicating this trifling piece of intelligence will be its best apology." It is perhaps surprising that such information could be described as "trifling" by a high priest of eighteenth-century literary antiquarianism, at a time when the chronology of the Shakespearean canon was a matter of considerable concern and the date of Shakespeare's first publication not yet firmly fixed. A piece of intellectual architecture that we take for granted was not yet in place, and as Margreta de Grazia has shown, a great deal hung on its successful realization.[10]

Perhaps the nonchalance that Douce exhibits here is strategic, masking his hope that the older scholar will be dazzled by a nugget of evidence so casually dropped. A surviving manuscript shows that he took extensive notes on the Stonley journals, devoting some effort to working out who had written them and to making sense of the activities they document.[11] Certainly, when an actual copy of the first edition of *Venus* finally turned up in 1805, nonchalance was in short supply. Malone bought it from the Manchester bookseller William Ford for what he called "the enormous price of Twenty five Pounds"—"so extravagant a price that I am ashamed to mention it."[12] However embarrassed Malone may have been, the volume (bearing the ownership inscription of the seventeenth-century Staffordshire gentlewoman Frances Wolfreston) remains the only surviving witness to the first edition and is now a treasure of the Bodleian Library. But none of this does much to help our literary factoid. To see it arriving in the world as an afterthought does not encourage us to linger over it.

Before we dismiss it, however, we might put some pressure on the idea of the "trifling" evoked by Douce as he offers "this trifling piece of intelligence." The trifling can of course be telling. "There is nothing so important as trifles" was how Sherlock Holmes put it, in "The Man with the Twisted Lip," when he noticed a telling difference between two shades of ink in the addressing of a letter.[13] Holmes's gimlet eye for detail is anticipated by Shakespeare's Iago, as he hangs the tragic plot of *Othello* on the wanderings of a handkerchief: "trifles light as air / Are to the jealous confirmations strong / As proofs of holy writ."[14] Equally celebrated is Autolycus, who announces himself in *The Winter's Tale* as "a snapper-up of unconsidered trifles." All three examples concern material things, and the power they can accrue in part because they are so easily belittled and overlooked.

A trifle is, first and foremost, an item in the market. When Autolycus calls himself "a snapper-up of unconsidered trifles," he elides his thieving and his pedlary, which is reliant on small things: "Lawn as white as driven snow, / Cypress black as e'er was crow, / Gloves as sweet as damask roses, / Masks for faces and for noses."[15] In the sixteenth century as much as in the modern world, small but pretty objects oiled the wheels of commerce. The *OED* derives the word "trifle" from the Old French *truffe* or the Italian *truffa*, suggesting (according to Florio) "a cozening, cheating, conicatching," or in the *OED*'s words "a false or idle tale, told (a) to deceive, cheat, or befool, (b) to divert or amuse; a lying story, a fable, a fiction; a jest or joke; a foolish, trivial, or nonsensical saying."[16] "The shades of sense cannot always be distinguished," the lexicographers add, but they have already sketched a set of highly suggestive relationships between the insignificant, the deceptive, and the literary. We might infer that the trifling is a commercial fiction: the kind of story the pedlar tells in order to sell his wares, or the fabulous ballads that Autolycus retails along with his pins and poking sticks. Our love of the tall story—of romances, fables, and fairy tales—is our love of the foolish and trivial, which is also our guilty, disavowed love of items in the pedlar's pack or the shopwindow.

For early modern Protestants, meanwhile, the word "trifle" was just one among several linked terms for describing the objects of Catholic religiosity: it took its place alongside "trinkets," "trumpery," and "trash" in a vocabulary of disdain.[17] In one utterly typical example, a broadside poem of 1641 unwrapped a bundle of Jesuitical trumpery, beginning with

A Trusse of Trinkets, holy Crosses, beades,
Religious Reliques, Ave-Maries, Creedes;
Our Ladies Image, Images of Saints,
That waxen Lamb, that the shav'd Priest depaints
By th'name of *Agnus Dei*, Indulgences,
Pardons, for veniall, and for foule offences.[18]

Such lists of Catholic artifacts sought to drive home the enormity of false religion, exposing its dazzling plenitude in contrast to the supposed unity and simplicity of the true church. Alliteration focuses iconoclastic energy; there is verbal pleasure to be had in banishing a "trusse of trinkets" or "the whole packe of the Popes pedlary wares." To itemize the rags of Rome was a way of leveling them down and emptying them out. The list confounds any effort to particularize by forcing so much stuff on the reader's attention in so short a time.

As James Kearney has argued, Shakespeare's Autolycus exposes the inter-twining of commodity culture and false, fetishistic religiosity when he criticizes the country folk for their susceptibility to his wares: "They throng who should buy first, as if my trinkets had been hallowed and brought a benediction to the buyer" (4.4.687–89).[19] When he reports that he has sold everything and has "not a counterfeit stone, not a ribbon, glass, pomander, brooch, table-book, ballad, knife, tape, glove, shoe-tie, bracelet, horn-ring, to keep my pack from fasting" (4.4.684–87), Autolycus recalls the Protestant dissections of Romish trumperies. The most deliciously ambiguous item in his pack is the "tawdry-lace," mentioned when Mopsa reminds the Clown that he "promised me a tawdry-lace and a pair of sweet gloves" (4.4.276–77).

Tawdry laces, from which our word "tawdry" descends, were silk neckties that were sold at Ely on 17 October, the feast of St. Audrey or St. Etheldreda. The seventh-century princess died of a throat tumor that she regarded as divine punishment for her youthful overindulgence in splendid necklaces.[20] The sale of tawdry laces in her memory looks like an object lesson in the barefaced cheek of the market, which finds ways of milking human vanity no matter what. But the lace was often understood as a devotional object, as when William Patten attacks that "very Antichriste the Bishop of Rome" for promoting a religion of "Pardon Beades, Tanthonie belles, Tauthrie laces, Rosaries, Collets, [and] charmes."[21] Tawdry lace thus blurs the line between trivial knack and soul-destroying trash.

The Winter's Tale suggests that Autolycus's trinkets are, like Catholic toys, things to be wary of. When Polixenes rebukes Florizel for failing to "load [his] she with knacks" from "the pedlar's silken treasury," Florizel responds that Perdita "prizes not such trifles as these are. / The gifts she looks from me are packed and locked / Up in my heart" (4.4.382–83, 391–93). A little later in the scene, Polixenes reveals his true identity and tells his son that he will be barred from the succession "if ever I may know thou dost but sigh / That thou no more shalt see this knack" (4.4.482–83). The angry patriarch, the materialist who would "load his she with knacks," is the man who proves capable of seeing the woman *as* a knack. Tawdriness, trifles, trinkets, trash—these trivializing terms represent stuff as it turns deceitful, papistical, leeringly commercial. But although the play may repudiate him, Autolycus proves to be a crucial mediating figure in the plot, which in the manner of romance depends upon trifling things—Hermione's mantle with "her jewel about the neck of it" (5.2.35–36), Antigonus's letters—for its resolution. There is no escape from materiality.

The idea of the trifling serves ultimately to inoculate us against our embroilment in a world of stuff. Those who fall for trifles are the quasi-idolatrous dupes of the market, who are being sold sex rather than love, false religion rather than true. Here we arrive back at the analysis of fetishism in the work of Ann Rosalind Jones and Peter Stallybrass, touched upon in my Introduction. To accuse the other of fetishism is a way of shoring up one's own "proper" approach to material things, which is (in the spirit of Protestant empire building) thoroughly detached and thus open to any opportunities that might arise to turn attractive things into liquid profits. This inheritance is compounded by what Daniel Miller has identified as the "somewhat unexpected capacity of objects to fade out of focus and remain peripheral to our vision, and yet determinant of our behaviour and identity."[22] The triviality of a journal entry showing a copy of *Venus and Adonis* being bought for sixpence derives from the ways in which philosophical, religious, and economic currents have conditioned our attitude to objects. Before it is a popular erotic poem or a major cultural landmark, the first edition of *Venus* is merely a trifle.[23] When it is just an item in a list, before it is read, it does not signify.

My aim in this chapter is to shape a kind of material reading, a thinking through stuff that recovers the life in the supposedly obdurate things juxtaposed in Stonley's account book. The collision of food, clothes, and books on Stonley's page looks banal at first sight, but pursuing the depths within and the connections between these items can change our sense of the book and its place in early modern culture. If understanding reading means understanding its circumstances, as my Introduction proposed, then material things are among the most basic and significant of those circumstances. To see the significance of Stonley's journal entry means confronting our impulse to belittle goods in the marketplace; which means reading it in a spirit of attachment rather than detachment. By the term "attachment" I hope to capture a receptivity to material things and an attitude to texts (as proposed by Rita Felski) that acknowledges past and present investedness in them, rather than standing by in a pose of disinterested or disenchanted critical objectivity.[24] I also use the term to suggest the relations between things that are brought, however fleetingly, into proximity, and so come to exert a mutual influence. We are all familiar with the effect of a still life in which the juxtaposition of objects creates a dialogue between them, a set of resonances that invites us to see them as a meaningful assemblage. Here I read Stonley's journal entry as a transient and accidental still life that transforms its individual elements, revealing congruities between superficially dissimilar items—such that Shakespeare's Ovidian poem undergoes its own metamorphoses.

Textual Attachments

To begin with, we should note that the list itself provides a material metaphor for attachment, since one of the six entries that Stonley made on 12 June 1593 was for the purchase of "thre dosen of Scotishe Buttons," costed at twelve pence. A button was in the early modern period one of the most dismissible of material things. The phrase "not worth a button" was commonplace, and you could upbraid a triviality by saying "tush a button."[25] Button making was among the homeliest of "mechanic" trades, and button makers were regular targets of satire in attacks on Protestant nonconformity.[26] Yet buttons are culturally revealing objects that are capable of infinite variety. "In their making they reveal our impulse to enhance even the most familiar and minute details of everyday life, and in their collecting they represent our ever-present desire to find the extraordinary in the commonplace."[27] Books that promote button collecting as a hobby tend to begin in the eighteenth century, supposedly the "golden age" of button making, and to skip over the time "five hundred years ago" when "you could tell status and wealth at a glance by the materials and workmanship of a person's buttons," and when "buttons might cost more than the clothes they adorned."[28] Like so many material things, like the material in general, buttons are at once trivial and important.

Quite what was distinctive about Scottish buttons is not known. The only qualitative statement that I have been able to uncover comes from a passage in Thomas Dekker's work *The Batchelers Banquet*, which discusses the "trouble and vexation of mind and body" caused to a husband whose wife is pregnant: "She must have Cherries, though for a pound he pay ten shillings, or greene Pescods at foure Nobles a pecke: yea, he must take a horse, and ride into the Countrey, to get her greene Codlings, when they are scarcely so big as a scotch button."[29] Exactly what we should infer from this about the size of Scottish buttons is not clear, but perhaps they were distinctively large. Although one struggles to find any reference to them in the literature on early modern Scotland, it is clear that Scottish buttons were an established commodity. A tailor named Thomas Ludwell, who had a shop in the parish of St. Antholin, Budge Row, that Stonley visited on several occasions, was employed by the court in 1568 to provide the Italian jester Monarcho with a new jerkin "of fine copper golde brayde doble gilte," adorned (among other things) with "two dossen and a half of skottyshe buttons of copper golde."[30] The account books of John Petre show that he paid twenty pence in 1585 for "2 dozen and a half of black Scotch buttons . . . for a doublet," while Edward Dering's accounts for December 1623 record a payment of thirteen shillings and four pence to one Sinolphus Bell for "3 grosse and 4 dozen of Crimson purl'd scotch buttons."[31] In 1598 a thief was indicted for stealing thirty-eight dozen black silk Scotch buttons, worth nine shillings, from Thomas Stone, mercer of London.[32] Taken together, these references show that Scottish buttons were a well-defined category and an exception to the rule that buttons were defined by their materials—pewter, glass, hair—rather than their place of origin.[33]

If the precise nature of Stonley's buttons remains somewhat elusive, their quantity is far easier to gloss. Stonley bought three dozen buttons because (as previous quotations have suggested) buttons and other attachments such as laces, ribbons, and points were needed in large numbers for early modern outfits. Stallybrass and Jones draw attention to "the myriad eyelet holes through which laces were passed to attach hose to doublet, sleeves to kirtle, busk to bodice, codpiece to hose, one part of a 'body' to another part to make 'a pair of bodies' (i.e. a bodice)."[34] They also note the growth in the number of buttons in men's clothing across the sixteenth century, as a result of which a jerkin might require five dozen buttons, a doublet four and a half dozen, a cloak two dozen.[35] Such figures had immediate social consequences, since they increased the importance of servants to the process of dressing and thereby expanded opportunities for the performance of hierarchy. They also point us to a fundamental feature of early modern clothing: its reliance on detachable parts. In this period, any outfit was a complex composite in which numerous elements joined together to form a whole. As well as creating endless possibilities for layering and customization, this dispensation facilitated the giving of separate pieces of clothing (think of Troilus's sleeve) and enhanced opportunities for "translation" or recycling.[36] It also suggested the possibility that identity might be a composite, a notion that became a mainstay of satirical representations of clothing. Considering her suitors in Shakespeare's *The Merchant of Venice*, Portia complains that Falconbridge, the English baron, cannot communicate with her, since he has no languages. But his clothing at least is multilingual: "How oddly he is suited! I think he bought his doublet in Italy, his round hose in France, his bonnet in Germany, and his behaviour everywhere."[37] Falconbridge's identity registers both as a deficit in attachment (his costume does not hang together) and as an excess of attachment (he comes from too many places at once). Such a critique, in a more muted form, could conceivably have been leveled at the identity that is created by Stonley's brief journal entry, thanks not only to his Scottish buttons but also to another transnational item bought on 12 June 1593: canions.

Canions were ornamental rolls worn below the breeches; their name, from the French *canon* and the Italian *cannone*, registered their resemblance to the barrel of a gun.[38] The earliest citation of the word in the *OED* comes

from Philip Stubbes's 1583 dialogue *The Anatomie of Abuses*, which includes
a survey of outrageous modern fashions.³⁹ There are several kinds of hose,
Stubbes's Philoponus explains; "some be called french-hose, some gally-hose
and some Venetians." Of the French hose, there are two kinds, one round,
the other narrow, "whereof some be paned [decorated by cutting into strips],
cut and drawne out with costly ornaments, with Canions annexed reaching
down beneath their knees." Here the references to "drawing out" and "annex-
ing" help to suggest the "wunderful excesse" of contemporary fashions, which
are (in Stubbes's view) at once ugly, impractical, and sinfully costly.⁴⁰

The fashion for canions was noted in print slightly earlier in France. In
one of the satires of Nicolas Margues, published in 1563, a critique of inflated
hose is followed by an attack on their extension:

> Et qui plus est d'une nouvelle ruse
> Pour mieux enfler, d'une seringue on use
> Et puis au bout en forme de canon
> La decoupure, à la brusque façon,
> Le taffetas tout autour du genou
> Peur qui soit veu, d'estre au iarret galou

> [And what's more, for a new trick to blow them up better, they use a
> syringe; and then at the base in the form of a cannon they cut out, in
> the newest fashion, taffetas all around the leg; afraid to be seen as flaccid
> in the haunch.]⁴¹

Margues anticipates the structure of Stubbes's attack, treating canions as an
outgrowth of the swelling abomination of the hose and symptomatic of a
fashion pursued by poor blinded sots ("vous pauvres sots aveuglez") who are
oblivious to the threat of divine vengeance.⁴² Still heavier artillery was trained
on the canion in Henri Estienne's *Deux Dialogues du Nouveau Langage François,* the earliest surviving copy of which dates from 1578. Celtophile has been
away from France, so Philausone updates him on the changes that have been
wrought in language and clothing during his absence. These days, he says,
courtiers are never caught without cannons on their legs ("ils ne sont jamais
sans canons en leurs chausses"). But, lest this militaristic embellishment
should seem to blunt the claim that effeminacy is on the increase, Celtophile
should note that these cannons are made of silk, of velvet, of satin, of taffeta

("notez que ce sont canons de soye . . . de velours, satin, taffetas").[43] Celtophile is nonplussed by this and can only assume that his friend is talking about pistols covered in fabric. No, says Philausone, and what's more, these canons are made by tailors (cue an exasperated digression on the fact that "cousturiers" must now be called "tailors"). When Celtophile finally twigs that the mysterious "canons" are items of clothing, he asks what fly has bitten these clothiers, that they have to steal a military word for their fashions.[44] But Philausone has already warned him that the first rule for speaking like a courtier is to require neither rhyme nor reason in the words you utter.[45] A gentleman would be delighted to hear his tailor telling him that "this clothing arms you well." And perhaps these absurd new fashions in clothing and speaking are chiefly designed to relieve the superrich of their money.[46]

The shocking fashion for canions had reached England by the 1570s. In 1575 the court fool William Shenton was made a pair of "gascons" (hose) "with canyons with lyninges of lynen, wollen, cotten, heare, canvase, with pockettes, poyntes, silke garters: & a peire of nether stockes to them," while a "litle blak a More" received "a peire of gaskens . . . with canvase cotten heare pockettes of fustian and lyninges of fustian in the canons."[47] But canions seem to have been circulating in France at least a decade earlier. The strong implication is that they were a French invention that was rapidly taken up in England; thereafter they straddled the English Channel just as they bridged the gap between hose and stockings. Insofar as canions accentuated the upper leg, fitting tightly around the thighs, we might see their invention as part of a process that Ulinka Rublack has argued was integral to early modern clothing culture, toward "tightly sewn and shorter clothing for men," which "brought different parts of the body separately into view for the first time"—a trend that is also legible in the increased use of buttons. (Rublack quotes the anthropologist Claude Lévi-Strauss reminiscing about Lucien Febvre, who said that he wished his fellow historians would address "problems such as the origin and spread of the button," since he had a hunch that "the presence or absence of this item demarcated important ways of human behaviour.")[48]

Stonley had caught on to the vogue for tightness by 1582. The first volume of the journals contains a payment to Thomas Trotter for the charges of making a fustian doublet, and for "ij yardes of sylke lace for a pere of Canions" (price two pence). In volume 2, the reference of 12 June 1593 is the first of several in that year. On 20 June, Stonley recorded a payment "for ij yardes quarter di[midium] of Ashe Coller [color] durance at ijs the yard for canions to two pere of upperstokes of Lether" (11r); on 31 July, he paid "Peter" two shillings and sixpence "for a quarter of an elne of Taffate to mend the Canions of my hose with Lace," with another sixpence for "the workmanship" (20r); and on 8 December he purchased two yards of "Jenue fustian" for just over two shillings, "for ij pere of Canions for my hose" (45r). The materials Stonley chose were not always the most extravagant. Taffeta and lace hint at a courtly sheen, but serge and ash-colored durance would probably have looked relatively subdued. Meanwhile, "Jenue fustian" was fustian from Genoa, and was a name that mutated over time to give us "jean," from which our "jeans" are made. Stonley's canions might with some justice be said to be an avatar of modern jeans.[49]

The idea that the first reader of Shakespeare may also have been one of the earliest wearers of jeans is delightful, but it does not seem to bring us any closer to understanding Stonley's reading. How can we make the move from velvet to *Venus*, from canions to canon? How might the materials in our Elizabethan shopping basket illuminate literary culture?

Clothing the Book

Buttoning together England, Scotland, and France (with a bit of Genoa for good measure), Stonley's marketplace was a site of cultural bricolage. Putting together an outfit was a process of assemblage that involved a complex choreography of materials, measurements, and prices, many of which were recorded in the account book. Here is an entry for a doublet, paid for on 26 June 1581:

	for iij yardes dimidium of Silke Dutch	
	fustian to make a doblet at iijs	
	iiijd the yard	xjs viijd
Apparell	for one elne & half a quarter	
dublet	of Taffata Sarsnet at viijs	
	the yard to Lyne the sleve	ixs
	for iij yardes whit Lyning fustian	
	at xd the yarde	ijs vjd
	for Pyncking the same	[blank]
	for Silke & Buttons	[blank]
	The makinge done by Trotter[50]	

While Stonley may not have understood many of the secrets of tailoring (and tailors were notorious for showing off their wares in dimly lit surroundings, so as to dupe their customers), he was clearly aware of the different stuffs that were going into his doublet, and of the way that they would relate—here through the "pyncking" or ornamental slashing of the surface material in order to display the lining. Clothing appears repeatedly in the account book as a composite of materials and workmanship that yields a hefty expense at the end. In one of the most spectacular entries, stretching over three pages, Stonley spends more than £9 on three doublets (the most expensive of which, made of tawny satin, cost more than seventy shillings), a pair of black satin sleeves, a mourning gown, and a frize jerkin.[51] But this kind of bricolage was not restricted to clothing. An entry for a book could look surprisingly similar:

| Byble | To Mr White Stacioner for a new Byble all gylde with Silver Claspes the Bokes xvs xd the Claspes per oz j oz dimidium quarter vijs iijd the makinge iijs iijd in all | xxvjs vd[52] |

Like a doublet, a Bible requires raw materials, including expensive silver clasps, which join with the gold tooling and the cost of the original volume, plus "the makinge," to produce the finished article and the final price. There is a strong overlap between the textual and the textile, both of which fostered a culture of the composite.

This overlap should not surprise us. Scholars such as Alex Walsham and Helen Smith have shown us how early modern people wore their books, integrating small devotional volumes into their clothing, or have discussed the willingness of writers to reach for sartorial metaphors when discussing books—for example, by calling the printed volume "a black gown furred with white."[53] As usual, Rabelais comes up with the most pungent version of this kind of thinking, when he describes how Pantagruel went to Bourges to study law, "and sometimes he used to say that the law books seemed to him a beautiful golden gown that was bordered with shit. 'For,' he said, 'there are no books in the world so beautiful, so ornate, so elegant, as are the texts of the *Pandects*; but their border, to wit, the gloss by Accursius, is so foul, so unspeakable, and smelly, that it's nothing but sewage and sludge.'"[54] Books could be parts of one's clothing, or could resemble clothing, but this was also a period in which books *wore* clothes, being dressed in the same leathers, velvets, and embroidered fabrics that people wore on their bodies. Richard Sackville, third Earl of Dorset, whose attire regularly "dazzled the eyes of all who saw," had eight folio volumes bound up in red velvet stamped with his initials "R E D," identifying himself with the luxurious material covering of his books.[55] The clasps and laces that tied early modern books together were often color coordinated with the clothing of their owners; in extreme cases, such as the copy of *Eikon Basilike* to which Charles I's Garter ribbons were posthumously attached, there was a particularly clear exchange between the bibliographic and the sartorial.[56] It was even possible for books to sport buttons. In July and August 1649, the Ferrars of Little Gidding bound up large numbers of copies of *Eikon Basilike* to send for distribution by sale and gift in Virginia, Barbados, and Bermuda. Among the copies described in their accounts are three "in Vellome done by N[icholas] F[errar] with Silke strings and Buttons in Middell at—2 sh per [book]" and 197 copies that were "Stringed with Silke Ribbine of Severall Cullers and the small ones have strings and gould buttons: some in leather Blacke and some of the Smaller in blacke leather and Coullerd Vellome."[57] The textual relics of the martyred monarch hoped to cut a dash in the New World.

It is the composite, stitched-together nature of the early modern book that allows us to connect the texts and textiles in Stonley's journal entry for 12 June 1593. Looking back at his entry for binding a Bible, we might note that it refers to "the Bokes," not "the Boke." This is presumably because the Bible comprises two testaments, each of which is itself full of "books." The Bible is, for Stonley, a plural entity. But such plurality was by no means unusual:

Bookes	For the four bookes bounde up to gether in forrell [parchment] called youthes wytte et al —————————	xxd
Bookes	For the nosegay of Morall Philosophe iiijd the recreacion for weyfaringe men: the disputacion betwene the Gaylers wyf & the prisoners & The dolfull discourse of a dutch gentlewoman &c — vjd	xd

Bookes	For the Seven Sobbes of the Sorrowfull Sowle per William Hunnes with his handfull of Huny Succles and pore wydowes myte ———————	vjd
Bookes of utopia et aliis	For Sir Thomas Moores worke of Utapia with others in Past borde ———————————	ijs viijd[58]

Some of the books mentioned in these entries were published as composites. William Hunnis's *Seven Sobs of a Sorrowfull Soule for Sinne*, a popular devotional work for which the first surviving edition dates from 1583, promised on its title page to provide the text of the seven penitential psalms "framed into a forme of familiar praiers"; "whereunto are also annexed his Handfull of Honisuckles; the Poore Widowes Mite; a Dialog betweene Christ and a sinner; divers godlie and pithie ditties; with a Christian confession of and to the Trinitie."[59] Although the book is continuously paginated, each of the works in the collection has a separate title page, reinforcing the idea that you were getting more than one delectable duodecimo for your money. *The Nosegay of Morall Philosophie*, a translation of a French work by Gabriel Meurier, survives in a single edition from 1580, but "the recreacion for weyfaringe men" and "the disputac[i]on betwene the Gaylers wyf and the prisoners" appear to be lost.[60] The last work in this compilation, "The dolfull discourse of a Dutch gentlewoman," is also lost, but we learn from the Stationers' Register that it was itself a composite, published together with "*the harde Happe of Twoo Norfolke gentlewoman*" (hence Stonley's "&c").[61] *Youthes Witte, or, The Witte of Grene Youth Choose Gentlemen, and Mez-dames Which of Them Shall Best Lyke You*, published in 1581, was (as Chapter 7 shows) a book that could not make its mind up about how many titles it had, or about its contents. Stonley's "four bookes bounde up to gether" may be an attempt to guess how many parts there are to *Youthes Witte*, but it is also possible that the volume was bound with other titles. The latter must have been the case with his copy of *Utopia*, which was not included in More's *Workes* of 1557, but which was published on its own many times in different languages after its initial appearance in 1516.

Taken together, these volumes point to the importance of the compilation and the Sammelband in sixteenth-century book culture. The work of

Jeffrey Todd Knight and Alexandra Gillespie has done a great deal to make us aware that many early modern books were heterogeneous compilations in terms of their production, which were then gathered by their readers into still more miscellaneous assemblages.[62] The fact that books were usually sold unbound encouraged readers to bring works together in customized collections, and publishers seem to have played to this practice by creating pick-and-mix editions of authors such as Daniel and Spenser. In many cases, the act of compilation can be taken as an implicit form of interpretation. Each anthology creates a new set of circumstances and hence new horizons of interpretation for the works contained within it. Such practices might appear to be very different from those that related to clothing in the early modern period, since binding a book looks like a final and irreversible act, quite unlike the continuous processes of recreation that were made possible by textiles. But a great many compilations were temporary, and were created by rough-and-ready stab stitching or by homemade bindings; and there were other ways in which a bound book might be unmade.[63]

Viewed in this light, Stonley's journal entry for 12 June 1593 is notable partly for the way that it refuses to treat *Venus and Adonis* as a singular entity:

Bookes	for the Survey of Fraunce with the Venus & Adhonay per Shakspere	} xij d

Venus is an appendage, an add-on, to another book: John Eliot's *Survay or Topographical Description of France*. The entry presents the two books for a single price, preventing us from knowing exactly how much Shakespeare's poem cost for its earliest known purchaser. There is no evidence that the brace in his entry indicates that the two books would have been bound or stitched together, but the formula Stonley employs here ("for *x* with *y*") is anomalous. Usually, if he buys multiple books on a single day, he lists them in sequence under the same generic marginal heading ("Bookes"). Notably, the two works coincide in terms of their physical format—they are both quartos—and it is likely that, as a slight pamphlet consisting of eight folded sheets or twenty-eight leaves, *Venus* would have needed some kind of physical support, which might well have involved tacking it on to the much more substantial *Survay*.[64]

Although very few copies of the earliest editions of the *Venus* survive, it is striking that many of them have been bound into *Sammelbände*. Equally striking is the fact that these compilations are exclusively poetic in their contents. The sole surviving exemplar of the first edition, now in the Bodleian Library, joins Shakespeare's work with Giles Fletcher's *Licia, or Poemes of Love* (poems also dating, the prefatory matter suggests, from 1593). While the book is not in its original binding, both volumes are signed by a seventeenth-century owner, the Staffordshire gentlewoman Frances Wolfreston, and were probably conjoined from an early date.[65] A third-edition *Venus* of 1595 was once bound with a mouthwatering collection of poems, all published in the same year: Spenser's *Amoretti*, Daniel's *Delia* and *Rosamund*, Barnfield's *Cynthia*, Constable's *Diana*, and the Countess of Pembroke's play *Antonie* (a translation from the French of Robert Garnier).[66] A sixth edition of *Venus*, an octavo dated 1599, is bound in vellum with a 1600 *Lucrece* and several other works of poetry: E.C.'s sonnet sequence *Emaricdulfe* (1595), Thomas Middleton's *Ghost of Lucrece* (1600), and the semi-Shakespearean poetic miscellany *The Passionate Pilgrim* (1599–1600).[67] Another copy of the same edition survives in its original binding together with *The Passionate Pilgrim* and the *Epigrammes and Elegies* of Christopher Marlowe and John Davies. This last composite, now in the Huntington Library, was part of a cache of books rediscovered in a lumber room at Lamport Hall, Northamptonshire, in 1867—a haul rich in poetry of the 1590s, much of it probably bought by the blind Thomas Isham (1555–1605) or his son and heir, John (1582–1651).[68] Material attachment points us to readerly investment: *Venus* signals by the company it keeps that it is being read by a dedicated follower of fashionable erotic poetry. Taken together, these copies situate *Venus and Adonis* in the midst of a poetry craze. We might well want to situate Stonley's purchase of *Venus* in relation to that craze, as a purchase that (like buttons and canions) tells of his embroilment in the world of fashion.

That said, Stonley's purchase of "the Survey of Fraunce with the Venus & Adhonay per Shakspere" pulls Shakespeare's poem into a different kind of assemblage from these later poetic compilations. Putting the two texts together as he does feels distinctly uncomfortable for a modern reader nourished on the established literary canon. First, it undoes our sense of priorities. In his account-book entry, Shakespeare's poem plays second fiddle, and this in a society in which linguistic precedence mattered.[69] (It doesn't help that Stonley gets the title of Shakespeare's work slightly wrong, rendering "Adonis" as "Adonai," one of the Jewish epithets for God.) Second, the pairing presents a collision of literary with the nonliterary and (in retrospect) of the highly popular with the utterly overlooked. Whereas *Venus* went through numerous editions in its own day, Eliot's *Survay* was never reprinted after its first publication in 1592.[70] And whereas *Venus* has generated vast amounts of critical debate and discussion, the *Survay* has to my knowledge never been written about. The journal entry thus reproduces in miniature the challenge of Stonley's life records, and of a library that rides roughshod over generic distinctions. The heterogeneity here is also geographical: like Stonley's buttons and canions, the collision of Shakespeare and Eliot snaps us out of a closed focus on England, reminding us of the proximity of France in Elizabethan London and of the deep dependency of English publishing on imported and translated materials from its nearest neighbor.[71] Our sense of what *Venus and Adonis* might have meant begins to shift in a new field of force, a widened interpretative horizon. But is it possible to be more precise than this, and to say what becomes of *Venus* in these unfamiliar circumstances? To answer this question, we need to undertake the first-ever survey of *The Survay of France*.

Surveying France, Surveying Shakespeare

Although it was published anonymously, and entered in the Stationers' Register without any ascription, it is relatively easy to establish a publishing context for *The Survay of France*.[72] A copy of the book in Cambridge University Library has, pasted on the back of the title page, a unique printed dedication to Sir John Puckering from the author, John Eliot of Warwick.[73] Not much is known about Eliot, save that he was regularly employed by John Wolfe as a translator of French texts. Among these were news pamphlets, such as *Advise, given by a Catholike Gentleman, to the Nobilitie & Commons of France* (1589), a treatise on Christian warfare (Bertrand de Loque's *Discourses of Warre and Single Combat* of 1591), and a text offering spiritual advice to those afflicted by illness (Jean de L'Espine's *Sicke-Mans Comfort*, 1590). These works appeared soon after their initial publication in French, suggesting the conscious determination with which Wolfe was importing new materials for the English market. Eliot may have been commissioned by Wolfe to provide a work of French geography that would serve as a companion for readers keeping up with the latest news from France.[74]

For all the promises of pleasure on its title page, the *Survay* offers a very stripped-down account of the terrain it describes. It is essentially a gazetteer, which sets off from Paris and proceeds in a somewhat haphazard order around the capital and from the north to the south of the country. The entries routinely remark on the lie of the land, the quality of the soil, the strength of fortifications, and the character of the people. But there are plenty of places for which entries are straightforwardly enumerative, setting out spatial relationships and political dependencies:

> *Renes* the parliament seat for all *Brittaine*, standing on the river of *Vilene*, not farre from *Chambourg* and *Guerch*.
> *Rohan* an auncient house.
> *Guymenay*, descended of the marshals of *Gye*.
> *Nantes* uppon Loire, there is a chamber of accounts. In the territorie of *Nantes* are *Ancenys* upon *Loyre: Clipson, Montagne*, on the coast of *Poictow*.[75]

The parsimony of the *Survay* comes more sharply into view when we consider its sources. Eliot claims to be digesting the work of many authors, but the only source that he cites explicitly is François de Belleforest, whose massive *Cosmographie universelle de tout le monde*, building on foundations laid by Sebastian Munster, appeared in three volumes in 1575.[76] Explicit acknowledgments of Belleforest are confined to the first few pages, but it is clear that Eliot is heavily reliant on his work throughout.

We might compare the English translation with that of another adaption of the *Cosmographie*, the *Theatre Francoys* of the French cartographer Maurice Bouguereau, printed in Tours in 1594. Tom Conley has contrasted Belleforest's copia, his "rivers of words," with Bouguereau's "dry style," in which "fancifully motivated etymons are replaced by the description of the limits of the area and its chateaus, its bailiwicks, its presidial court, and its country seat; other towns, natural resources, *singularitez en ce pays*, and points of interest are enumerated: fountains, subterranean rivers, windmills, and paper mills; limestone formations and mineral waters."[77] If Bouguereau hacks Belleforest back to topographic essentials, Eliot is more savage still. Take, for example, their accounts of the city of Laon, in Picardy. Belleforest tells us its physical situation, speculates about its antiquity (or not), and sets out the terms in which Clovis established the bishopric of Laon in A.D. 500, before listing all of the bishops of Laon and the villages that lie within the bailiwick. His account occupies the best part of two folio pages.[78] Bouguereau reduces this to a single short paragraph, although he still manages to discuss the city's age and to name a few bishops.[79] Eliot gives us a single sentence: "The territorie of *Laon* is comprised betweene the rivers of *Ayne* and *Oyse*, whereof *Laon* is the cheefe town which standeth, it is a bayliwik wheron do depend *Soissons, Noyon, S. Quintin, Riemont, Coucy, Chauny, Guise, Peronne, Mondidier, Roye*."[80] Viewed comparatively, what Eliot gives us is the triumph of the spatial over the historical. The France of the *Survay*—a flourishing country replete with well-fortified towns, navigable rivers, and plentiful natural resources—exists almost exclusively in the present tense. Eliot mentions the ravages of civil war in his preface, but there are no references in the text itself. Nor is there any comment on the confessional difference of this land with its innumerable religious houses and holy shrines. Ideology gives place to neutral physical description. It is possible that this neutrality would have seemed novel and perhaps even fashionable to the book's first readers; the *OED*'s first entry for "survey" as a "a general or comprehensive view or look" dates from 1589.[81]

The priority of space in the *Survay* was driven home by the additional selling point advertised on the title page: the book came "with a new Mappe, helping greatly for the Surveying of every particular Country, Cittye, Fortresse, River, Mountaine, and Forrest therein." The map, which folds out to become four times as wide and twice as high as a standard quarto page, and which includes England as far north as York and Italy as far south as Rome, is an impressive piece of engraving. The work of the Flemish cartographer Petrus Plancius and the engraver Baptista Duetecum, it was imported from Amsterdam, where it was sold separately.[82] In England, Eliot's title page proclaimed that the *Survay* came *with* a map, but the order of significance might have been quite the reverse for its purchaser. Books, like clothes, could be taken apart. When Stonley bought John Derricke's *Image of Ireland*, a book originally accompanied by twelve or more woodcuts, he recorded it in his journals as "the discripcion of the Irishe men with the boke to the same."[83] Having bought the 1581 *Habitus variarum orbis gentium* of Jean-Jacques Boissard in a pasteboard binding for twelve shillings on 19 December 1582, he may have broken it up to make what the 1597 inventory described as "xj little pictures in frames of the fashions of strange Countries."[84] He might well have viewed Eliot's book as an adjunct to his map. In most extant copies of the *Survay* the map is nowhere to be found—a case of readerly attachment resulting in practical detachment.

Despite the seeming dryness of the *Survay*, early readers were attuned to its moments of strangeness and color. In the presentation copy for Lord

Keeper Puckering, an attentive annotator (perhaps Puckering himself) has gone through the whole text adding marginal crosses, lines, and manicules. This reader is by no means hostile to the book's enumerative aims—he or she adds numbers to the book's initial list of eight regions and parliaments. But the majority of the annotations seize on more curious details. They direct us to the "wood of *Treason*" near Paris, an oak forest where twigs sink in water like stones and where damaged oaks have ceased to grow, ever since "the treason (whereof it taketh the name) was there contrived" (B2v). They draw attention to a description of a stream near Blois that presages plague or famine if it overflows during the dog days (B4v), to the odd claim that Chartres cathedral "was founded long before the coming of Jesus Christ" (B3r), and to the legend that Mary Magdalene died at Sainte-Baume (L1r–v). Another surviving copy, now in the Bodleian Library, was annotated by Robert Burton.[85] The anatomist of melancholy was more interested in features of the terrain than was the annotator of Puckering's copy; he seems to have been reading for textual resources, prospects, and natural advantages, the lie of the land. But he too kept an eye out for marvels, including a gulf near Angoulême so deep "that there can no bottome be founde thereof, heretofore covered with swannes" (H1v), or another gulf in the Auvergne "whereinto casting a stone you shall heare a most wonderful noise and roring, which also in summer it maketh though nothing be cast therein" (I2v). Such singularities of nature were perhaps marked out in a Baconian spirit, as worthy of further investigation. Elsewhere, Burton challenges his author: when Eliot claims in his preface that the population of Paris numbers "many millyons," Burton adds "mentitur," "he lies" (A3r).

Early modern readers may have been more alert to the *Survay*'s pleasures than we can be today. Yet the *Survay* remains a recalcitrant text, because it is—like the account book in which it is embedded—basically a list. The case for thinking of lists as a fundamentally anti-literary form has been forcefully made by the critic Paul Tankard. Drawing on the work of Jack Goody, he argues that lists are "literate but pre-literary," the result of "a very early function of writing"; they stop us reading and start us counting, browsing, or skimming.[86] Making lists of books is (he suggests) a substitute for reading them, and tidy-minded listing is the enemy of the rambunctious creative imagination. "Non-fictional prose texts are often framed by list-like paratexts: tables of contents, running heads, indexes," but "lists are not natural adjuncts to literary texts," because their discontinuity clashes with the flow of narrative.[87] Even a professed listophile like Umberto Eco finds it hard to get excited about real lists. In *The Infinity of Lists* he offers a list of such lists: "The practical list can be exemplified by a shopping list, the list of guests invited to a party, by a library catalogue, by the inventory of objects in any place (such as an office, an archive, or a museum), by the list of assets in a will, by an invoice for goods requiring payment, by a restaurant menu."[88] But it is clear that Eco prefers the poetic list, the chance meeting of an umbrella and a sewing machine on an operating table, to its practical cousin. Robert Belknap's *The List* has more time for utilitarian lists—"how inviting to the imagination they can be, and how personal as well"—but still banishes them from consideration after the preface.[89] The nonliterary list is just a collection of things demarcated by a frame (such as "places in France"). It is unlikely to engross us unless we have an immediate practical interest in the things described. It is to be used, not read.

These stark distinctions are beginning to dissolve in more recent criticism of early modern literature, which is alert to the discontinuities of texts and to their propensity to break apart in the hands of their readers. Contrasting the codex with the scroll, Peter Stallybrass has argued that the book is a multiple-entry-point technology, which is in some ways a paradoxical vehicle for continuous narration.[90] Studies by Heidi Brayman Hackel and Bill Sherman, among others, have taught us that "book use" may be a more helpful category than "reading" for dealing with the variety of ways in which early modern readers approached their books, which could certainly include making indexes for fictional texts.[91] As Mary Thomas Crane and Ann Moss have reminded us, commonplacing was one of the dominant modes of reading in the period, partly because it eased the transfer of classical materials to a culture with radically different mores.[92] More recently, the work of Juliet Fleming and Adam Smyth has taught us to think of commonplacing as a kind of cutting and pasting, and as one version of the excerption (the detachment and reattachment) that is involved in all reading.[93] The Latin verb "legere" meant not just to read but also to gather, pluck, or select. So reading and listing may not be antithetical phenomena.

Of course, there is a kind of aptness, a fractal quality, to the fact that Eliot's *Survay* should be lurking in this entry from Stonley's journals, a list within a list. But it is an aptness that does not apply only to the *Survay*. As Sasha Roberts demonstrated, commonplacing was one of the key modes by which *Venus and Adonis* was appropriated by its early readers. Men who stole shreds from Venus's speeches in order to woo women were regular butts of satire. Yet while some readers turned it into an "erotic sourcebook," "others transformed the poem into grave sayings and wise *sententiae* on a range of topics, demonstrating in so doing how light literature could be used for utilitarian, even didactic purposes."[94] In manuscript miscellanies and commonplace books, as well as in printed commonplace books such as *England's Parnassus* and *Belvedere*, excerpts from *Venus and Adonis* were removed from their (often ironic) contexts in the poem and offered up as general truths about "Love" and "Lust," "Affection" and "Anger," "Beauty" and "Use." Shakespeare's poem plays, deliciously, with the fact that a speaker can use moral arguments to immoral ends; Venus spouts commonplaces like the devil quotes scripture. Yet by the same token, the poem (particularly in its couplets) powerfully engages its reader's instinct to whip out a notebook or table book to write down its nuggets of wisdom.[95] And in succumbing to this instinct and ranging its excerpts under commonplace headings, readers were turning the poem into a series of lists.

We cannot know that Stonley would have read his *Venus and Adonis* in this way, but it is likely that he did. This is partly because, as the next chapter shows, his journals were not just journals; they were also commonplace books, which testified to his daily reading of improving excerpts from the Bible and the classics. Further evidence of Stonley's investment in the culture of the excerpt is a payment of three shillings "for printinge of poesies with goldne Lettres upon vj Bybles," which made bookbindings into vehicles for moral edification.[96] But there is something more fundamental here too, which has to do with the kinship between the commonplace book and the account book. Commonplacing is the application of mercantile practice to texts. The commonplacing reader identifies a bundle of textual stuff—often aided and abetted by a marginal note, which serves as a label or a handle—and exports it to her or his own notebooks for later repurposing and recycling.[97] The partible and recombinant nature of early modern texts is another way in which they resemble textiles, discussed earlier. It also provides a link to the culture of food—to Margery and her "vittell," Stonley's other expense of 12 June 1593—since the process of transporting the textual extract was frequently figured as a process of digestion, which would ensure that the wisdom of the commonplace would lodge in the memory.[98]

The mercantile logic of commonplacing was rendered explicit by Francis Bacon, who in his *Commentarius Solutus* (a notebook dating from 1608) resolved to keep collections of undigested notes, as in "a Marchants wast booke where to enter all maner of remembrance of matter, fourme business, study, towching my self."[99] A second book would, like "the marchants leggier booke," allow "those thinges (which deserue it)" to be set down, and to "have Contynuance." Beyond that, Bacon planned to keep "seuerall title bookes" in which a servant would enter items "in order, and vnder fitt Titles."[100] His prescriptions model his notetaking on the practice of double-entry bookkeeping; Angus Vine suggests that this also conditioned his step-by-step approach to natural philosophy, which proceeds "from particulars to lower axioms, then to middle ones, each higher than the last until eventually we come to the most general."[101] Bacon's plans were put into practice (probably unwittingly) by numerous institutions that moved information from journals to ledgers, including the Royal Society of London and the Académie des Sciences of Paris.[102] They may also have influenced Thomas Hobbes's account in *Leviathan* of how thinking is like mathematics, a simple matter of the addition and subtraction of ideas. "The Latines called Accounts of mony *Rationes,* and accounting, *Ratiocinatio*: and that which we in bills or books of account call *Items,* they called *Nomina*; that is *Names*: and thence it seems to proceed, that they extended the word *Ratio,* to the faculty of reckoning in all other things."[103] And "when a man *Reasoneth*, hee does nothing else but conceive a summe totall, from *Addition of* parcels; or conceive a Remainder, from *Substraction* [*sic*] of one summe from another."[104] Whenever we add "I reckon" to some statement of our views, we are registering this similarity between accountancy and thought. And to talk about "telling" a story, or to call a story an "account," points up the deep interconnections between narrative and numeracy.[105] It is hard to sustain any hard-and-fast distinction between narration and numeration, reading and listing.

Love Songs in Age

If Stonley treated his *Venus* as a source of wisdom rather than (or as well as) of titillation, turning Adonis into Adonai, this may help us to absorb the most delightful and strange aspect of his journal entry, which is the fact that the first known purchaser of Shakespeare's poem was around seventy-three years old when he bought it. Although it was not unusual for people to live to an advanced age in this period, provided they survived infancy, Stonley was by the standards of his day a very old man.[106] (The very fact that he was in the city buying books in the summer, in a year in which, by his own tally, more than ten thousand Londoners died of plague, perhaps says something about his resilience.)[107] This is not at all the reader that we imagine when we attempt to make sense of Elizabethan textual culture today. A long-standing critical narrative puts the golden age of literature in the age of Shakespeare, Spenser, Marlowe, and Donne down to a surfeit of youth. In the theaters, drama was being revitalized by a band of university-trained playwrights who brought a new intellectuality to what had previously been a noisy, bodily performing tradition.[108] In prose fiction, a generation of writers including Lyly, Gascoigne, and Sidney compulsively reiterated the role of the prodigal son, whose bad example had been excoriated in the Latin dramas they had been made to read and perform at school.[109] At court, young men deprived of preferment were forced to turn their talents to the production of poetry, veiling their thwarted ambitions in sonnets.[110] Among the primary audiences for literature and theater was the ever-increasing body of young men who were at the "finishing schools" of the Inns of Court, and the swelling ranks of apprentices whose youth made them apt to seek entertainment beyond their workplace.[111] There is no place in these narratives for old men, who are usually cast as enemies of the literary imagination.

Fitting with this model, *Venus and Adonis*—"the first heir of [Shakespeare's] invention," according to the dedication—is a song in the key of youth. "Rose-cheeked Adonis," his face "hairless" (487), his years "unripe" (524), seems barely pubescent, the kind of sexually inexperienced boy that in early modern English could be called a "maid." Venus, as a goddess, is no spring chicken, but possesses eternal youth:

> Were I hard-favoured, foul, or wrinkled old,
> Ill-nurtured, crookèd, churlish, harsh in voice,
> O'er-worn, despisèd, rheumatic, and cold,
> Thick-sighted, barren, lean, and lacking juice;
> > Then mightst thou pause, for then I were not for thee,
> > But having no defects, why dost abhor me?
>
> Thou canst not see one wrinkle in my brow,
> Mine eyes are grey, and bright, and quick in turning,
> My beauty as the spring doth yearly grow,
> My flesh is soft, and plump, my marrow burning.
> > My smooth moist hand, were it with thy hand felt,
> > Would in thy palm dissolve, or seem to melt. (133–44)

The goddess is, or claims to be, protean: one minute a fairy, the next a nymph who can dance on the sand yet leave no print. One of the key elements in her persuasion to love is the carpe diem; she urges Adonis to seize the day and sow his wild oats while he can, since sex is a young man's game. When death misses its usual mark, "feeble age" (941), and lights instead on Adonis, the goddess does not spare the elderly in the curse she lays on love. "Sorrow on love hereafter shall attend," she decrees, and love will henceforth turn the world upside down by "teaching decrepit age to tread the measures." Love "shall be raging mad, and silly mild, / Make the young old, the old become a child" (1148, 1151–52).

We might infer from its disparagement of age and its louche subject matter that *Venus and Adonis* aimed to attract a youthful demographic; and according to Gabriel Harvey, it found it. Annotating his copy of Chaucer's *Workes* probably at some point between 1598 and 1601, Harvey noted that "the younger sort takes much delight in Shakespeares Venus, & Adonis: but his Lucrece, & his tragedie of Hamlet, Prince of Denmarke, have it in them, to please the wiser sort."[112] Stonley, as a member of the *older* sort, would seem to be a representative of the defunct order that erotic poems such as *Venus and Adonis* set out to offend or perplex. Katherine Duncan-Jones notes this incongruity, claiming that the poem was, for him, "an uncharacteristic purchase. Other books he bought in 1593 included two sermons by Henry Smith, anti-Catholic works by Richard Bancroft and Thomas Bell, and Hooker's *Lawes of Ecclesiastical Polity*." She goes on: "Stonley bought the poem, but possibly did not read it. He was attracted to it by its dedication [to the Earl of Southampton], for Southampton's guardian, Lord Burghley, was, as Lord Treasurer, Stonley's boss. He is unlikely to have shared Shakespeare's empathy with Venus's eloquent desire, for he was fond of such misogynistic maxims as 'Be thou not moved with the weeping words of the wife when she is angry, for a woman when she weepeth goeth about with her tears to work deceit.' Nevertheless, his habit of buying brand-new books and punctiliously recording his purchases is useful. It tells us that *Venus* was on sale by 12 June, and at the price of *6d.*"[113] All the signs line up—a devotion to the elderly William Cecil, rather than to his nineteen-year-old ward; a penchant for misogynistic commonplaces; and a "useful" habit of writing things down.

Yet it is not true to say that *Venus* was an uncharacteristic purchase for our aged reader. Among the books in his library, besides printed drama, in the form of unspecified "Enterludes and Commedies," were works by Gascoigne, Greene, Lodge, More, Whetstone, and (probably) Spenser, amid a host of European and classical "literary" authors. Stonley owned story collections by Painter and Bandello, jest books, emblem books, and translations of

Seneca's tragedies into English that have long been thought to be key to the development of Elizabethan drama. If his journals show Stonley buying books of theology and religious controversy, they also show him buying poetic miscellanies and catchpenny pamphlets in the latest style. (A few days after he bought *Venus*, he paid two pence for Nashean squib entitled *Bacchus Bountie*; allegedly written "By Philip Foulface of Ale-foord, student in good felloship," this was a scatalogical celebration of drunkenness that would have washed down well with the wine bought on the same day.)[114] Stonley was personally acquainted with Arthur Golding and Geoffrey Fenton, translators whose labors brought swathes of classical and continental literature to English readers (including Stonley himself), and he received a presentation copy of the 1562 *Woorkes* of John Heywood from the author. To think of his purchase of *Venus* as a mistake is to underestimate the capaciousness of textual culture in the period, and the variousness of the attachments that were licensed by that culture. (It is perhaps also to underestimate the liveliness of its jeans-wearing old men).

In this chapter, I have sketched a series of relationships between the things that Stonley bought on 12 June 1593, and in the process I have offered a sustained meditation on the relationship between textual and material culture in the period. Exploring the parallels between the material stitching and unstitching of clothes and books offers us a model for thinking about the human investment—by which word I mean to suggest both "financial outlay" and "investiture"—in texts. By putting *Venus and Adonis* back into the marketplace, we have begun to locate in it a malleability that is fundamentally mercantile, a matter of transmissible and exchangeable stuff. Though we might be tempted to reach for a tidy distinction between reading and book use, we might equally argue that what Stonley does as he pulls the poem into a new assemblage is already a kind of reading. Material choices, reframings, and reclothings of the text are powerfully interpretative and need to be recognized as such.

Of course, this endeavor to educe a material reading from the pages of an early modern journal is fraught with difficulty. The assemblage in question is partly a product of happenstance, and is troublingly evanescent—as evanescent as the commodity phase of an object, which comes to an end when it is removed from the marketplace and inserted into new circuits of ownership and use. We might argue that the list furnished by an account book offers us far too much interpretative liberty; as Belknap has suggested, "If the items display no obvious relationships, no discernible patterns, the brain will invent relationships, imposing some arbitrary order on the disorderliness of the material."[115] And we might worry that, for all our sensitivity to its textuality, we are taking the account book as some sort of transparent window on to the world (which, as the next chapter shows, would be highly problematic). These are reasons to be cautious, certainly, but they ought not to blind us to the logics revealed in Stonley's journals, which can do much to advance our understanding of early modern texts as things in the world.

Chapter 2

Accounting for the Self

Commonplace Selves

Scratch the surface of a piece of early modern life-writing and you often find the arts of accountancy lurking not far beneath. Samuel Pepys's diary was written up in a ledger book from accounts of his daily expenses, so that its record of each day's business and pleasure plays a set of variations on the ground bass of a financial record.[1] Matthäus Schwarz, compiler of the celebrated *Trachtenbuch*, or "book of clothes," in which he memorialized the numerous costumes that he wore between 1520 and 1560, was accountant to the Fuggers of Augsburg and the author of the first northern European manual on double-entry bookkeeping.[2] The account books of Benvenuto Cellini, who asserted his singular genius in a boisterous autobiography, still survive in Florence.[3] Thomas Whythorne, who recorded his more modest life story as a contextual frame for his manuscript "book of songs and sonnets," kept accounts for William Bromfield, lieutenant-general of the Ordnance, taking care to file different writings in "several boxes, in [his] counting house or desk made for the purpose, to the end that when I should be called to mine account I might the readilier find them."[4] When spiritual autobiography and diary keeping became widespread in England in the seventeenth century, economics offered a standard model for understanding the tribulations of the soul; many a devout Calvinist would refuse to go to bed until she had "call[ed] herself to a strict Account in every particular, that the Errours of every Day past might be avoided in those, that were to follow."[5] Other forms of inner life proved comparably receptive to the language of bookkeeping. In Sonnet 30, Shakespeare summons the "remembrance of things past" to an internal court hearing, "the sessions of sweet silent thought." But recollection rapidly turns into a kind of emotional accountancy, "tell[ing] o'er / The sad account of fore-bemoanèd moan, / Which I new pay as if not paid before."[6] Shakespeare was following in the footsteps of Sir Philip Sidney, who (in the guise of Astrophil) described how painful it was for a besotted lover to submit to "reason's audit," "and by just counts myself a bankrupt know / Of all those goods, which heaven to me hath lent."[7]

Taken together, these examples suggest that bookkeeping was in some way crucial to self-understanding and self-expression in the early modern period, and that it has a strong claim to consideration in the scholarly search for what Charles Taylor has called "sources of the self."[8] But the workings of the relationship between accounting and identity are as yet thinly understood. Account books have been mainly the preserve of the economic and social historian, searching for factual information about past lives. There appears on the face of it to be a good fit between the purpose for which the records were created—the bare enumeration of income and expenditure— and the needs of historians seeking raw data relating to prices, living standards, the development of markets, and the movement of commodities.[9] Inartistic, utilitarian documents taken up with the itemizing of dates, places, commodities, and prices, account books are not intrinsically readerly texts, and they offer little to tempt the literary historian. Nonetheless, the burgeoning of interdisciplinary interest in early modern autobiography and an increasing fascination with the history of the archive has rendered the project of understanding such life records more pressing.

One of the most important recent interventions in this field is Adam Smyth's book *Autobiography in Early Modern England*, which brings a literary critic's generic and linguistic attentiveness to materials that are usually left out of critical accounts of life-writing, including almanacs, commonplace books, parish registers, and account books.[10] Smyth innovates principally by leaving open the question of what might count as "autobiography" in the early modern period. While some would dismiss that term as straightforwardly anachronistic, a nineteenth-century coinage that necessarily distorts any older texts that it attempts to subsume, Smyth argues that its retention can be productive, so long as we are prepared to abandon many of our presuppositions about what autobiography might look like. The versions of self-writing that Smyth finds in the archives unsettle our assumptions in a variety of ways. Commonly, they have more to do with likeness than difference: they are less keen to assert the singularity of the subject than to find exemplary models or structural continuities with lives already lived. They are often fissured and fragmented, not making any clear differentiation between public

and private history and not troubling to create a narrative logic to give meaning to the succession of events. Particularly where they are found in account
books, these texts are more closely engaged with objects (things in the world
and their financial values) than with subjects (insofar as that term implies
subjectivity and inwardness). Finally, they are always in process, moving from
one form of record to another, rather than being planned and produced in a
singular creative act. Thus we might witness a fragment of autobiographical
text migrating from an almanac to an account book to a diary to an autobiography, sometimes over many years, with each of the different formats leaving
its imprint upon the trace of a life.[11] In Smyth's view, we need to learn to
respect the multiplicity of this writing, rather than trying to impose a false
unity on it, or to search for a "true" life that lies beyond its textual manifesta-
tions. We also need to recognize the significance of a text's materiality. Different configurations of ink and paper shape life-writing and are in turn shaped
by it.

The strength of Smyth's analysis is that it is radically open to the strangeness of writings that we habitually go to in the firm expectation that we shall
meet familiar forms of the self. The powerful sense of the first-person singular
that we encounter in the writings of Cellini, Montaigne, and Pepys is absent
from such works, so we need to recalibrate our expectations and to recognize
the role that genre plays in defining not only the ways that a self can be
expressed but also the versions of selfhood that are in play in a given period.
The underlying proposition here is that representations of the self, even at
their most individualistic, are socially constituted. As well as being elaborated
from sets of accounts, Pepys's diary is full of physical stuff, and money, and
social relations; it builds a sense of self partly by its willingness to record
personal opinion, but partly also through its relentless attentiveness to the
changing social status of the diarist and to his appearance as registered in the
eyes of other people. This means that, for all of his distinctiveness, arising
from his sense of himself as a curiosity, there is something communitarian
about the self that emerges from the diary that Pepys created. A century
earlier, Thomas Whythorne's "autobiography" offers a sense of the particular
predicament of its musician-author, but it also shows us how he rendered his
life predictable by assimilating it to certain set patterns: in childhood he was
childish, in adolescence he was adolescent, and so on. Whythorne's autobiography is steeped in proverbs and commonplaces, perhaps in part because of
his early association with John Heywood, a collector of proverbs, but also
because (as we saw in the previous chapter) commonplacing pervaded the

literary and intellectual culture of the period.[12] This matters to autobiography because, as the work of Juliet Fleming and Margreta de Grazia has shown, the commonplace was a form of discourse that bucks all of our assumptions about the privately owned and inevitably self-revealing nature of language and literature.[13] Commonplaces are often authorless, and are marked out by their iterability; they are also distinctively material, inscribing themselves on the mind only when (as Erasmus instructs) they are first inscribed on rings, knives, windows, and books. The "shared" self that Smyth begins to identify—a self distributed among people, things, and documents—is perhaps also the "commonplace self," a self that is not remotely concerned to vaunt its own singularity.

Richard Stonley offers a challenging case for thinking about the representation of the self in the period, since his journals are not straightforward accounts. Instead, as the last chapter hinted, they present us with an innovative hybrid that splices together elements of the account book, the commonplace book, and what we would now call the diary—a yet-to-be-invented genre in this period. Stonley's method was to commence each day with a heading, indicating the day and date. Next he entered a textual excerpt, copied by rote from a printed book. In the first volume these snippets were taken from the Geneva Bible; in the second and third they came from collections of proverbs and adages gathered by Erasmus and translated by Richard Taverner from the late 1530s.[14] Then, when his day had involved some expenditure, Stonley noted the details of his purchases, usually adding marginal categorizations such as those we have already seen for "vittell," "bookes," and "apparell." Finally, he added what we might think of as a diary entry: a short summary of the day's activities. This composite structure looks at first sight like an evolutionary mutation of the account-book form—the bare record of expenditure mutating and clambering up onto the shores of selfhood. Such a perspective has its attractions, but our curiosity about this amphibious life form is thwarted to some extent by the highly formulaic nature of the "diary entries" in the journals. Though there are many variations, major and minor, there is clearly an archetypal form of such entries for Stonley, which is something like: "This day after morning preyer I went to westminster kept ther till xj came home to dynner kept home all the Afternone at my bokes & so ended that day with thankes to god at night." The template, repeated hundreds of times across the journals, appears almost specifically designed to obstruct our desire to find subjectivity and individuality in the archive. There could be no better example of the distance that can open up between the first person and the singular in early modern writing. For the historian of reading, there is the additional opacity that comes from not knowing whether "at my bokes" means reading in general or what Stonley on one occasion calls "makinge up my Accomptes" (459/3r)—although, as the last chapter suggested, these two activities may not have been so different from each another.[15]

So much for the template, but what about the variations? The most obvious variation, which is itself formulaic, comes on Sundays, when Stonley usually claims not to have been "at my bokes" but instead to have spent the afternoon "readinge of the Scriptures."[16] He often takes care to chart his movements: day trips from home to work within the city, or longer journeys from his London townhouse to his estate at Doddinghurst in Essex, often with a stop for dinner at the home of his daughter Anne Heigham in East Ham. He makes brief notes on matters of business. Sometimes these record the mind-boggling sums that he was disbursing from the exchequer ("payd there m'm'cccliijli ijs to master Dale & others for gone powder" [459/15r]); elsewhere they document property transactions and keep tabs on legal proceedings ("This morning I went to Estham to mete May the goldsmyth at a Cort but his Stuard came not nether wold the Tenantes appere & ther for went home with his cumpany as he came" [459/6r]). In the summer months Stonley makes frequent reference to his having occupied himself "abrode in the feldes" (460/26r), gathering fruit with his servants. He often mentions his dining companions, and come the second volume he has adopted a practice of listing "Strangers at Dyner" and "At Supper" after his main diary entry. Christmas and New Year are particular social high points, with long lists of dinner guests and of gifts given and received. Very occasionally, usually where it is of practical import, Stonley will note the weather ("This day . . . I kept home by reason of the fowle wether" [459/75v]), and intermittently he reports an item of news or rumour ("This day yt was reported the L Treasorer was dead but after proved a false lye god kepe hym many yeres emonges us to the common weales sake" [460/57v]). Significant personal or public events are marked with a marginal manicule or pointing hand, for his own benefit or to direct the attention of an anticipated future reader.

It would not be fair to deny that Stonley intermittently ventures a personal opinion. When he writes "This day for lacke of service at our parishe Churche by our obstinate Curate I red the service at home to my famelie" (459/10v), he is clearly passing judgment on the inadequacies of a local churchman. When he registers the death of his patron Lady Anne Petre by commenting "she was a good almes woman lyved al hir lyf vertuously and so ended the same" (459/50v), this looks like a heartfelt personal tribute. As the shadows gather around him, Stonley notes that he has been "preparing to Answer all persons agenst this terme especially my L Treasorer who sercheth earnestly my doinges . . . yet a man [of] good nature & in thend sheweth much frendship to the honest mynded" (460/58r). Here he seems to be trying to convince himself about the probity of the man in whose hands his fate rested. Later, incarcerated in the Fleet, Stonley would be openly critical of Edward Coke, whom he described as "enve[igh]ing sore agenst [him] & denyinge the Allownce of all [his] peticions," because "though he knew the Lawes yet in this matter he understande not the course of thexchequer" (461/17r). He also spoke out against his mistreatment when his son-in-law Daniel Donne sent him word that his wife "continewed very sicke at my howse in Essex." "God helpe her & send us some conforte yf yt be his will," he wrote, "for yf my service were concederd as yt ought to be or yf her majestie knew yt I shuld be otherwise considered to my owne comfort & my frendes &c" (461/24v). Such intrusions of opinion are sometimes hedged about with modesty and references to "my Simple Judgement."[17] Still, the question remains: why, given that Stonley was able to state his point of view in this way, is the journal so frustratingly short on what we have come to recognize and value as the signs of selfhood? To think through this question, we need to read some guides to the art of accounting.

"Debitor & Creditor"

Among the books listed in the sale inventory of Stonley's goods as having been kept in his bedchamber, between Calvin on the Pauline Epistles and the works of Duns Scotus, is an entry for a volume entitled "Debitor & creditor," valued at two shillings.[18] Editing the inventory in 1949, Leslie Hotson ascribed this book to "Peele," meaning James Peele, and in this identification he was probably correct. Peele (d. 1585) was a member of the Salter's Company and clerk of Christ's Hospital, the school for the education of poor boys that had been established by Edward VI on the site of the former Greyfriars buildings on Newgate Street. He published two books on the subject of double-entry bookkeeping that were among the earliest vernacular works to propagate the method in England. The fact that Peele's son George would go on to become a noted poet and playwright has not been lost on critics exploring the intersection between literature and economics in the period.[19]

Peele's first manual, *The Maner and Fourme How to Kepe a Perfecte Reconyng after the Order of the Moste Worthie and Notable Accompte, of Debitour
and Creditour* (thought to have been published in 1554) introduced English
audiences to the multiple-notebook method that was a cornerstone of double
entry. A merchant following this method would need to maintain at least
three separate manuscripts in order to keep track of his affairs. The first was
the "Memoriall or booke of remembraunces," into which servants would
enter details of all incomings and outgoings as they occurred. The second
was the "Journall or daiely booke," a fair copy of the items recorded in the
memorial. Finally, there was the "Quaterne or great booke of accomptes," to
which entries were transferred from the journal, each being divided in two
and placed on facing "Debitor" and "Creditor" pages.[20] Peele's treatise then
went on to induct the student into the arcane language of double entry,
which turned the raw materials of trade into "debitors" and "creditors"
according to whether they been received or delivered:

Moneie is Debitor to remaine of the balaunce of laste yeares
accompt, for .viii. royals, at xv.s. the royall, amounteth to xxxvi
pounde, I saye. ◊ ————————————————————— 2 036 00 00

Norwiche Worstedes is Creditour by partable accompt,
betwene Thomas Thruston & me Fraunces Bond,
for xij. peces for a voyage into Normandy, at iij.
pounde the pece. ◊ ——————————————— 6 036 00 00[21]

These entries are found among the numerous ruled yet mostly blank specimen pages that Peele provided after his comparatively brief expository text,
to show how a bookkeeper's "great book" should look in practice. Still more
sheaves of blank ruled paper would roll off the presses in 1569, when Peele
came to recast his work as *The Pathe Waye to Perfectnes, in th'Accomptes of
Debitour, and Creditour.*[22] Now the main text was cast as a dialogue in which
a schoolmaster instructed a servant in the arts of accounting. If the long-
winded title of his first foray into print suggests a certain status anxiety, this
second publication was still more concerned to assert the value of bookkeeping and to insist on its relevance for a broad readership that might include
gentlemen and farmers as well as merchants. This is nowhere clearer than on
the work's woodcut title page, which depicts allegorical figures of Wisdom
and Science supporting an architectural surround, laden with armorial
shields, that gives pride of place to the figure of Fame, trumpeting human

16.

August.

¶Wiſdome and Science, Preuent Indigence.

¶ Practiſe procuereth perfection: Ia. Peele.

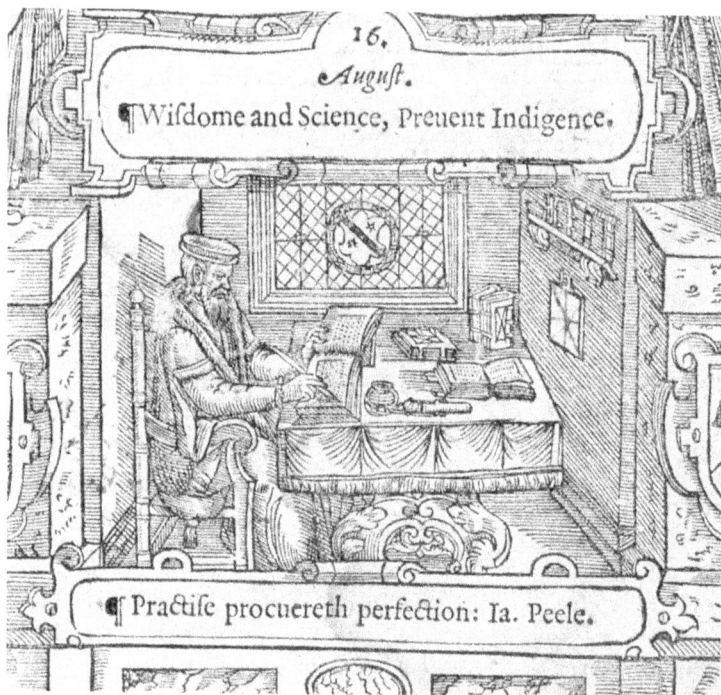

FIGURE 2. Title-page author portrait from James Peele, *The Pathe Waye to Perfectnes* (1569). San Marino, CA, Huntington Library # 80066.

virtues to eternity. But the most striking feature is hidden away at the bottom of the page, where a man is shown sitting at a desk, amid his books, casting up accounts (Figure 2). The window behind him has an armorial worked in stained glass, and the arms are those of Peele, suggesting that the image is a portrait of the author—still a considerable rarity in an English book at this time.[23] The early modern bookkeeper was potentially something of a celebrity.

Stonley's "Debitor & creditor" was most likely one of Peele's two manuals, though there is a rival candidate in the form of Hugh Oldcastle's 1543 work entitled *Here Ensueth a Profitable Treatyce called the Instrument or Boke to Learne to Knowe the Good Order of the Kepying of the Famouse Reconying, Called in Latyn dare et habere, and in Englyshe Debitor and Creditor.*[24] No copy of this manual now survives, but its text was reproduced in 1588 in *A Briefe Instruction and Maner How to keepe Bookes of Accompts after the Order of Debitor and Creditor* by John Mellis, who helpfully confessed in his preface that he was "but the renuer and reviver of an auncient old copie printed here in London the 14. of August, 1543."[25] Published for sale at a bookshop "at the North dore in Christes Hospital, next unto the Cloyster, going into Smithfield"—next door to Peele's place of work and a stone's throw from Stonley's house on Aldersgate Street—Mellis's recycling of Oldcastle reaffirmed the associations of this part of London with education in mercantile mathematics.

In practice, it does not much matter which of these books was in Stonley's library, since they overlap substantially in content and presentation, and they are all heavily indebted to the classic formulation of double-entry method offered by the Italian mathematician Luca Pacioli in his *Somma di aritmetica* of 1494. (Oldcastle's text was a direct translation, Peele's a paraphrase). Through them, Stonley wired himself up with the rhetoric and practice of double-entry bookkeeping, a technology often credited with the transformation of European capitalist economies and hailed as an invention of comparable significance to those of Copernicus and Gutenberg.[26] Bookkeeping might appear to be a purely practical art, a technique for managing the increasingly complex world of early modern trade. But recent studies have emphasized the rhetoric quite as much as the utility of double entry, understanding it as a form of impression management that aimed to confer an aura of predictability, transparency, and virtue on business dealings that were frequently uncontrollable, opaque, and (in the eyes of the church) damnable. According to James Aho, double entry emerges as a direct response to the prohibition of usury and the increasing insistence of ecclesiastical authorities on rituals of confession and penance. The new-model bookkeeping offered a form of self-scrutiny to parallel the newly intense internal auditing required of the Christian undergoing penitential confession. And in its insistence on openness and balance, double entry also appeared to demonstrate that the merchant who employed it had a clear conscience: "The appeal that the ledger makes as a rhetorical composition is that the business in question is honest and its profits just. How, it might be asked, can a written document lend credence to such claims? At a minimum, by being brief, concise, orderly, lucid, comprehensive, and above all, consonant with reality. Or, in Cicero's words: *brevis, aperta* (clear), and *probabilis*."[27] Crucially, double entry created a laborious system of internal self-ratification, requiring the accountant to check at regular intervals that entries in the journal had been correctly transferred to the ledger, and that the doubled credit and debit entries in the ledger answered to one another. This process of "balancing the books" offered itself as a display of rightness and righteousness, a simulacrum of order and justice.[28]

Commentators on the history of bookkeeping have called particular attention to the insistence of Pacioli and his followers—carried into practice in many surviving manuscripts from the period—that account books open with a genuflection. As Pacioli puts it, "Every business man . . . must always commence his affairs in the name of God, whose name must appear at the beginning of every manuscript, always bearing his Holy Name in mind."[29] The gesture reveals what is implicit in the apparently "neutral" and mathematical arts of accounting, which is their promise to bring the scandalously worldly into alignment with the divine. Aho finds account books that proclaim their transactions "a nome di dio Guadagnio," "in the name of God and profit"; or that begin by invoking the Virgin, John the Baptist, and all the saints in Paradise "that by their holy pity and mercy they will grant us grace for a holy, long, and good life, with growing honour and profit, and the salvation of our soul and body."[30] Such formulae pin their hopes on the possibility that divine favor and worldly prosperity might walk hand in hand.

Early modern accounting was a salutary fiction for a society struggling to adjust to the logic of capital, but it also helped to assuage anxieties afflicting the individual. Alongside the negotiation of moral and theological concerns about usury and greed there ran a strong current of concern for economic self-preservation. Account books were promoted as a means of acquiring a form of self-knowledge that was specifically financial. Their carefully cross-referenced and cross-checked entries gave the bookkeeper supposedly instantaneous access to the core of his being: his solvency. As the prefatory poem by "A.G." to the 1569 *Pathe Waye to Perfectnes* urges:

> Peruse this worthy worke then, pend by *Peeles* most painefull hand:
> And learne by just and trew accompt thy state to understand.[31]

"State" and "estate" become keywords in Peele's text, denoting at once "personal condition," "financial standing," and "social status," all of which are set out to view in well-kept account books. Peele's dialogue begins with a merchant approaching a schoolmaster and asking him, "Helpe me to renewe frendship betwene me and my selfe." Insufficient self-surveillance has resulted, we infer, in a kind of inner divorce. The merchant says he brings with him his "Estate: which I moste instantlye desyre you to peruse."[32] This "estate" is not a pile of possessions or of titles to property; it is a statement of the self's financial worth set down on paper, so that it can be inspected at a glance. As a later writer put it, "In an Instant [the compiler of the account book] can see (as he doeth his Person in a mirror) his whole estate and what posture it is in at the time."[33]

If financial self-scrutiny is cast as instantaneous, it is nonetheless the product of continuous labor. Accounting requires an insomniac, paranoid gaze, the kind of gaze that (in ancient Greek mythology) Hera employed to guard Io from the attentions of Zeus. "A marchant may be applied vnto *Argus*, which as Poetes shewe, had a hundreth eyes, so shoulde a marchaunt be circumspect in his businesse, worde and deede."[34] Close your eyes for just one moment and all might be lost; hence the urgent imperatives of Matthäus Schwarz of Augsburg: "Don't forget anything, write everything down; discover all you can about yourself and your situation."[35] Pepys regularly registered his anguish at his failure to keep up with his accounts, "so that I know not," he wrote, "what condition I am in the world," and expressed delight when he succeeded in balancing the books "to [his] heart's wish and admiration." There were times when he could scarcely bear to look at himself in such an unflattering mirror: "I have for this last half-year been a very great spendthrift in all manner of respects, that I am afeared to cast up my accounts."[36] But just as often there were reasons for celebration. Pepys frequently took the last day of the month, or of the year, as an opportunity to calculate his personal assets and to thank God for the growth of his estate.

As well as being many-eyed, the bookkeeper also needed to be sharp-eyed. To have their full rhetorical force, account books had to record every last detail. "Every *perticuler* man shold right well perceave upon presente viewe of his bookes, the state of all his thinges with all men, aswell generall as *perticuler*," writes Peele, echoing the title of Pacioli's chapter on double entry, "Particularis de computis & scripturis."[37] Jane Gleeson-White situates Paciolian method among a number of technical innovations of the thirteenth and fourteenth centuries "which emphasized precision, mathematics and the quantification of phenomena"—among them spectacles, maritime charts, perspectival paintings, and clocks.[38] As Smyth argues, "Perhaps the most fundamental lesson of financial bookkeeping was the need to attend to, to take notice of, the very smallest transaction; to give it consideration and textual space equal to the largest of sums; and to move, quickly, from part to total, from small to large."[39] Every penny and halfpenny had to be accounted for. This appetite for lynx-eyed observation is legible in the fastidiousness with which Matthäus Schwarz detailed the moments when he had his portraits painted, the measurements of his waist ("an astonishing 60 cm"), and the number of slashes on his extravagant outfits (which could be as many as 4,800).[40] While some of these details doubtless fed other technologies, such as astrology, it is hard to believe that they had nothing to do with Schwarz's practice as a ceaselessly self-monitoring accountant. If the financial account was "what truth looked like on the early modern page," that truth was in large measure secured by its accommodation of minutiae.[41] No purchase, however "trifling," was unworthy of note.

Although Stonley had probably read up on the double-entry method, his own account books are (like most account books kept in England at this date) single entry.[42] But they are nonetheless governed by rules articulated in the bookkeeping manuals. The use of multiple, interrelated manuscripts, for example, was not exclusive to double entry, and Stonley would have been familiar with an alternative yet equally elaborate system of cross-corroborated accounting from his work in the Exchequer.[43] To pay money into the national treasury required a laborious ritual that gave material form and solidity to the fleeting transaction. First, the teller noted the sum received into a book and recorded it on a strip of parchment (known as the teller's bill). This strip was then thrown down a pipe into a lower chamber known as the tally court, where the transaction was entered into two more books. Finally, the two deputy chamberlains of the court picked up their knives and mallets and struck a tally, a piece of wood on which the nature of the payment was recorded in writing while the sum of money involved was notated via a series of notches, rising in size from a scratch for a single penny to the width of the palm of the hand for £1,000. Once it was cut, the tally was split down the middle; one half (the "stock") was given to the payer, the other half (the "foil") retained and filed in the court. In any future reference back to the transaction the two halves of the tally could be reunited, like the parts of a legal indenture, offering an unfalsifiable record to corroborate the various paper accounts.

So forms of multiple documentation akin to those proposed by the double-entry textbooks would have been Stonley's bread and butter. And there is ample evidence that his journals were not static volumes, but were sites of transfer, of "textual traffic."[44] As we have seen, the accounting entries in the journal are distinguished with brackets and grouped under headings ("Lawe," "Almes," "Bote hire"). These headings allow different kinds of expenditure to be aggregated so that their extent can be gauged. Some of this aggregation may have gone on in a separate ledger, but the 1581–82 volume allows us to see it in action, since it includes a list of expenditure for 1581, which totals just over £253. A variety of items (unspecified) were bundled together as "Inventarye" (£63), and another group, perhaps of less permanent goods, as "Empcions" (£71).[45] Other significant costs were for clothing (£45), servants' wages (£43), building (£16), and law (£11).

These are the results of the exporting of entries, but the first volume of the journals also allows us to see the exporting taking place, since entries for the whole of 1582, from January to December, are struck through.[46] The manner in which they are deleted is telling. Instead of crossing through each individual entry in the accounts, Stonley deletes only his marginal headings, putting a diagonal line (or a cross) through the summary headings that categorize his purchases (Figure 3). Then, in the most extravagant graphic gesture in the journals, he swoops a vertical line through the various deleted headings, as if to certify that they have all been "processed." (While most of the deleted marginal headings referred to different kinds of expenditure, the first marginal heading of each entry supplied the locus for his daily textual excerpt, making visible the homology of moral/religious commonplaces and commodities.)

Stonley's crossings out follow the prescriptions of the bookkeeping literature. Oldcastle's manual recommended a "line overthwart" to cross out entries moved from the merchant's inventory or memorial to the journal, and elsewhere suggested that "yee shall launce or make a stroke in the manner as is saide before."[47] The crucial point was that, even when they had all been processed and deleted, entries had to remain fully legible, since legibility was crucial to maintaining the accountability of the account book. Medieval notaries could be cast out from their guild for defacing an account book, and in the eighteenth century excise men were warned not to "erase, deface, or alter any figure, letter, or character" in their minute books, "on pain of being discharged."[48] The same anxieties about tampering governed bookkeepers' dealings with white paper. To assure the integrity of his record, Stonley made frequent use of space fillers, usually in the form of a series of diagonal pen strokes at the foot of his pages (Figure 4).[49]

So much for transfers out of the journals; what about incoming traffic? How were these lists of expenses composed? The key point to make here is that the journals are *not* a rough draft, the equivalent of Pacioli's waste book, into which the merchant would enter "all his transactions, small or big, just as they happen to come to him day by day and hour by hour" in the *furia* of trade.[50] These manuscripts are on display, and accordingly they exhibit a high

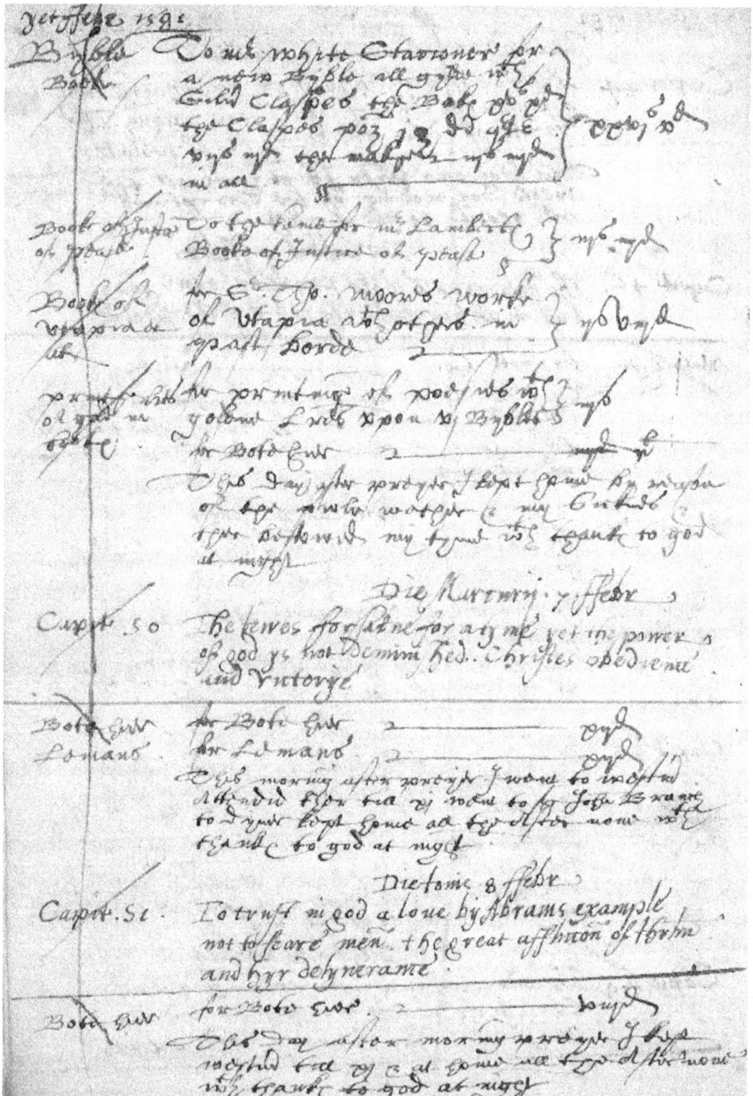

FIGURE 3. Folger Shakespeare Library, MS 459, fol. 46v, showing deletion of entries.

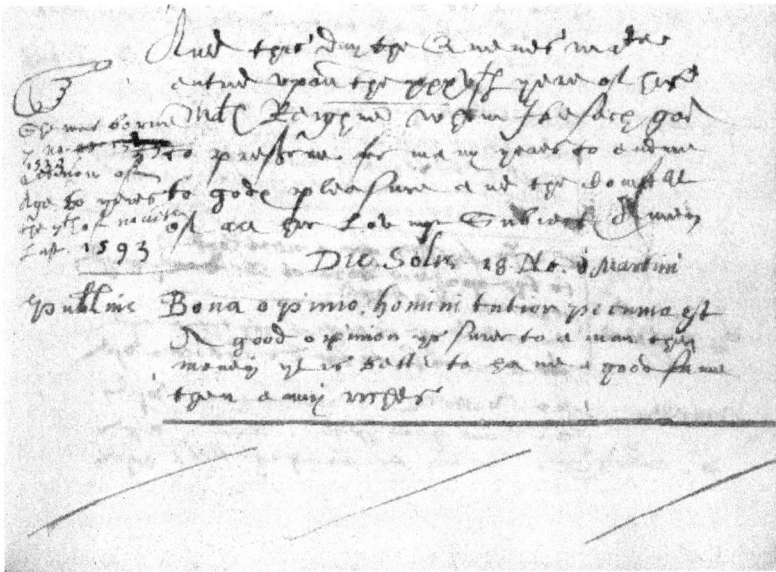

FIGURE 4. Folger Shakespeare Library, MS V.a.460, fol. 40r, showing space fillers.

degree of visual regularity. Although he did not always succeed, Stonley was concerned to maintain a consistency of format and thereby to create the firm impression of completeness and order in his accounts. However gnarled and difficult Stonley's hand may appear to our eyes, the journals are "fair copies" worked up from preexisting notes, whether those notes were rapidly jotted down in a notebook, incised in the wax-treated leaves of a table book, scribbled in almanacs, or kept as loose-leaf receipts.

There is some evidence to suggest that Stonley employed almanacs for the initial transcription of the notes that came together in a more polished form in the journals. From an early point in the second volume and continuing, albeit patchily, across the course of that volume and on into the third, Stonley splices a new element into his daily entries, noting saints' days and "red-letter days" alongside the date. Thus 8 June 1593 is "Medard," the 9th "Trans Edmond," the 10th "Trinite sonday," the 11th "Barnabe apostle," the 12th "St Basilide." Contrary to what one might expect, calendars circulating in Elizabethan England were often thick with saints' days, offering information that went far beyond the twenty-seven holy days (besides Sundays) that continued to be recognized by the *Book of Common Prayer*.[51] The calendar that prefaced the 1568 "Bishops' Bible," which Stonley owned, offered its readers a saint for all but a handful of days in each month.[52] Such calendars differed widely in the information they offered, and I have been unable to trace the precise source of Stonley's annotations. (It is of course possible that, since Stonley composed the journal entries in several different locations, he relied on multiple sources). The strong likelihood, however, is that he used almanacs for his notation of the religious calendar. In one section of the 1597–98 volume he records not just saints' days but also astrological information relating to phases of the moon and the movements of the sun and through the signs of the zodiac. So 20 March 1598 is "Cuthbert capricorn last quarter," while 25 March is "Annunc. marie pisses [Pisces]." Stonley goes still further in April 1598, noting not just star signs but also the parts of the body that they governed; so 5 April has "Leo the hart & back," 9 April "Libra the reines [kidneys] and longes," and 11 April "Scorpio secretes [genitals] and bladder." Although there is occasional misreading ("longes" on the 9th should be "loynes," for example), the wording that Stonley employs here is taken directly from the images of the "astrological man" that were a standard element in printed almanacs, whether they were sold as folded pamphlets or as single folio sheets designed for posting up on walls. The journals also allow us to see Stonley buying multiple almanacs—in London on 14 December 1581, he bought seven for eight pence, alongside four pence worth of oranges and a copy of the *Diamond of Devotion* at ten pence.[53] The unavoidable implication here is that he was stocking up for the New Year, though whether he was planning to distribute the almanacs among members of his household or to post them up in a variety of places for ease of consultation, we cannot know. He paid five shillings "for a pere of writing Tables" in 1581 and twelve pence for "a pere of writing tables & Brasse penne" in 1594, suggesting that he had a variety of options available for rough notetaking.[54]

My claim that the journals are fair copies may be somewhat contentious, because the daily entries are full of gaps, errors, and *currente calamo* corrections, the writing often suggests a degree of haste, and the protocols for what constituted an entry were subject to ad hoc revision on a fairly regular basis. But some of these imperfections offer forceful evidence of the compiler's aspirations. Gaps in the record—as when we read

This day was

Arrayned in the Kinges benche
For

—indicate that Stonley intended to return to a passage later, and they tell of his desire for accuracy and completeness, even though that desire was visibly unfulfilled.[55] Running corrections, while they might spoil the visual effect, suggest a comparable effort to get things right. Meanwhile, there are several corrections to the diary entries in the journal that are particularly helpful in allowing us to cement the claim that there is nothing especially "immediate" about its composition.

The entry for Friday, 5 August 1581, for example, begins by mistakenly reporting events that happened on Saturday, 6 August—Stonley goes to Doddinghurst and dines with his son William Heigham, his wife, and various gentlemen "cuminge owte of Suffoke." This entry is deleted and replaced with a corrected record, which states that Stonley stayed at home that day, venturing out only to dine with his brother-in-law ("at the L. Mayers"); the Saturday record follows after. Evidently, the entry for Friday cannot have been penned until after the events of Saturday had taken place.[56] The same thing happens in 1582, when a day trip to Kingsbury that took place on Sunday, 29 July, is at first mistakenly attributed to Saturday.[57] In these cases, it is possible that the date of transcription was not widely separated from the date described—we are dealing with a time lag of perhaps a day or two. But in at least one section of the first volume, the consistent hue of the ink, backed up by an unusual degree of consistency in the writing, suggests that perhaps two weeks' worth of journal entries may have been penned retrospectively, at a single sitting.[58] It is no coincidence that this is also a period in which Stonley was seriously afflicted by illness. Presumably his "Cough and Agewe" prevented him from keeping up his journals, as well as confining him to his house in London with no possibility of venturing out. (Several of the entries report that the ague kept him coughing "all the night longe," and so breach the tidy distinction between one day and the next.) Although these entries are exceptional, they confirm an impression that the journals are not rough, spontaneous notebooks but a perfected record.[59] Once we have observed this, it seems significant that Stonley opens his record of the day's activities with the words "This day," or "This morning," and not "Today."

For all their neatness, it should be admitted that the journals are engagingly fluid in form and full of odd variations and unexpected extras. The first volume begins with a list of payments that Stonley made to his wife for housekeeping and ends with a list of miscellaneous receipts, probably repayments on loans; as we have seen, the entries for the whole of the year 1582 in this volume are deleted, something that happens nowhere else.[60] In the second volume, in January 1593/4, perhaps as the result of a misguided new year's resolution, Stonley starts noting "Profit" and "Losse" at the foot of each page, but he gives this up within three weeks, presumably because there is never any profit to be noted in what is essentially a record of outgoings. Midway through volume 2, at the end of 1593, he adds a note of the numbers of people who have died and been christened in London in the past, plague-stricken year. Then he moves on to tot up his various outgoings for the year in a table that he calls "The Pye of my Expences this yere ending at Christmas 1593."[61] The second volume ends with a list of "Arrerages of desperat debts Recevid since the xiiijth of May 1593," reflecting Stonley's impending financial calamity and his need to chase his debtors (460/89r). In the third volume of the journals, written in the Fleet, Stonley starts recording not only his dining companions but also what he had for dinner and supper. This was presumably a way of compensating for the comparative paucity of day-to-day expenditure in this period. But midway through the volume he stops transcribing his bills of fare, adding this note: "from this day ther is a nother booke which I terme the weekboke or kytchin book wherin I note all thinges & somes of money laid out all kynde of weyes . . . that in the end of the yere I may raye owt every thinge in ther proper places" (461/36r). After this, his entries are bipartite, comprising textual excerpts and diary entries but no "stuff"; the only intrusion of money now comes in the form of fortnightly receipts, signed by the deputy warden of the Fleet, for chamber rent. The bareness of the record in the last months of Stonley's life tells us something about its mobile, experimental quality. The rules of Stonley's record keeping were open to renegotiation right up to the end. This restlessness and unpredictability in what is intended to be a neat and tidy record may help to explain how this new mutation, the tripartite format of the journals, was able to happen.

For all their local quirks, though, the journals are the product of a formidable discipline. They present life as orderly and structured, and they doubtless helped to make life *feel* orderly and structured. To understand how they worked, we need to dig deeper into their material form and the relationship of that material form with time, space, and morality. In the process, we shall come to understand why the self as we know it has absconded from Stonley's proto-diaristic discourse.

Life in a Box

Stonley's journals originally came with labels. At the end of the second volume, for 1593–94, there is a note that instructs: "Loke the next boke of LL."

It is just about possible to make out a faded "KK" inscribed on the back of the vellum binding of the same volume and a faint "OO" on the third volume (for 1597–98), indicating that we have lost the three intervening volumes, LL, MM, and NN. A mark on the back of the first surviving volume (for 1581–82) is likely to be a "Z," suggesting that the doubled letters were a second alphabetic sequence that followed on from the first. If we assume that the lost volumes were roughly the same size as those that survive, this means that Stonley began keeping his journals around 1560. The fragments that survive are the remnant of a much larger archive.

As well as telling us how much we have lost, Stonley's labeling of his account books is significant because it chimes with his labeling of other storage devices in his house. On 19 June 1581, he made a payment of forty-nine shillings and ten pence "To Mr Abdey for charges in Lawe this mydsomer terme as by his bill in the Box of A. may appere" (359/3v). After listing the guests at his house on Christmas Day and Boxing Day 1581, Stonley notes: "The fare for bothes [both these] dayes apperethe in a Booke of the diettes emonges my other matters in the Box of D" (359/38v). Less happily, on 5 August 1593, Stonley made an interest payment of four pounds "To master Serche Scrivener dwelling in foster lane" for a loan of four hundred pounds that was evidently secured on a quantity of plate. After noting the payment, he added: "Memorandum the bill of the parcelles of plate remayneth in the Box of P. in the Gallary under & master Serch hath the Bill of Sale under my hand & Seall to be delyvered to me with all the parcelles mencioned in the same at thend of vj monethes . . . viz ultimo Januarij 1593" (460/20v). These references capture something of the web of documentation in which the journals were caught up—and Stonley also mentions "my note boke of sermons" (459/47r, 70r) as well as the "weekboke or kytchin booke" referred to earlier. They also show that a manuscript journal was just one of the alphabetized receptacles that Stonley used to organize his affairs. These books were, effectively, boxes.[62]

Stonley's daily entries also have something box-like about them. Although it is not immediately clear to the eye, the pages on which he wrote were laid out as a grid, a frame made up of vertical and horizontal lines. Discussing Jan Gossaert's *Portrait of a Merchant* (c. 1530, Figure 5), Peter Stallybrass has called our attention to the extraordinary care with which Gossaert rendered the paper on which the merchant (recently identified as Jan Snoeck, collector of river tolls at Gorinchem in Holland) is writing.[63] Before he takes up his pen, Snoeck has folded his paper so as to make four vertical columns that will provide the mise-en-page for his accounts. Stonley uses

FIGURE 5. Jan Gossaert, *Portrait of a Merchant*, c. 1530. Oil on panel. Courtesy of the National Gallery of Art, Washington, DC.

exactly the same technique to articulate his page space. (There is a cautionary tale for users of digital facsimiles here, because the high-grade digital reproductions of the journals in the Folger's "Luna" image collection render the folds invisible.) Cutting across the vertical lines created by paper folding are the horizontal lines that Stonley drew with a ruler. These rules are not used to divide one day from the next, as we might expect and as indeed we would demand in a printed diary today. Instead, they divide the textual excerpts from the daily expenses and the diary entry that follows. The excerpts are also often distinguished by their use of Latin, rendered in italic script; in some sections of the journals there are pairs of rules, separating the Latin sentence from its English translation, and the English translation from the quotidian affairs.[64]

The proximity between the ruled line and the moral or biblical excerpt should prompt us to reflect on the ambiguity in the word "rule" and the connections that were widely drawn in early modern culture between straight lines and moral rectitude. References to the "rule of reason" or the "rule of righteousness" are commonplace in the literature of the period, and are often elaborated in ways that make it clear that these rules are by no means dead metaphors but are imagined as physical rulers. The exiled English recusant Benet Canfield offers an example of this kind of thinking when he writes in *The Rule of Perfection* that "as the materiall rule is the thing wherby to drawe a line straight, and wherby wee trie whether any thing be right or crooked; so the *will of God* is that wherby wee may drawe only the course of our life, and the intention of our works, words, or thoughts, and wherby wee may knowe whether they bee straight by right intention, or crooked by any blind affection."[65] "What is more certain," asked William Chillingworth in his *Religion of Protestants* (1638), "then that he may make a streight line who hath a Rule to make it by, though never man in the world had made any before: and why then may not he that beleeves the Scripture to be the word of God, and the Rule of faith, regulate his faith by it, and consequently beleeve aright without much regarding what other men either will doe or have done?"[66] Anyone familiar with allegorical writing or allegorical images from the period knows that the primrose path of dalliance is always winding and "errant," while the straight and narrow path leads directly to virtue. All of this means that as he drew his horizontal rules, underlining the moral or spiritual points that he had transcribed, Stonley may have been focusing the self-regulating energies of his writing practice in his journals more generally—driving the verbal point home on a haptic level.

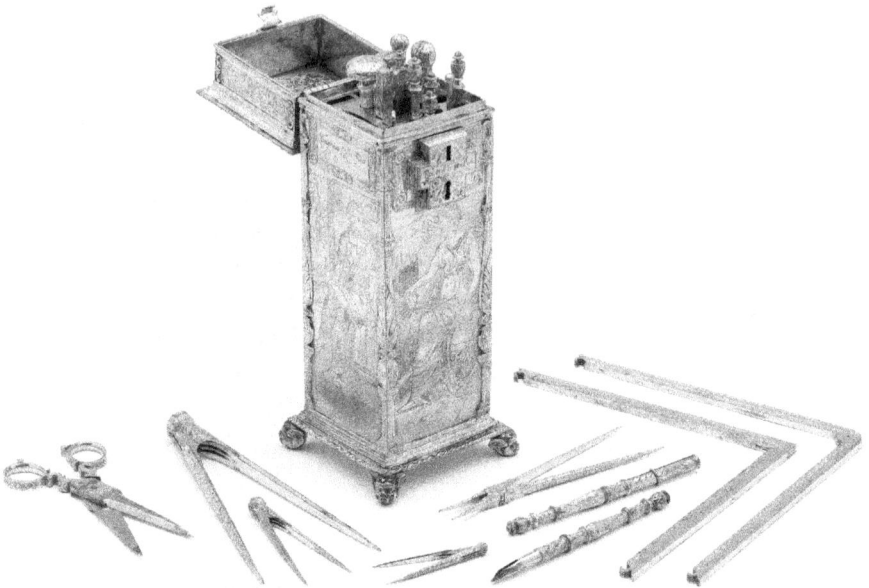

FIGURE 6. Bartholomew Newsham, gilt brass instrument case, c. 1570. British Museum 1912,0208.1.

While a ruler is, to us, an everyday implement, it is possible that Stonley's version was a more exclusive product, and one that came (fittingly) in a box. The British Museum holds "the sole surviving example of an Elizabethan drawing set," which is dated c. 1570 (Figure 6).[67] Made of gilt brass, this tall case of instruments is engraved on four sides with allegorical figures of Peace, Abundance, War, and Poverty; inside it has spaces for scissors and knives, a pen, a pencil holder and pricker, a whetstone, several sets of compasses and dividers, and a folding rule. The case is signed by Bartholomew Newsum or Newsham, a clockmaker active in London from the 1560s, who during the 1580s seems to have served as mender of the Queen's clocks. The *ODNB* cites him as one of the first English clockmakers whose skills could bear comparison with those of his foreign contemporaries and as a harbinger of London's later growth as a European clockmaking center. We know that Stonley was acquainted with Newsham, since on 1 June 1582 he recorded a payment of 15s. 4d. "to Bartholmew Newsham for mending my Clockes at sondry times" (459/61r). Meanwhile the inventory of Stonley's London house includes "a little latten [i.e., brass] ymplement belonginge to a standishe [inkstand] to putt bodkin in. Compasses &c in."[68] Since this was appraised at six pence, it was presumably smaller or less elegant than the British Museum's example, but it sounds like a close relation of Newsham's kit.[69]

Newsham's surviving oeuvre creates a kinship between the regulation of time and the regulation of writing that is also clear in the format of Stonley's daily diary entries, with their curiously insistent yet tokenistic genuflections to clock time. Stonley bookends the day with morning and evening prayer, the week with services and scripture reading on Sundays, and the year with prayer: "And so ended this day And the yere with thankes to Almighty god for the preservinge me to this day And humbly besech hym to graunt me grace to procede in this next yere in his feare & love" (459/99r). Less obtrusive is the fact that Stonley almost invariably stays at his Westminster office "till xj.," although his time of arrival there, or of other events in the day, is rarely deemed to be worthy of note. The significance of "xj." is presumably that it heralds dinner time, and in the journals the naming of the hour frequently serves as a prelude to the detailing of dinner arrangements. It may be relevant to note here that, as well as perhaps providing Stonley with writing implements, his clockmakers were regularly employed to set up or mend the mechanical turnspits that were a feature of his kitchens.[70] The significance of time discipline and regular dining to Elizabethan officialdom is encapsulated in an anecdote about how one of the barons of the Court of Exchequer became known as "Baron Tell-Clock": "And that nickname Baron *Tellclock* came up first in Baron *Southertons* time, who when he felt the Chimes ring in his Stomach towards dinner, he was us'd to tell chief Baron *Tanfield, My Lord 'tis twelve a clock.'"[71] The clockwork baron in this story was Stonley's Aldersgate neighbor John Sotherton (1562–1631?).

My contention is that the physical form of the journals is tied to forms of moral and temporal regulation: to the ruling in of the self, rather than its expression. Once we have absorbed that possibility, it is impossible not to be struck by a feature of the diary entries that I have not hitherto discussed, which is their pervasive and vociferous interest in the regulation of the social order. The first volume provides us with ample evidence to suggest that Stonley was preoccupied by infractions of the peace. On 30 June 1581 he hears of "a disorder a bowte Smythfeld in takinge a wey of one Butcher from the Cart that was ponished ther for sturringe up the people to make a rebellion agenst gentle men & Servinge men" (459/6r); on 15 July he reports that "a Bowt Wenesday Last at the Cort at Grenwich therles of Sussex and Leicestre fell owt at great wordes one a genst a nother but the Queenes majestie as ys thought will take up the matter which I pray god graunt" (459/9r); and on

27 September he learns of "a bill . . . set upon the gate [of the Lord Mayor's house] by some envious person a geynst the seyd Lord mayer blaymyng hym of many vices & all most false" (459/21v). (The Lord Mayor mentioned here was Stonley's brother-in-law Sir John Branche, who is always referred to in the journals by his title during his time in office.) During the same period Stonley twice makes detailed notes on the misdemeanours of the "obstinate Curate" at Doddinghurst, recording the scriptural passages that the unnamed clergyman had cited while he was ostentatiously "refuzing the Servise of the day" and proceeding "without preyer at all for the quenes Majestie."[72] The diarist also participates in a bit of low-level spying, when "Master Butler a neighbur by had his child Christenyd ther beinge ther hym self & not at his parishe churche which was notyd yet in my opinion both he & his wyf lyve veery vertuouslye so farr as I can here" (459/12v). This concern with social order was still operative when Stonley was in prison in 1597; on one occasion he reported: "This evenynge at Supper Master Strowd & one kirton fell at such hote wordes as master Strowde called the other Pillerye knave the other with that began to rise to go to hym after yt was axed what he wold have done. mary quod he in my fury I wold have kylled hym. But after ther fury was mitigated and folded up in the Table clothe" (461/15r). For "folded up in the Table clothe" we might substitute "put back into the box"; the desire of Stonley to contain disorder was a transposition of his textual practice. His strong emphasis on social discipline runs parallel to the kinds of internal discipline that we have begun to uncover in the journals.

If Stonley's journals are boxes, it is important to emphasize that they are full boxes. The most significant feature of the "template" diary entry—"This day after morning preyer I went to westminster kept ther till xj came home to dynner kept home all the Afternone at my bokes & so ended that day with thankes to god at night"—is its insistence on temporal coverage, its carving of the day up into segments each of which is accounted for, from start to finish. Contrary to some claims, Pepys did not invent the dawn-to-dusk diary entry that propelled its subject from "Up" to "And so to bed."[73] Stonley's completist diary entries are, I want to suggest, the temporal equivalent of the "boxed-in" page space that, if it is not completely filled in with text, needs to be filled out with space fillers. Pushing this idea a little further, we might say that the diary entries are *themselves* space fillers, which assert the industry and piety of the subject rather than doing any of the work that we would today expect a diary to do. Such an argument brings us back to Aho's claims about the primarily rhetorical function of early modern bookkeeping—claims that can be ballasted in Stonley's case by the regularity with which the numbers fail to stack up. The first volume contains fifty-one sums, twelve of which Stonley gets wrong (23.5 percent). The second contains seventy-three sums, of which Stonley miscalculates nineteen (26 percent).[74] These troubling statistics may just be evidence of the financial incompetence (or was it corruption?) that led to his ruin. The more compelling implication is that there is something cosmetic about the account book as a form: the appearance of financial probity is more important than the reality. The journals may be less about trustworthy record keeping, more an elaborate front. When Stonley stayed at home of an afternoon "makinge up my Accomptes" (459/3r), the emphasis may have been on the makeup. In this light, we may wish to revise our notion that his journals were a means of self-regulation, and suggest that they were a means of creating the *appearance* of self-regulation. Far from seeking to construct a self, they seek to construct an alibi—or a paper trail. Future chapters draw out some of the things that he may have been hiding.

This chapter has shown us Stonley's journals as a technology for the management and projection of the self that is fundamentally inhospitable to modern notions of inwardness and subjectivity. It has traced their connections outward to manuals of double-entry bookkeeping and to the material culture of Stonley's study and of his wider household, adumbrating the place of reading and writing in relation to the ordering of daily life and the management of a domestic archive. The journals took shape in an environment in which business and leisure were scarcely distinguishable, and in which the spiritual and the monetary were perfectly harmonized. My next chapter explores that environment in more detail, via another source that requires careful handling.

Chapter 3

On Aldersgate Street

Besides the journals, the other key source for the book life of Richard Stonley is the household inventory that was drawn up when his goods were sold off to defray his debts in 1597. In this chapter, I consider what we can learn from the inventory, a mode that (like the account book) casts the self as a financial entity, a product of property and perhaps also a property in itself. Reconstructing the circumstances in which the inventory was compiled, and with due attention to its likely occlusions, I use it to take the reader on an imaginary tour through Stonley's London townhouse, seeing what we might infer from the mix of books and other kinds of stuff that the appraisers found in each room. Stonley's domestic spaces bring together lavishly illustrated books with maps, prints, and paintings, and I explore in some detail the role of the visual in mediating between books and physical furnishings. I also pursue the idea of the home as a mirror, in which the decaying of property and the yellowing of books might have reflected the old age of its owner, who was nonetheless (I suggest) a committed purchaser of new books. Finally I consider the relationship between books and the proliferating chests and boxes in Stonley's domestic environment. This leads to a consideration of the ways in which books were objectified in the early modern period, and to an appreciation of Stonley's investment in the fashionability of a particular kind of commoditized book.

People and Things in the Household Inventory

In act 2, scene 2, of Shakespeare's *Cymbeline*, the villainous Iachimo climbs out of a trunk in the dead of night to embark upon an extraordinary mission —the visual, virtual rape of the sleeping Imogen. Having failed to persuade her to betray her beloved Posthumus, Iachimo sets about gathering the evidence that will allow him to claim that he has slept with her after all. "Our Tarquin thus / Did softly press the rushes," he remarks as he draws nearer to her bed, identifying himself with a fellow countryman and the rapist of Lucretia as a prelude to his own act of purely ocular invasion.[1] For a moment he marvels aloud at Imogen's beauty; then he catches himself—"But my design—/ To note the chamber"—and pulls out a portable writing tablet, or table book:

> Such and such pictures; there the window; such
> Th'adornment of her bed; the arras, figures,
> Why, such and such; and the contents of the story [historical painting].
> (23–27)

Having itemized the furnishings in the room, Iachimo turns to Imogen herself—"Ah, but some natural notes about her body / Above ten thousand meaner movables / Would testify, t'enrich mine inventory" (28–30). In pursuit of this more intimate evidence, he purloins her bracelet, the "manacle of love" that Posthumus had given her when they parted (1.1.122); and he observes "on her left breast / A mole cinque-spotted, like the crimson drops / I' th' bottom of a cowslip" (37–39). There is no need to write this down; it is, Iachimo says, "riveted, / Screwed to my memory" (43–44). Before he leaves, he notes one last detail:

> She hath been reading late
> The tale of Tereus; here the leaf's turned down
> Where Philomel gave up. (44–46)

"I have enough," he says, and climbs back into the trunk, urging the "dragons of the night" to hasten the dawn (46, 48).

The rendering of these events is breathtaking, from the most basic tensions of its mise-en-scène (how can Iachimo say and do so much in Imogen's presence without waking her?) to the way that it translates violence into rapt voyeurism. But for the modern spectator or reader, one of the startling things about the scene is the way that it elides people with inanimate objects—a process that begins in Iachimo's choice of hiding place. His trunk is being stored in Imogen's chamber supposedly because it contains "plate of rare device, and jewels / Of rich and exquisite form" (1.6.189–90)—a gift for the emperor that needs looking after. But what the trunk really contains is Iachimo. Meanwhile the sleeping Imogen becomes just another item, albeit a more precious item, to enrich Iachimo's inventory. The "natural notes about her body" will weigh more heavily than "ten thousand meaner movables," but they seem (as "movables") to be readily comparable.[2] We are accustomed to early modern texts that treat women as objects, but there is still something unnerving about the mingling of awestruck reverie with bureaucratic efficiency in Iachimo's swoop from the domestic furnishings of the princess to her body.

That "something" comes in part from the application of a familiar legal process—the making of a household inventory—to an object that usually falls within a different jurisdiction. Iachimo's conflation of the domestic and the amatory produces an effect that borders on the uncanny, as the borders of the body and the room start to blur. Would the play's first audiences have found this so weird? The shimmering strangeness of the scene may be the product of a modern tendency to make a rigid moral and evaluative distinction between people and things, signaled most powerfully in our repugnance for slavery.[3] John Donne's first surviving sermon states as a matter of course that "in a right inventary, every man that ascends to a true value of himself, considers it thus; First, His Soul, then His life; after his fame and good name: And lastly, his goods and estate; for thus their own nature hath ranked them, and thus they are (as in nature) so ordinarily in legal consideration preferred before one another."[4] This puts financial worth in its place, third place, although the second-place fame and good name were scarcely separable from goods and estate. Donne echoes the bookkeeping literature surveyed in the last chapter in acknowledging "estate" as a crucial component of human identity; who you are is inseparable from what you own. An episteme that could so readily inventory the self might well have been more comfortable with the rendering of the body's object status. Olivia, in Shakespeare's *Twelfth Night*, flippantly proposes to publicize her beauty by making an inventory of it, "as, *item*, two lips, indifferent red: *item*, two grey eyes, with lids to them: *item*, one neck, one chin and so forth" (1.5.179–80). Her thumbnail sketch is a version of the blazon, a poetic inventory that turns people into lists of physical attributes. Such lists were often just lists of female body parts, but they could be more exalted, as when Olivia says of Cesario later in the same scene, "Thy tongue, thy face, thy limbs, actions and spirit / Do give thee five-fold blazon" (1.5.226–27).

When early modern writers made the process of inventorying an occasion for wit and satire, they often included a playful conflation of people and

things. Itemizing property inevitably leads to the thought that the self is itself
a property, made up of its material wealth, or lack thereof. Take for example
a single-sheet broadside published in 1641 entitled *The Welch mans inventory*,
which offered its readers (in a cod-Welsh accent) "Han Infentory of the
Coudes [Goods] of William Morgan, ap Renald, ap Hugh, ap Richard, ap
Thomas, ap Evan, ap Rice, in the County of Clamorgan [Glamorgan], Shen-
tleman."[5] The broadside proceeded to itemize the goods of this gentleman,
rich in ancestry but poor in property, which were distributed between a pantry,
a "napery," a wardrobe, a dairy, a kitchen, a cellar, an armory, a garden, a
"leasway," a common field, a "broom close," a barn, a study, a closet, and a
bed. If the house sounds substantial, the goods it contains are distinctly down-
market. The wardrobe holds an Irish rug, a frize jerkin, a sheepskin doublet,
two Irish stockings, two shoes, and six leather points. The kitchen has a pot and
a pan, "two Redhering," and "nine Sprat." The sumptuous garden contains a
bed of garlic, nine onions, and twelve leeks—all notoriously smelly foods, associated with the poor—together with twelve worms and six frogs. In the study
is Morgan's paltry shelf of books, staples of cheap print mixed up with farm
animals: "one welch piple [Bible], two Almanack, one *Errapater*, one seven
Cha[m]pions for St. *Taffie* sake, twelve pullet [i.e., chickens], one pedigree."[6]
Then, as the penultimate item, we get the family, who are just more stuff:
"Item, more lumber about the house one wife, two shild [i.e., children], one
call her plack shack [Black Jack?],[7] and the t'other little *Morgan*." Welsh gentlemen (the broadside suggests) are interchangeable commodities, and their children barely need individuating names.

   Another text that plays with the inventory is an epigram addressed by
Sir John Harington to his wealthy widowed mother-in-law, Jane Rogers:

   To his wives mother, reproving
      her unconstancy.

Last yeare, while at your house I hapt to tarry,
of all your goods you took an Inventary,
Your Tapistry, your linnen, bedding, plate
Your sheep, your horse, your cattell you did rate
and yet one moveable you did forget
More moveable then theis therein to set
   Your wav'ring minde I mean which is so moveable,
   That you for it, have ever been reprovable.

What looks like a standard misogynist gibe about female changefulness has, in this poem, a sharp edge, since Harington was interested in the possibility that he and his wife might inherit his mother-in-law's property, including the "Tapistry, . . . linnen, bedding, [and] plate" inventoried here. Her "wav'ring mind"—her *will*—was, we infer, prone to change.[8] The epigram's concluding joke renders the testator's mind material, but it also testifies to the material underpinnings of the poet's identity. Without more money, there will not be much more wit.

Sources like these point to the ubiquity of the inventory, which in early modern culture was a key technology of self-evaluation. Everyone would have been familiar with the making of lists of goods, whether for intermittent stocktaking (as, for example, at the opening of a new account book) or in preparation for the transfer of property, often but by no means exclusively after its possessor's death. In many European countries this process was placed in the hands of professional notaries, but in England it was frequently undertaken by the creditors of the deceased or by persons to whom a legacy was due.[9] Proceeding room by room through a property, the inventory's compilers listed the moveable goods they encountered in varying degrees of detail. The terms they employed were usually conditioned by the practical need to differentiate items from one another and (where goods were to be sold) to provide a thumbnail justification for the prices at which particular items were appraised.

As Lena Cowen Orlin and Giorgio Riello recently pointed out, inventories are heavily inflected by the practical circumstances of their composition and have many blind spots that limit their value as historical records.[10] Inventories are highly partial in their representation of property. They tell us only about moveable property, not about fixtures and fittings, and there were many motives for excluding individual goods, and sometimes entire classes of goods, from particular inventories. Inventories are also silent about the mobility of movables, giving us no sense of how objects might have traveled both within and beyond a household, and presenting an illusion of stasis, a still life rather than a tableau vivant. Nor do they present us with personal associations and emotional investments. Filtered (in the majority of cases) through the gaze of an outsider, they present a stripped-down list of deracinated articles rather than of things with deep roots in personal and familial histories. A will might tell you that a particular brass pot "was mine owne mothers and her fathers afore her"; an inventory will rarely open up such a vista.[11] Inventories also fail to offer a reliable picture of domestic spaces. They only take note of rooms that contain goods to be inventoried, and they tell us little about physical relationships between rooms or about patterns of usage. And inventories mask a number of interests, depending on who was making them and their relationship to the objects that they were cataloguing. Those with a financial stake in a post-mortem inventory might well have adjusted prices upward or downward in order to serve their own immediate ends. For all of these reasons, these sources offer no transparent or unmediated record of historic living spaces.

Inventories are key sources for the history of the book. They have been used to give us a much more detailed picture of the curriculum at the universities and to advance our understanding of the spread of literacy.[12] But like inventories in general, lists of books are perilous and problematic sources, and Stonley's list is (as we shall see) dogged by difficulties endemic to the genre. Its entries are often too imprecise to permit texts to be identified; it does not date editions; it fails to itemize ephemera, bundling pamphlets together in single generic entries; it documents only those books that the owner kept in a particular site, not the whole collection; and it offers no copy-specific detail to explain its pricing.[13] Any instinct toward scholarly completism can only be frustrated by such a list, and in this chapter I take the blurred edges of the booklist for granted. My aim is, indeed, to blur the edges still further, not separating the books out from the other material stuffs in the inventory, but using it holistically to address the questions compassed in my earlier chapters about the relationship between literature, material culture, and the human subject.[14] I use the inventory that was drawn up when Stonley was sent to the Fleet in 1597 to explore the place of books in the larger material constitution of an individual and a household. This aim is rendered problematic by the nature of the evidence, since the inventory is itself a fissured document. The books were inventoried separately from the other goods, and apparently at a later stage. Then someone stitched the two lists together, dividing the books between three of the rooms and listing them after the rest of the goods in each room. But while we could wish for a more detailed document, the list as we have it offers a rich opportunity to attend to the multiple interactions between books and their environments; to think about the book as unbound, or bound outward, rather than bound in. This chapter continues my project of thinking about books in terms of their attachments to the wider world of objects, which is simultaneously the subject's attachment to (or entanglement within) those books and that world.

Through the Keyhole

The inventory of Stonley's goods describes a substantial townhouse on a street that would become renowned for its elegance (Figure 7). As James Howell commented in his *Londinopolis* of 1657, Aldersgate Street "resembleth an *Italian* street, more then any other in *London*, by reason of the spaciousness & uniformity of Buildings, and streightness thereof, with the convenient distance of the Houses; on both sides whereof, there are divers very fair ones."[15] One of the fairest, in Howell's estimation, was the house that had formerly belonged to Stonley's patrons the Petres, on the west side of the street between the turnings into Long Lane and Little Britain, the frontage of which took up forty-eight feet. Surviving inventories show it to have had more than thirty chambers, plus garrets, cellars, and outhouses. On the evidence of the inventory, Stonley had to make do with just seventeen rooms, along with a number of outhouses, a yard or two, and a garden, in what he was apt to call his "pore howse."[16] The approximate location of the property can be established through an entry in a City Lands Grants Book, dated 10 November 1597:

> Memorandum that the xth daye of November 1597. Anno 39.
> Elizabethe Regine. Edward Jones of the Cyttye of London Esquyer is
> lycenced by Tho. Wilfod Chamblen of the Cyttye of London to sett owt
> a pale and porche before the sayd Jones his Howse or Tenement in
> Aldersgatestreete Betweene the Inne called or knoven by the name of the
> white Bell And the mansion howse of Master Stonley theare: the sayd
> pale & porche to be sett towardes the streete equall with the pale and
> porche before the sayd Stonley his house / next adjuoyninge, payend
> yearely thearefore to the Chambleyn of london the use of the Maior
> Cominaltye & Cittizens the Some of syxeteene pence. /
>
> Edw: Jones[17]

Stonley's next-door neighbor was the M.P. and "earnest place-seeker" Edward Jones, who served as secretary to Lord Keepers Puckering and Egerton and was later Francis Bacon's deputy as a clerk of Star Chamber.[18] I have found no other evidence of a "White Bell" tavern, but it seems reasonable to assume that this was the same as the Bell, which was on the east side of the street opposite the entrance into Long Lane. (A letter from Henry Knowlis

ALDERSGATE WARD
and
St Martins le Grand
Liberty
Taken from the last
Survey, with Corrections

Part
of
Cri-
ple
gate
Liber-
ty

73. Cates Court
74. Cherry Tree Court
75. Smiths Court
76. Cates Passage

G.O.S.W.E.L.L STREET

PART

BARBICAN

OF

CRIPLE

GATE

A Table of Refferences
to this Mapp

Aldersgate Ward
within the wall

1. Prists Court
2. Rose and Crown Court
3. Dark Entry
4. Goldsmiths Hall
5. St John Zachary Church yard
6. St Richard Levets
7. Staining Church yard
8. Dolphin Court
9. White Horse Court
10. Scriveners Hall
11. Foxes Court
12. Hides Court
13. St Anns Church and alley
14. Quakers meeting house
15. Bull and mouth Inn

Aldersgate ward
without the wall

16. Narrow Court
17. Castle Inn
18. Cooks Hall
19. Green head Court
20. Stone fives
21. Bull Alley
22. Golden Lyon Court
23. Rose & Raindeer Ct
24. Nicholson Court
25. Maidenhead Court
26. White Hart Inn
27. Thanet House
28. Trinity Court
29. Westmoreland alley
30. London House
31. Angell Alley
32. Horne alley
33. Cockpitt yard
34. Cradle court
35. Black horse alley
36. Black horse Court
37. Halfe moon Court
38. Halfe moon alley
39. Crown Court
40. Swan Inn
41. Lauderdale House
42. Bell Inn
43. Sun Tavern
44. Cock Inn
45. Devonshire Court
46. Red Lyon Inn
47. Three Cups Inn
48. White Horse yard
49. Staines alley
50. White horse Inn & alley
51. White Lyon Court
52. Artichoke Court
53. George Inn
54. Cross Keys Court
55. Red Cross alley
56. Carpenters yard
57. Pelican Court
58. Montague Court
59. Great Montague Court
60. Axe yard
61. Dr Fryers Rents

St Martins le grand

62. Round Court
63. Mould makers Rents
64. New Rents
65. Great Deans Court
66. Three Crown Court
67. George Street
68. St Johns alley
69. Cock alley
70. Christophers alley
71. Four Dove Court
72. Kings head Court

PART OF

FARRING-

TON WARD

WITHOUT

ALDERSGATE STREET

Thanet
house

PART

OF

FARRINGTON

WARD WITHIN

St Buttolphs
Church
yard

W

A

R

D

G.O.S.W.E.L.L STREET

Blow Bladder Street

A Scale of 600 Feet

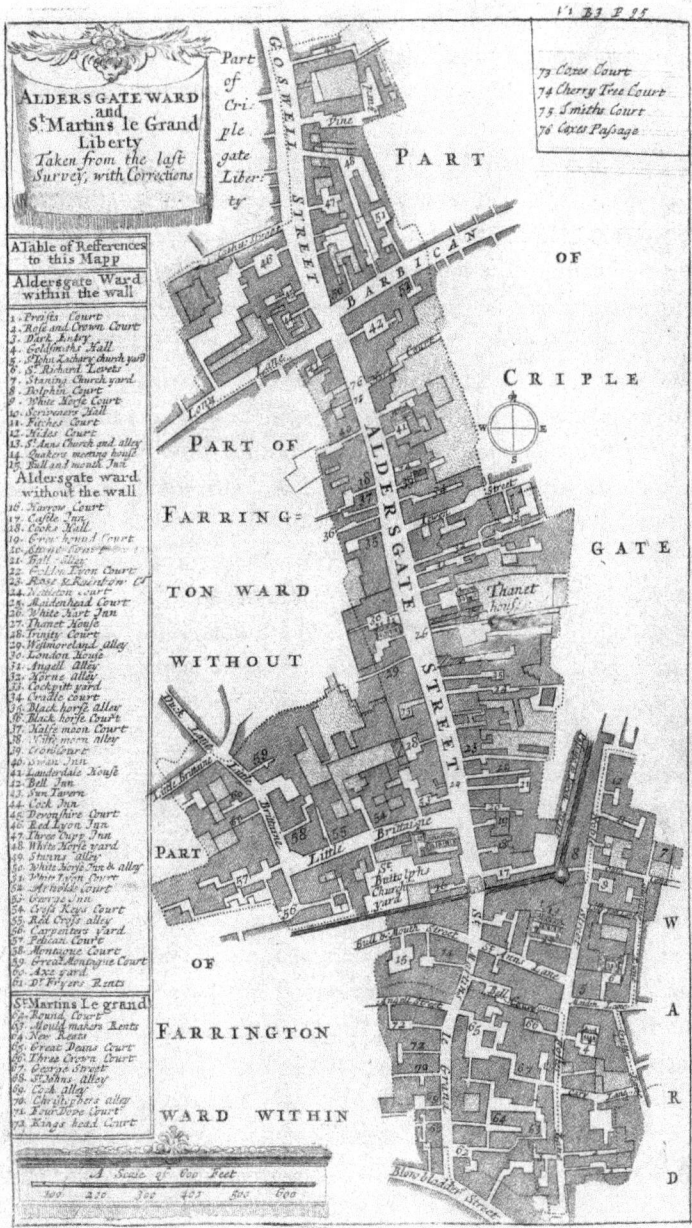

FIGURE 7. Detail from a map of Aldersgate Ward, showing the former residence of William Petre (30) and the Bell Inn (42). From John Stow, *A Survey of the Cities of London and Westminster*, rev. John Strype (1720). Cambridge University Library.

to Robert Cecil, dated 18 October 1600, is signed off "From the Bell in Aldersgate Street over against Long Lane end.")[19]

This was a lively place to be. Long Lane, which led down to St. Bartholomew's and Smithfield, was notorious for its pawnbrokers, selling secondhand clothes and other out-of-date wares; as Thomas Nashe wrote in *Pierce Penilesse*, "this is an yron age, or rather no yron age, for swords and bucklers goe to pawne apace in Long lane."[20] Stonley makes several references to the street in the journals; in the second volume he pays eighteen pence to "the upholster at Long lane end for Covering my deske with grene Lether," two shillings to "Thomas Garet my shomaker at Long Lane end by Thomas Poole his forman for a pere of Showes," and twenty pence "To John fysher in long lane" for two locks.[21] Aldersgate Street was a site for drama in the decades before London could boast dedicated playhouses; Trinity Hall, a building attached to the church of St. Botolph's, is known to have been rented by players in the 1550s and 1560s. Stonley reports having gone with his wife to a dinner in Trinity Hall to celebrate the marriage of two neighbors in May 1581.[22] And the street had rich associations with printing, most notably through John Day, who was based in the parish of St. Anne and St. Agnes from around 1548 until his death in 1584. William Baldwin's *Beware the Cat* suggests that Day's printing house was more or less built into the city wall at Aldersgate, where the severed heads of traitors were hoisted up on poles and where cats gathered for their nocturnal councils.[23] A little later, from 1589, Thomas East would publish from the sign of the Black Horse on the western side of Aldersgate Street. (East became known as a printer of music, thanks to his association with the composer William Byrd, who held a monopoly on music printing, and Byrd was closely associated with the Petres, so this move may have been designed to consolidate a set of existing relationships.)[24] In any case, Stonley would not have had to go far from home to find books.

The 1597 inventory was made when Stonley had already been consigned to the Fleet prison for debt, and his prison journals record several payments relating to the document.[25] On 23 April 1597, he paid twenty shillings "to [blank] Phelips master hilles clarke for making a Coppy of the Inventory of my goodes & a Coppy of my bondes to be delyvered to Thexchequer" (461/14r). More than a month later, on 27 May 1597, there is a payment of ten shillings "To Phelips master hilles Clarke for making an Inventary of all my Bookes in Aldersgat strete" (461/25r). So the inventorying was a two-stage process, with the books left until later and spliced into an existing list of furnishings. Perhaps Stonley initially hoped to save his library, and only later realized that it too would have to go.

Who was the Iachimo who made this inventory? Stonley's "[blank] Phelips" was Francis Phillips, a Londoner, born in 1572 and baptized at St. Andrew Undershaft.[26] Like many of his colleagues, he married into an Exchequer family; he would go on to enjoy a lengthy career as an auditor of the Exchequer.[27] A letter he sent to his uncle Robert in October 1596 gives us some insight into his life at this time, when he was preoccupied with the fallout from his father's death five years earlier.[28] His brother, the celebrated cryptographer Thomas Phelippes, was deep in debt to the Queen and was himself imprisoned (along with Stonley) in the Fleet.[29] Another brother, he reported, "is now seated in a shop in wood strete with his deske, lettice [furred gown], and papers, like a skrivener." Francis's own literacy is attested by the fact that (although he was a younger son) it was he to whom his father chose to leave his books in his will.[30] He would have been very much at home amid the dusty volumes, and all too familiar with the financial scenario that was playing out around him.[31]

The rooms named in the 1597 inventory were presumably spread over two or three floors. The appraisers began upstairs, in the master's bedroom, then moved to the "gallery next the bedchamber" and a succession of bedchambers, not forgetting the "jackhouse," or privy. Descending through the house, the inventory surveys the brushing chamber, the hall, parlor, study, and office, and finally comes to the buttery, the kitchen, and various outhouses. As the wealth of material details suggests, this would have been an unusually large and differentiated house with spaces for work, leisure, study, and sociability as well as for the necessities of eating and sleeping. It also had a garden that (according to the account book) required regular weeding, and that included a rose arbor and a graveled garden "walk" or "gallery"— conceivably a covered space for outside dining.

The inventory has a number of strange gaps. The most obvious is that it contains no plate, which would usually be the most obvious concretion of wealth in an elite house at this time. The absence is more noticeable because there is "an olde Cupborde of Wainscott to sett plate on" in the parlor. We can infer that Stonley's silver had already been sold off (in 1593 at least some of it was held in pawn by a scrivener and usurer named William Serche).[32] Nor is there any clothing, perhaps because Stonley had taken such personal effects away with him. These are among the blind spots in the inventory, the things that it will not let us see. Another oddity is that the first room to be assessed, "Master Stonley's Bedchamber," turns out to have no bed. (Could Stonley have moved it to the Fleet? Or was this prized item simply removed from the list?) These are just a few of the ways in which the inventory proves (as Riello and Orlin foretold) a refractory document.

The sense of incompleteness is exacerbated by the fact that this was not the only inventory that was made after Stonley's descent into bankruptcy. Another list, much of it rendered illegible by dirt and wear, survives for an unidentified house—conceivably at Doddinghurst—that contained a gallery, a "servant mans chamber," an armoury, a "chamber over the gat[e]," and a "great studie," as well as a kitchen, buttery, and brewhouse.[33] A rural location is suggested by the list of "Chattle of the said Master Richard Stonleye"— including horses, livestock, and quantities of crops. Unlike the London inventory, this list does mention plate, including a gilt salt, a pepper box, and a set of thirteen white silver apostle spoons, totaling £43. There are signs of lavish living: the "chamber over the gat[e]," perhaps the main bedchamber, has a bed extravagantly decked with purple silk curtains worth more than £4, a tapestry coverlet with blankets (forty shillings), three great chairs (thirty shillings), and plentiful window curtains for insulation. A relatively bare room described as the "great studie" contains two tables and a chair, a "greate Iron chest" valued at a massive £3 6s. 8d., and "sondrie bookes devinitie & others," worth five pounds. Since the books in London were priced up at a sum of just over £25, this may mean that there was quite a substantial library at Doddinghurst, containing perhaps around eighty books. But since the titles are not individually itemized, we cannot say anything more about this collection.[34]

Having registered some of the things that we can't see in the Aldersgate Street inventory, let us turn to consider what it does tell us. The room designated "Master Stonleys Bedchamber" (Figure 8) may not have a bed in it, but it has some substantial furnishings, including a wooden table and two chairs, a desk covered with red leather, and a smattering of smaller items—a bone candlestick, gold weights, a touchstone, a casting bottle for perfume "garnished With a little sylver," and a brass lamp. The room is by no means a space of private leisure: questions relating to the weight and purity of metals, which might have preoccupied Stonley in his work at the Exchequer, are to the fore here. There is "a battle axe with A mille" (meaning, perhaps, with decorative edging), presumably hanging on the walls, and an unspecified "picture With a frame."[35] The room also has an abundance of containers, including "a Case of Boxes of Wallnuttree with a Frame," "A lyttle case of

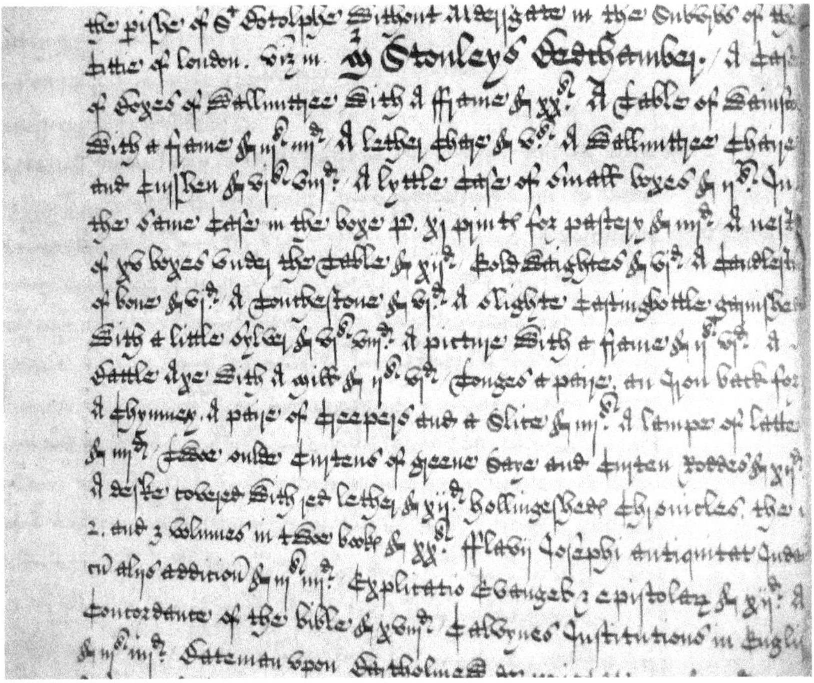

FIGURE 8. The start of the 1597 inventory. National Archives, London, E159/142/435.

smalle boxes," and "a nest of xv boxes under the Table." These may also speak to the life of the bureaucrat, which was (as we have seen) carefully boxed up.

It is conceivable that some of the boxes were originally used to store the slew of books that are listed as present in the room, in 193 separate entries. The list is as unlike the standard early modern library catalogue as it could be; in place of a careful hierarchical arrangement by subject and size, with books of divinity in pride of place, the inventory offers a crazy miscellany. Occasionally it is possible to sense the vestiges of organization, as clusters of books emerge from the general chaos. Thus it is notable that the larger, more expensive books are mostly found in the first half of the list. We kick off with Holinshed's *Chronicles* in the 1587 edition (twenty shillings), followed not long after by more heavyweights: Augustine's works in four volumes (thirty shillings), the biblical commentary of Nicholas of Lyra in six volumes (thirteen shillings, four pence), and Foxe's "Book of Martyrs" (twenty shillings).[36] A number of other books—by Josephus, Calvin, Plutarch, St. Bernard, Peter

Martyr—add to the impression of theological bulk, as does a copy of Wolf-gang Musculus's *Common Places of Christian Religion* and William Alley's religious compendium *The Poore Mans Librarie*.[37] One of the most massive books on the list, assessed rather surprisingly at just four shillings, is recorded as "Regestrum libri Cronicorum." This was the colophon of the celebrated Nuremberg Chronicle, one of the most ambitious publications of the first phase of print (Figure 9).[38] There is also a copy of William Turner's pioneering *Herbal*.[39]

In the wake of these behemoths comes a plethora of smaller works; books of travel, religious controversy, biblical commentary, law, rhetoric, and literature (Ovid's *Heroides,* Brant's *Shyp of Folys,* Seneca's tragedies in Jasper Heywood's translation, Heliodorus's *Æthiopian Historie,* Painter's *Palace of Pleasure,* Gascoigne's scandalous *Hundreth Sundrie Flowres* and supposedly chastened *Posies*).[40] A collection of "Songe books of diverse kyndes" must have been quite substantial, since it is appraised at ten shillings; a bundle of "Enterludes and Commedies" made less of a claim, at just eight pence. There are sheaves of ungathered items—five "Bundells of Pamphlets in quarto" (twenty pence) and eleven "Bundles in viij°" (a respectable four shillings). The list contains a Hebrew grammar and a number of books in French (including a "Testament in Frenche," "A tretise of the lords supper in frenche," the *Tresor des livres d'Amadis de Gaule,* "Institucion of princes frenche," and "Meditacions of holy Fathers frenche").[41] There is a small clutch of emblem books, including works by Andrea Alciato in Latin and Spanish and Claude Paradin in French. Here too we find Stonley's copy of "Debitor & Creditor," discussed in Chapter 2.

Was it unusual for a bedchamber to be so cluttered with books? One can certainly find depictions of bookish sleeping quarters, including Carpaccio's *Dream of St. Ursula,* which shows a little study area in the corner of the saint's bedroom. But this is not a library on Stonley's scale. Architectural historians have, however, found a firm association between the early modern book room and the master bedchamber of the house.[42] It is quite possible that the bedchamber would have had an unacknowledged closet tacked onto it for the storage of books, or that a section of the room had built-in shelves; this might also imply a certain position of dominance for the collection held in this room. The presence of the desk, together with the curtains (implying natural light), a lamp, and a candlestick, make the room feel like a space that could have been used for study and prayer, using the rich resources of the library listed here.

FIGURE 9. Hartmann Schedel, *Liber cronicarum* (1493), title page. Cambridge University Library, Inc. 0.A.7.2.

It is, however, the second room to be inventoried that represents the real powerhouse of the building. This is "the Galery next the Bedchamber," a designation suggesting that this space was strongly associated with the paterfamilias.[43] This room has three times as many object entries as the bedchamber (fifty-one to the bedchamber's seventeen), and boasts a comparable number of bibliographical entries (187 to the bedchamber's 193). Reading the inventory, one senses the sheer quantity of space that would have been needed to house this welter of things; it is likely that (as with other examples from this period) the gallery would have run the entire length of the house. Such long galleries capitalized on the views from their high windows, and were designed to allow their owners to take exercise during periods of bad weather, as a prestigious indoor equivalent to a garden.

If the objects inventoried in the gallery were all fixtures there, then the most striking feature of this room is its multifunctionality. Here we find materials for work, including a table and two desks, a great press or cupboard for letters, and an elaborate standish or inkwell, made "of wood and Iron garnyshed with silver in a lether boxe" and priced up at forty shillings. Here too we find that "lyttle latten ymplement belonginge to a standishe to putt bodkin in. Compasses &c in" (discussed in Chapter 2). Associations with Stonley's day job are strengthened by a variety of chests and boxes, with two of the chests explicitly described as "to cary mony in." Also on hand are objects of knowledge, such as celestial and terrestrial globes, which would in time become standard library furnishings, and a number of recreational objects, including a chess set and a set of bowling balls—the latter providing evidence that the room was indeed used for exercise. There are signs too that eating and drinking went on here, among them a silver gilt crystal salt cellar priced at just over twenty-three shillings, some tigerware stone jugs "covered with sylver and guylt," and a wine cellar. And the room also appears to function as a gallery in the modern sense—a picture gallery, with paintings of the Queen, prominent courtiers, family members such as the merchant John Braunche (Stonley's father-in-law), and an array of other images: maps, fashions of the world, classical goddesses, and the Ten Commandments.

The books in the gallery are again a very mixed bag, but there is a serious concentration of law books in one section of the inventory, which again suggests that the room was a place for work as well as leisure. "Le grand Abridgment," "dyvers Statute bookes bounde up together," "Bracton de legibus Anglie," "Ploydens Reports," and the rest are among the most expensive books in the list. They are set alongside more big, imposing books. Stonley turns out to have owned some of the leading collections of maps and city views of his day—the *Civitates orbis terrarum* of Braun and Hogenberg and Saxton's "Mappes of England."[44] He also had Jacques Tortorel and Jean Perrissin's landmark series of prints documenting recent French history, the *Wars, Massacres and Troubles* (another book that is strangely cheap at twelve pence).[45] "A Byble gilded" may be a copy of the 1568 Bishops' Bible, an illustrated folio with Stonley's arms painted on the front and back, which now survives at Trinity College, Oxford (it was priced at six shillings).[46] Euclid's *Elements* and parts of Gesner's *Historia animalium* drew the eye into still other realms of knowledge.[47]

Yet, as in the bedchamber, the luxury books are just a part of the larger torrent. There are more songbooks and pamphlets, including a bundle of forty pamphlets for two shillings and sixpence, and twenty-four songbooks for five shillings. Then there is a range of educational and literary texts that one might plausibly link with the intellectual leisure signaled by the room's furnishings. These cluster toward the end of the list, where we find Terence's comedies and Nicholas Udall's schoolboy *Floures for Latine Spekynge Selected and Gathered oute of Terence*; an epitome of Erasmus's *Adages* and various editions of Cicero's "Offices"; Richard Rainolde's *Foundacion of Rhetorike* and Robert Whittington's *De octo partibus orationis*; a "poetical dictionary" to help out with classical allusions; and a number of modern prose works.[48] These include English translations of Boccaccio's *Filocolo* ("xiij questions of Bocace"), Diego Hurtado de Mendoza's *Lazarillo des tormes* ("The Spaniards liefe"), and a French version of the *Celestina* of Fernando de Rojas, recorded as a "Traicte des deceptions de servitures envers leur Maisters."[49] Joining them is a jest book in French, entitled *Les joyeuses adventures et plaisant facetieux devis fort recreatif pour rejouir tous esprits mélancolique* (now known from a 16mo. edition printed at Lyon in 1555, of which one copy survives), and another in Italian, Ludovico Domenichi's *Facetie, motti et burle di diversi signori et persone private*, which was (judging by the density of his annotations) a favorite book of Gabriel Harvey.[50] Stonley also took his witty tales in English, in the form of Thomas Blague's *Schole of Wise Conceytes*, and in Latin, from such books as Joannes Hulsbusch's *Sylua sermonum iucundissimorum* (now evidenced by a single edition published at Basel in 1568).[51]

The close relationship between recreational reading and language learning is cemented by a copy of *The Pretie and Wittie Historie of Arnalt & Lucenda with Certen Rules and Dialogues Set Foorth for the Learner of th'Italian Tong*, a translation by the language teacher Claudius Holyband, who plied his trade "in Paules Churchyarde by the signe of the Lucrece."[52] Stonley's gallery also contained a copy of Holyband's *Frenche Littelton* (1581), a manual so called because it was as indispensable to learners of French as Littleton's *Tenures* was for novices in the law.[53] (In the inventory, *The French Littelton* sits quite close to two copies of the *real* Littleton, and to a number of books in law French.) Taken together, the books in this section of the inventory might remind us that our septuagenarian reader had seen his stepchildren through their education and had also been involved in the education of a ward and a godson.[54] Youth and age seem to be in dialogue, rather than opposed, in this bustling space.

The rest of the rooms in the upper part of the house are free of books. "The Greene Chamber" contains a substantial bed, various chairs, and a court cupboard. Another chamber ("betwene the grene Chamber and the Jackhowse") has a couple of chests, a bed, some cushions and "an oulde Turky Carpet" worth thirteen shillings and four pence. Then we come to an "oulde Galery," which is mostly a storage area for linen, with four chests full of sheets, napkins, and cupboard cloths galore, all carefully distinguished by their different grades of fineness. (Eight pairs of fine sheets promise to bring in sixty-four shillings.) Apart from the napery, the room had some weapons ("Twoe Rapiers, ij swordes, iiij hangers and iiij daggers," worth twenty shillings), and a suggestively juxtaposed pair of maps—"A map of the Creacion" and "A mappe of London."[55] "Mistress Stonleys Chamber" has a bed, chairs, hearth furniture, two chests for linen, and "Old hanginges of paynted Clothe" for decoration and insulation. Finally on the upper levels there is a maid's chamber with a halberd and some painted cloths, a room called "Gostwikes Chamber," which again boasts a chest full of linen, and a "Brusshyng Chamber," a service room with another Turkish carpet (this one worth more than fifty-three shillings), cushions and pillows, and a chest containing candlesticks and pewter dishes.[56]

The first room to appear in the inventory that assures us that we have reached the ground floor is the hall. In a medieval house this would have been the hub of activity, but this hall feels rather empty and unloved, with scant furniture for dining and "olde painted clothes" about the walls. A few pictures served to enliven the space; these included Old Testament narratives ("Twoe oulde pictures in frames of the storie of the iij Children and of Hamon and mordokay"), a moralizing allegorical image ("An oulde Table of Cebes"), and nationalistic historical portraiture ("A table of the kinges of this lande in a frame of Wainscote").[57] But the overall tenor of the room is captured by another item: the "Iron Backe in the Chymney cracked." The action has clearly moved to the parlor, a more intimate space that boasts a court cupboard for the display of plate, a hierarchy of chairs ("A greate olde Chaire of Wainscot," "Another lesser Wainscot Chaire," and "A little stoole of Wainscot with a backe"), and furnishings for the hearth, as well as a pair of virginals, a variety of pictures, and a "little olde Clocke with plomettes" (i.e., weights).[58] It also had carpets and cushions for comfort, curtains for the windows, andirons for the fire, and a single book ("an olde Frenche bible").[59] After the parlor, we come to "The Studdy beneth" ("beneath" implying perhaps a lower-level still), which has nothing to show except books—thirty-two entries, characteristically miscellaneous but here predominantly religious.[60] Books of prayers and devotion ("Christian prayers by Henry Bull," "Godly prayers and meditacions," "A tretize againste the feare of death") rub shoulders with various Bibles and testaments, with psalters and books based on the psalms ("vij Sobbs of a sorrofull soule," "A goulden Chaine out of the psalmes," "septem psalme penitentiali cum aliis"), which were a key model for prayer in the period.[61] We might imagine Stonley's sabbath-day scriptural reading taking place in this room. Meanwhile a room called "The office" was presumably the one dedicated space for working in the house, although this room has just one item in it—"A countinge table of bordes covered with olde greene cloth." The word "Exchequer" derives from the use of just such a table in reckoning up sums of money: a board with black and green stripes in a checker pattern.

All that remained for the appraisers to itemize were the buttery and kitchen, with their clangor of hardware and vessels for drinking and dining, representing a world of vibrant sociability that was now coming to an abrupt end. The house seems to have had two outhouses (designated a "little back-howse" and a "lyttle howse") and a number of external spaces (including "The office yarde," "The firste Courte," and "the Backe yarde," as well as the garden). In these spaces, we might appear to have left the book-stuffed spaces of the house far behind and to have entered a world of hard-edged materiality: brass, iron, pewter, copper, stone. But the kitchen, which would likely have contained the one fireplace that was lit throughout the day, laid in a chimney that would have given the house its spine, was of course an engine of the home.[62] It is in the kitchen that we find that crucial innovation, "A Jacke and iij leades," where a jack is "a machine for turning the spit in roasting meat; either wound up like a clock or actuated by the draught of heated air up the chimney."[63] As we saw in Chapter 2, these mechanical turnspits (perhaps a recent invention, since the *OED*'s earliest reference to "the jacke whiche turneth the broche" dates from 1587) were wired into the regimen of self-regulation represented in Stonley's journals. They are an indirect link between the activities of the kitchen and those of the bedchamber, gallery, and study.

There is a still more startling way of crossing any imagined gap between the putatively "upper" and "lower" parts of this house. For the very first item that the appraisers inventoried, in "Master Stonleys Bedchamber," was a "lyttle case of smalle boxes," and there they reportedly found "in the boxe P. xj printes for pastery." Such "printes" (filed alphabetically?) were presumably molds for producing texts or images on foodstuffs. As Wendy Wall has shown, "the domestic world was filled with inscribed, engraved, and printed objects that included edible visual signifiers."[64] Letters could be shaped out of marzipan, cinnamon, pastry, or root vegetables; posies could be printed on sweetmeats or written in walnuts faked up from sugar paste and were ubiquitous on knives and fruit trenchers. Even Erasmus, as Wall notes, "advised baking letter-shaped treats to familiarize pupils with the alphabet"; "the master could reward a student by giving him permission to eat his lesson."[65] Printing was an art that furnished Stonley's household with hundreds of books, but it also played a part in the preparation of food. It is possible that the prints were used to impress improving moral messages onto comestibles, turning them into "objects of virtue" that would in turn impress moral messages onto their consumers.[66]

What was printed onto pastry, as onto pages, might be text, image, or a combination of the two. In the next section of this chapter I explore the overlaying of words and pictures in Stonley's domestic sphere.

The Rage to See

Interactions between visual and literary culture are a striking feature of the inventory of Stonley's goods. Just as many of his books—especially his large-format books of maps, city views, and military reportage—were collections of printed images, so his small but significant collection of paintings and prints worked to disperse the materials of the library across the wider physical environment.

On the evidence of the inventory, most of Stonley's pictures were to be found in the "Galery next the Bedchamber." Although we do not know for sure that they were hung on the walls, the presence of the pictures permits us to imagine this space as something akin to our modern idea of a gallery, a room or series of rooms designed for simultaneous walking, talking, and viewing. The appraisers grouped the pictures together, clearly thinking of them as a discrete category of object. But they were no connoisseurs, and the bluntness of their judgments forces us to rely on speculation, imagination, or sheer guesswork as we struggle to see these images through the inventory's clouded lens. It is worth making the effort, however, since the visual culture of this London mansion intersects with the life of its owner and his reading in many ways.

The list of pictures in the gallery begins with portraits, and (perhaps with a nod to hierarchy) with "A litle picture of her majesty." Despite its small size, the painting was valued at ten shillings, twice as much as the portraits that follow. These proceed from "a little picture of Sir Christopher Hatton late lord Chauncellor" and "A picture of the Lord Dyer" (an eminent judge) to "An olde picture of A merchant called master Branche as is saied" and "An olde picture of a merchant as it should seeme." A little later in the list come "Twoe olde pictures of Sir Walter mildmay and the lord Tresurer that nowe is" (William Cecil), images that bump us back from the city to the court.[67] Public figures seem to be readily identifiable, family members less so. We might note the increasing presence of the word "olde," as the portraits take us back in time, into an area where memories fade and identities start to dissolve. Yet this dispersal of meaning, attendant upon the dispersal of the collection, points us to the intended function of the paintings, which was to plug their owner into a network, materializing his social and familial connections and loyalties. Through his portraits, Stonley situated himself in relation to key figures in the state, the establishment, and the mercantile family into which he had married. To compose a gallery was to situate one's identity in a cat's cradle of outward links.[68]

Besides the portraits, Stonley's gallery contained a variety of other images: "A picture upon Clothe of twoe Friers at a banquet," "The ten commaundementes in a frame," "A smalle picture of Flora covered with glasse," "iiij pictures in Clothe of the vij deadly synnes," "xj little pictures in frames of the fashions of strange countries," and "a picture in oyle colors discribing the ages of the world." There were also numerous maps, including "viij smalle mappes in frames colored of diuerse forren Countries," "xiiij smalle mappes of diuerse Countries in paper put in frames white and vncolored," and "twoe large mappes in frames uncolored."[69] Such miscellaneity was a hallmark of late Elizabethan visual culture. Tarnya Cooper cites an inventory of Ingatestone Hall made in 1600, which sets a portrait of Sir William Petre alongside images of Henry V, Henry VIII, Cleopatra, Diana, and a male and female Turk, plus "nine painted sheildes with poseys upon them."[70] Such a mélange requires a viewer capable of moving rapidly between different frames of reference and modes of attention. One minute we are contemplating the wider world and new ways of visualizing that world, through cartography and costume; the next we are imbibing the stern written edicts of the Ten Commandments or relishing allegorical moralities (the seven deadly sins in painted cloth).[71] There may also have been some religious satire in the mix, if the image of "twoe Friers at a banquet" was (as seems likely) an anti-Catholic image.[72] What unites the images is a certain relationship between seeing and knowing. Just as the gallery would have had windows looking out over the busy London streets, so it opens a series of windows onto the world.[73] To be high up in this house was to gain a surview, a perspective on the world and one's own place in it.

Many of the images in Stonley's gallery would have been prints, and might well have been cut from books or originally issued in book form. When the appraisers tell us that he has eight maps of "forren Countries," eleven of "strange Countries," and fourteen of (simply) "diuerse Countries," the likelihood is that the last (not strange, not foreign) countries are in fact counties. Those images are likely to be, or to derive from, Saxton's county maps of England—the very same maps that Stonley kept in book form in his gallery, where they were valued at a lavish twenty shillings. The fold-out map of France from John Eliot's *Survay*, bought back in 1593, may have been hanging on the wall as one of "twoe large mappes in frames vncolored," but the inventory of the gallery also lists a book of French maps, the *Galliae tabule geographicæ* of Gerhard Mercator. Other images could have been cut from books: the "xj little pictures in frames of the fashions of strange Countries," for example, may (as suggested previously) be all that remains of the copy of the *Habitus variarum orbis gentium*, a collection of sixty-five plates that Stonley bought in a pasteboard binding a few days before Christmas 1582.[74]

Bringing portraiture and print together, Stonley's gallery also contained "a boxe of diverse printed portraitures in paper and pastbord, some colored and some uncolored." These could have been purchased individually: according to Malcolm Jones, "portraits formed the bulk of the presses' production of prints, satisfying that voracious human curiosity to know what those we currently call 'celebs' look like."[75] But it would have been tempting to bulk out such a collection with portraits cut from the title pages of books, or from compilations of historical portraits such as Guillaume Rouillé's *Promptuaire des medalles* (1553) and Antoine du Verdier's *Prosopographie* (1573), copies of which were owned within Stonley's extended family.[76] Such books offered fanciful heads reaching all the way back to Adam and Eve, taking in a wide variety of biblical, classical, and modern figures. They built upon the human-istic notion of history writing as a fundamentally visual phenomenon that set exemplary deeds and cautionary misdeeds before the reader's eyes. Pictures of the heroes and villains of the past were not so much an addition to reading as its consummation.[77]

Links between the visible and the legible are also evident in the "oulde Table of Cebes" found in Stonley's hall. Moldering in that neglected space, with its painted cloths and cracked chimney back, the image nonetheless resonates with the "Cebes table" that is listed among the books in the gallery, valued at a single penny. *The Table of Cebes* (Figures 10 and 11), an anony-mous work probably written in the first century A.D., was first translated into English by the diplomat Sir Francis Poyntz (c. 1487–1528); it was printed posthumously in around 1531.[78] Hugely popular throughout the early modern period (fresh translations followed in 1616 and 1708), the *Table* began by describing the perplexity of a group of visitors to the Temple of Saturn on seeing "a picture very strange" that had been left as an offering there. "A fatherly man standynge by" offers to explain the image, an allegory of human life from birth to its ideal goal—the attainment of true happiness. He "toke then a rod, and poincted to the picture" (A4v), leading the viewers step by step across its surface and pointing out the various enticements and missteps that wait on men, from their initial encounters with Deceit and Fortune, via meetings with the likes of Incontinence, Riot, and Flattery, and so onward and downward to Sorow, Wailyng, and Sluggishnesse. From this prototype of the Slough of Despond, Repentaunce leads the lucky ones on to Untrue Learnynge, whose followers are poets, orators, logicians, mathematicians, and philosophers of various sects. Some will rest content at this point, but others will pass through the strait gate and onward to meet (true) Learning, who points the way to Felicitee. All of the abstractions bar one—an old man called Genius, who fills the soul with wisdom before it is born—are women, some of them dangerously alluring emblems of deception, others firm friends of the wayfarer on his journey through life.

Once a man has achieved felicity, he can return to the world he left behind and see "how evyll and how wretchedly they live, the whiche dwell

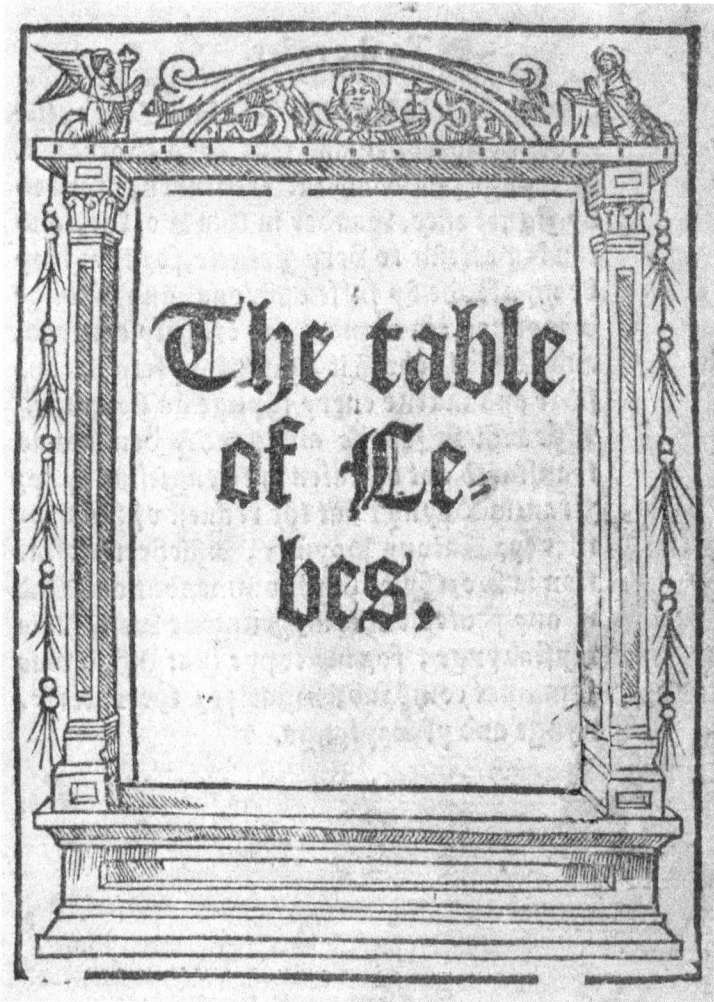

FIGURE 10. *Table of Cebes,* trans. Francis Poyntz (1531?), title page. San Marino, CA, Huntington Library, # 99540.

stil there, and in what great daunger and peryll they live, and howe they erre and wander, and are ledde, as it were by their ennemies" (C1r). The happy man has a privileged perspective on the rest of the world: "he him self liveth well and doeth beholde other, the whiche lyve evyll" (C2r). This beholding is also, of course, what *The Table of Cebes* allows its readers to do; we do not have to go through the whole assault course to recognize the evils of the

FIGURE 11. *Tabula Cebetis*; Nuremberg, Erhard Schön, c. 1531. London, British Museum, E, 8.5.

world, since they are pointed out to us by the "fatherly man" at the Temple of Saturn. When they came to recreate the "table" as an image, reconstituting the lost original described in the text, sixteenth-century artists such as Holbein and Goltzius festooned their images with labels and banderoles, identifying the allegorical figures and providing detailed verbal keys to the visual detail. Viewers thus gained immediate access to unvarnished reality, bypassing the false appearances of the world. But in a sense the engravings remain true to the spirit of the book, since each image at first presents a riot or blur of information, which has to be processed slowly by the eye, preferably in the presence of an expert interpreter wielding a rod. The image possesses what Alfred Gell (discussing intricate designs of all kinds) calls "cognitive stickiness." As a maze of information that demands extended attention, it functions as a kind of "mental flypaper" that catches the viewer, sticking its moral lessons upon the soul.[79]

The 1597 inventory leaves us gasping for information at several points. What are we to make, for example, of the painting of Flora—the only picture in the gallery that was said to be "covered in glass"? Had Stonley looked up Flora in his copy of the *Elucidarius poeticus*, he would have found her glossed as follows: "Flora, meretrix, quæ hæredem pop. Rom. reliquit: unde Floralia, in eius honorem. Huius meminit Cic[ero]."[80] The goddess of flowers and springtime was supposedly a prostitute who left her ill-gotten gains to the Roman people, thereby winning immortality in the festival of the Floralia. "Of such force is wycked *Mammon*, that he can make an Harlot, counted for a Goddes," railed Stephen Batman, although he also blamed "Pope, and Poet" for turning this harlot into a saint.[81] How far did the image Stonley owned indulge the lascivious possibilities of its subject? It is just conceivable that his painting was a derivative of Titian's Flora, a half-length portrait of a beautiful woman with loose locks and revealing décolletage, originally painted around 1515 and widely reproduced in the period.[82] This may be the closest we come to *Venus and Adonis* in Stonley's pictures.

Just as tantalizing are the two religious images—"a little picture of Saint Gerome" and "a little picture in glasse of Joseph and Mary." The latter is strange, since the representation of Mary and Joseph without Christ was unusual; the most common mode in which one finds it is in depictions of the Marriage of the Virgin. As for the St. Jerome, we might imagine that the Protestant prohibition on images of saints would have ruled it out, but other examples are known.[83] But which Jerome was this: the penitent in the wilderness or the humanist hero, set in his study amid all the lovingly rendered paraphernalia of reading and writing?[84] Stonley, with his gilded red-leather inkstand, his desk topped with green velvet, and his brass desk-tidy stuffed with bodkins, compasses, and folding rulers, is recognizably a denizen of the culture of writing immortalized by artists such as Dürer and Antonello da Messina. The little picture may well have been a kind of self-portrait.[85]

There is just one painting in Stonley's collection for which we might be able to name the artist, and it also suggests the proximity of paint and print. This is the first painting listed in the gallery, the portrait of Elizabeth I. The picture (priced at ten shillings) may well be the same painting for which Stonley paid ten shillings on 27 April 1594, noted in the journals as "for the Quenes Picture bought of John Gipkyn picture maker at Shordiche" (46o/8or). The name is familiar to historians of Jacobean art, since Gipkyn was the painter employed for Lord Mayor's shows between 1604 and 1618, in which he collaborated with writers including Jonson, Middleton, and Munday.[86] In 1620 he was employed by another man of the theater, Edward Alleyn, to supply a series of paintings of the Sibyls to the new College of God's Gift in Dulwich; he may have been responsible for supplying sequences of English monarchs, of Christ and the Apostles, of Protestant reformers, and of poets to the college at around the same time.[87] But his finest work was completed a few years before this, in 1616, when he was set to work by a scrivener named Henry Farley, who was agitating for the renovation of London's dilapidated cathedral.[88] Gipkyn's celebrated diptych of St. Paul's, now owned by the Society of Antiquaries, is a rich evocation of the world of the Churchyard. A man whips a dog; horses stamp; the shops built against the walls of the cathedral belch smoke from their chimney pots. Ranks of well-dressed gentlemen sit listening to the sermon, conscious that the King is looking down from the royal box. We catch a snippet of conversation, one man asking another, "I pray, Sir, what is the text?" To which the reply comes back, charmingly, in mirror writing: "The second of Chronicles, chapter xxiv"—a chapter telling how a King set about repairing the Lord's temple.[89]

Paul's Churchyard, the center of the London book trade, was a site with which Gipkyn would have been intimately familiar, since he had been apprenticed as a stationer by his father. The elder John Gipkyn (d. 1596) had been made free of the Stationers' Company in 1586 but could not be sworn in the traditional manner, since he was deaf and could not speak. His father before him (another John, apparently an immigrant from Holland) had sold books "in Paules church yarde, nexte the great Schole, at the sygne of the sprede Egle." It is possible that Stonley's copy of William Turner's densely illustrated *Herball* was the edition for which this Gipkyn had held a ten-year privilege granted in 1551, the year before his death.[90]

But Stonley's reference to buying a painting from a John Gipkyn in 1594 is a surprisingly early one. This was the year in which Gipkyn began his apprenticeship as a stationer, and there are no other records of his artistic output until a decade later. It is possible, therefore, that the portrait of Elizabeth was the work of the deaf father.[91] We know that he was also an artist, thanks to a letter sent by "John Gipkinge" junior to Robert Cecil, probably in 1604, offering his services and saying that he has learned from his father, a German, "to pourtray in picture the image of life and living creatures, agreeable with proportion of true life, so far as art can discover."[92] So it seems that the book arts and the visual arts ran side by side for three generations of a family that would eventually give iconic form to Paul's Churchyard, the center of London's discursive universe.

Something Old, Something New

One last image that we might linger on in Stonley's gallery is described as "A picture in oyle colors discribing the ages of the world." This was probably a version of "The Four Ages of Man," a popular subject for prints and paintings that anatomized the inexorable movement of human (usually male) life as a process of rise and fall from cradle to grave. A surviving late sixteenth-century example carries verses from Thomas Tusser's *Five Hundred Points of Good Husbandry*, linking the ages of man to different animals:

> *Ape* Like Apes we be toieng, till twentie and one,
> *Lyon* Then hastie as Lions till fortie be gone:
> *Foxe* Then wilie as Foxes, till threescore and three,
> *Asse* Then after for Asses accounted we be.[93]

The painting would have cast an unflattering light back on a man who was well past threescore and three and whose flawed accounting might have led him to be "accounted" an ass. How might Stonley's age have inflected his relationship with his property, and with his books?

In Chapter 1, we considered the challenge that Stonley, as a septuagenarian reader, might pose to standard narratives of Elizabethan literary history, with their emphasis on youthful vitality. When we come to consider the 1597 inventory, we cannot help but notice that it has a single dominating adjective: "old." Admittedly the main rooms are largely exempt: in Master Stonley's bedchamber only one item is called "old" ("Twoe oulde Curtens of greene saye and Curten Roddes"), while in the gallery the word applies only to portraits ("An olde picture of A merchant," "Two olde pictures of Sir Walter mildmay and the lord Tresurer that nowe is"). But other rooms are full of old. The Green Chamber's chairs are covered with "oulde black Clothe" or "olde red velvet," while the court cupboard is covered with "an oulde greene carpett," the chimney has "Iron olde crepers," and there is also "An oulde peece of portrature in A frame." The "oulde Galery" has two "olde Danske chest[s]" and a lot of old napkins ("olde diaper napkyns ij dozen," "olde playne napkyns xvij"). Mistress Stonley's chamber is hung with "Olde hanginges of paynted Clothe," and she makes do with old blankets, an old green rug, an "oulde lyttle Chayre," and "an oulde Chest" that contains "diverse peeces of oulde course lynnen." She is considerably luckier than the maid, who has to sleep on "an oulde broken bedstead." Downstairs, the hall is (as we have noted) hung with "olde painted clothes," but it is the parlor that is more noticeably faded. Here we find an old wooden cupboard, a "greate olde Chaire," and "Twoe little olde stooles." The virginals are old, as are the creepers in the fire, the clock, the carpets, the cushions, and various pictures ("a little olde picture of the queenes Armes upon Wainscot," "An old picture of the late lord Tresurer"), not to mention one of the few books that attracts any kind of physical description, "An olde Frenche bible."

We know that Stonley had been living in Aldersgate since at least 1549, as that is the date of the mortgage document that is recycled to form the vellum wrapper to the third volume of the journals. The document, relating to the lease on a property in Fleet Street, refers to Richard Stonley "of Alderichgatestrete, London, gent." The age of many of the items in his house might be taken merely as a reflection of the fact that almost half a century had passed since he first moved into the house. If the chest full of linen in Anne Stonley's bedchamber was the one she had taken with her on her first marriage, to Robert Donne, probably in the early 1540s, then no wonder it was full of "ould course lynnen." But "old" was also a favorite word of appraisers. Keith Wrightson finds it generously applied in the inventories compiled by Ralph Tailor of Newcastle, linking it to the use of "small," which "seems to imply diminished value as well as small size."[94] The word appears fifty-eight times in the Exchequer court inventory of the goods of Armagil Waad, chief clerk of the Privy Council, made following his death in 1568.[95]

TABLE 3.1. Price Depreciation in Selected Volumes Owned by Stonley

Title	Purchase price	Sale price
Chillester, *Youthes Witte* (459/10r)	20d.	6d.
Hutchins, *Davids Sling* (459/41r)	12d.	4d.
Hunnis, *Seven Sobs* (459/41r)	6d.	3d.
Strigelius, *Harmony* (459/62v)	14d.	6d.
Mexía, *Foreste* (459/65r)	12d.	6d.
Batman uppon Bartholome (459/95v)	8s.	20d.
Bilson, *Perpetual Governement* (460/43r)	3s.	12d.
Bancroft, *Survay* (460/43r, 51r)	3s. (or 3s. 4d.)	10d.
Hooker, *Lawes* (460/61r)[97]	3s.	12d.

In Stonley's inventory "old" appears fifty-six times, closely followed by "small" and "little," which together appear thirty-four times. While some of these disparaging adjectives were used to tell objects apart ("Spittes greate and smalle viij"), their proliferation suggests that the appraiser was attempting to produce a low estimate for the purposes of a quick and easy sale.[96]

In the case of Stonley's books, it is sometimes possible to assess the extent of price depreciation over time, since the journals show him buying books that are later priced for sale at substantially lower sums. As Table 3.1 shows, the prices at which Stonley's books were appraised were typically between a third and a half of the prices that he paid for them.[98] We have already noted a number of books appraised for peculiarly low sums. The 1493 *Nuremberg Chronicle*, perhaps the oldest clearly identifiable book on the list, goes for four shillings—a high price for this list, but scarcely commensurate with the scale of this landmark publication, unless its condition or its age counted against it. Another book that is almost certainly very old, *Thordynary of Crysten Men*, printed by Wynkyn de Worde in Fleet Street between 1502 and 1506, goes for eight pence.[99] A Coverdale Bible in Latin and English, dating from the late 1530s, is worth twelve pence, Hardyng's verse *Chronicle* of 1543 just six pence.[100] Books printed in Marian England receive short shrift: Thomas Watson's *Twoo Notable Sermons . . . Concernynge the Reall Presence* (1554), an octavo in twenty-four sheets, commands two pence; John Standish's *Discourse Wherin is Debated Whether the Scripture Should be in English* (1554–55), at half the length, a single penny.[101] But ideology played little part: Tyndale's *An Exposicion Uppon the. v. vi. vii. Chapters of Mathew*, probably published between 1533 and 1549, will fetch a penny, while Cranmer's *Confutation of*

Unwritten Verities, published by the Marian exiles at Wesel in 1556, comes in at two pence.[102] We could multiply examples, but the basic point is clear. When it came to books, this appraiser was no great respecter of age.

As he viewed himself in the glass of his possessions, Stonley would have seen his age reflected back in the preponderance of objects that had grown old in his company. His library appears to be something of a midden, inviting us to dig down through the layers until we hit antiquities such as *Thordynary of Crysten Men* or the *Nuremberg Chronicle.* But, just as we have already seen Stonley as something of a follower of fashion, so the evidence of the journal suggests his book buying was, even toward the end of his life, mostly up to the minute. Thus, in the first volume of the journals, of the books that we can assign any kind of date to (that is, books that were not hardy perennials like the Bible, or Aesop's *Fables,* or "ballads"), fully twenty-seven were published between 1580 and 1582. Only five—Nowell's *Catechism,* More's *Utopia,* Aristotle's *Organum,* a medical work called *Guidos Questions,* and Pedro de Mexía's *The Forest or Collection of Histories*—were not newcomers to the print marketplace (though they may have been bought in new editions).[103] The same pattern is observable in the second volume, where thirteen purchases were freshly minted in 1592–93; another (Jeninges's *Discoverie of Dangers*) dated from 1590, and only one title (Becon's *Governaunce of Vertue,* perhaps first published in 1544) was of long standing.[104]

Stonley's purchase of Shakespeare's *Venus and Adonis* and Eliot's *Survay* thus falls squarely into a broader pattern of book buying. Stonley was demonstrably in the market for the new; indeed, he may have been the sort of reader that John Webster mocked in the preface to *The White Devil,* when he complained that most of the people who came to see his play were like "those ignorant asses (who visiting Stationers shoppes their use is not to inquire for good bookes, but new bookes)."[105] What Webster's fit of sour grapes misses is the potency of the intersection between new books and news. Stonley's journals testify to a world in which the publishing industry was increasingly servicing a desire to know about current events. This is nowhere clearer than in the first volume, which allows us to see Stonley following the stories of the Catholic priests Everard Ducket and Edmund Campion from day to day, and also buying "the Booke of the Arraynment of Everard Ducket" (459/12r), "Bookes and Ballades touching Campion & Ducket" (459/12v), and "Whittacre agenst Campion" (459/25r). Elsewhere he buys two books of Continental news (459/13v, 460/79r) and a proclamation (459/73r).

Proclamations are frequently considered "jobbing work" that falls outside the usual rules of the print marketplace, but such items could evidently also be bought like any other.[106]

The inventory, with its preponderance of "old," seems at odds with the newfangledness of Stonley's book buying. But the comparative absence of "old" qualifiers in the most significant rooms of the house tells its own story. Furthermore, the inventory lists around twenty-five books that must have been bought in the 1590s—less than half the figure for previous decades, but a reminder that Stonley was still buying books as his finances collapsed. One of his latest purchases, Andrew Maunsell's *Catalogue of English Printed Bookes* (1595)—a pioneering bibliography of divinity, physic, surgery, and the mathematical sciences—suggests that there was a degree of self-consciousness to his book collecting at the end of his life. The tidily organized printed booklist points up the scandalous disorganization of the inventory in which it is found.[107]

Like Stonley's library, with which it overlaps considerably, Maunsell's *Catalogue* marks a certain stage in the development of vernacular publishing. There are now enough books printed in English for a bibliography of English books to be useful. But Maunsell's project is underwritten by an anxiety about memory. Maunsell was moved to compile the work when he observed "many singuler Bookes, not only of Divinitie, but of other excellent Arts, after the first impression, so spent & gone, that they lie even as it were buried in som few studies." Although publication ought to have rendered them publicly visible, printed books were prone to disappear from view: "men desirous of such kind of Bookes, cannot aske for that they never heard of, and the Bookeseller cannot shew that he hath not."[108] Anticipating Webster, Maunsell admits that some readers don't care about this, "for some soare so hie that they looke not so low, as on their owne countrie writers, and some regard not old Bookes, but aske what newes? Or new writers?" But sixteenth-century publishers have set forth religious works that are as good as any "since the Apostles time," and (as Maunsell wrote in his dedicatory epistle to Elizabeth I) these lost sheep needed to be found again:

> What great account (most gracious Soveraigne) hath beene made of godly bookes, may evidently appeare by the value set uppon the bookes of curious Artes, brought to the Apostles feete to be burnt: For if those bookes were valued to two thousand markes, Of what estimation shall we account the bookes, whose author is God himselfe, who by his holy

spirite hath inspired the Prophets, the Evangelists, the Apostles, and his true Ministers, to write and set forth the same for the instruction of his owne people and Church? All the goods upon the earth cannot value them. The booke of God hath bene alwayes of his children more accounted of, than their lives, or anie thing else in this worlde whatsoever.[109]

Maunsell makes the case for the transcendent value of divinely inspired writing, protesting against the fickleness of a print marketplace that allows it to fall into oblivion. But this was of course just another eminently forgettable point of view, jostling for attention in an ever more crowded field of public discourse. Francis Phillips added the *Catalogue* to the pile, pricing it up for eight pence.

Books, Chests, and the Objectification of Discourse

The disorganization of his library as inventoried in 1597 is at odds with the rage to order that we have seen Stonley displaying in his journals, which is also reflected in the material culture of his house. To conclude this chapter, I want to follow a trail that leads from the chests and boxes in his domestic environment, via the material structure of the early modern book, to the question of how discourse was objectified and commodified in the first age of print. As we shall discover, Stonley's entanglement in the newness of books was also an embroilment in a mode of literary production and consumption that was vital to this phase of print culture.

In the sixteenth and seventeenth centuries, the profusion of household goods led to a corresponding growth in the number of receptacles that were required to tame it.[110] The phenomenon is visible in dictionaries of the period: take, for example, the "young clerk's vocabulary" from 1685 that suggests Latin equivalents for "A Trunk," "A Male Trunk, or Portmanteau Trunk," "A Chest," "A Pannel Chest," "A Cabinet, Casket, or Little Coffer," "A Desk," "Drawers or Boxes in a Cabinet," and "A Case-Box, or Nest of Drawers," as well as for "A Little Chest," "A Chest to keep Books in" (*Librarium*), "A Chest or Press to keep Apparel in," "A Chest wherein Mercers put their Wares, a Shop-Chest," and "A Chest where Evidences or such like Writings are kept." There follow terms for dedicated boxes (spice boxes, jewel boxes), and various kinds of cupboard ("A Cupboard to set Plate in," "A

Cupboard to keep Victuals in," A Bread Cupboard").[111] There was doubtless some reassurance in the idea that a classical language could capture every thing in the modern world, but such a list gives a vivid sense of the copiousness of things in the period.

Early modern wills and inventories make frequent references to chests, trunks, and boxes. In his will of 1615, William Neile of Westminster (brother of the churchman Richard Neile) bequeathed to seven of his children a total of 880 books, each of which had been labeled on the title page with the name of its intended recipient. Six of his children also received a chest. Mildred got "the lesser wainscote chest," Richard "my best Trunke," William "my second best Trunke," John "the wainscote chest with the nine worthies on it," Dorothy "the boxe which was sometimes Charles Newells," and Frances "one Cedar boxe" (only Robert, a newborn, went boxless).[112] Equally eloquent is the will of Henry Darell, "Citizen and fishmonger of London," written on 9 January 1620 when he was "at sea in the good shipp Called the hart of London bound for *Persia*, where by gods assistance I am to remayne for a Certaine time." The inventory of Darell's shipboard goods is clearly his own loving enumeration of the things in his life, which includes a small collection of books (Spanish and English Bibles, accounts of foreign travels, a nautical almanac and a guide to shipboard medicine, two dictionaries, a popular letter-writing manual, and a copy of "peeles booke of Accompt").[113] But before we are treated to these, we are invited to admire his sea chest: "a verie fayre Truncke with 3 drawers for Lynnen covered with a good Cowhide made of oake and Elme (timber) planke and the boxes of wainscott the cover under the lether bound with Iron 3 bands Cleane over the lidde cost in England and is worth here = 3—16 0." Darell also has a second chest, a hat case, and three cases of wine.

Documents like these help to prepare us for the proliferation of boxes in Stonley's house, especially in the bedchamber and gallery. The inventory of the former room kicks off with "A Case of Boxes of Walnuttree with a frame," "A lyttle case of smalle boxes," and "A nest of xv boxes under the table," while the list for the latter begins:

A Joyned Table with a Cupbord	vs
A greate Case of boxes with gilt lock and keys and a frame	xls
A case of boxes with Iron lock and keys ungilt and a frame	xxs
Twoe smale Chestes to cary mony in	vjs viijd
A smalle case of boxes of Joyned worke	vs

A case of boxes covered with black lether	xiijs iiijd
A greate bard Flaunders Covered with tand lether	xxvjs viijd
A Flaunders Iron Chest	xls
. . .	
A chest for lynnen covered with black lether	vs
A waynscot little chest	vjs viijd

As if this were not enough, the same room contains an inkstand "in a lether boxe," two square combcases, "A wainscot box with A lokinge glasse," "A Seller for wyne," and a great presse [i.e., a cupboard] for letters." Some of the pictures in the room are also ferreted away in boxes. Nicholas Penny comments that "no-one reading sixteenth-century household inventories can fail to be impressed by the number of chests," and Stonley's is no exception to that rule.[114] As well as containing valuables, chests were themselves among the most valuable items in a house, and just as they helped to separate and differentiate different kinds of thing, so they were themselves highly differentiated in terms of size, material, and place of origin (the appraisers can recognize a "Flaunders" and a "Danske" when they see one).

The fact that two of the chests in the gallery are described as being designed "to carry money in" connects them firmly to Stonley's professional identity. His journal entries reveal that Stonley spent many of his days paying often vast sums of money into the "Chest" at Westminster, as when he writes: "This morning after preyer I went to westminster delyverd up to the Chest vjMli."[115] On a number of occasions he turns the word "chest" into a verb, as in: "This morning after preyer went to westminster Chested up ther by makpes MMMCC li."[116] (According to Michael Clanchy, the Exchequer, or royal treasury, itself originated as the collection of chests and documents that followed the King around the country.)[117] Chests also figured in Stonley's battle against impending bankruptcy. Explaining his debts, Stonley requested an allowance "for the losse of money stollen from me when the Receipt was robbed out of my Cheste which I had contented in a sheet of paper to be [£4,000] and found at my cominge left but [£1,900] or there about at which tyme the Lo: Thresorer that nowe is tooke a patterne of the Theeves feet upon my telling boord—[£2,000]." His financial meltdown seems to have been occasioned in part by a blurring of public and private that is implicit in the fact that these chests for carrying money are to be found in his house. Stonley claimed that "his debt first grew by purchasing land with part of the money he had received for first fruites, & kept in his handes without controlment."[118]

Although there is no evidence that the Aldersgate Street books were stored in chests, this was one of the commonest modes of book storage in the medieval and early modern periods.[119] That fact is registered explicitly in one work in Stonley's collection, the translation of Girolamo Cardano's *Comforte* by Thomas Bedingfield, which begins with an exchange of printed letters. In the first, Bedingfield asks the Earl of Oxford to keep the manuscript of his translation secret. In the second, the Earl of Oxford explains that he has turned down Bedingfield's request, since it would have been an unpardonable error "to have murthered the same in the wast bottomes of my chestes." Hence the printed book that we have in our hands.[120] Another of Stonley's books, James Calfhill's *An Aunswere to the Treatise of the Crosse* of 1565, attacks Jewish phylacteries and other "external" uses of religious texts and objects, citing Jerome to the effect that "the commaundementes are to be caryed in the heart, and not in body," "for otherwyse studies and chestes have bokes, and have not the knowledge of God."[121] This is another version of the dialectic that we observed in Maunsell's *Catalogue*: the vessels that facilitate preservation and remembering are by the same token sites of death and oblivion.

Thinking about the relationship between books and boxes can help to deepen our understanding of the materiality of the early modern book. For if it was taken for granted that chests would hold books, this was also a culture in which books could be turned into chests. The Dutch antiquary Abraham Gorlæus was depicted in 1601 with his collection of coins and medals, many of which were stored in small chests shaped like books, which shut with metal clasps (Figure 12).[122] Another Dutchman, the poet and polemicist Philips van Marnix, in his *Bee Hive of the Romishe Church* (a work translated into English in 1579), told the story of an "old wife" of Venice who set herself to fast and pray in a cell for six days, assisted only by "two great bookes . . . both of equall bignes, & like fashion."[123] While one of the books was a Bible, the other was a cunningly disguised chest stuffed with "flat bottles ful of Malmesie, and with good fine Marchpanes, which she her selfe made, of the brawne of Capons and Partridges, with Sugar and Almondes (like a lickerous Ladie)." Had she not been found out, this edible book would have produced "a wonderfull miracle" that would have been the making of the self-mortifying sect that the unnamed lady was striving to promote.

We have already explored the extent to which Stonley's account book is at once cognate with boxes and is itself a series of boxes; and in this it would

Gorlæus hîc in ære scalptus, æs cui,
Argentum, & aurum, Roma quod vel Græcia
Signauit vnquam, gemmaque & carus lapis
Olim vetustis destinatus annulis
Perennitatis gratiam debent suæ.
Nunc experitur an Metalla a sæculis
Qui vindicata sæculo nostro dedit,
Ipsum futuris dent Metalla sæculis.
H. Grot,

FIGURE 12. *Portrait of Abraham Gorlæus* (c. 1549–1608); engraving by J. de Gheijn, 1601. British Museum.

have been quite typical. Compare a letter that Edward Dering wrote to his wife in 1632, in which he informed her: "I have sent this messenger on purpose to bringe me a boxe and a booke that are upon the nearest corner of my study table next the doore: the boxe is a little firre boxe with a fewe papers and some evidence[s] in itt, the booke is an olde long booke in my grandfathers hand of payments, and lyes beside the boxe. they do both concerne our house in Dover."[124] The accounts and the evidence box sit next to each other on the study table, and perform comparable storage functions.[125] The larger space of the study or closet could also be imagined as a kind of lockable book box, as in Donne's *Satire I*, where the student calls his chamber a "standing wodden chest" in which he is "consorted with these few bookes," and in which, he says, he hopes to be "coffind, when I dy." Donne's satirist here wittily proposes to take advantage of the burial options that are elsewhere imagined as the enemy of literary culture.[126]

The material overlap between books and boxes becomes even more conspicuous when one starts to call up titles from Stonley's inventory in a rare books room, in an effort to imagine what this library might have looked like. Many of the larger books turn out not to be in the light pasteboard bindings that would come to dominate in the later sixteenth century, but are instead bound in solid wooden boards with metal clasps (Figure 13).[127] The resulting volumes are distinctly weighty, and they do not just fall open; you have to turn them on their side and unclasp them like a box before they can be read. A chest of such books would have been something like a nest or case of boxes.

This aspect of the book's physical disposition is often echoed at the level of content. A surprising number of Stonley's books harbor ambitions to put the whole world of knowledge between two covers. Whether they are encyclopedias such as the *De proprietatibus rerum* of Bartholomaeus Anglicus (which Stonley owned both in the "original" and in Stephen Batman's revision), universal histories like the Nuremberg Chronicle, biblical compendia like William Alley's *Pore Man's Librarie*, theological commonplace books such as those of Peter Martyr or Wolfgang Musculus, or one of the many herbals, dictionaries, *silvae*, and other compendia in the collection—the sheer scale of many printed books and the persistence of the medieval idea of the book as thesaurus or treasury are striking.[128] Other books in Stonley's collection invite a similar kind of analysis, as when R. W. Maslen describes William Painter's *Palace of Pleasure* and Geoffrey Fenton's *Certaine Tragicall Discourses* as "two inexhaustible treasure-chests of narratives."[129] This notion of the

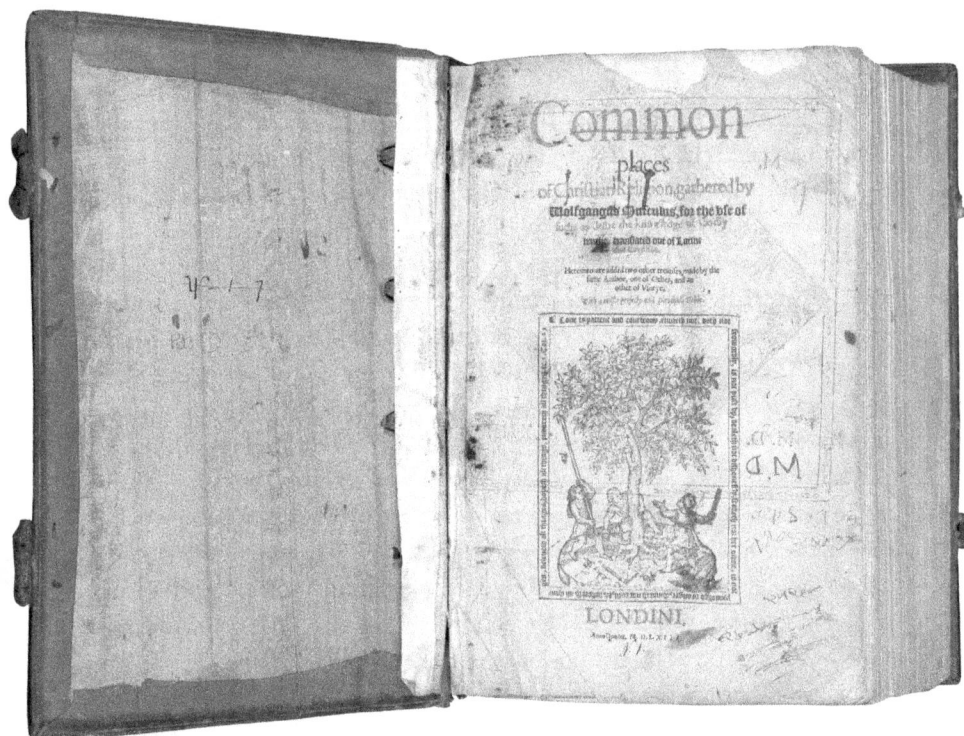

FIGURE 13. Wolfgang Musculus, *Common Places of Christian Religion* (1563), in a wooden binding. Cambridge University Library, Pet. O.5.6.

book as chest survives in the modern thesaurus, a bibliographical receptacle for the riches of language.

Several of Stonley's books propose themselves either as treasuries or as jewels to put in a treasury. Stonley owned a book about human anatomy called *The Englishemans Treasure* and two works by Conrad Gesner, *The Treasure of Evonymus* and *The Newe Jewell of Health*, that linked distillation, health, and wealth.[130] He owned Thomas Cooper's English-Latin Dictionary, the *Thesaurus linguae Romanae et Britannicae*, and Augustine Marlorat's Biblical digest, the *Thesaurus sacrae scripturae*.[131] He also had John Blagrave's treatise on the astrolabe, *The Mathematical Jewel*.[132] To focus on titles like these is, however, immediately to notice how many more of his books have objectifying titles. Stonley bought *A Christall Glasse of Christian Reformation*, *The Forest of Histories*, *The Rock of Regard*, *The Palace of Pleasure*, and *The Haven of Health*.[133] He bought *The Posye of Flowred Prayers*, *The Seven Sobs of a Sorrowful Soul for Sin*, and *The Diamond of Devotion*.[134] Nor should we overlook *A Hundreth Sundrie Flowres* and the *Shepherd's Calendar*.[135] Not all of these items suggest storage (a forest, a palace, or a sob will not fit into a chest), but taken together they suggest the insistence with which early modern writers and their publishers imagined books as places and things.

The penchant for giving books, especially devotional books, quaintly objectifying titles was pilloried by Rabelais in his catalogue of the library of Saint-Victor, in the seventh chapter of *Pantagruel*. Among the works that Pantagruel finds in the Parisian monastery are (in Donald Frame's translation) "The cart of salvation," "The codpiece of the law," "The pomegranate of vices," "The nest-egg of Theology," "The mustard-pot of penitence," "The gym-shoe of humility," and "The handcuffs of Piety."[136] The satire here is usually taken to be aimed at scholastic theology; in parodying titles that yoked the familiar with the ineffable, Rabelais was attacking the presumption and hypocrisy that passed for learning in his day.[137] His parody seems to have had little or no impact on the world of sixteenth-century publishing; books called "The X of Y" became a mainstay of the presses.[138] Why was this such a common formula? The answer presumably has to do with the question of how words can be packaged up for sale in the first place. A number of celebrated works from the first half of the sixteenth century have seemingly redundant titles, such as *The Book of the Courtier* and *The Book named the Governor*, suggesting that the book needed to announce itself as a book; compare incipit-like titles such as *In this Booke is Conteyned the Names of the Baylifs Custos Mairs and Sherefs of London* (1503?) and *This Boke Sheweth the Maner of Measurynge of All Maner of Lande* (1537?).[139] By the later sixteenth century, the problem of how to objectify discourse has been solved by basing the title either on an established genre or on a particular act (often a speech act). A book is an anatomy, a dialogue, a discovery; or it is a protestation, relation, reply, or survey. To cast your book as a thing—as a mirror, or a garden, or a touchstone—was another way of giving it a place in the world.

The modern reader is likely to share some of Rabelais's skepticism about the vogue for "the x of y." Books with such titles were often the work of writers whom we might dismiss as hacks, but who are more properly thought of as "polygraphs" or "polygraphers" (on the model of the Italian *poligrafi* and the French *poligraphes*). The idea of the polygraph was first explored in detail by Paul Grendler, in his 1969 book *Critics of the Italian World*.[140] These were "adventurers of the pen," disciples of Aretino who eked out a living away from the suffocating courts and who wrote vernacular texts that aimed at broad popularity: "tales, poetry, plays, moral fables, travel literature, satires, social and literary criticism, letters, and burlesques."[141] In the gaps between their appearances in print, they worked as editors or translators "and sometimes operated their own presses."[142] Grendler hoped to redeem his Italian polygraphs from the taint of literary prostitution or of "mere" mercantilism —the charge that they "sold their words with the detachment of a merchant selling a bolt of cloth"—by identifying the intellectual ramifications of their writing.[143] These were not hacks; indeed, Italian polygraphs often look like polymaths.

Moving from Italy to England, the polygraph label fits a good many miscellaneous writers who played an important part in the development of vernacular print culture. Perhaps the most obvious is Anthony Munday, a Proteus of the literary marketplace whose works (many of them translations) included prose romance, news, moralized biography, chronicle and urban history, ballads, paradoxes, polemic, and devotion.[144] Like several Italian *poligrafi*, Munday was close to the institutions of print; the son of a stationer, he was apprenticed to a printer, and at one point seems to have worked as an in-house translator for John Wolfe. Among many other things, he was the author of *The Mirrour of Mutabilitie* (1579) and *A Banquet of Daintie Conceits* (1588), and editor of *Archontorologion, or the Diall of Princes* (1619).[145] Another candidate is Abraham Fleming, translator of Virgil and John Caius, editor and indexer for numerous London presses, compiler of *A Panoplie of Epistles or a Looking-Glass for the Unlearned*, and author of devotional works, such as *The Diamond of Devotion, The Conduit of Comfort*, and *The Foote-Path to Felicitie*.[146] Other writers who might be considered polygraphs include John Norden, Lodowick Lloyd, and John Philips.[147]

Stonley was clearly attracted to these kinds of objectified texts, and his book buying was highly miscellaneous, so we might want to think of him as a "polyreader". Where the polygraph replenished the presses with "diverse foods," the polyreader was the lapper-up of that fare.[148] Exalted book collectors like John, Lord Lumley, constructed polymathic libraries in a conscious attempt to master the full range of human and divine learning, but men-about-town like Stonley read variously because the press supplied them with miscellaneous materials.[149] Where the press led, this reader followed, creating a template for later urbanites like Edward Dering and Samuel Pepys.[150] These were the readers that print built in early modern London.

"The readers that print built": the conceit relies on the idea that we are made out of the things we read, as a composite of books like that which is rendered grotesquely literal in Arcimboldo's painting *The Librarian.*[151] This chapter began with the tendency of inventories to elide people and property and to imagine the self as materialized in the stuff that it possesses. The delight that Samuel Pepys took in viewing himself in the mirror of his growing wealth might be taken to exemplify this conception of the self. While in the case of Stonley it is harder to track his investment in stuff from his inventory, this chapter has suggested some of the ways in which objectified discourse took its place in the home, and blurred into the life of its owner. His books offered themselves as a prosthetic lenses with which to view the world, as mirrors with which to reflect on the passing of time and the process of aging, as indexes to the new, and as storage devices that allowed precious things to be simultaneously remembered and forgotten.

On Aldersgate Street, we have focused on the entanglement of the human with its constitutive stuff; my next chapter goes on to think about the book as an object mediating human relationships, drawing on the smattering of books that survive from Stonley's collection. As we cross the threshold, we might glance back into Imogen's bedchamber to observe that the most startling thing that happens there, from the point of view of book history, has nothing to do with Iachimo and his inventorying. It is the simple fact that the princess should ask her maidservant to fold down the leaf for her when she has finished reading.

Chapter 4

People of the Book

Ties That Bind

When we turn to the books that survive from Richard Stonley's library, we find little or no annotation, and so no evidence of reading as it is usually understood.[1] Some, it is true, contain quantities of underlining, the most frustrating kind of annotation since it is usually impossible to pin it on any individual reader. Here, however, the distinctive style of the underlining (emphasizing the edges of the text block) means that it can often be firmly ascribed to his stepson, the ecclesiastical lawyer Daniel Donne.[2] More broadly we may say that the books Stonley owned say much less about his reading than about his relating. If, as Bill Sherman has complained, book history has too often been technological and mechanical, leaving out the social and delivering a world that is "curiously unpeopled," these books constitute an antidote to that malaise.[3] They want to tell us about social connections, and they want to tell us about status.

The books discussed in this chapter figure first and foremost as possessions. We only know that they belonged to Stonley because of the care he took to mark his ownership of them, usually with a notation of the price. To argue (as my previous chapter did) for the kinship between the books and the chests in his household thingscape is to see the books as receptacles, places for storing up knowledge. Stonley may have been accumulating books rather as he accumulated the parchment bonds that proved his rights to lands: in order to store up wealth.[4] A number of the books have elaborate gold-tooled bindings, and the journal shows us both how much such bindings could cost and what the sums involved might mean. On 20 January 1582 Stonley paid the publisher and bookseller Edward White thirty shillings "for iij Bybles in 8° very well bownde at xs the pece." On 6 February 1582 (as we have seen),

he paid him twenty-six shillings and five pence for "for a new Byble all gylde
with Silver Claspes the Bokes xvs xd the Claspes per oz j oz di[midium]
quarter vijs iijd the makinge iijs iijd."[5] Ten shillings, the cost of a well-bound
octavo Bible, could buy you a pair of winter boots or four pairs of winter
shoes from "John Shomaker," or forty horseshoes for your geldings from the
blacksmith at Doddinghurst; it was also the sort of money you might give to
reward "To Mr Wrothes man for bringing of a Bucke."[6] Twenty shillings (two
Bibles) might buy you a court cupboard or a chair from Andrew Weston, or
it could be a quarter's wages for your cook Thomas Fyssher.[7] Thirty shillings
(three Bibles) represented a year's wages for "Agnes the mayde."[8] Twenty-six
shillings, the cost of a gilded Bible with silver clasps, got you a luxurious
beaver hat from "Richard Perkyns at the Hartes Horne in Suthwarke" (60v),
or a saddle and saddlecloth of "fustian naples" for your daughter from "Richard Bywell Sadler."[9] So a well-bound book could be seriously expensive.

If the books that Stonley acquired were acts of investment, they were
also acts of attachment. His most imposing binding is also his most extravagant gesture of status, a claim to have arrived. It is found on a copy of the
Bishops' Bible of 1568, now at Trinity College, Oxford (Figure 14).[10] Within
a gold-tooled surround inlaid with colored leathers, the covers of this large,
lavishly illustrated folio volume are painted on the front with Stonley's arms
and on the back with the same arms, impaled with those of his wife. The
colors are still bright, the effect garish, but there is no denying the force of
this statement of familial prestige. (This may be the Bible that Stonley bought
new in 1582 for twenty-six shillings, stripped of its silver clasps, and it might
also be the "Byble gilded" listed in the gallery in the 1597 inventory, priced
up at six shillings, but this can only be a speculation.) The binding has been
identified as the work of the "MacDurnan Gospels Binder," one of the most
prominent purveyors of gold-tooled bindings in Elizabethan London, and
has been linked with another binding on a smaller book in the Bodleian
Library in Oxford. This is a copy of *The Psalmes of David* from 1571, in a
gilded corner-and-centerpiece binding that has the arms of Stonley's brother-
in-law John Braunche painted on the front board, and the same arms impaled
with those of his wife on the back (Figure 15).[11] While the volumes cannot
be said consciously to allude to one another, there is a strong family resemblance, and it is particularly striking that the "chain" tool (made up of a series
of interlinked, rounded lozenges) found on the front of the Bible should also
have been used on the spine of the psalter. A version of the tool is also found
on the spine of the only other surviving book from Stonley's library to bear

FIGURE 14. *The. Holie. Bible.* (1568), armorial binding showing arms of Stonley impaled with Branche. Oxford, Trinity College, K.10.3.

FIGURE 15. *Psalmes of David and others* (1571), gold-tooled binding. Oxford, Bodleian Library, Broxb.29.2.

a MacDurnan Gospels binding, which is a copy of Antoine du Verdier's *Imagines Deorum* (1581) now in the Cambridge University Library (Figure 16).[12] This book was signed by Stonley and annotated by Daniel Donne, who transcribed an excerpt from Psalm 115 (a locus classicus about the deadness of idols) on the flyleaf facing the title page. Again, it would be a stretch to suggest that these bindings were intentionally interconnected. But the chain design furnishes an apt visual metaphor for the ways in which bindings might bind families as well as books. If, as I have suggested elsewhere, the designs of early modern bookbindings were visual displacements of the knotting and ligaturing of quires that is going on under the surface, they were also ways of creating links between groups of objects and the groups of people who were invested in those objects.[13]

Witnessing and Giving

Bindings are by no means the only material feature of a book to have such social valencies. The library of the University of St. Andrews has Stonley's copy of the *Confessio Catholicæ fidei Christiana* (1559), a defense of Catholicism by the Polish cardinal Stanislaus Hosius.[14] At the head of the blank final leaf of the book Stonley writes: "I bought this book cuming from the Minores xiiij Februarij *1586* Teste Rogero Batte." The witness here, Roger Batte, was a servant of Stonley's whose name first appears midway through the first volume of the journals, on 23 March 1581/2, in a bill for livery coats (459/52r). In the second volume he is paid several times for wine, and on one occasion is reimbursed for two shillings "that he leyd owt to the gardners wyf for weding the garden at London" (460/7r). But now he also accompanies Stonley's daughter Dorothy Dawtrey on a journey to her home in Sussex, and he is treated to another act of investiture as he is given mourning clothes to attend the funeral of Robert Petre (460/24v, 46v). During Stonley's imprisonment in the Fleet, Batte was a constant presence; on one occasion, Stonley dispatched him "with [his] rentes to westminster which is lockyd up in a Chest ther wherof Roger hath the key" (461/13r). And he was still with the family in 1611, when Anne Stonley left him £5 in the schedule attached to her will.[15] On the Hosius, Batte is merely called upon to witness Stonley's purchase of a second-hand book. But it is striking that the inscription on this Latin book should slide into Latin at the moment of witnessing ("Teste Rogero Batte") (Figure 17). Just how literate was this liveried servant? It also

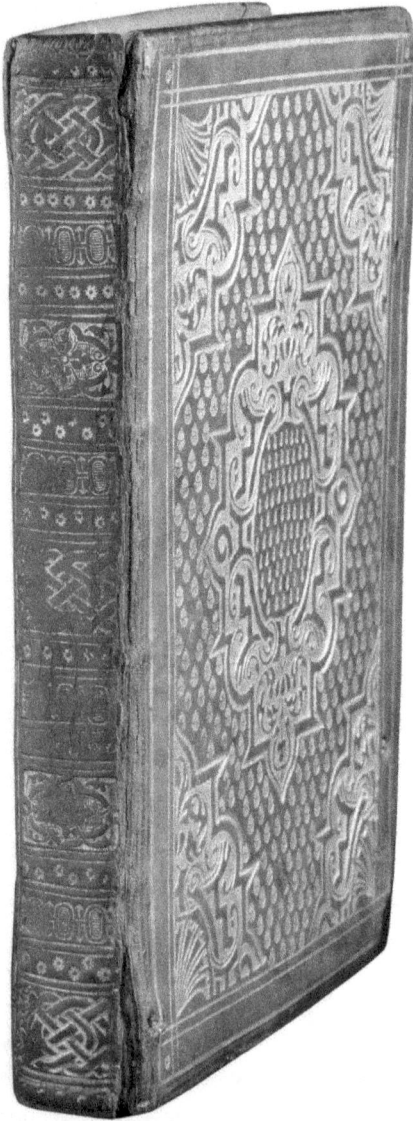

FIGURE 16. Antoine du Verdier, *Imagines deorum* (1581), gold-tooled binding. Cambridge University Library, Rel.C.58.3.

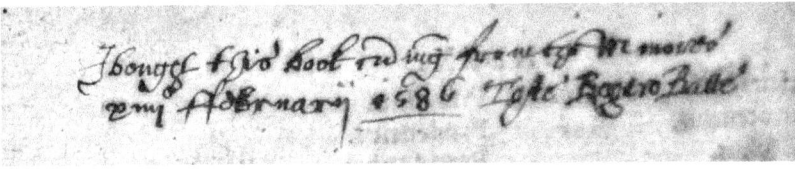

FIGURE 17. Inscription on final leaf of Stanislaus Hosius, *Confessio catholicæ fidei christiana* (1559). St. Andrews University Library, TypNAn.B59SD.

matters that the whole inscription is in Stonley's hand. He signs for his servant, effectively acting as a witness for himself.

The witnessing of book ownership was a widespread phenomenon in early modern England, and one that has so far escaped the attention of book historians. Some entirely typical versions are found in a copy of Christopher Sutton's popular devotional treatise *Disce vivere*; in 1611, John Davyds, "Cambrobrytanus," got a fellow Welshman, Richard Burches, to witness his ownership of the book, and in 1637 the same volume was claimed by Mary Jones in a Latin inscription witnessed by John Smith.[16] John Finet was more artful. Signing his name nearly fifty times in a tiny Latin prayer book, he made one of the signatures curl round in a circle, adding the words "me tenet teste edwarde bell" around the edge of it.[17] There is a good deal of evidence that witnessing was a game that schoolboys played with their books. Thus a thirteen-year-old Anthony Wood wrote in his copy of Francis Meres's *Witts Academy* (1634) "Anthony Wood his booke Wittnesse John Cowdrey 1645," along with various schoolboy notes, including one that reads "Wood is a foole."[18] Such youthful witness statements could also be teasing forgeries. A copy of *Fabularum Ovidii interpretatio* (Cambridge: Thomas Thomas, 1584) is inscribed "Daniel Evans his booke. witness Arthur JDonne"; apparently John Donne had signed the book, possibly as a schoolboy, and Evans subsequently inscribed it, co-opting Donne as a witness. (He turned him into an "Arthur," apparently not noticing the "J").[19]

This kind of game playing did not stop in adulthood. The title page verso of a copy of George Sandys's *Relation of a Journey* (1615) in Cambridge University Library declares that John Parish of Sudbury in Suffolk owns the book, with "Elizabeth stiles wittness to it / February 4the / Ano Domini 1691/ 2."[20] The front flyleaf has both "Elizabeth styles not her book" and "Elizabeth stiles Her book / John Parish witnes to it 1689." On other flyleaves we find further doodles involving Parish and Styles, as well as signatures or names of Thomas, Isaac, and Samuel Parish (Samuel claims to be the owner of the book, with "John Parish witness to it," in 1688). On the final flyleaf we have what may be the consummation of a relationship: a flourished inscription of "Elisebeth Parish." We can establish from other sources that John Parish was a substantial Suffolk clothier and nonconformist who had married his first wife, Sarah Gunton, in 1673; his children Samuel and Isaac were about eleven or twelve years old when their names were written in the book. Meanwhile John's will, proved in 1694, referred to Elizabeth as his "now loveing wife."[21] Witnessing seems here to be a ritual played out at a liminal moment in the lives of the Parish family, as they welcomed a new wife and mother into their midst. Sandys's Middle Eastern travels become the exotic substrate for an altogether different kind of journey.

Elsewhere, witnessings seem to be part of a process of habituation to bureaucratic culture. A copy of Anthony Colynet's *True Historie of the Civill Warres of France* (1591) in the Bodleian Library has inscribed along the edge of one leaf: "Andrew Boreman of Tilehurst in the County [of] Berks / yeoman oweth this Book witnes william wickens of / Tilehurst aforsaid decemo die Septimbris ano domi 1623" (Figure 18).[22] But another leaf has, in the same hand, "William wickines of Tilehurst in the Com[itis] of Berks / yeoman sendeth greeting in our lorde god euerlasting / know ye that I william Bush-mill of Tilehurst." A single opening has, on one side, "By me Andrew Bore-mane of Reading in the County of / Berk waterman oweth this Book" and, on the other, "By me william wickens of Reading in the Com[itis] of Berks Chandler sendeth greting." It is not clear quite who is holding the pen here, but all of the inscriptions feel like semiofficial formulae, akin to other formulae (such as "know all men by these presents") that were regularly scrawled in early modern books.[23] Such marks are often categorized as "pen trials"; the "sendeth greting" example in particular suggests someone testing out nib and ink before writing a letter. But it might be better to think of these inscriptions by watermen and chandlers as exercises in a certain kind of literacy, a proficiency in the set forms of written communication. Another conclusion we might draw from this brief survey of witnessed inscriptions is that our modern understanding of the signature as an authenticating mark does not apply. Such inscriptions are usually in a single hand, and whether the hand is that of the owner or the witnesser is often unclear.

"I bought this book cuming from the Minores xiiij Februarij *1586* Teste Rogero Batte": the inscription offers us a fleeting glimpse of an event, like an entry recovered from a missing volume of Stonley's journals. We cannot know what had taken Stonley to this area on the eastern side of the city, outside the walls, by the dissolved abbey of St. Clare, nor where he could

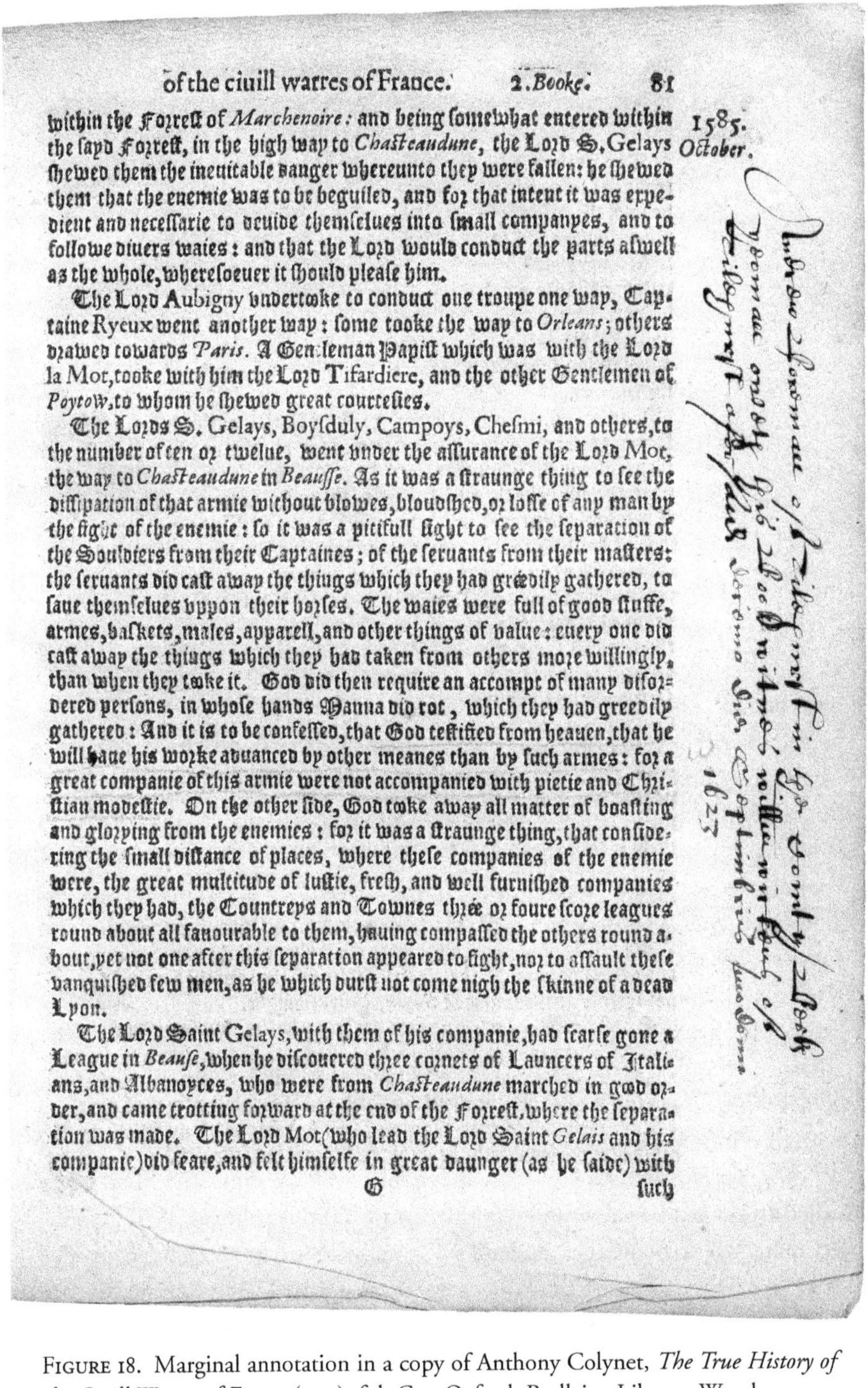

within the Fo2rell of *Marchenoire* : and being fomewhat entered within
the fayd Fo2rell, in the high way to *ChaSteaudune*, the Lo2d &,Gelays
fhewed them the ineuitable danger whereunto they were fallen: he fhewed
them that the enemie was to be beguiled, and fo2 that intent it was erpe-
dient and necellarie to deuide themfelues into fmall companyes, and to
followe diuers waies : and that the Lo2d would conduct the parts afwell
as the whole,wherefoeuer it fhould pleafe him.

&he Lo2d Aubigny vndertœke to conduct one troupe one way, Cap-
taine Ryeux went another way : fome tooke the way to *Orleans*; others
d2awen towards *Paris*. A Gentleman Papill which was with the Lo2d
la Mot,tooke with him the Lo2d Tifardiere, and the other Gentlemen of
Poytow,to whom he fhewed great courtefies.

&he Lo2ds &, Gelays, Boyfduly, Campoys, Chefmi, and others,to
the number of ten o2 twelue, went vnder the affurance of the Lo2d Mot,
the way to *ChaSteaudune* in *BeauSse*. As it was a ftraunge thing to fee the
diffipation of that armie without blowes,bloudfhed,o2 loffe of any man by
the fight of the enemie : fo it was a pitifull fight to fee the feparation of
the &ouldiers from their Captaines ; of the feruants from their mafters:
the feruants did caft away the things which they had greedily gathered, to
faue themfelues vppon their ho2fes. &he waies were full of good ftuffe,
armes,bafkets,males,apparell,and other things of value: euery one did
caft away the things which they had taken from others mo2e willingly,
than when they tœke it. God did then require an accompt of many difo2-
dered perfons, in whofe hands Manna did rot , which they had greedily
gathered : And it is to be confeffed,that God teftified from heauen,that he
will haue his wo2ke abuanced by other meanes than by fuch armes: fo2 a
great companie of this armie were not accompanied with pietie and Ch2i-
ftian modeftie. On the other fide, God tœke away all matter of boafting
and glo2ying from the enemies : fo2 it was a ftraunge thing,that confide-
ring the fmall diftance of places, where thefe companies of the enemie
were, the great multitude of luftie, frefh, and well furnifhed companies
which they had, the Countreys th2ee o2 foure fco2e leagues
round about all fauourable to them, hauing compaffed the others round a-
bout,yet not one after this feparation appeared to fight,no2 to affault thefe
vanquifhed few men,as he which durft not come nigh the fkinne of a dead
Lyon.

&he Lo2d &aint Gelays,with them of his companie,had fcarfe gone a
League in *Beaufe*,when he difcouered th2ee co2nets of Launcers of Itali-
ans,and Albanoyces, who were from *ChaSteaudune* marched in gœd o2-
der,and came trotting fo2ward at the end of the Fo2reft,where the feparation was made. &he Lo2d Mot(who lead the Lo2d &aint *Gelais* and his
companie)did feare,and felt himfelfe in great daunger (as he faide) with
                    G   fuch

FIGURE 18. Marginal annotation in a copy of Anthony Colynet, *The True History of the Civill Warres of France* (1591), fol. G1r. Oxford, Bodleian Library, Wood 475.

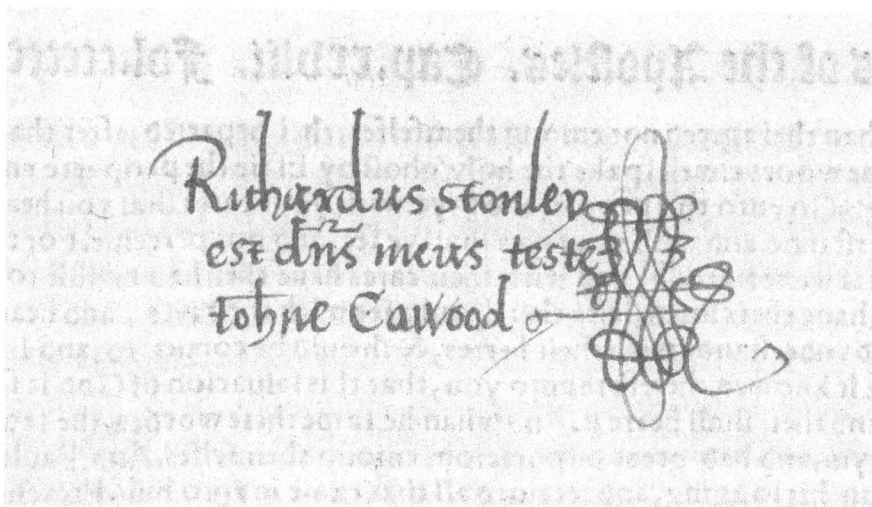

FIGURE 19. Inscription on Erasmus, *Paraphrases*, vol. 1 (1548), fol. 4G8v. New York, Pierpont Morgan Library, E3 098 C.

have bought a book so far from the centers of the trade in London, nor why he felt compelled to explain the circumstances of this purchase. The two other books from his library that bear witnessed inscriptions offer comparably occluded glimpses into social exchanges buried still deeper in the past. One is found on a substantial and beautifully preserved folio, the first volume of Erasmus's *Paraphrases*, now in the Pierpont Morgan Library in New York. The book speaks, proclaiming "Richardus stonley est dominus meus teste Johane Cawood" (Figure 19).[24] Another comes from another folio volume, a 1550 translation of Thucydides' history of the Peloponnesian War, bought by Stonley for five shillings and now in the Middle Temple Library.[25] Before the colophon, Stonley wrote, again ventriloquizing the book, "Richardus Stonley est Dominus meus, Teste Williamo hill. et williamo Spark" (Figure 20). To both inscriptions he added a large flourish flanked by his initials.

Neither of these inscriptions is dated, but both are suggestive. The name of John Cawood is well known to historians of Tudor printing. A Yorkshireman, he was a bookseller in Paul's Churchyard from 1541 and a printer "dwelling at the signe of the holy goste" from 1551.[26] In the summer of 1553 he was appointed Queen's Printer to Mary Tudor, a post that he continued to serve in under Elizabeth. The evidence for his confessional identity is ambiguous. On the one hand, his press was the official voice of Marian

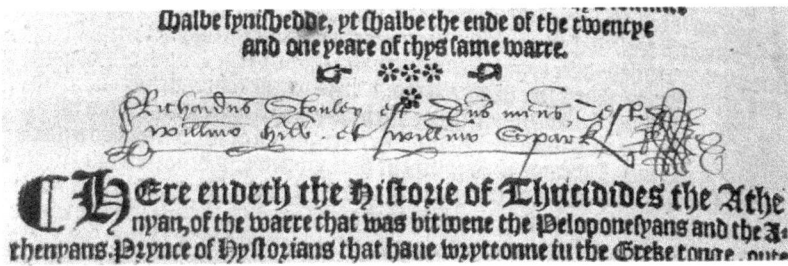

FIGURE 20. Inscription on Thucydides, *The Hystory* (1550), fol. 2P3v. London, Middle Temple Library, L(D).

Catholicism, and in 1556 he was named as a warden of the Fraternity of the Holy Name of Jesus, the revived form of a late medieval guild that met in a chapel beneath St. Paul's Cathedral. On the other, he managed to weather the change of monarch and to become a printer of English Bibles and prayer books under the new regime. His witnessing of the Erasmus volume may have been a shopkeeper's favor to an unusually possessive customer, but it perhaps reveals that Stonley was cultivating substantial book-trade connections in his early years in London.

Something similar is hinted at by the Thucydides. The names of William Hill and William Spark are not linked by any other document that I have been able to uncover, but they were close neighbors in the parish of St. Gregory by St. Paul's; that is to say, they worshipped at a church that was built against the south wall of the cathedral. Sparke was a Merchant Tailor from a Cheshire family who married in 1562 and died in 1566; Hill was described as a "howsholder" when he died in 1564.[27] In 1551, William Cecil and Lawrence Eresby sold "Certain Houses in Saint Pauls Church Yard and a large peice of void ground" to William Sparke and John Battene.[28] While the nature of Stonley's relationship with these men cannot be determined, the inscription seems again to put him in the Churchyard. It is likely that the book was purchased and inscribed soon after its publication in 1550. The price that Stonley paid, five shillings, is the same as that noted on a copy in the Huntington Library that was purchased on 19 August 1551; and as well as signing the title page Stonley wrote his name on the title page verso beneath the prefatory poem wishing a long reign to Edward VI, which may imply that he was writing before the king's death in 1553.[29]

Book-trade connections are also visible in a book with a gift inscription rather than a witnessing of ownership, a copy of Richard Howlet's *Abcedarium Anglico Latinum* of 1552 now in the Houghton Library at Harvard

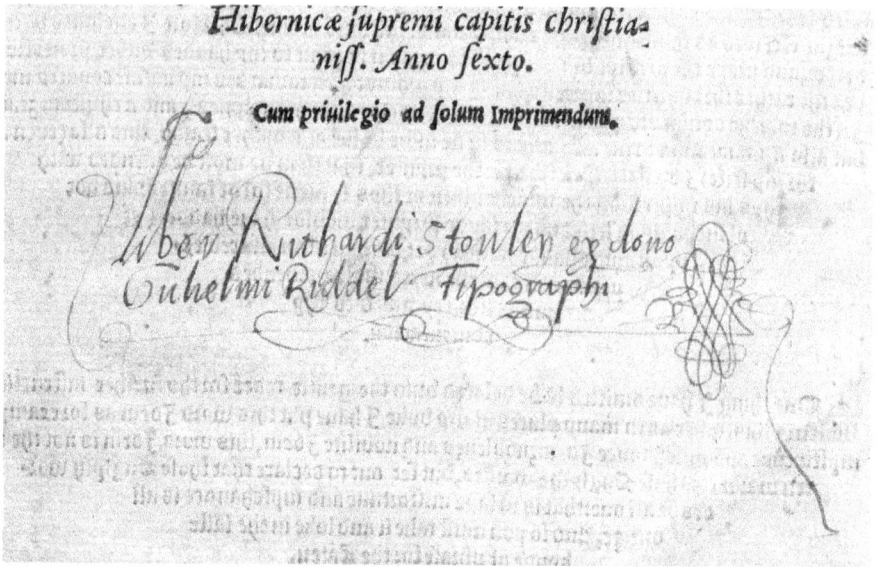

FIGURE 21. Inscription on Richard Huloet, *Abcedarium Anglico Latinum* (1552), fol. 2N4r. Houghton Library, Harvard University, Cambridge, MA, STC 13940.

(Figure 21). The product of almost a decade of painful labor for Howlet, this was the first newly compiled English-Latin dictionary of the sixteenth century, in the tradition of such works as the *Promptorium parvulorum, sive clericum* of around 1440, which Stonley also owned.[30] Stonley's *Abcedarium* has, on the final leaf beneath the colophon: "liber Richardi Stonley ex dono Gulielmi Riddell Tipographi."[31] Riddell, who seems to have printed the volume for the publisher John Day, was a stationer based in Paul's Church-yard and Paternoster Row in the mid-1530s, who was associated with a smattering of publications between 1548 and 1556; most of these gave his address as the sign of the Eagle in Lombard Street.[32] He was also listed as a member of the Stationers' Company in the charter of 1557. For all of his experience in the print trade, his handiwork did not please the author; Howlet left a number of notes of his dissatisfaction in the text, including one that complained of "cacographis . . . literis" (badly written letters).[33] Again, with so little to go on, we cannot know why Riddell made this gift to Stonley, but such inscriptions from printers are unusual. This one offers more evidence for Stonley's proximity to the institutions of print in the years immediately preceding his appointment in the Exchequer. The first volume of the journals shows that in 1581–82 Stonley obtained many of his books from Edward White; perhaps these inscriptions are testimony to earlier fidelities of this kind.[34]

The three early inscriptions we have looked at thus far share another feature that craves further consideration. As well as participating in a display of different hands (since Stonley tends to sign these books several times, sometimes in italic and sometimes in secretary), they also bear a conspicuously showy knot, with the initials "RS" on either side of an intricate series of symmetrical loops. Although many scribes incorporated elaborate flourishes into their signatures—to such an extent that they come to seem routine rather than distinctive—Stonley's knot finds its most precise parallels in the "Common Paper" of the Scriveners' Company, the volume in which all those admitted to the company were required to sign their names (Figure 22).[35] Although the practice fades out toward the end of the sixteenth century, scribes signing the book seem to have felt obliged to perform a graphic pirouette as they did so, often dividing their names or their initials across the knot just as Stonley does. Although we have no reason to believe that Stonley trained as a "writer of the court letter," it is tempting to see his flourish as a further elaboration of the claims to higher literacy that, I have argued, are embedded in the witnessing of books. The knot is a sign of technical accomplishment that intensifies the inscription's claim to status.

A second ex-dono inscription in a surviving book from Stonley's library takes us forward to the early 1560s, and to a personal association with a major author. On the title page of a copy of Heywood's 1562 *Woorkes* now in the Beinecke Library at Yale, Stonley has written "liber Ric. Stonley. ex dono Johanis Heyw[ood]" (Figure 23).[36] Again the inscription is undated, but it seems likely to date from soon after the date of printing; it was almost certainly made before July 1564, when the religious climate finally became intolerable to this staunch Catholic and Heywood was forced into exile on the Continent, where he joined "numerous relatives already dedicated, at some sacrifice, to persevering in the Catholic religion despite political and religious developments in England."[37] What does Stonley's (otherwise undocumented) association with Heywood signify? The gift is perhaps some kind of kin with the earlier gift from William Riddell, since Riddell was the publisher of one of Heywood's works, a ballad on the marriage of Mary Tudor and Philip II of Spain. We might also see links with the copy of Erasmus's *Paraphrases* as inscribed by Cawood, in part because Heywood's *Woorkes* are so palpably Erasmian. The 1562 volume, which omitted Heywood's plays, opens with a

FIGURE 22. A page from London, Guildhall Library, MS 5370, the Scriveners' Company "Common Paper," fol. 40r.

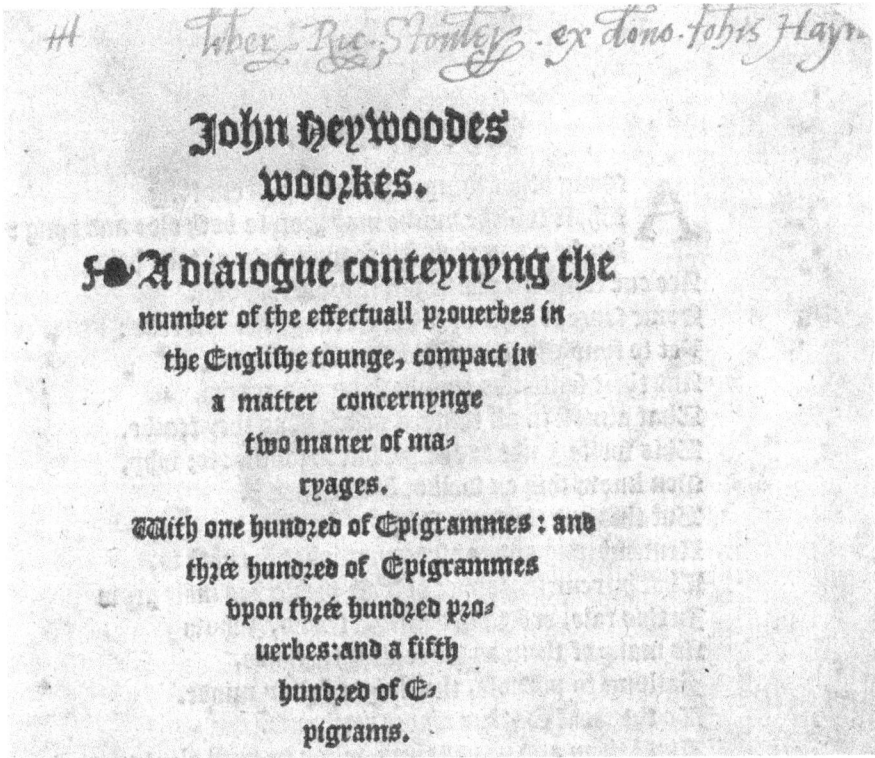

FIGURE 23. Inscription on John Heywood, *Woorkes* (1562), title page. Yale University, Beinecke Library, If H51 a562.

long versified debate on whether it is better for a man to marry a young and beautiful woman with no money, or an old and haggard widow with a large fortune. That debate is conducted through proverbs—hundreds of them, the majority hurled like grenades between bickering spouses. The rest of the *Woorkes* volume is made up of Heywood's six hundred epigrams, most of which are based on proverbs too. The debt to Erasmus's *Adages* is palpable. But there is also a rhyme between Cawood and Heywood that goes beyond sound, since both printer and author came into their own under the Catholic Mary Tudor. So too (one might suspect) did Stonley, who received his Exchequer post by royal patent in the first year of her reign. So this paper trail winds round to the vexed question of Stonley's religious complexion. And to begin to compass that, we need to consider an entirely different kind of book-ownership record.

"On a Table in His Chambre an Evyll Papystycall Booke"

On 27 August 1584, at the instigation of one Master Owen, an associate of the notorious recusant-hunter Richard Topcliffe, Sheriff John Spencer conducted a tense investigation of a London house:

> In the house of Roger Smythe gentleman in
> holborne
>
> Phillip Bassett of Collom John in the Countie of Devon Esquier
> on a table in his chambre an evyll papystycall booke
> which master owen hathe   *Phillip Bassett* [signature]
>
> John Bolte servant to the said master Bassett
>
> William Dawtrey gentleman: bothe thes were expullsyd owte of
> 3. papystycall bokes./   lyncollnes Inne for papystry –
>
> John Meres his servaunte & a lackey / William hill servant to master
> dawtrey
> we fownd being denyed
> by smythe & therfore comytted
>
> . . .
>
> In Roger smythes chamber certen papysticall bokes
> & xij prynted superstycyous pyctures.//[38]

This declaration opens up a series of connections that reveals a great deal about Stonley's cultural identity. The most proximate figure is the "William Dawtrey" who had been expelled from Lincoln's Inn; a decade earlier, in 1574, this man had married Stonley's elder daughter, Dorothy. Stonley appears to have been devoted to his son-in-law; on his death in 1589, he placed an armorial wall tablet ("amoris et Pietatis simbolum" [a symbol of love and piety]) in the chancel of St. Dunstan's Church, Stepney, calling him "Viro ingenii acumine, Mentis acie, et non Vulgari Municipalium Angli;ae legum Scientia, Præcellenti" (a man surpassing in shrewd intellect, sharp mind, and uncommon knowledge of the civil laws of England).[39] Dawtrey had impeccable Catholic credentials. His father was another William Dawtrey, who outlived his son and died in 1591, who had married Margaret Roper, a granddaughter of Sir Thomas More.[40] Through his daughter's marriage,

Stonley was thus networked with one of the country's most prominent Catholic families—a family of which John Heywood had been a member since his marriage to Eliza Rastell in the early 1520s.[41]

Phillip Bassett was another connection that Stonley gained through that marriage. He was the son of James Bassett, servant of Stephen Gardiner and private secretary to Mary Tudor; his mother was Mary Roper, Margaret's sister, and he was named after his godfather, Philip II of Spain. At her death in 1572, Mary bequeathed her son a heap of treasures rich in Catholic associations:

> my best ring of golde that king phillip gave me set with a greate ruby and a crosse of golde set of eche corner with thre poynted dyamondes and thre pearles hanging at it which crosse was my grandfather [Thomas] Mores with all that is within the same and a greate hope of golde that Master Basset gave me for my wedding ring halowed / Also my tablet of unicorne and a flowre of golde set with a rocke rubye and a greate blewe saphire having a greate perle hanging at it and a gilte cuppe with a cover to the same which cup King Phillip gave hym at his christening.[42]

(There were legacies for her sister and brother Dawtrey too, and, Mary directed, for "my godsonne and cosen William Dawtreye," who received "a claspe of golde for a partelet set with a diamonde which I will shalbe made into a ring for him.")[43] Whether Bassett managed to hang onto these precious relics for long is doubtful. His letters of the 1580s and 1590s were "(like Davids psalmes) full of lamentationes," prompted by his growing debts; he was also caught up in numerous legal wranglings over loans.[44] By 1595 he could write that "at this present I have not the revenew or certainty of one penie in the world."[45] When Stonley was trying to recover his own finances in the 1590s, he listed Bassett among his debtors, noting that he had contracted a debt of £100 in partnership with a London goldsmith named John Mabb back in February 1582. This was the most "desperate" of debts.[46] We also have a record of Stonley socializing with Bassett in London on Friday, 14 December 1582: "had with me to dyner Master Basset, Master Patten, my Sonne Dawtrey master Bullerde Master Johnson & his Brother master Fuller &c."[47]

Stonley and Bassett moved in overlapping circles. Petitioning for his release from the Fleet in 1585, Bassett named three men who might "stande bounde" for him: his "brother" Richard Verney of Compton, Warwickshire; Henry Ferrars of Baddisley in Warwickshire; and William Dawtrey the younger.[48] Verney had married into the Grevilles, a prominent Warwickshire family, who were connected to the Petres thanks to the marriage in 1560 of William Petre's elder daughter, Thomasine, to Ludovic Greville.[49] These social ties were also shared by "John Bolte servant to the said master Bassett" who was present during the raid on Roger Smyth's house in Holborn. In March 1594 "John Bolte of the Cyty of Exceter of the age of xxxte yeares or ther about" was caught up in another investigation of papist books, following a raid on a house "in the upper end of goldinge lane." He reported that "he serveth not any nor hathe doen this half yeare or moore / & dyd lastly serve Sir John Peter & sythence hym not any and was dyscharged out of his service abowt mydsomer last past." Before that he had gone "into warwicksher to mr verney his howse to teach master Bassettes children to syng & play on the virgynalles," and after that he had served one Morgan Robyns in Finsbury Fields.

Bolt confessed to a good deal of Catholic book production: "one booke bound in parchement begynninge with a pece of scripture viz Ther is no other name vnder heaven & c is a booke & of his wrytynge," "and also one lytell booke wrytten called St Peters Complaynte is hys but of whose wryting it is he knoweth not," and a book "conteynyng matter of Campion . . . is his and that he wrote the same with his own hand."[50] Another investigation provoked the confession that "certeine leaves conteyneinge divers & many verses beginninge why do I use my paper penne and Inke & c and endinge thus, to Jesus name which such a manne did raise is all of his owne hand wrytinge, and that he wrote the same aboute five yeares past in london . . . and that he hath readd the same sithens aboute five or sixe tymes."[51] A third investigation, this one signed by the notorious torturer Richard Young, revealed that Bolt had not been to church for two years and had not received the sacraments for seven years. He refused to say who had converted him. Asked whether he would support Elizabeth or the pope during a Catholic invasion of England, he evaded the question: "To this he will not answer."[52] Bolt's name is found in the Petre accounts from 1586/7 to 1593, and his movement from Bassett's to Petre's service and back again suggests the closeness of the ties between recusant households in Essex and Warwickshire. Meanwhile Bassett's dealings in Warwickshire extended (probably not coincidentally) to the very village in which Stonley was born and in which he continued to hold property in his old age: from 1582 there survives a "Mortgage by bargain and sale to secure £1,000 from Edward Fisher of Fishers or Bishops Itchington esq. to Philip Bassett of Colum John, Devon, esq. of the manor of Tachbrook, which refers to another £1,000 owed by Fisher to Bassett."[53]

This slew of associations, combined with Stonley's lifelong ties to the Petres, might prompt us to wonder what Master Owen would have made of Stonley's library, had he broken into the Aldersgate Street house to inspect his property. If William Dawtrey had "3. papystycall bokes. /," his father-in-law could boast many more. Passing over the paintings of St. Jerome and of Joseph and Mary, the pursuivant's eyes might have alighted on what looks like a copy of the *Golden Legend*, or the decidedly antique *Ordynary of Crysten Men*, or one of Thomas More's responses to Luther.[54] Owen might have pored over Thomas Watson's *Twoo Notable Sermons* affirming the Real Presence, originally delivered before Mary Tudor, or William Peryn's 1557 *Spirituall Exercyses*, one of the earliest attempts to bring Ignatius Loyola's prescriptions to England, and the work of the prior of nearby St. Bartholomew's, Smithfield.[55] He might have dwelt on John Standish's Marian *Discourse Wherin is Debated Whether it be Expedient that the Scripture Should be in English for Al Men to Reade that Wyll*—which concludes, predictably enough, that it is not expedient—or on Cardinal William Allen's *Apologie . . . of the Two English Colleges*, published at Rheims in 1581.[56] He might have wondered why Bishop Bonner's *Articles* of 1554 needed to be preserved, while shaking his head over Pierre Doré's flagrantly idolatrous *L'image de vertu, demonstrant la perfection & sainte vie de la bien heurée vierge Marie, mere de Dieu*.[57] Various Latin works, including the *Authoritatum Sacrae Scripturae et sanctorum patrum* of the Jesuit Peter Canisius and the *Liturgiae, siue Missae sanctorum patrum* of the Parisian theologian Claude de Sainctes, could also be added to the pile of suspicious titles.[58] It is possible that Stonley's note on his copy of the *Confessio catholicae fidei christiana*, asserting that he bought the book, rather than having it passed to him through illicit recusant channels, aims precisely to deflect suspicion.[59] But the haul we have assembled thus far might well be enough to warrant further investigation.

Stonley would have had plenty of ammunition to rebut allegations of backsliding. He may have owned Standish's treatise advocating the burning of all English Bibles, but among his numerous Bibles and testaments there were several in English, including Coverdale's Latin/English New Testament, his decorated Bishops' Bible, and the Geneva translation from which he drew daily excerpts for his journals.[60] Yes, he owned Marian books, but he also owned Cranmer's *Confutation of Unwritten Verities*, published by the Marian exile community at Wesel.[61] He had Watson's sermons on the Mass, but he also had Robert Crowley's response to Watson's sermons on the Mass.[62] And for every book printed by his conservative associate John Cawood he could have pointed to four by his radical Aldersgate neighbor John Day.[63] His library was stuffed full of reformed materials, including works by Luther, Calvin, Beza, Bullinger, Musculus, Marlorat, and Peter Martyr. Alongside some unstinting anti-Catholic diatribes, he owned numerous defenses of the Royal Supremacy and of the Elizabethan Settlement by the likes of John Bridges, John Jewel, Thomas Rogers, and Richard Hooker.[64] In April 1582, Stonley had noted in his journal, "This day master Nowell dean of Paules preached at the Spittle where my hart was but my body cold not for weaknes And therfore I served god at home with thankes to hym at night"; his inventory contains two copies of Nowell's *Confutation*.[65] His adherence to the English via media was equally clear from the many counterblasts to Presbyterianism in his collections.[66] On 28 November 1593, Stonley bought himself a copy of "Mr Bancroftes Book of the Survey of the pretendid holly discipline" for three shillings; as a New Year's gift for 1594 he bought Sir John Petre a copy of the same book for three shillings and four pence.[67] Stonley also owned books that asserted the necessity of attendance at church services, in the teeth of recusant objections.[68]

The evidence we have surveyed is thoroughly equivocal. It was no crime for the learned to be well versed in the arguments of their opponents, and as Alexandra Walsham has pointed out, the dominant mode of religious disputation in the period, the animadversion, involved the verbatim quotation of opposing arguments and hence the recycling of enemy propaganda.[69] We are increasingly aware of the subtle shades of theological and doctrinal opinion that circulated in the wake of the Reformation; Stonley's library is perhaps just evidence of how hard people worked to negotiate the welter of controversies that rumbled on down the decades. Yet there is something odd about the cohabitation of Catholic and Protestant writings in the inventory. Perhaps they testify to Stonley's broad religious sympathies. Perhaps they merely consolidate our sense of Stonley as polyreader, buying whatever is new and enticing, with no desire to construct a library that will be the tidy reflection of a neatly bounded self. But they may also show us someone protesting too much, struggling to suppress an earlier Catholic identity but failing to erase it completely.[70]

Evidence of confessional latitude comes from the presence in Stonley's collection of a number of books that straddle the great divide. These were Catholic devotional works repurposed for English-speaking Protestant audiences, including such Elizabethan best sellers as the works of St. Bernard of

Clairvaux, Thomas à Kempis's *Imitation of Christ*, and the minimal Protestant rewriting of Robert Persons's *Booke of Christian Exercise*. Ian Green and Alec Ryrie have helped us to make sense of the popularity of à Kempis, whose work attacked relics and pilgrimages and emphasized an inward, Christocentric piety that was deeply congenial to Protestant readers.[71] For Green, Edmund Bunny's translation of Persons offers a clear example "of what was common to both Counter-Reformation Christianity and Protestantism: the desire that believers should be not merely nominal but real Christians, whose souls experienced God and whose beliefs dictated their every thought and action." Ryrie, meanwhile, emphasizes the sincerity of Bunny's desire for interconfessional "pacification," part of a widely shared suspicion that religious disputation was in itself irreligious, a rending of Christ's garments.[72] Another of Stonley's Catholic/Protestant works was the *Methode unto Mortification* of the Spanish Franciscan Diego de Estella; this could be published without offence, according to its editor, "seeing the ground, subject, and substance of the booke is such, as . . . the wisest of both sides do agree in, namelie that *the worlde, and the vanities thereof are to bee contemned*."[73] Stonley's ownership of these books fits with his broader fondness for works of popular religiosity and prayer books, often of a conservative cast.[74]

As for the theory that Stonley was papering over the cracks of a complex religious identity, which was as layered and multifarious as his library, we might look for our evidence to those moments in the journals when a curious sense of detachment sets in. So, for example, throughout the second half of 1581 he commented on the trial and execution of Edmund Campion and his abettors. He bought a number of "Bookes and Ballades" relating to Campion's case on 4 August 1581, and Whitaker's reply to Campion's *Rationes Decem* on 13 October; on 27 May 1582 he bought "the Quenes declaracion of the undutifull affection borne agenst her majestie by Edmond Campion & other Traytors."[75] All of this suggests considerable interest. Stonley also appears to have witnessed Campion's execution first-hand, noting in a significant change to the standard formulae that "this day After morning preyer cuming thorough Chepside ther came one Edmond Campion [gap] Sherwyn & [gap] drawen upon hurdles to Tyborne & ther suffred execucion at which tyme a pamphlet boke was redd by wey of Advertisment agenst all thos that were busye flateres favorers or whisperers in his cawse."[76] Although he makes it sound like an accidental encounter ("cuming thorough Chepside"), this was clearly a significant event for Stonley—that much is, paradoxically, suggested by the gaps that indicate his desire to get the facts straight.

But it is notable that, in all of these references, the Jesuit remains "one Edmond Campyon"; he is held at arm's length, failing to become familiar despite repeat appearances. We might at the very least have our suspicions raised by this. Slightly more blatant is the tribute that Stonley makes to Lady Anne Petre when he notes her death in his journal: "This night my good Lady Anne Petre wydowe departed to god at Ingatstone . . . god I trust hath recevid hir sowle in to his mercifull handes. She was a good almes woman lyved al hir lyf vertuously and so ended the same."[77] Here the seeming unexceptionable emphasis on the virtue of charity looks like a calculated effort to gloss over Lady Anne's adherence to Catholicism. By recasting the Catholic commitment to a theology of good works as almsgiving, Stonley puts it in terms that an anti-Puritan English Protestant would find acceptable.[78]

Perhaps Stonley was bifurcated—a closet Catholic—or perhaps he possessed the kind of layered and multiform religious identity that was required to weather the storms of the sixteenth century. Whichever was the case, his books must have served as a kind of material memory, opening up vistas into distant pasts and other ways of being. A rough count of the datable books in Stonley's collection suggests that it got going in the 1530s (eleven titles), expanded during the 1540s and 1550s (twenty-four titles and thirty-one titles, respectively), reached a peak in the 1560s (fifty-eight titles) and 1570s (sixty-eight titles), remained strong throughout the 1580s (fifty-six titles), and trailed off significantly in the 1590s (twenty-five titles).[79] To sell off such a library must have seemed like selling off a life.

Devolving Ownership

Surviving volumes from Stonley's library, set alongside other life-records, provide some evidence for the giving and sharing of books within the family and immediate social networks. A copy of George Buchanan's *Rerum Scoticarum historia* of 1583, which bears much underlining and a few scattered annotations that may be in Stonley's hand, came from a stepson; it is inscribed on the title page by the recipient: "Liber Ric. Stonley ex dono Danielis Donne legum doctore."[80] Stonley was also a giver of books such as the two copies of Richard Bancroft's *Survay of the Pretended Holy Discipline* (1593) that he purchased in 1593, the first seemingly for himself, the second as a New Year's gift for Sir John Petre. At three shillings and four pence, this was a slightly less expensive present than the capons that he sent to Lady

Petre at the same time, and far cheaper than the perfuming pans and gilt bowls that he sent to colleagues and patrons at court.[81] When we see him buying multiple gold-tooled Bibles and prayer books, we can guess that these too were intended as gifts; his multiple copies of almanacs were presumably intended for dispersal across his properties.[82] One unusual entry in the journals for March 1582 shows Stonley giving a cache of books "which I lent hym Longe synce" to his thirteen-year-old godson Harry Browne, son of Roger Browne, who had been vicar of Doddinghurst since 1567.[83] Striking here is the determination with which Stonley prices the gift up at £6 13s. 4d.; this offers more evidence for the readiness with which books could be equated with their cash value.

There is just one entry in the journals that points to the purchase of books for educational purposes. On 3 August 1581 Stonley bought "an Isops fables & Master Nowells Catachisme for Richard Stanton," at a price of sixteen pence for the two; in the margin he added, "Bookes for the warde."[84] The first volume of journals contains a number of entries relating to Stonley's ward, who seems to have been outhoused at Kingsbury, to the northwest of London; these include payments "To Mr Whytinge for teaching of Richard Stanton to this day," "To John Clewley for his Boording to that day," and "To Katheryne Clewley to by a hatte & a pere of showes for Richard Stanton."[85] In 1584 "the warde" married Stonley's daughter Mary (who was at the time about twenty-four). The purchase of Aesop for his young charge resonates with two other facts of what we might call Stonley's biblio-biography, his book life.

The first is that the only marginal annotations that we can confidently ascribe to Stonley are Aesopian. Joannes Ferrarius's treatise *The Good Orderynge of a Common Weale* (1559) includes a discussion of the power of fables to persuade people to virtue. In this section of his text Ferrarius retells several stories by Aesop, commenting on their moral significance. Stonley adds marginal notes to each tale:

of the man with
the sparrow and
appollowe.

The lyon the
Asse & the fox
with the pray.

of the Asse wth
the Image of
gold.[86]

That these should be the only annotations in the book suggests Stonley's enthusiasm for Aesop, a fact that also registers in the 1597 inventory, which lists two Latin copies of the *Fables*.[87] The second salient fact is that the only surviving book with a *printed* dedication to Stonley is an edition of Aesop translated and published in London in 1577 by Richard Smith, a member of the Drapers' Company who had recently distinguished himself as publisher of three books by George Gascoigne (*A Hundreth Sundrie Flowres*, *The Posies*, and *The Steele Glas*). Addressing Stonley as "his worshipfull and especial good friend," Smith strove to requite "that great good will that you have borne unto me and mine, since the time of my first acquaintance with you" by giving him this book, a translation from the Middle Scots verse of Robert Henryson, which had recently been printed at Edinburgh.[88] While I have found nothing to illuminate the nature of the relationship between Stonley and Smith, the former's marriage into a family of Drapers is presumably part of the story. The involvement of Drapers' Company members in publishing was highly controversial, and was finally brought to an end in 1600 when the Stationers were given exclusive control over the production of books in the capital.[89] Smith activates text/textile associations in a prefatory poem to his edition, in which he describes how, "late passing thorowe Paules Churchyarde," he saw "Sir *Esope*" "apparelled both brave and fine, / After the Scottish guise," begging to be turned into English.[90] More broadly, Stonley's various dealings with Aesop tell of that author's special place as a denizen of the schoolroom who continued to captivate his readers for the rest of their lives.[91] The ganglion of associations here suggests how the "ownership" of books might be dispersed across a household, and across the life cycle of a single individual.

While various of Stonley's surviving books have been annotated by his illustrious son-in-law Daniel Donne, we have no direct evidence for the reading of the women of the household. The single exception to this statement is one of the most evocative survivors from the library, an octavo Sammelband now sadly broken up and bound in eleven separate volumes, in the Hunterian Library at the University of Glasgow. This is not so much a miscellany as a unified compilation: nine out of the eleven books were printed by Robert Wyer across the breadth of his career, from around 1530 to perhaps 1554.[92] The books are sharply focused around Wyer's stock-in-trade: "the influence of the weather, of the moon, of the planets, of precious stones, and of herbs, upon the health and destinies of man."[93] Given the compatibility of format and subject matter, it seems likely that Wyer was expressly designing his books to be sold in pick-and-mix gatherings of this kind; the printer had a line in woodcuts and decorated letters to enliven his little volumes. Poorly proofread, often with typos in key words of their titles, and almost all undated, the books survive today in tiny numbers. The Glasgow copies are often the only extant witnesses to their editions, and so can be read on *Early English Books Online*. What is remarkable about this Sammelband for our purposes is that it was signed at the front not just by Richard Stonley (in what looks like an early version of his signature) but also by his wife, Anne (Figure 24)—presumably because medicine was in this period frequently a female domain.[94]

What would Anne have held in her hands when she leafed through this volume? The bulk of it came from two substantial books, which were followed by a shoal of short pamphlets. First up is Sir Thomas Elyot's *Castell of Helth*, printed in 1541.[95] This was a comprehensive introduction to Galenic humoral physiology and its implications for diet and sickness. The work's status was somewhat equivocal: Elyot, as a noted diplomat and theorist of government, was obliged to offer a "Proheme" in which he denied that he was a mere dabbler in physic, usurping the prerogatives of the Royal College of Physicians. Next comes Thomas Moulton's *Glasse of Helth*, advertised as "a great treasure for pore men, necessary and nedefull for euery person to loke in, that wyll kepe theyr body from syckenesses, and dyseases." The book explains how the twelve signs govern the months, days, and hours, influencing human nature and determining the success or failure of physic; it goes on to provide "Remedyes for many dyvers Infyrmyties and dyseases that greveth and hurteth the body of man," beginning with the plague and ending with "the yche or scabbes."[96] Lest it should be overlooked, a crucial piece of advice from the volume was reprinted on the title page: "These ben the iii. Peryllous mondayes in the yere to let blode or to take any medicin or purgacion, that is for to say. The fyrst Mondaye of August, the seconde is the last Monday of Apryll, and the thyrd is the last Mondaye of Decembre."[97]

Elyot and Moulton sound keynotes that continue to resonate in the collection's less substantial texts. Plutarch's *Governaunce of Good Helthe*, translated from the Latin of Erasmus, teaches its reader how to stay well through moderation in eating and drinking, exercise, and bathing; the title page promises "Thou wylt repent that this came not sooner to thy hande."[98] Should moderation fail to keep you well, the Sammelband goes on to offer several treatises offering remedies for ailments. *The Anthidotarius* offers to teach "how thou shalt make many, and dyuers noble playsters, salues, oyntementes, powders, bawmes, oyles, and wounde drynkes," which are useful

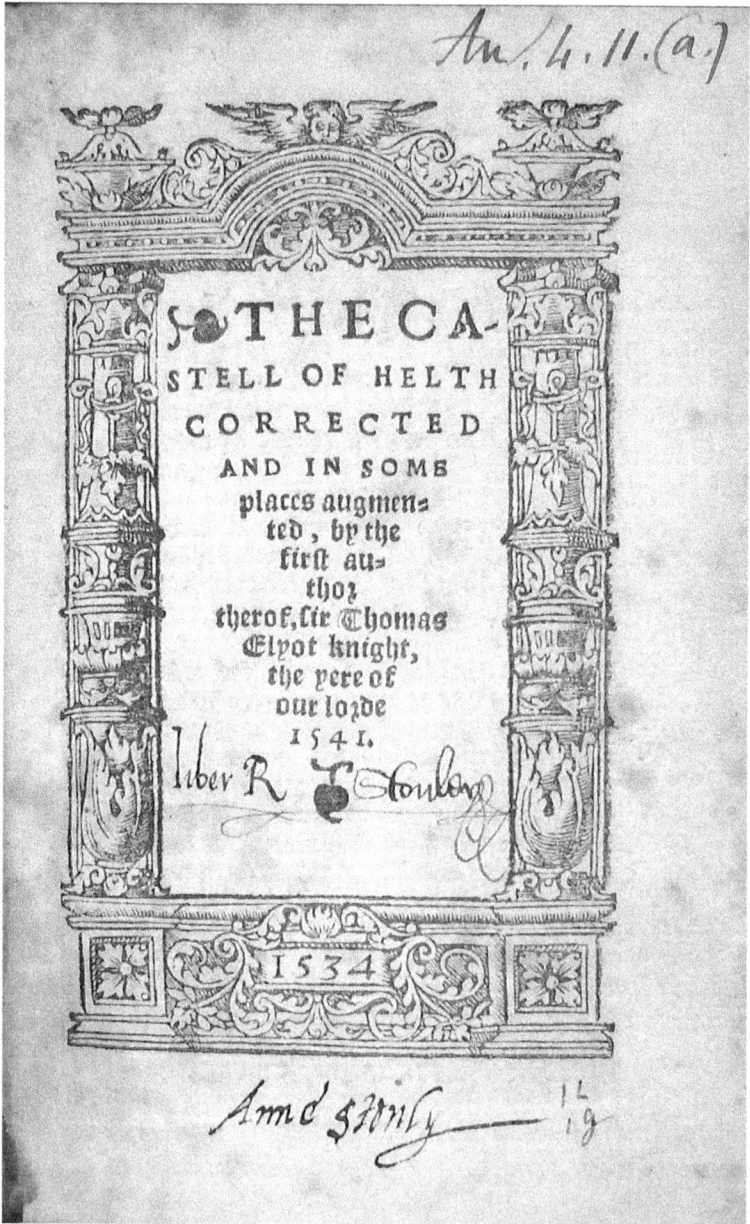

FIGURE 24. Thomas Elyot, *Castell of Helth* (1541), title page. Glasgow University Library, Hunterian Au.4.11(a).

"for euerye Surgyan, therin to be experte, and redy at all tymes of nede." Full of complex recipes requiring multiple ingredients from the apothecary, this book seems to be appealing to the professional rather than the lay reader. A second pharmacopoeia, *This Lytell Practyce of Joha[n]nes de Vigo in medycyne*, "translated out of Laten in to Englysshe," offers another range of remedies, including a terrifying recipe "for the Letarge in the hynder parte of the heade" that involves disemboweling a black cat, roasting it on a spit, and using the moisture that falls out as a salve for the neck.[99] A third pamphlet, entitled *This Boke Doth Treate All of the Beste Waters Artyfycialles* and billed as the work of "syr Roger Becon Frere," sings the praises of many different infusions, starting with the water of gold, to be made by warming wedges of fine gold and quenching them forty-two times in the water of "a good well or fountayne," which "exalteth & comforteth the herte merveylouslye."[100]

While these remedies were being prepared, the reader of the Sammelband could gaze nervously into the future using two pamphlets on medical prognosis. The first, entitled *Prognosticacion, drawen out of the bookes of Ipocras, Avicen, and other Notable Auctours of Physycke*, is a relatively sober work distinguishing forms of diseases that are deadly from those that are curable.[101] Rather more baleful is a tiny treatise called *The Boke of Knowledge: Whether a Sycke Person Beynge in Peryll Shall Lyve, or Dye. &c.* that claimed to draw from Galen and Hippocrates a series of clues, such as "If the sycke tourne hym ofte to the wall, it is an evyll sygne." Falling sick on particular days of the month is perilous: "yf [a man] fall sycke fyfth daye, he shall be sore sycke, yet he shall escape," but "yf he falle sycke syxte daye, he shall seme to be hole, yet he shall dye some daye of the next moneth."[102] This emphasis on timing is taken up in *Here Begynneth the Nature, and Dsyposycyon [sic] of the Dayes in the Weke*, a versified treatise purportedly derived from "a laten Boke of Aristotiles de Astronimis." According to this text, each day of the month has a different character; so the nineteenth, for example, when "I wote well that / Isaac, Jacob his sone begat," is a good day for buying and selling, and for crossing the sea, while children born on the nineteenth will be wise, true, and worshipful.[103]

These ideas about time are set in a broader perspective by *A Litell Treatyse of Astronomy* by Antony Askham (brother of the humanist Roger Ascham), a work that served as a kind of companion volume to the almanacs that the same author issued between 1548 and his death in 1559.[104] Written "not for leraned [sic] men but al onelye for the unlerned Englishe reader, that they may partly perceyve the workynge of the omnipotente power . . . in al thinges that are made of the .iiii. elemente," it offered guidance on the herbs, stones, gums, and metals to use under different astrological dispensations.[105] Finally, the Sammel-band also pulls in a miniature survey of the cosmos, in *The Descripcion of the Sphere or the Frame of the Worlde,* translated from Proclus by William Salysbury of Thavies Inn, via the Latin of Thomas Linacre. Describing the poles, the five parallel circles, the zodiac, and the celestial signs, this book allows its reader to contemplate the "wonderful, goodly and dyvine fabricature" of the earth.[106]

What does Anne Stonley's signature in this Sammelband tell us? Signatures in wills and other kinds of archival document have provided historians with baseline evidence about literacy levels in early modern England, although there has been much controversy about their interpretation.[107] A signature on a book makes a stronger statement. We can be confident that Anne Stonley could read the medical pamphlets gathered here. Given the dates of the books, it seems likely that the volume was acquired in the mid-1550s. We might want to speculate about how she would have read it. Did she use it to understand the different humoral constitutions of her two husbands, and so to explain why the fruits of her first marriage were boys, while those of her second were girls?[108] Did she turn to it as we today ransack the internet during times of illness, as when her husband was in prison in London while she was in Essex, "dangerously sick with a gref in her side"? (And had she done so, would her son William, by this time a licentiate of the Royal College of Physicians, have approved?)[109]

The private fascinations of this fizzingly weird compilation are, however, only part of the story. What the majority of the surviving books from this collection disclose is not private reading but a network. We see not one man alone but a pair (husband and wife, master and servant, giver and recipient) or a group (like-minded readers patronizing the same bindery, recusant community, livery company). Irrespective of whether or not you read it, taking possession of a book is a ritual, social act, the occasion for the assertion of status, the playing of games, the firming-up of social bonds, and the creation of familial resources. Books allowed their owners to proclaim their attachments: to splice themselves into the ranks of the gentry or the invisible congregation of an outlawed faith. They may have allowed someone like Stonley to lay another false paper trail, projecting wisdom and godliness outwardly while burying controversial religious convictions in the multifariousness of a collection. But if (as my last chapter suggested) he was a polyreader, his books also answered to the polymorphousness of early modern print, which regularly played across religious divisions in ways that upset modern expectations.[110]

Chapter 5

Paper Travels

For Francis Bacon, texts were like ships, remarkable vehicles that brought people together across vast distances: "So if the invention of the Shippe was thought so noble, which carryeth riches, and commodities from place to place, and consociateth the most remote regions in participation of their fruits: how much more are letters to be magnified, which as Shippes, passe through the vast Seas of time, and make ages so distant, to participate of the wisedome, illuminations and inventions the one of the other?"[1] The technologies that Bacon presents as rivals were, of course, frequently used in tandem. Writing may be like a ship, but it usually requires a ship, or several ships, in order to appear at its most ship-like. The power of texts lies in their ability to wander, and to invite their readers to wonder about the foreign lands and alien experiences they describe. Books cross boundaries with impunity, even where censorship is threatened, and they license fantasies about distant times and places that are always also reflections on the local. This chapter investigates the other worlds to which Stonley had access thanks to two books in the inventory that ought not to have been there: the first, because it was banned; the second, because it seems to have been otherwise utterly unknown to English readers. The former was a published account of Russia, and to frame Stonley's possession of it, I draw on a fascinating set of legal documents that allow us to push deeper into his family connections and the global reach of the mercantile circles into which he married. The latter title, which we might very loosely call a dirty French novel, points us to the transnationalism of Stonley's book culture and shows how print, travel, and sex could coalesce in the literature of the period.

Imagining Muscovy

So far as we know, Richard Stonley never traveled overseas, but his life was anything but static or neatly circumscribed. His journals depict a highly mobile Elizabethan, traversing the city every working day from the northern suburbs to Westminster and back again, and regularly returning to his home in Essex at weekends and on holidays. His job in the Exchequer would have given him a powerful sense of the financial capillaries that ran through the nation, and some of his larger payments would have put him in contact with the world of international warfare. Thus on 26 August 1581 he delivered £6,114 to Lord Henry Seymour to take to the Netherlands to aid the military campaign of the Duke of Anjou, while on 31 October of the same year he paid out £5,000 for the wars in Ireland.[2] On 15 February 1582 he paid out £6,400, partly in "barbary gold," to the Genoese alum trader and financier Horatio Palavicino, probably also part of the bankrolling of war in the Low Countries.[3] As a Londoner, he would have rubbed shoulders with all manner of immigrants. One of his tenants in London was Peter Bryart, a merchant originally from Rouen, who claimed that "bycawse of his Religion, [he] was not onely enforcid to flye for savegarde of his lyfe, But also there lost alle his goodes Cattayles and landes And dare not repayre thyther for that all the dayes or the moste parte of his lyfe he hathe always trafficked in this Realme in the citie of london." (Bryart's story emerged when he complained to the Privy Council in 1564 that Stonley was trying to evict him in order to hand the lease over to another merchant, a Portuguese Jew named Dunstan Anes, who was the Queen's grocer.)[4] Among the "returns of aliens" for the parish of St. Katherine Colman in 1568, we find an entry for "Domynick Bouchear, merchant, borne in Italie; Frauncis Falconere, Italion; and James Mytham and his wif, Nicholas theire sonne, and Nicholas and John, theire servantes; of the Italion churche; tenauntes to Mr Stonley. Italions persons, vij."[5]

Thanks to his own mercantile connections, Stonley would have interacted regularly with agents on the Continent. An exchange of letters in 1561, for example, shows him attempting to recover a debt that had been due to Robert Donne, his wife's first husband, from one "John Johnson late merchant of the Staple." Johnson had become bankrupt, so could not pay the full £200 that he owed, but he had £100 in goods in Seville that Robert had attempted to seize. The pursuit of the goods had involved one "Anthonie Marswellys" or "Antony Mazzuello," "a marchant straunger ther," and an attorney, Lewis de Pace, who moved between England and Spain; it had also involved an obligation witnessed by Sir William Petre and letters from King Philip II of Spain himself. Despite all of these efforts, it was still going to take some fancy choreographing of notaries in Seville and in London's Lombard Street to bring the business to a happy conclusion. Early in September 1561, Stonley petitioned the ambassador, Sir Thomas Chaloner, to pursue his cause, "albeyt this matter be somwhat troblesome and must axe tyme in the travell to bring yt to good effecte."[6] It seems that Chaloner made some very slow headway; Stonley sent an effusive letter of thanks "from London leasorlesse" [i.e., "leisureless"] on 12 October 1562, more than a year after the initial inquiry.[7] In December of the same year, Chaloner reported that the documents had finally arrived in Madrid, where he would "travayle no lesse in the same then if it concerned myne owne self," trusting "to send yow good newes by my next." Chaloner's motives for pursuing Stonley's cause were anything but disinterested. As the rest of this letter makes clear, Stonley was paying Chaloner his wages, and given how long it took to get the money transferred to Spain, the ambassador was worried about any delay. "I assure yow I thinck my self very strangely handled of late that I am so long unpayde behinde my daye . . . to be delayed as I am (in whome soever the fault resteth) is such a wrong as my nede can nat endure."[8] This was mutual back-scratching over a long distance.

Still greater distances were traversed when Stonley was called upon, along with his brother-in-law John Branche, to act as an executor to the will of William Rowley, "Citizen and haberdasher of london." Rowley was a fairly close relative; he had married John Branche's sister Ellen at some point in the early 1540s. His will, composed in April 1565, looks like a straightforward document. Rowley bequeathes his soul to Christ, his body to the earth, "and as for all my goodes, Cattells, plate, Jewells, readie monie, wares, marchaundizes and worldlie substaunce," once his debts are settled he leaves them to his children Martha, Mary, and Joan, to be paid at the age of majority or at marriage. (Rowley's oldest daughter, Grace, was not mentioned, presumably because she was already married by this date.) Richard Stonley and John Branche are the only other legatees; they are each to have three pounds and six shillings as a reward for their executorship. The will was witnessed by the public notary who penned it, and by the notary's servant.[9]

Despite its simplicity, a long time passed between the drawing up of Rowley's will and the completion of its business. This was no deathbed will; it was not to be proved until December 1575. And once matters had been brought to this apparently satisfactory conclusion, a storm blew up and threw

everything into confusion again. To begin to follow this paper trail, we need
to take stock of one crucial fact that the will does not reveal: our citizen and
haberdasher of London was also a member of the Muscovy Company, or (to
give it the long-winded name under which it was incorporated in 1555) the
"marchants adventurers of England, for the discovery of lands, territories,
iles, dominions, and seignories unknowen, and not before that late adventure
or enterprise by sea or navigation, commonly frequented." And Rowley was
not just any company member; he was a central figure in some of the earliest
efforts to establish trading relations in the Baltic and Russia. In August 1566
we find him in the northwestern city of Novgorod the Great, where an outbreak of plague prevented him from obtaining a license to travel onward to
Moscow.[10] By April 1567 Rowley was head of the Muscovy Company's operations in Russia, instructed by his paymasters "to have continually in remembrance that we have appointed you upon a singular trust to be our chef Agent
in those forraine partes; you sustaine therby no small expectation of your well
doeing and passing of our affaires." It fell to him to ensure that the company's
vessels were laden with the finest commodities, all clearly labeled to prevent
fraud; to see that nobody encroached upon its privileges by engaging in private trade; to manage the accounts; and to keep watch over the members,
who were forbidden from drinking, whoring, dressing above their station,
and keeping "dogges, beares and other superfluous burdens."[11] His oversight
of the company's affairs involved Rowley in innumerable dealings with individual traders, some of which would come back to haunt his executors after
his death.

Executing the will of a Muscovy trader was, as Stonley and Branche
would discover, no easy matter. Among the decrees of the court of Chancery
there survives a lengthy judgment that was handed down when they
attempted to recoup money that they believed was owed to Rowley by the
Muscovy Company. They claimed unpaid wages to the tune of £360 and
miscellaneous expenses that brought the total to £863. The company's refusal
to cough up would, they said, be "the utter undoyng of the poore fatherless
chillderne of the said William." The company counterattacked, claiming that
Rowley's wages had already been paid, and that he had in fact died with all
manner of debts owing to it. A special commission, comprising two lawyers
and four merchants, was set up to take witness statements and to investigate
the claims on both sides. The commission threw out most of the company's
demands and awarded Rowley's estate about £330 after various debts had
been cleared. The investigation had been a difficult one, the commissioners

reported. But their job appeared to have been done; the will was finally settled, with (one imagines) sighs of relief all round.[12]

But it was around this time, early in 1577, that Stonley and Branche themselves began to come under fire, as legal proceedings were initiated against them by one William Copeland. Copeland does not figure in histories of the Muscovy Company, but he was a friend of Thomas Greene, a goldsmith or "assayer" (tester of metals) who in 1567 had been sent to Russia along with an apothecary, an architect, and a doctor, at the tsar's request.[13] In return for the generous trading privileges he had granted to the Muscovy Company, Ivan IV (later known as Ivan the Terrible) had made a series of outlandish demands for reciprocal benefits. Perhaps the most remarkable of these was his demand for the right of asylum in England were he to be ousted from power. (Graciously, he offered to extend the same privilege to Elizabeth I, promising that in the event of a coup at Westminster she would find a safe haven in Russia; this was a favor that she felt unable to accept.) Tsar Ivan also requested shipments of arms, military pacts, and the kind of "knowledge transfer" arrangements that saw Thomas Greene packed off to Russia.[14] The chief complicating factor in Greene's life story was that, while he was transferring knowledge in Moscow, he married a woman named Darya (or "Doria"), said to be a native either of "lefe land" (Livonia, a Baltic province of Russia) or of Poland. They had had children together, one of whom, named Anthony, had survived beyond infancy. Then both Thomas and Darya had died, probably around 1570–71.

Here William Copeland enters the picture, since it was he who undertook to bring young Anthony back to England to be raised and sent to school. At stake in Copeland's lawsuit was the question of how wealthy Anthony's father had been at the time of his death, and how much of his property had lain in the hands of the Muscovy Company's Agent, William Rowley. If Copeland could prove that part of Rowley's estate had really belonged to Thomas Greene, he could win some compensation for the costs of raising Greene's son; hence his lawsuit. The problem was that all of the relevant events had happened in another country, and all Copeland had to rely on were the fragile memories of his fellow tradesmen.

The archival paper trail begins with a flurry of signed witness statements from some of the key players in Anglo-Russian relations in the period. There is a deposition from Anthony Jenkinson, the man who had pioneered the trade route via Moscow across the Caspian Sea and into Persia in 1561–62 and had subsequently become one of Elizabeth's ambassadors to the tsar.

There are testimonies from two more Russian ambassadors: Thomas Randolph, the man who had been sent to clear up the mess after an irate Ivan IV had revoked the company's privileges in 1568, and Daniel Sylvester, a fluent Russian speaker who had conducted similarly sticky negotiations in 1575–76. (Sylvester would be killed on a later mission by a lightning bolt that struck while he was trying on "a newe yeolow satten jackett" on the upper floor of the English house in Kholmogory; the tsar, "much amassed [amazed]" when he heard of it, said "God's will be donn.")[15] Also deposing in this case were smaller fry—the mercers, clothworkers, and merchant tailors who had dealt with Greene in Moscow, several of whom claimed to have been at his wedding. The stories that these men tell convey a strong sense of the precariousness of the English situation in Russia in the early decades of the new trading partnership.

So what had Thomas Greene been worth at the time of his death? Jeffrey Ducket said that he had visited him in Moscow around 1569 with a view to making him the new company agent; Greene had replied that "it was A thinge which he loked not for and yet never theles if he had the same he wold be contented to lay in stock with the said marchauntes a thousand Rubbells or twayne which Rubbell is abought the valew of xiijs iiijd." Nicholas Walker had heard his cousin Henry say that Greene was worth two thousand marks (about £1,300) at his death. Anthony Jenkinson had picked up similar rumors from Thomas Glover, a sometime agent of the company.[16] But several witnesses reported that Greene had suffered severely at the hands of the tsar. Daniel Sylvester heard him say shortly before he died that "he had had los[s]e by the prynces dysplesure of muscoe and yet that not withstandinge he saide he had sufficient to be in as good lykinge and prosperitie as he was before." According to Nicholas Proctor, though, Greene "died in povertie." Imprisoned by the tsar, "he did see his goodes taken away by the kynges offycers of Muscovia to the number of viij or ix sleades which may be so moche as viij or ix Cartes Can Carye."

And then, supposing Greene did have any money when he died, how much had the company's agent William Rowley seen of it? John Saris, a skinner, recalled that he had bought some of Greene's clothes from Rowley, who had said, "I pray the gyve me as moche as you may because it is deads mens goodes." Rowley was hoping (Saris reported) that he might be able to raise from them "a hondred Rubbels or twaine to the use of his [Greene's] sonne." Others said that Rowley had taken goods from Greene's wife after her death; Ducket recalled "ij Ingattes of gold & A bag of money . . . worthe

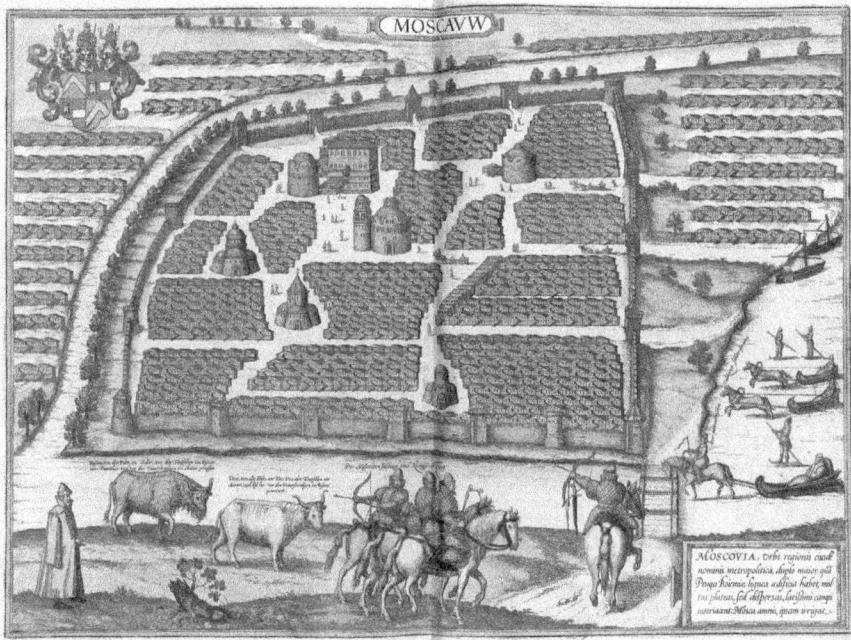

FIGURE 25. "MOSCAVW" from Georg Braun and Frans Hogenburg. *Civitates orbis terrarum* (1572–1618). Cambridge University Library, Atlas.4.57.3.

one hundred Rubbelles," while Christopher Fawcett remembered a vessel full of "the Swepynges and washinges of gold and sylver of the said Thomas greanes which . . . the deponent . . . did Imagine to be worthe ij C [200] Robbles." John Sparke, meanwhile, was able to supply the missing context for the handing over of Greene's goods to Rowley. Darya had entrusted her husband's commodities and money to the English Agent "for that the Cyty [was] in great danger of Burnynge." This is a reference to the fire that engulfed Moscow during the invasion of the Crimean khan in 1571, destroying huge swathes of the wood-built city and causing incalculable loss of life.

"The number of those that wer[e] burnte, besydes such as wer[e] caryed away captyves by the said *Crymmes* [Crimeans], ys thowghte to be above iiiᶜ thowsand [300,000]," Anthony Jenkinson reported in a letter to William Cecil, Lord Burghley, before pointing the moral: "A juste punyshment of God for such a wycked natyon."[17] But the fire affected the English company as well as the Russian nation; twenty-five of its members were reportedly stifled to death in the beer cellar of the English House, and the Muscovy traders claimed to have sustained 10,000 rubles or £6,600 of losses as a result of the devastating blaze.[18] William Rowley was one of those who lived to tell the tale, although according to some accounts he lost significant sums of his own money in his efforts to save the company's property. The earlier Chancery suit brought by Stonley and Branche to recover money owing to Rowley contained some grisly speculations about who owned the ducats that were found on the body of one Thomas Field, "after that he was smothered in Musco."[19]

As is often the case with early modern legal documents, we have the witness statements but we do not know how the case was resolved, so we cannot know whether Copeland ever recovered the money he claimed to have spent bringing up a goldsmith's orphan. What confronts a reader of the documents relating to these lawsuits is not a completed narrative but a process of translation—translation in its broad meaning of "transport," the changing of places and the transfer of commodities, as well as in its linguistic sense. When English merchants set out to pioneer the northern sea route in the 1550s, they were transporting themselves in the quest for new sources of profit, and they were earning for their country a new place in the pecking order of nations. Richard Hakluyt's *Principall Navigations* of 1589 gathered testimonials from several foreign commentators who were awestruck at the possibilities opened up by this surprising development. Giovanni Battista Ramusio, "Secretarie to the state of Venice," reports in 1557 that the English have found the supposedly "frozen sea" to be navigable; this means that there might be a "North-East Passage" to the Spice Islands or East Indies, the cynosure of global trade in the period.[20] Gerard Mercator, the renowned Flemish mapmaker, confesses that "the most famous navigation of the Englishmen by the northeast sea" has given him clues "for the reformation of the Mappe of Europe."[21] Best of all among these testimonials, the humanist Jean Matal (Joannes Metellus Sequanus), chronicling the deeds of the king of Portugal in 1574, denies that "the whole glorie of discovering the Ocean sea, should be ascribed to the *Spaniards*," since "the English men about 20. yeeres past, by a newe navigation into *Moscovie*, discovered the northeast parts." The result is a lucrative new traffic in numerous wares. "They cary thither old plate, and course linnen cloth, and all kind of small mercerie wares, serving for the apparelling of men, and women, as linnen, and silk girdles, garters, purses, knives, and many such like things. And they bring away from the *Moscovites*, all kind of pretious furres, and Salmons salted, and dried in the smoke."[22] "Translation" here means the transfer of goods and the improvement of England's reputation as the country began to cut a more conspicuous figure on the global stage. Hakluyt's work as a compiler was not just to render England more estimable by advertising the mobility of goods in the mobile medium of print; it was also (as is suggested by the work of Bruno Latour) an effort of mobilization, of amassing the textual resources that would exert pressure where it was most needed.[23]

In the documents relating to William Copeland's lawsuit, translation is at once linguistic and material, and its effects are frequently bizarre. Take the claim that Thomas Greene "did see his goodes taken away by the kynges offycers of Muscovia to the number of viij or ix sleades which may be so moche as viij or ix Cartes Can Carye." The translation here feels redundant from the start, since it claims precision in a situation where the real point is rhetorical (a *lot* of property was confiscated). But it also sticks out for its blending of the mundane and the strange. For if a Russian sled is identical to an English cart in terms of its storage capacity (it can be translated into English terms just as readily as the tsar's officers can steal your property), it is worlds away in its power to evoke an alien landscape and traditions. (The depiction of Moscow in the second volume of Braun and Hogenberg's *Civitates orbis terrarum* of 1575 [Figure 25] makes sledges very prominent, as shorthand for the peculiarities of the Russian climate and culture.)[24] Monetary translations, by contrast, appear comparatively fluid. The pound-ruble exchange rate is conveniently pegged at 3:2 ("every rubble amountyng to the value of thirtene shilling fowre pence"), and few feathers are ruffled when Rowley is described as engaging in currency speculation by converting the Muscovy Company's rubles into "olde dallars" at the port of Narva and then creaming off a 10 percent profit when he exchanges them for "muschoes" in the capital.[25] We find slightly less liquidity (linguistic and financial) when Stonley mentions that he received some of his brother-in-law Rowley's goods—"Certayn Jewells platte money and Rynges"—"in a Chest Called A Corrobye." The "corob," "corobia," or "coroby" crops up regularly in documents relating to the Russia trade. Although it may have its roots in the Latin *corbis*, the word was clearly strange to Stonley, expert in chests though he was.[26]

Stonley had another chance to engage in imaginary travel to Russia when he acquired a copy of Giles Fletcher's *Of the Russe Common Wealth* (1591), a book that displays the same uneasy play of likeness and difference as this earlier paper trail.[27] Fletcher's systematic dissection begins with "A description of the Countrie of Russia, with the breadth, length, and names of the

Shires" (B1r). Even though we are assured that these "Shires" are "far greater & larger then the shires of England," the word still struggles to render the vastness of the country assimilable to English understandings. Russia's mighty rivers—Volga, Dneiper, Don, Dvina—are "of very large streames, the least to be compared to the *Thames* in bignesse, and in length farre more" (B6r). Again, a local reference struggles to overcome the difference of scale. Describing the political structure of the country, Fletcher informs us that "*Gubnoy Starust* . . . signifieth an Alderman, & . . . *Sotskoy Starust* . . . [the] Bailief of the soake or hundred" (H1v). Like coins, some words can be exchanged with little difficulty. Yet the text also establishes a strong sense of difference as it discusses Russia's harsh climate—"you lose your nose, your ears, your cheeks, your toes, your feet with the cold" (B4v)—and still harsher political regime. This was a barbaric nation, in which cruelty and rapacity were integral to the social order. It was also a tyranny in which subjects enjoyed no legal protection and no political representation. Ivan IV, "to show his Soveraintie over the lives of his subjects," had been known to command the decapitation of people whose faces he disliked (D5v); meanwhile the heir to the throne looked like a chip off the same block, delighting "to see sheepe and other cattel killed, and to looke on their throtes while they are bleeding (which commonly children are afraid to beholde) and to beate geese and hennes with a staffe till he see them lie dead" (C8v). The absence of any check on power went hand in hand, in Fletcher's analysis, with the country's depraved Catholicism. Russian churchmen did not merely lack learning, they were actively opposed to it—witness the burning down of a printing house that had been set up in Moscow some years previously (M5v). Meanwhile the country supported an "infinit rabble" of friars, many of them men who were fleeing the shark tank of politics and seeking the sanctuary of religious life. "To speak of the life of their Friers, and Nunnes, it needes not, to those that know the hypocrisie, and uncleannesse of that Cloyster-broode" (M5v, N1v). At many points in Fletcher's account, the abuse of power and Catholicism merge until they appear to be two sides of the same coin. In Russia, a poor man has to fall down in the presence of his social superiors, "knocking his head to the very ground as he doth unto his Idoll" (G6r). Tyranny was state idolatry.[28]

On the face of it, Fletcher intends his reader to deplore the portrait he paints in *Of the Russe Common Wealth*. This is, he assures Elizabeth I, "a true and strange face of a *Tyrannical state*, (most unlike to your own)" (A3v). By

contrast with Russia, England appears to be a land of civility and opportunity, where the legal system guarantees the safety of the subject, Parliament keeps monarchic desires in check, and education has an emancipatory
force. English society represents a veritable free market in virtuous self-
improvement, whereas Russia fails "to advaunce any vertue, or to breed any
rare or excellent qualitie in Nobilitie or Commons: as having no farther
rewarde nor preferment, whereunto they may bend their endeavours, and
imploy themselues to advaunce their estate" (H1r). But the presentation of
this negative exemplum may well have been a subtle attempt to shape readers'
understandings of their own polity.[29] Contrasts between Russian tyranny and
English enlightenment are not always especially clear-cut. Fletcher's description of the methods of torture used to extract confessions in cases of treason,
murder, and theft ("as scourging with whips . . . or by tying to a spit and
rosting at the fire, sometimes by breaking and wresting one of their ribbes
with a payre of hote tongues, or cutting their flesh under the nayles" [M4r])
might not have seemed so very distant to English readers.[30] And his account
of how the tsar allows the monasteries to grow rich on donations and then
periodically steals all of their wealth (G2v–3r) might well have brought to
mind the activities of Henry VIII in dissolving the equivalent institutions in
England. Translation becomes not so much of a challenge, more a temptation
that the text dangles before the armchair politician.

There are other moments in this treatise when Russia becomes a compet-
itor to England rather than a mere foil for native glories. At one point
Fletcher refers to his diplomatic mission to Moscow of 1588—an unhappy
experience that paved the way for his depiction of the country in 1591. The
anecdote he tells concerns his refusal to address the tsar with his full "style"
("Emperour of all Russia, great Duke of Volodomer, Mosko and Novograd,
King of Cazan, King of Astracan," and so on). "The rest I omitted of purpose," he reports, "because I knew they gloried, to have their stile appeare to
bee of a larger volume then the Queenes of England" (D3v). In the event,
the gesture proved futile, because the chancellor refused to allow the audience
to go ahead without a full acknowledgment of the tsar's titles, enforcing
Fletcher's capitulation. In the annals of ambassadorial coups de théâtre, this
ranks rather low.[31] Whether Tsar Theodor I really prided himself on his
superiority to Elizabeth I of England is hard to say, but Fletcher's anecdote
would have prompted his reader to remember the style of the English Queen,
who was "by the grace of God Queen of England, France and Ireland,

Defender of the Faith, &c." The antiquated claim to France and the hopeful
"&c" might well have suggested similarities between the Russian despot and
the English queen.

Vexed dealings between Russia and England in the second half of the
sixteenth century repeatedly weighed Elizabeth against the tsar, and they
throw a sometimes comical sidelight on the new prominence of merchandizing in English society in this period. As we have seen, Ivan IV's grants of
privileges to English merchants had strings attached; in return for the right to
trade in Russia, the tsar wanted military aid and military alliances. Whenever
Elizabeth, striving to keep trade and politics apart, baulked at his demands,
the tsar was prone to revoke the privileges he had granted to the Muscovy
Company and to accuse the Queen of failing to lead her people. "Wee per-
ceive that there be other men that doe rule, and not men, but [boors] and
marchaunts, the w[h]ich seeke not the wealth and honnor of our majesties,
but they seeke there owne proffitt of marchandize," he wrote, adding: "And
you flowe in your maydenlie estate like a maide." Elizabeth was forced to
protest that "no merchants govern our country, but we rule it ourselves, in
manner befitting a virgin queen, appointed by the great and good God."[32]
Such an assertion of dignity was in itself a considerable indignity, and suggests the volatility of a world in which monarchs and merchants were working out the terms of their coexistence. Richard Stonley lived his life between
the two worlds of the court and the city. He would have experienced every
day the tensions that became startlingly visible at the distant boundaries of
English mercantile and diplomatic expansion.

Stonley's ownership of Fletcher's treatise tells of his attachment to the
circuits of global trade and to an urban elite that was entranced by the possibilities for exploitation that were opening up in a world reconfigured by
mercantile exploration. But *Of the Russe Common Wealth* was also a book
that Stonley ought not to have owned. After its publication in 1591, members
of the Muscovy Company complained that the book, "dedicated to her
Majestie[,] . . . will turne the Companie to some great displeasure with the
Emperour and endaunger both theire people and goodes nowe remayninge
there." They feared that the book's negative portrayal of Russia and the Russians would "utterlie overthrowe the trade forever." Their petition for the
book to be called in was carried through. A copy surviving at Trinity College,
Cambridge, contains a letter from one W. Dallye to his "ever honored freind
master Palmer Esquire secretary to the right honorable the lord Keeper,"
saying "The booke was called in and rare, and therefore I pray you be carefull

of it."[33] The work did not thereafter disappear; censored versions of Fletcher's text, playing up the possibilities of trade and excising any critique of tyrannical rule, were reprinted in the second edition of Hakluyt's *Principall Navigations* (1598–1600) and in Samuel Purchas's *Hakluytus Posthumus or Purchas his Pilgrimes* (1625).[34] And sixteen copies of Fletcher's banned book are known to survive today, suggesting that the attempt to call it in was not especially successful. The appraiser of Stonley's library had clearly not heard about it, since he priced up the juicy octavo for a single penny. Its presence in his inventory offers us an opportunity to reflect on the interdependence of representations of the other and understandings of home, and on the unruly mobility of the medium that could prompt such dangerously relativistic thoughts.

Imagining Europe

A very different kind of journey. Two young men, Guenelic and Quezinstra, are traveling around the Mediterranean, pursuing adventures like many a hero of romance before them. They start out from the city of Sirap, where they set sail on "Neptune's salty waves."[35] The first port of call is Goranflos, where they are dubbed knights and engage in a jousting tournament. Then they depart for the isle of Cythera, sacred to Venus, after which they are blown off course to the Barbary Coast and eventually to Cyprus. From Sidon in Syria they set out to find the ruins of Troy, where they see the tombs of Hector and Ajax. Next they sail into the port of "a very beautiful city, which was named Eliveba," where a beautiful young princess finds herself besieged by an admiral with an enormous fleet, a man "aged, weak, and broken" whom she has refused to marry, who is eventually seen off by our heroic duo.[36] On they go to Athens, Mycenae, and "a little city named Basole," before heading on to Italy and a town called Buvacca, where a "perverse and iniquitous people who did not want to obey or have any superior" needs to be taught a lesson and have their rightful prince restored.[37] Quezinstra persuades the prince to show clemency in victory, and the rebellious people respond by renouncing their crimes. But all of these glorious feats are just so many distractions for Guenelic, for unlike his friend Quezinstra he is in love, and his only goal is to find the tower in which his beloved has been imprisoned by her tyrannical husband. On numerous occasions he is dissuaded from his quest, assured that love corrupts the soul. But he resists all efforts to persuade him to shake off the memory of his beloved, "accompanied," he relates, "by a desire that continually urged me on."[38] Eventually our wanderers chance upon the tower and succeed in freeing the lady, but no sooner is she in Guenelic's arms than she swoons away. As life fades, she tells her love that it is good that they have not consummated their desire: "The divine clemency has taken pity on us, since it has not wished to allow the sin of adultery to be committed by us."[39] They can repent and be forgiven in heaven. With a prayer for redemption, Guenelic follows his lady's example and dies forthwith.

The story comes from another book that should not have been in Stonley's library, if only because his inventory is the only evidence we have for its circulation in early modern England. "The Works of Madame Helessenne in French" are listed, valued at two pence, in Master Stonley's bedchamber—an apt locale. For "Madame Helessenne" turns out to be a French writer, Marguerite Briet (c. 1515–50), who went under the nom de plume Hélisenne de Crenne, and whose collected works were first published as *Les oeuvres de ma dame Helisenne* in 1543.[40] First and foremost among her *Oeuvres* (Figure 26) was a story entitled *Les angoysses douloureuses qui procedent d'amours*, first published in 1538 and recently translated as *The Torments of Love*. The work was highly popular in its day—the *Universal Short Title Catalogue* lists eight editions of the *Angoysses* and seven editions of the *Works* between 1538 and 1560. Thereafter, however, the work was not reprinted, and little more was heard of Hélisenne until her revival by feminist critics in the late twentieth century.

What they rediscovered was a remarkable thing: a story of adulterous love told in the first-person singular by a female narrator who is identified with the author. The first section of the *Angoysses,* which describes the eruption of desire and its initial, shattering consequences, reads like a sixteenth-century premonition of Flaubert's *Madame Bovary*. Hélisenne, a woman so beautiful of body that crowds gather to admire her wherever she goes, is married off at the age of eleven. Fortunately, the gentleman in question is "very agreeable," so there is no great trauma in this.[41] But one day, when she is in the city with her husband to pursue a legal dispute over land, she catches sight of a young man at a neighboring window. "I found myself wretchedly ensnared," Hélisenne writes, proceeding to catalogue her desperate efforts to make contact with the young man in the temples and law courts of the city, his cat-and-mouse games with her emotions, and her husband's increasingly punitive reactions.[42] Desire proves to be a violent force that drags Hélisenne

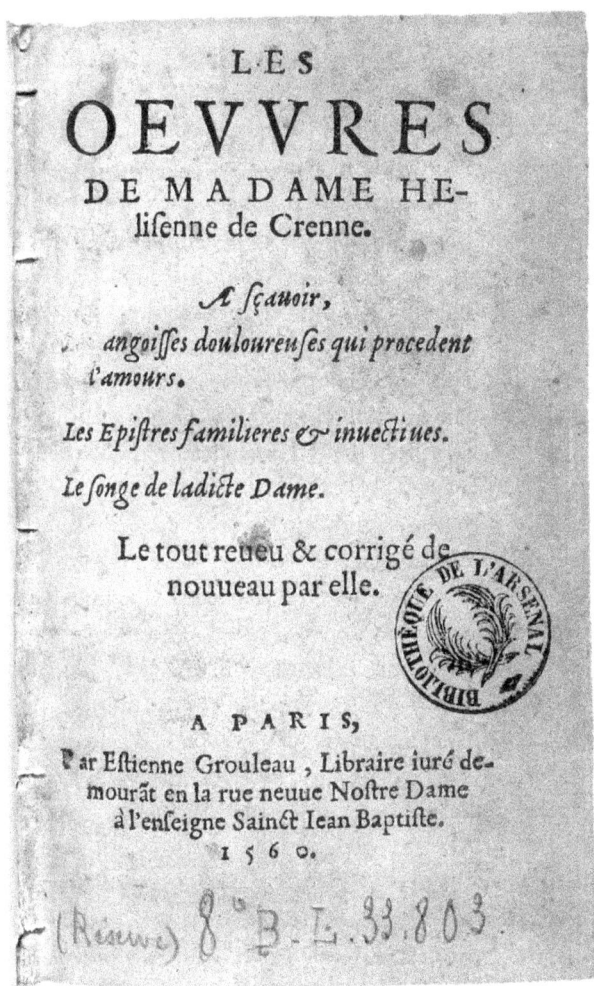

Figure 26. Hélisenne de Crenne, *Les oeuvres* (1560), title page. Paris, Bibliothèque nationale, département Arsenal, Reserve 8-BL-33803.

from the path of reason into corruption: "The impetuousness of love had broken in me all the bonds of temperance and moderation, and made me exceed every sort of feminine audacity . . . I was completely ablaze with erotic fire."[43] Her brief interviews with her beloved (who along the way acquires a name, Guenelic) are described with a moment-by-moment intensity that forces the reader to share every emotion with the quaking protagonist. Emotional extremity rapidly turns physical thanks to the actions of the jealous husband, who hits his wife on several occasions; one blow, Hélisenne relates, "made me fall and break two of my teeth, which caused me such extreme pain that I remained a long time without giving any sign of life."[44] The unnamed husband also tells his wife how he would like to catch her lover, subject him to "great and innumerable torments," and, he says, "after my appetite was sated with torturing him . . . make you a present of his body, all broken and lacerated." "And at the same time I'd shut you up in a tower where by force and constraint I'd make you lie with him."[45] And eventually, after finding her incriminating writings, he does send her away from the city to live locked up in a tower—not with her tortured lover but alone, with "only two maids."[46] There she recomposes the autobiography that her husband had burned, hoping that it might fall into the hands of her beloved and win his heart; and our attention shifts to Guenelic's heroic voyages in search of her.

The first book of *Angoysses* represents one of the most extraordinary eruptions of eros in early modern literature. This is a literature that abounds, of course, in representations of unruly and lascivious women; the tradition of prose narrative that descended from Boccaccio is especially preoccupied by the ungovernable appetites and resistant wills of the female sex, and plays such as Webster's *Duchess of Malfi* pick up on the energies of this tradition, playing out patriarchy's nightmares with fascinated horror. What is so remarkable about the *Angoysses* is that here the ungovernable woman speaks, in the first person, about her own tormenting desires. (A powerful influence on the work, Boccaccio's *Fiametta*, written c. 1343–45, provides a model for first-person erotic confession but does not earth the discourse in the life of the author.)[47] Compellingly, Hélisenne speaks simultaneously from within *and* beyond the framework of external moral condemnation. She is capable of identifying her own love as lascivious, and of identifying her beloved as (very likely) a rapacious male who seeks merely to rob her of her honor and leave her broken. When she writes to Guenelic, or converses with him, she delivers moralizing sermons on the unsuitability of his attentions, but always with a concluding swerve in which she confesses that, *were* she the sort of woman who might betray her husband, he would be the man with whom she would deceive him. At the same time, she depicts herself as reveling in her sinfulness. Forced by her husband to go to confession, she laments the tiresomeness of the operation: "It seems to me folly to divulge [my love] to this old man who has grown all cold, impotent and useless for nature's purposes. He will scold and blame me for what he earlier found pleasant." But then she reconciles herself by imagining the pleasure of reporting her desire: "He cannot force me to follow his advice, and so I shall take pleasure in talking about the man I love more ardently than any lover was ever loved by his lady."[48] Her love is irresistible, and it braves the torments of hell: "I believe there can be no place so painful to [my soul] as my wretched body . . . I, poor wretch, am tormented in body and in soul by love's flame."[49] Throughout the first book, meetings between the two lovers take place in "temples"—fairly transparent coding for "churches"—which seem to be places for dangerous flirtation rather than religious observance. Such flagrant blasphemies might have shocked early audiences in a distanced, third-person rendition, but coming from the mouth of their perpetrator, a female author, they are explosive indeed.

The *Angoysses* was prefaced by a letter, "Lady Hélisenne's epistle dedicating her work to all honorable ladies, offering them her humble salutations" and exhorting them "thereby to love well and honorably by avoiding all kinds of vain and unchaste love." By passing on the cautionary tale of her amorous sufferings, Hélisenne suggests that she will enable women "to avoid the dangerous snares of love."[50] Yet the Hélisenne we read about in the story is passionately committed to her desire and scheming to win her love right up to the end. Once she has died, the same Hélisenne is judged favorably by Minos and allowed to spend eternity roaming in the Elysian fields, arm in arm with the object of her unruly desires. The story sets moral compasses spinning—are we supposed to be reveling in this tale of unchaste love, panting for its satisfaction to the last, or should we condemn the narrator for her depraved behavior? At the same time, our narrative sense-making is thwarted, because if Hélisenne dies in the course of her narrative, she cannot be identical with the narrator or the author. The third book of *Angoysses* is said somewhat troublingly to be "Composed by Lady Hélisenne . . . Including the death of the said lady." This feels to a modern reader like a primitive kind of error in the plotting, although there is currently a rather full Wikipedia page devoted to "fiction narrated by a dead person."[51] Finally, the book sets the distinction between fact and fiction at sixes and sevens; it casts itself as quasi-diaristic, and at times reads that way, yet it is also larded with literary artifice—nothing can be said without a host of classical allusions—and full of fictional elements (beginning with that romance pseudonym, "Hélisenne").[52] Those fictional elements at times mask something real; so the city of Sirap, from which the young men set sail, is Paris; the beautiful city of Eliveba, not far from Troy, is Abbeville, Marguerite Briet's hometown in northern France (and the beautiful woman besieged by the aged admiral looks like another of the author's avatars). Goranflos, where our heroes are knighted, is a village a short distance from Abbeville. Such identifications do precious little to give us a sense of direction.[53]

After the deaths of the lovers, there are further surprises in store that directly implicate the medium of print. In a coda narrated by Quezinstra, the souls of the lovers are transported to the underworld by Mercury, god of eloquence, who descends through the air in a dazzling light. As he embalms their physical remains, Mercury perceives "that near Hélisenne's body there [is] a small packet wrapped in white silk, which he pick[s] up very promptly." In it is Hélisenne's book, which he thinks would make a splendid present for Pallas, "who took special pleasure in reading."[54] The gift causes a minor fracas among the gods, since Venus ("very curious to see new things") considers the matter of love her domain; but Jupiter helps to settle things down by suggesting that Mercury have the book printed "to show the world the anguish, travails, and painful torments that proceed from love."[55] Mercury asks where he should go to accomplish this, and Jupiter replies "that to do so there [i]s no place more suitable than the renowned and populous city of Paris."[56] Pallas expresses her love of that learned place and asks Mercury to inquire on her behalf "of the noble orators, poets, and historiographers whether they have newly composed anything."[57] The gods on Olympus turn out to be avid readers and perhaps not much unlike "those ignorant asses" castigated by Webster, "who visiting Stationers shoppes their use is not to inquire for good bookes, but new bookes."[58]

The fact that the *Angoysses* should turn out to be not just an admonitory tale, or a come-on to a lover, but a gift from the gods resonates with the strong vein of self-aggrandizing fantasy in the narrative. It fits with the extraordinary beauty that Hélisenne ascribes to herself ("I exceeded all other women in beauty of the body; had my face been equally fair, I should have boldly dared to call myself one of the most beautiful women in France"), and with the presumption that led the author to produce her collected works in her own lifetime.[59] But more important, the coda acts as a celebration of print and the capacity of this technology to "tell the world" the news of Hélisenne's sufferings. The book was published in Paris, but it might as well have been published in Sarip: it is expected to wander, turning the local into the global.

The *Angoysses* was an avowedly modern book, in what it represented, the way that it represented it, and its embrace of the power of print to cross borders. It was one of a number of late fifteenth- and early sixteenth-century best sellers that used vernacular print to pioneer a new brand of urban realism.[60] Other books in this category that wandered into Stonley's library are the *Celestina* of the Castilian lawyer Fernando de Rojas, which Stonley had in a French translation, and the picaresque classic *Lazarillo de Tormes*, which he owned in English.[61] The former is a tragicomedy of love, powered by the larger-than-life presence of Celestina, "laundress, perfumer, a master hand at making cosmetics and replacing damaged maidenheads, procuress, and something of a witch."[62] The latter details the witty shifts of a much-abused servingman who, having been exposed to the hidden corruptions of the world by a succession of masters, finally achieves a modicum of stability as the common crier of Toledo. The translator of *Lazarillo*, David Rowland of Anglesey, was attracted to the work by the fact that "in France so many delighted therein, being turned into their tongue," and he dedicated it to the merchant Sir Thomas Gresham, "who both for travaile, dailie conference with divers nations, and knowledge in al forein matters is knowen to be such a one, as is well able to judge, whether these reports of litle Lazaro be true or not."[63] Gresham, founder of the Royal Exchange, was a fitting patron for the transnational literature of sixteenth-century England: imported texts, printed on imported paper using imported technologies, often under the direction of immigrant workers, which allowed armchair travelers to experience alternative worlds with dazzling and often alarming vividness.[64]

Further work will need to be done to establish whether the *Angoysses* succeeded in achieving an audience outside France; the *Universal Short Title Catalogue* currently lists sixteen editions of Hélisenne's works printed in Paris, one in Lyon, and two without date or location. The fact that her writings were lurking in a London bedchamber in 1597 demonstrates that they were available to English readers, and again gives us cause to wonder at the insularity of early modern English literary studies. Few scholars of sixteenth-century English literature are aware of Briet or of the scholarly ferment around her oeuvre. More than that, the idea that a sixteenth-century woman writer might have published her collected works would strike us as distinctly counterintuitive. The record of Stonley's book buying suggests that we need to redraw our maps of literary culture to take account of the porosity of national borders in the period.[65] The next chapter develops this point as it uncovers a merchant of culture who was at once Stonley's close relation and his distorted mirror image.

Chapter 6

A Booke in Commendacion of
the Ladye Branche

Fracas in a City Churchyard

On Thursday 8 May 1594, Richard Stonley noted two expenses in his diary: four pence for "Bote hier" for his journey back and forth to Westminster, and one penny "for a Booke in commendacion of the Ladye Branche."[1] It is a tiny reference, but an intriguing one, and not just because it marks a rare eruption of Stonley's private life into what we habitually think of as the public medium of print. Helen Branche was Stonley's sister-in-law, the wife of Sir John Branche, citizen, Draper, and (in 1580–81, during the period covered by the first surviving volume of journals) Lord Mayor of London (Figure 27). Stonley seems to have been close to his brother-in-law; we have already seen the pair of them acting in concert as executors of William Rowley's will, and it seems that Richard took every opportunity to dine with Sir John (always referred to as "my Lord Mayor") during his spell in high office. So it is unsurprising that he should have wanted to read a book in praise of Branche's wife when she died in 1594, five years after her husband. This is, however, one of those areas where the smooth surface of the diary hides complexities. For there is no reference to the Lady Branche's death in Stonley's journal entry for 10 April.[2] And although there is a reference to her funeral, marked for attention with a manicule, it appears that Stonley did not trouble to attend it—although he was in London at the time.

It is quite possible that the demands of business, rather than any coolness or hostility, kept our busy Exchequer clerk away from St. Mary Abchurch on the day in question. (In a familiar pattern, he spent the morning at Westminster until eleven, then returned for dinner and "kept home all the day.")

Indeed, one might not suspect anything were it not for a tempestuous set of court depositions surviving from 1588, recording a familial dispute that centred upon Helen Branche. According to the deponents in the investigation undertaken by the bishop of London's consistory court, this venerable worthy of the parish of St. Mary Abchurch had (some Sundays past) been subjected to a series of verbal assaults both in the church and in the streets.[3] The tongue that lashed her belonged to her husband's niece Grace Dorrell, one of the four daughters of the Russia merchant William Rowley. In the words of one eyewitness, Helen Spicer, "after the communion ended and as they were departing owt of the church / the sayd Grace dorrell being in her pew hastely came owt & overtooke the Lady Branche and in the churche porche as she remembreth began after a raging sorte to rayle against the sayd lady Branche sayeing these worrdes . . . I mervale yow . . . can receave the communion and beare such mallice to me & Sir [John] Branches kynred for that you cannot abyde nor think well of any of them but wishe they were all hanged." Dorrell went on to accuse the Lady Branche of trying to have her killed, run through with a knife—the assassins being a prominent Draper, Edward Hyde, and the wife of another Draper, Katherine Osborne.[4] "And I wonder," she added, "yow will suffer that knave hide & his wiffe to come so daylie to yowr howse & table for he is a wicked person and practised the blak arte." "After this manner she brawled along the churchyarde," Spicer related, and "still she prosecuted her scandalous speches against the sayd Lady Braunche in the open streate from the churchyerde till she came to Sir John Branches in Canon streate." Another witness, Thomas Lees, reported the same sequence of events, but added one crucial detail. Dorrell had accused her aunt of fraternizing with sorcerers for a very particular purpose. She had reportedly said: "Madam one of thie feate is in the grownd alreddy & the other followeth and thow haste bene with mother davys the witch to know whether thie self or thie husband shall live longer."

The eyewitnesses to this outbreak of scolding were scarcely unbiased. Helen Spicer and Thomas Lees were both household servants of Sir John Branche; the former, a native of Hereford, said she had served him for fifteen years, while the latter, born in Cumbria, had served for seven. Lees had been holding the Lady Branche's hand, "to staye her by respecte of her age," as they left the church. Both had been asked by Sir John to testify against Grace Dorrell, whom they described as an "evell-woman envyous a brabler one that most unjustly seketh the vexacion of her nighbors." But their account of events must have been broadly accurate, since, far from denying their stories,

Figure 27. Sir John Branche as Lord Mayor; a generic image from the 1608 miscellany of Thomas Trevelyon. Washington, DC, Folger Shakespeare Library, MS V.b.232, fol. 321v.

Dorrell repeated them to the court on her own account. She had not thrown the first stone; in her version, it all began when Anne Hyde had called her "Queane" (whore) "and sayd she prayd to the devell" when Dorrell had refused to open a pew door for her. Dorrell had then noticed that Lady Branche was receiving communion—an act implying that she was at peace with her neighbors—which surprised her, seeing that the old lady "had gone abowt to work her what mischeiff she might uppon private grudges."[5] So no sooner had she crossed the church porch than Grace accosted her. Why, she asked, had the Lady Branche set Edward Hyde to "corrye" her (to "curry" or beat her like leather)? Why did she entertain Hyde and his wife at her table, "seing he the said hide is comonly called for his extreme uses [his high rates of interest on loans] the blak usurer and the develles blak byrd among the clothiers"?[6] And had she not sent to Mother Davies, "reputed a sorceror," "to know somewhat abowt Sir John Branche her husband"—as she thought, "what tyme he the sayd Sir John shold live"?[7] Dorrell stopped short of confirming her other rumored insults, but went a long way to confirm her reputation for "scolding."

The records of church courts in this period are full of such disturbances of the peace, but it is hard to establish the underlying causes of this raucous outburst in the precincts of St. Mary Abchurch. Grace Dorrell was twice widowed; her first husband, William Kettell, a Clothworker, had died in 1573, and she had remarried in 1574 to Christopher Dorrell or Darrell, a Merchant Taylor, who had died in 1581. Kettell seems to have been a firmly committed Protestant—not only did his will beg "with the prophet David lorde enter not into judgement with thie servant for [in] thie sight shall no man be justifyed," he left £50 "to the Frenche churche or dutche churche in London . . . towardes the setting owte of souldiers or otherwise for the mayntenaunce of gods gospell." Christopher Dorrell was, like Grace's father, a Freeman of the Muscovy Company (we know this because he tried to bequeathe his Freedom to his son-in-law in his will). Stonley *did* trouble to attend Dorrell's funeral, recording on Monday, 4 December 1581, "This day was buryed my Coxin Christopher Darrell gente in the parishe Church at Abchurche London whom I trust almighty god hath takne to his mercye."[8] Grace herself lived on until 1612, leaving a very full will that demonstrated her closeness to Stonley's son-in-law Sir Daniel Donne, her care to provide for her own grandchildren, and her pride in her lineage (she asked for twelve shillings to be spent on "schutchions of Buckram with my armes" for her funeral).[9] This, then, is a brief profile of our railer.

On the face of it, the story of the victim, Helen Branche, is rather similar. Granted, she was the child of a vanished age. Her father, the London Draper William Nicolson, left elaborate provision in his will of 1531 for chantry priests "to sing for my soule my Father and mother soules and all my frendes soules / and all christien soules," as well as a legacy for "my doughter margaret a none of Elstowe Abby to pray for my soule." Helen's first husband, John Mynors, also a Draper, died in 1567, leaving £5 to the French Congregation in London; by his will, suggestive of considerable wealth, he bequeathed to his wife half of his property and the use for life of his mansion house "called the horsehedd" in Candlewick Street.[10] Like Grace, Helen remarried almost immediately, but she stuck with the same livery company when she took her neighbor John Branche as a husband in 1568.

This pattern of hasty remarriage was typical for the wives of London's merchant classes. We know that Anne Branche, whose first husband, Robert Donne, died in 1553, had married Richard Stonley by 1555, when the Petre accounts register a payment for the christening of his child.[11] It is difficult to recover the motives at play.[12] Does the conspicuous speed with which women found themselves new husbands speak of the weakness of the widow, cut adrift from the city companies and desperate to regain her links with the urban elite? Was Dorrell perhaps driven to "shrewishness" partly because she had not managed to reconnect in this way after the death of her second husband? Or did women remarry on their own terms, sensing the pleasure of their own autonomy and the likelihood that subsequent matches would be more freely made and hence more equal than the first? Was Dorrell anxious that, with the death of Sir John, the family property might be spirited away by her doddery aunt?

We cannot answer these questions, but a few facts are conspicuous. The first is that Sir John Branche made his will and died later in the same year in which Grace and Helen quarreled.[13] He gave half his goods and the residue of his estate to his wife, whom he twice described as "welbeloved." (Thomas Lees and Ellen Spicer, who had testified on his behalf before the consistory, were overseers and received £25 and £50, respectively.) So *his* marital devotion, at least, is not in question.[14] Helen Branche's will, meanwhile, asked for a burial in Abchurch, "as neere unto the place where my late husband John Mynors was buryed as convenyently may be."[15] And although there was technically no need for her to provide for the family of her second husband, it is notable that she did not leave a single legacy to any of the multifarious relations she had gained through her Branche marriage. So perhaps there was something in her niece's allegations.

The Phoenix Riddle

This is the context in which Stonley spent a single penny "for a Booke in commendacion of the Ladye Branche." But which book did he buy? Remarkably, on her death in April 1594, Dame Helen was commemorated by no fewer than four printed verse tributes. Those tributes are interesting in themselves, since in their diversity of literary style and bibliographic presentation they read as the product of several different times. Some are conspicuously fashionable, others lumpishly retro, but they all usher from a single moment and from a single point of origin.

The shortest of the elegies for Lady Branche is entitled *An Epitaph* and signed by one "S. P.," who remains unidentified (Figure 28). It fills two pages of a tiny pamphlet (a single sheet folded twice to make a quarto) and is written in jogtrot fourteeners, perhaps an archaic style in 1594. After a few generalizing lines about death, the poem moves quickly to make the pun that proved irresistible to all of the elegists:

> Compare our selves unto a tree, which springeth up with with sap,
> And brings forth branches goodly ones, which taste of Adams hap.
> And as this tree doth grow to strength, the owner of the wood,
> May lop away the branches faire, as them which are not good.
> So hath he lopt away from us, a Ladie *Branch* of price,
> That lived here right worshipfull, disdaining every vice.[16]

Given that one of the key facts in Dame Helen's biography was the early death of her four children by John Mynors, the simile is not without its difficulties, but the poem does not confront them. It proceeds to document Branche's charitable donations, before delivering her to the pearly gates:

> Mee-thinkes I see old *Abraham,* unbracing of his brest:
> Saying blessed *Branch* come here and sleepe, and take thy quiet rest.[17]

In heaven, at least, all the hurly-burly about marriage will be over and done: "Injoy the sweete melodious tunes, with husbands both rejoyce," Abraham instructs.

Two of the four elegies are by writers who have been identified but who are now entirely forgotten. *A Commemoration* is signed "I. P." on the title page (Figure 29), and has been assigned to one John Phillips, a writer in multifarious modes: as well as several single-sheet epitaphs commemorating aristocrats and London worthies, he penned pamphlets about earthquakes and monstrosities and a best-selling prayer book.[18] The poem anatomizes Helen Branche's biography as a model for women at every stage of their life cycles:

AN
Epitaph of the vertuous

life and death of the right worſhipfull Ladie,Dame
Helen Branch of London widow , late the wife of ſir *Iohn*
Branch Knight , ſometime the Right honourable
Lord Maior of London,and daughter to M.
William Nicolſon ſometime of London
Draper:

VVhichﬁaidLadie,deceaﬁed on VVedneſday the 10.of Aprillaﬆpaﬆ:
and lieth interred in the pariſh Church of S. Mary Abchurch
in London , the 29.of the ﬁame moneth.
1 5 9 4.

LONDON
Printed by Thomas Creede.
1 5 9 4.

FIGURE 28. S.P., *An Epitaph* (1594), title page. San Marino, CA, Huntington Library, #81090.

A

Commemora-

tion of the life and death

of the Right Worſhipfull and vertuous Ladie; Dame *Helen Branch* (late Wife to the
Rightworſhipfull Sir *Iohn Branch* Knight,
ſometime Lord Maior of the famous Citie of
London) : by whoſe godly and virtuous life,
Virgines are inſinuated to virtue, wiues to
faithfulnes, and widdowes to Chriſtian con-
templation, and charitable deuotion, &c.
Which godly Ladie left this mortall life (to
liue with Chriſt Iheſus)the 1 o.of *April* laſt:
and lieth interred in the Pariſh Church of
Saint *Marie Abchurch*, nigh vnto
Canwicke ſtreete,the 29. day
of the ſame month.

1 5 9 4.

Fidenti ſperata cedunt.

I. P.

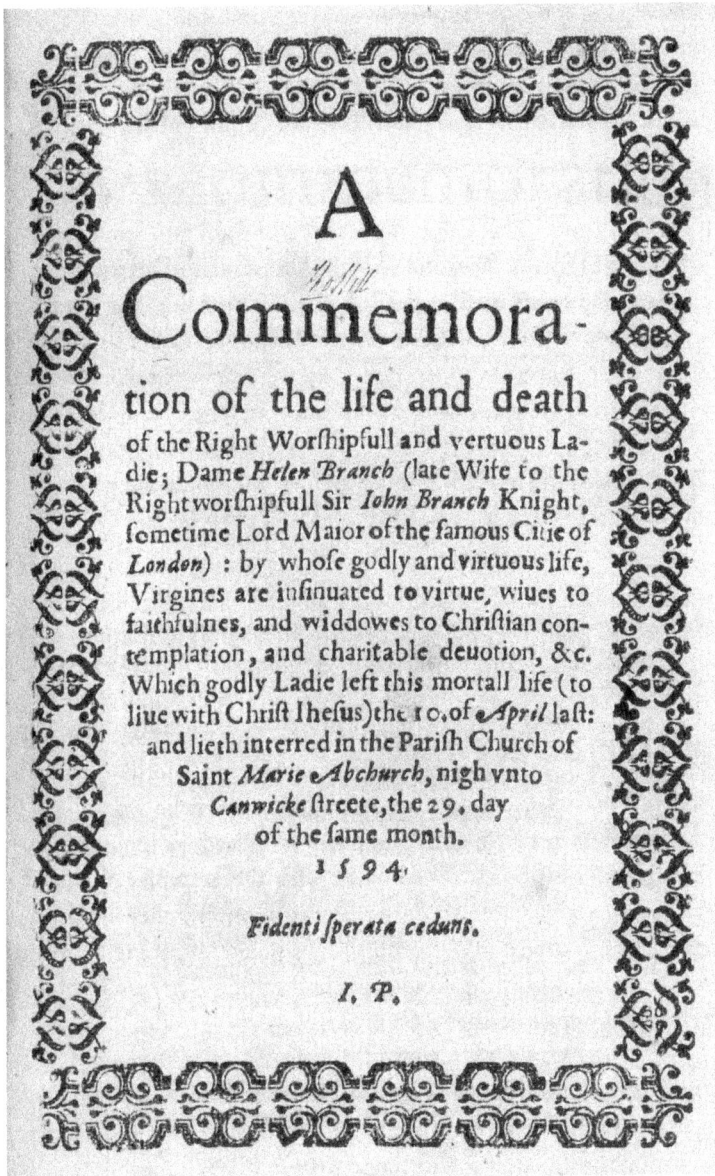

FIGURE 29. John Phillips, *A Commemoration* (1594), title page. San Marino, CA, Huntington Library, #81089.

Here Virgins yong are taught the way, to famous wisdomes bower,
Here may they feede to their contents, upon the finest flower.
Here married wives a loadstarre have, to leade them from abuse,
Here Widdowes are instructed still, vertue to put in use.[19]

Lady Branche's first name presents a bugbear—"I speake not I of *Helena* that fickle Gretian Dame / That causd the Greeks for *Paris* rape, to set all *Troy* on flame"—but this is soon forgotten in the praise of this particular Helen's exemplary obedience, chastity, and religiosity.[20] The children of her first marriage were blessings from the Christian God, coming to her as a "pledge of peace," but when he comes to tell how they were snatched from her, Philips segues into overblown classicism, invoking the myth of the three Fates:

Clotho the distaffe loathes to hold, *Lichesis* will not spin,
And *Parchas* for to cut lives thred in sunder doth begin.[21]

The death of John Mynors is (comparably) the work of Atropos, but after her own demise Dame Helen is brought, as in the *Epitaph*, to a Christian heaven: "Sweet Christ in heaven with glory great, hir happie head doth crowne."[22]

A third elegy, *Epicedium: A Funerall Song*, is signed "W. Har." (Figure 30), identified by E. K. Chambers as William Harvey (later Baron Harvey of Kidbrooke).[23] Harvey was a courtier and naval officer who won glory during the Armada campaign of 1588. If the poem is indeed by him, then it is his only known published work. By contrast with the examples discussed hitherto, the *Epicedium* is determinedly up to the minute, eschewing fourteeners for pentameters, arranged in twelve-line stanzas, and beginning with allusions to two very recent works, Shakespeare's *Lucrece* and Thomas Kyd's translation of Robert Garnier's tragedy *Cornelia*:

You that to shew your wits have taken toyle,
In registring the deeds of noble men:
And sought for matter in a forraine soyle,
(As worthie subiects of your silver pen)
Whom you have rais'd from darke oblivions den.
You that have writ of chaste *Lucretia*,
Whose death was witnesse of her spotlesse life:
Or pend the praise of sad *Cornelia*,

EPICEDIVM,

A Funerall Song, vpon

the vertuous life, and godly death, of the right
vvorshipfull the Lady *Helen*
Branch.

Virtus sola manet, catera cuncta ruunt.

LONDON
Printed by Thomas Creede.
1 5 9 4.

FIGURE 30. William Harvey, *Epicedium* (1594), title page. London, British Library, c.40.e.67.

Whose blamelesse name hath made her fame so rife:
As noble *Pompeys* most renoumed wife.
  Hither unto your home direct your eies:
  Whereas unthought on, much more matter lies.[24]

Cornelia was entered into the Stationers' Register on 26 January 1594, *Lucrece* on 9 May of the same year, apparently in anticipation of its publication. If the *Epicedium* was published for Dame Helen's funeral on 29 April, this allusion may therefore precede the publication of Shakespeare's poem, indicating Harvey's access to privileged circles of manuscript circulation (he would in 1597 marry the widowed mother of Shakespeare's patron, Henry Wriothesley, third Earl of Southampton).[25] Harvey opens his poem in combative mode, disdaining his rivals; compared with Lucrece and Cornelia, Dame Helen is a subject "whereof a poet needs not blush to write."[26] He negotiates the classical allusion buried in her name more elegantly than does Philips: a Helen for her beauty, she was a Phoebe or a Diana for her virtue. The death of her children elicits soothing metaphors that perhaps owe something to Shakespeare's earliest sonnets ("We daily see when *Phœbus* in the skie / Is highest mounted, straight he gins descend").[27] The familiar image of the tree is elaborated across three stanzas ("The *Branch* being dead, the blossome gan to droupe / Like to a parcht flower in the dogdayes rage"), and the poem ends in a bathetic enumeration of local detail:

Her faithfull end, was like her godly life,
Wedn'sday the tenth of Aprill, and no more
It was, when as was seene her breaths last strife
The year was fifteene hundreth, ninetie foure,
And gratefull *Abchurch* hath her bones in store.[28]

A few Latin verses asserting virtue's triumph over death bring the pamphlet to its conclusion.

If Hervey and Philips made barely a dent on literary history, the last contribution to this unlikely feast of commemoration comes from a positively illustrious hand. Josuah Sylvester was in his time both an extremely popular poet and a celebrated translator, renowned above all for his Englishing of du Bartas's epic account of biblical history, the *Sepmaines*, as *The Devine Weekes and Workes*. (According to Susan Snyder, Sylvester's modern editor, "everyone in pre-Restoration England who had received a literary education read the *Weekes* and almost all . . . admired it.")[29] By far the most elegant memorial to Dame Helen, Sylvester's *Monodia* (Figure 31) adopts a "weeping measure" of pentameter couplets arranged into substantial verse paragraphs.[30] The material is almost entirely commonplace, but the poet displays an impressive command of cadence, employing a number of mournful refrains to lend pathos to familiar ideas:

> But boughes & Branches, shrubs, & Cedars tall
> Wither and die and into ashes fall,
> So fel this *Branch*, for what draws lively breth
> But old or yong must yeeld at last to death?[31]

Like the other elegies, the poem moves to a happy ending, but although it emphasizes Dame Helen's ultimate spiritual fate (here delayed until "that great angels al-awaking blast") it also dwells upon a less obvious earthly legacy:

> And when you have drawn all your tear-springs drie;
> For her decease, heer let your comforts lie,
> That of this Phænix ashes there revives
> Another, where her vertue still survives.[32]

Sylvester suggests that, with her husbands and children dead, Helen Branche is left her own woman, "hir self, hir selfes commander."[33] The image of the Phoenix therefore seems apt to her, as it was apt to the childless Queen Elizabeth, a queen who was sure to succumb to death sooner or later. But if Elizabeth's successor was a mystery in the 1590s, so too was Dame Helen's; who is this "other, where her vertue still survives"?

The solution to this phoenix riddle lies in surviving copies of the other commemorative volumes, and in Helen Branche's will. The Huntington Library copies of the *Commemoration* and the *Epitaph* and the British Library copy of the *Epicedium* (Figure 32) have been marked up in the distinctive italic hand of one Robert Nicolson, Helen's nephew and the sole executor of her will.[34] The annotations that Nicolson supplied for these insubstantial pamphlets are startlingly elaborate. He added page numbers and running headlines, and he also added marginal notes to pick out the "narrative" of the elegies ("her virgin life," "maried to mʳ Jnᵒ Minors," "issue by mʳ Jnᵒ Minors").[35] What is striking about these handwritten contributions is their

MONODIA.

Imprinted by *Peter short.*

FIGURE 31. Josuah Sylvester, *Monodia* (1594), title page. San Marino, CA, Huntington Library, #31926.

impersonality; they do work that the compositors might have been expected to have done, rendering the text accessible by adding the kind of finding aids that had proliferated since the advent of print.[36] Nicolson also took pains to emphasize his own contribution to the commemoration of his aunt. When the *Epicedium* mentions "a yoong plant" springing at the feet of the inevitable tree, he added "R. N." proudly in the margin. At the end of the same volume he transcribed the text on the monument he erected to Dame Helen's memory in St. Mary Abchurch, complete with English verses of his own invention and others by Sylvester.[37] Finally, he pasted in armorials. What look like printed xylographics in the digital facsimiles on *EEBO* are in fact woodcuts, printed, cut out, and stuck down at points in the text where a pressman might well have added an ornament. The *Commemoration* has a large shield quartering the arms of Branche and Nicolson on the verso of the title page, the *Epitaph* a smaller Nicolson lozenge in the same spot.

Cutting has recently been integrated into our vision of early modern literary culture. As a special issue of the *Journal of Medieval and Early Modern Studies* entitled "The Renaissance Collage" has shown, it was not unusual for reading to be undertaken with scissors or knives in hand. Active reading could be boldly interventionist, involving the excision of material from the page and the transfer of that material via processes of sewing, stitching, gluing, and filing. These processes command attention partly because of their obvious kinship with commonplacing. But as Juliet Fleming (introducing the collection) suggests, the picking out of details is also a description of "what we all do when we read (from Latin *lego, legere,* 'to gather or pluck')": "cutting is not the exception but the rule" of reading, as of writing.[38] For Fleming, cutting means not destruction but pruning, grafting, tree surgery; it makes for growth. The process of cutting implicates not just the form but also the content of an armorial *wood-cut,* since heraldry is a matter of splicing arms and grafting people into a family tree. This might encourage us to revisit the play on Lady Branch's name in the 1594 elegies, with all of the growing and budding and drooping and lopping that it entailed. If death is a cut, Nicolson used the elegies to explore the idea that it might make for new growth—his own.

London's Ornament

So who was Robert Nicolson? He was born in 1561, the son of Benjamin Nicolson and his wife, Joan Parvis(h), and baptized at Holy Trinity, Guildford.[39] He married, on 26 December 1594, a woman almost twenty years his

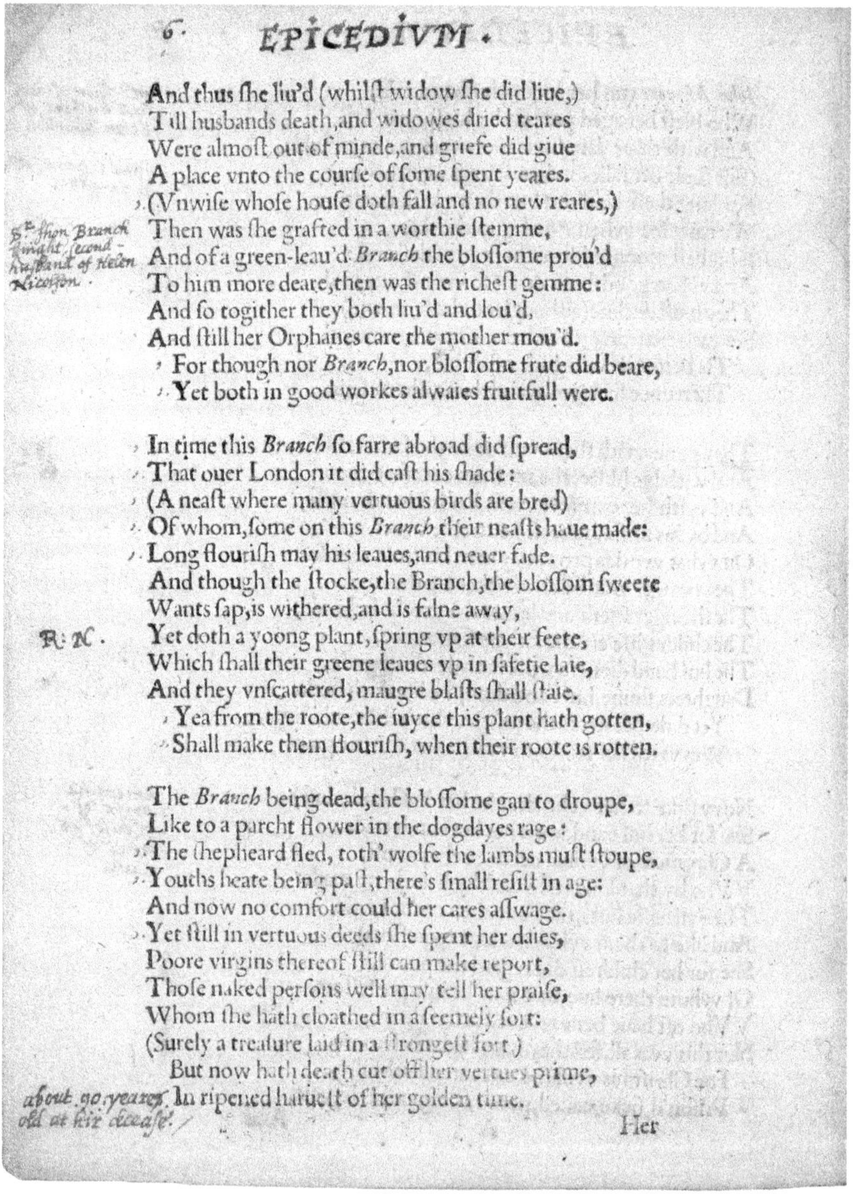

And thus she liu'd (whilst widow she did liue,)
Till husbands death,and widowes dried teares
Were almost out of minde,and griefe did giue
A place vnto the course of some spent yeares.
(Vnwise whose house doth fall and no new reares,)
Then was she grafted in a worthie stemme,
And of a green-leau'd Branch the blossome prou'd
To him more deare,then was the richest gemme:
And so togither they both liu'd and lou'd,
And still her Orphanes care the mother mou'd.
  For though nor Branch,nor blossome frute did beare,
  Yet both in good workes alwaies fruitfull were.

In time this Branch so farre abroad did spread,
That ouer London it did cast his shade:
(A neast where many vertuous birds are bred)
Of whom,some on this Branch their neasts haue made:
Long flourish may his leaues,and neuer fade.
And though the stocke,the Branch,the blossom sweete
Wants sap,is withered,and is falne away,
Yet doth a yoong plant,spring vp at their feete,
Which shall their greene leaues vp in safetie laie,
And they vnscattered,maugre blasts shall staie.
  Yea from the roote,the iuyce this plant hath gotten,
  Shall make them flourish,when their roote is rotten.

The Branch being dead,the blossome gan to droupe,
Like to a parcht flower in the dogdayes rage:
The shepheard fled, toth' wolfe the lambs must stoupe,
Youths heate being past,there's small resist in age:
And now no comfort could her cares asswage.
  Yet still in vertuous deeds she spent her daies,
Poore virgins thereof still can make report,
Those naked persons well may tell her praise,
Whom she hath cloathed in a seemely sort:
(Surely a treasure laid in a strongest fort.)
  But now hath death cut off her vertues prime,
  In ripened haruest of her golden time.

Her

FIGURE 32. William Harvey, *Epicedium* (1594), 3v–4r. London, British Library, c.40.e.67.

Her faithfull end,was like her godly life,
Wedn'sday the tenth of Aprill, and no more
It was,when as was seene her breaths last strife:
The yeare was fifteene hundreth,ninetie foure,
And gratefull *Abchurch* hath her bones in store.
You two strong props that vndershore the vine,
From whose ripe clusters sweetest *Nectar* flowes,
Whereof do drinke,the famous *Muses* nine,
Performe more full,what dutie doth impose,
Bring hither *Cypres* sad,see where it growes.
Embalme with *Mirrhe*,and sticke with *Rosemarie*,
Time is the onely hearbe which rests for me.

Quæ te propellat (nimium propensa)
Cura mors? O te properans veloci
Penna quis turbet? Dare terga cogat
Quod medicamen?

Aeque tu regis deruis superbi
Regias,& sic inopum cucumas.
Cura sunt morti iuuenes senesq,
Semper eadem.

Sola post mortem,remanet in æuum
Virtus,quæ nunquam peritura probis,
Fama florescet,licet ipsa cumbunt
Corpora in vrnis.

FINIS.   W. Har.

*Helen Nicolson,
Ladie Branch
deceased, the
10. Aprilis. 1594*

*Ladie Branch
buried in S.t Mary
Abchurch London.*

*Instigation of
Oxforde, &
Cambridg.*

Inter honoratos dignaris habere poetas. RL 1594

FIGURE 33. Detail from John Norden, *Surrey* (1610). London, British Library Maps C.2.cc.3.

junior. Martha, born in 1580, was the daughter of John Carrell or Caryll of Tangley, Surrey, across the fields from the Nicolson's home at Bramley, south of Guildford. The first of their twelve children was born in 1598.[40] Robert took possession of the family lands after his father's death in 1600, but his may not have been a substantial inheritance. Benjamin took care to spell out in his will that he bequeathed his goods to Robert "most willing-lie," given "his former dutyfulnes towardes me," but added that he "hartelie wishe[d] they weare better for him and that I had more to bestowe on him."[41]

These straitened circumstances may explain why Nicolson had already chosen to set himself up in London, where he worked his way into both the mercantile and the literary circles of the city. He acted as a patron to the cash-strapped cartographer John Norden, providing backing for the earliest engraved map of Surrey (another product of 1594, reissued in 1610) (Figure 33). Norden acknowledged the favor in the 1599 edition of his devotional manual *A Pensive Mans Practice* (1600), which he dedicated to "the Right Vertuous, & of singular good Hope, *M. Robert Nicholson,* Citizen and Merchant Adventurer of London," recalling "how well you were like to deserve many yeares since, when in your yong yeares and mine, you were wholy Dedicate to the study of Grammaticall rudimentes."[42]

Nicolson was also closely associated with Josuah Sylvester, whose writings (published in numerous editions, culminating in the ever-expanding folios of 1621 and 1633) provide rich testimony to their friendship—friendship that was (typically for the period) entwined with the provision of financial support. Several of Sylvester's poems have prefatory poems and epistles to Nicolson; occasionally (as in the case of the translated *Devine Weekes* in 1605) they bear commendatory verses penned by Nicolson.[43] The most striking testimony to their amity is Sylvester's dedication prefacing his translation of Odet de la Noue's paradoxical poem *The Profit of Imprisonment* (probably printed just a month or two after the *Monodia* of 1594):

> To you, youth's Loadstar, London's ornament,
> Frend to the Muses, and the well-inclinde,
> Loving, and lov'd of euery vertous mind:
> To you these tuneles accents I present.[44]

The friendship was an enduring one. At least one of the six verse epistles that Sylvester addressed to Nicolson was written after the death of Prince Henry (and the consequent death of Sylvester's hopes of court office) in 1612.[45] And the 1621 folio contains a revised version of the sonnet just quoted in which the dedicatee has become "his long approved friend" rather than merely his "approved frend." The (un)changed poem becomes emblematic of their unchanging amity:

> To thee the same, I the same Song present
> (Our mutuall love's eternall Monument)
> Wherein, our Nephewes shall heer-after finde
> Our constant Friendship how it was combinde
> With links of kindnesse and acknowledgement.[46]

Sylvester calls *The Profit of Imprisonment* "this simple pledge of my sincere affection / To *Tangley*, Thee, and thy *Soon-calm-in-heart*"—this last an anagram of the name of Nicolson's wife, Martha. Sylvester regularly refers to Martha in his occasional writings. An epithalamium for Robert and Martha includes an acrostic poem on "MARTHA NICOLSON," sententiously instructing the fourteen-year-old on how to deport herself, "That naught may trouble the *Soon calm in hart.*" A "Winters Posie" or device presents her (seemingly) with his heart ("this little brittle piece of me"), and may have been written on the back of a two-of-hearts playing card. And a "Canzone delle :3. Grazie" is dedicated "To the most faire and vertuous President of all female perfection, the *Soon Calm in Hart.*"[47]

Such inclusions remind us that Sylvester was one of the most materially playful of early modern writers: the massive folio collections of his works of 1621 and 1633 in particular are stuffed with shape poems (pillars, pyramids, castles), foldout posters on the mysteries of the Trinity, and poems that are also pairs of spectacles.[48] Sylvester was a lover of the anagram, which we need to see as something other than a debased and trivial form of wit. Frederick Ahl, attempting to undo our ideas about classical purity by arguing that Roman literature is in fact full of puns and anagrams, insists that for ancient writers the alphabet was an "element of language which could be rearranged, just as the natural elements which make up substance could be rearranged, to form a new being": Sylvester delights in such textual recombinations.[49] It matters that he was not just a man of letters; he was also a merchant, who interpolated praises of English mercantilism into his translation of du Bartas, and whose translation was in turn praised by Samuel Daniel as bringing "the best of treasures from a forraine Coast."[50] The patronage relationship between Nicolson and Sylvester was a multiply material affair. One of its most extravagant outcrops is something called a "Sonnet Acrostiteliostichon," a pair of sonnets, set side by side to be read across a double-page spread of the folio, and organized around four acrostics, one on Sylvester's name and three on Nicolson's.[51] There is a deep connection here between friendship, patronage, merchandizing, and textual playfulness.

Once we have identified Robert Nicolson as the patron who "commissioned" all of the elegies for Helen Branche, we can see why those poems look less like poems than versifications of her will. This shows particularly in their documentation of Dame Helen's charity. She followed the practice of many Londoners (and, notably, of her first husband, John Mynors) in making substantial donations to a variety of charitable causes: ten pounds in cash and coal to the poor of St. Mary Abchurch, twelve pounds to the London hospitals, ten pounds for "twenty poore maydens at theire severall marryages," twenty pounds for the poor prisoners in eleven named London prisons, and fifty shillings for the universities of Oxford and Cambridge.[52] Those donations are itemized couplet by couplet in S.P.'s *Epitaph*:

In Abchurch parish where she dwelt, the poore she alwaies fed,
With mony, meat, with coales for fire, somtimes with drink & bread.
To the Lunatickes of Bethelem, she gave right needfull things,
And not one prison she forgate, from faith such fruite oft springes.
To Maydes to helpe their marriages, (I meane the poorer sort,)
She left reliefe as bountifull, unto their great comfort.
To Oxford, & to Cambridge both, from whence good learning flows,
She hath them given liberallie, as sequell plainly showes.
To the Hospitals of London too, she gave a great reward,
And to the poore good store of gownes, she tooke so good regard.[53]

John Phillips offered a similar list.[54] Josuah Sylvester invited Oxford and Cambridge to requite their gift in the form of yet more volumes of elegies, imagined to carry the full weight of learning:

You springs of artes, eies of this noble Realme,
Cambridge & Oxford, lend your learned teares,
To wail your own losse, and to witnesse theirs:
Tel you, that have the voice of eloquence,
This bounteous Ladies large benificence.[55]

The elegies thus fill out the portrait of Helen Branche's virtues with instances of her exemplary charity, cast as an offshoot of her reformed religiosity ("from faith such fruite oft springes"). They suggest that a will might be a very public document; our gaggle of poets are here akin to the sign painters who recorded the generosity of London citizens on notices posted up in churches and other public places.[56]

In "publishing" the will of Dame Helen in this way, the elegies also make public her nephew's position of privilege as the transmitter of all this munificence: "And ready stands the executor hir meaning to fulfill."[57] When Nicolson memorialized his aunt's funeral monument in a handwritten note at the end of the *Epicedium,* he pointed to the prominent role of the Lord Mayor, Cuthbert Buckle, at her funeral (Figure 34). Buckle, a Vintner originally from Westmorland, died in office in the summer of 1594, and in his will he left a mourning cloak "to [his] Late servante Robert Nicolson."[58] The larger story behind the spate of elegies would appear to reside in Nicolson's perception that his aunt's death offered an opportunity for him to increase his status by asserting his links with London's most prominent men of trade.

HELENÆ NICOLSON domina BRANCH
epitaphium, lapide lydio inscriptum, &
literis aureis inscriptum, in tumulum
delubro Sanctæ Mariæ Abchurche
LONDON decorissime extructum,
anno a partu virginis 1594.

In fœlicem memoriam piæ pulchræ & pudicæ fœminæ
Dominæ HELENÆ BRANCH, filiæ venerabilis
GVLIELMI NICOLSON olim civis & Pannarij LONDON
quondam per quadraginta annos (& eo amplius) vxoris
viri dignissimi IOHANNIS DIINOIS civis, & etiam
Pannarij LONDON, cui peperit filium vnum Rogerum,
& filias tres, Ioannam, Ripnam, & Margaretam,
omnes sine prole defunctos. Nuper (ad annum vsque
nonagesimum) vxoris venerabilissimi viri IOHANNIS
BRANCH militis aurati, quondam præclarissimæ
Civitatis LONDON honoratissimi Maioris.
ROBERTVS NICOLSON generosus ex fratre nepos
vtriusq[ue] heres & dictæ Dominæ solus executor, suis
sumptubus spontaneis hoc Monumentum posuit.

Nuper fui vti estis.
Nunc sum vti eritis.

Quam ter fœlicem pietas, opulentia, forma
Fecere in terris modo suffragante popello.
Suffragante Deo fidei constantia viuæ.
Æternum in cælis, te nunc iubet esse beatam.

Nonagenaria obijt 10mo Aprilis
Anno salutis: 1594.to

Cuius honoratissimæ Dominæ exequiæ mœrentes, splendente
Die Lunæ 29o Aprilis 1594to magna comitante caterua
tam ornatissimi Domini CVTBERTI BVCKLE tunc
turrigeri LONDINI Maioris, quam venerabilissimorum
Doctorum Generosorum, consanguineorum, affinium, proximorum
Caduceatorum, perhonorificentarum Dominarum, generosarum
aliorumq[ue] plurimorum pleratorum, amicorum, seruorum
& pauperum, honorifice celebratæ fuerunt.

Tetrastichon suprascriptum Anglice.
Ladie, whom Pietie, Plentie, Beautie rare
thrice happie made, on earth by peoples voices
By constant liuely faith, Heauen doth prepare
æternall bliss for thee while Ioue reioices
Per Robtu Nicolson dictæ dominæ nepotem

Idem Anglice
Whom pietie plentie, & beutie made,
thrice happie here in earth among the best,
Hee, liuely faith, whose true fruite neuer vade
made home weh God in heauen for euer blest
Robtu Nicolson : 1594

FIGURE 34. William Harvey, *Epicedium* (1594), 4v. London, British Library, c.40.e.67.

Public-Private Reading

Did Stonley know about Nicolson's agency in orchestrating this outburst of printed ephemera for his sister-in-law? Did he even know Nicolson? The action at a distance facilitated by print, which might allow you to buy a book rather than attend a funeral, also opens up a space of unknowing, a rupture in the paper trail. But there are echoes across the divide. Stonley's younger relative was, like him, energetically engaged in turning financial into literary capital through book buying. About twenty titles can now be traced from his library, of which a significant minority were printed in France. These include the 1573 *Prosopographie* of Antoine du Verdier (purchased in 1592), a work that contains biographies of every notable from Adam and Eve to the present, illustrated with portraits, and its precursor, Guillaume Rouillé's 1553 *Promptuaire des medalles*, which provides portrait medals for celebrities ranging from Adam to the physician Laurent Joubert, taking in an array of kings, emperors, and popes along the way.[59] Both books cater to the rage to see that we earlier identified as a hallmark of Stonley's library. Other French imprints include a *Danse macabre* dated to 1500 and inscribed "Le liure de Robert Nicolson, de Londres"; a 1510 edition of a volume of forged historical works by Annius of Viterbo; and Pomponius Mela's *De totius orbe descriptione*, printed in 1507 and signed "1591, Roberti Nicholsoni Londinensis liber Parisijs"—this last inscription suggesting that he had traveled to the French capital, where all three books were printed.[60] Returning to England, we can identify his copy of a pioneering edition of the Gospels in Anglo-Saxon, a landmark of antiquarian and reformist scholarship emerging from the circle of Matthew Parker in 1571, and his 1568 folio Bishops' Bible.[61] Currently unlocated is a copy of the 1527 folio of Ranulph Higden's *Polycronycon* that Nicolson received as a gift from Helen Branche in 1589, which once had a copy of the Norden map of Surrey that Nicolson had sponsored inserted into it.[62] Global interests are documented by his copy of the *Civitates orbis terrarum*, purchased in 1593, and by two travel books, the *Navigations . . . into Turkie* by Nicolas de Nicolay (published in 1585, purchased in 1590), which was illustrated with costume-book images, and Richard Hakluyt's *Principall Navigations* (in the first edition of 1589, also bought in 1590).[63] Medicine is represented by a massive compendium, *A Generall Practise of Physicke*, translated from the German of Christof Wirsung in 1598 and purchased in 1602.[64]

Unlike Stonley's books, many of the surviving volumes that Nicolson acquired are thick with his annotations. As in the printed elegies, there is a certain ambiguity to his interventions. Some of the notes are what we might call "public service marginalia," added as though Nicolson were a pressman in the printing house, marking the book up for a general readership and making its materials more visible. Such impersonality is, as Bill Sherman has taught us, a standard feature of early modern marginalia, which usually provide technical analyses of the text rather than personal responses.[65] Thus on a typical page early in his Hakluyt, Nicolson adds three notes on the narrative ("By what means one shippe, & men were sav'd," "The prince of Joppas trecherie," "Prince Edward wounded"), and he bulks out a printed marginal note ("The arrivall of Prince Edward at Acra") with a helpful date: "A°· D°· 1271."[66] Similarly, when Nicolay and his companions sail into a cave full of "straunge myce" and are forced to cover their heads with their cloaks "for feare they should pisse on our heades (their pisse being venimous)," Nicolson supplements the printed marginal note:

> Strange myce.
> *whose piss is*
> *venemous* /.[67]

Such information as this, which might (just conceivably) be useful to the traveler, and which reveals something about the world's bewildering variousness, was rendered more conspicuous by annotation, as well as by handwritten additions to the volume's printed index. In the same spirit, Nicolson inserted numerous cross-references into his books ("Reade more of the Moores: folio: 8. 9: before").[68] The sense that these are "public" annotations is reinforced by their visual appearance: penned in a tiny and formidably neat italic, they seem to be trying to emulate the scale and clarity of letterpress.

But the line between the public and the personal can be hard to draw. At one point, for example, Nicolay describes how women at the Turkish baths, "perceiving some maiden or woman of excellent beauty, . . . wil not cease until they have found means to bath with them, & to handle & grope them every where at their pleasures, so ful they are of luxuriousnes & feminine wantonnes: Even as in times past wer the Tribades." Sliding into Latin in the margins, Nicolson froths: "Frons ficta, / obscœni mores, / petulansque / libido: / Certàque / fœmineus / viscera tor= / =ret amor" ("dissembling appearances, repulsive practices and freakish lust: truly, feminine love burns the innards").[69] The vehemence of the response suggests an individual rather than a collective voice. The more time one spends with Nicolson's annotations, the more they seem to speak of bees in his bonnet and of interpersonal connections, as when he supplements Hakluyt's account of Persia with a note on the Bonaret, a herb that reputedly grew "on the topp of a living lambe"—a subject that one could read about "more largely In Eden of Du Bartas, translated by Josua Sylvester. pag.181. *1621.*"[70] Here a cross-reference is linked to a particular lifelong friendship, rather than being a matter of indifferent public knowledge.

At a further extreme still are the family materials that Nicolson references in the margins of his Hakluyt. A typical example is found at the foot of a page that discusses the elephant's head that can be seen at the house of "the worthie merchant sir Andrew Judde": "Sir, there is a shipp of Master Juds Alderman come out of Ginie riche. It lyeth at Dover; There be two shipps more, that went in their Companie thether that be lacking./. Sir Jn° Branch knight; In a letter.xj: June:1555.n° 74. to his brother Thomas Branch, then in Andwarpe: Merchant. /."[71] There are a number of comparable references to mercantile correspondence, often with a clear family connection, suggesting that Nicolson viewed himself as something of a secretary to the Branche family. From these marginal notes we also learn more about the family's connections with Russia. A few pages into the volume Nicolson notes "The great comendation of the comp[any] of Moscovie merch[ants] in England," and in the section of Hakluyt's text devoted to Muscovy he starts laying out his family connections:

> 1 John Branch merchant & Lo. Maier & knight of London, Anno 1580.
> 2 And Thomas Branch merchant, his brother: were also at this time,
> Anno 1555. adventurers to Muscouia; As by the said Sir John Branch his
> letter to his sayd brother Thomas Branch Dated in London the 10th day
> of March Anno 1555. appeareth.[72]

Nicolson was evidently absorbed by the history recounted in my last chapter, making a detailed note on the great fire of Moscow and his family's involvement in it:

> The Citie of Mosko, with both the Castles, was utterly consumed with
> fire by the Tartars Prœcopenses, on Ascension day, in May Anno *Domini*
> *1571* where a great & innumerable multitude of people were stifled,
> choaked, & burnt, with the flame, smoke, & fire; a fewe escaped by

flight, (& hydeing in vawtes whereof master William Rowley the Agent was one.) And one only Castle Kitaigorod was scarcely defended;. And the Tartars led away a great number of people in captivitie. /. Sir Alexander Guagnin, Rerum Polonicarum tomo secundo. pag: 173. edition: 1584: 8°. /. Translated by Robert Nicholson gent.[73]

From his Hakluyt we learn that Nicolson was himself a Russia merchant: "Robert Nicolson the elder; was also admitted into this Right worshipfull Fellowship [sc. the Muscovy Company]: the 15 of February Anno Domini 1588. . . . And was Chosen one of the Assistantes of the same Fellowship the 1: March *1598*."[74] The destruction of the records of the Muscovy Company, probably in the Great Fire of London in 1666, leaves us dependent on chance snippets of information like this for our knowledge of its membership and activities.[75] Nicolson's status as a rising member of the company offers a crucial framing context for his annotations in the *Principall Navigations*. The book offers a venue in which its user can assert his place in a family history of engagement with Russia, and perhaps also a tool with which he primes himself for future engagements in the East.

So much for the familial elements in Nicolson's annotations. Seemingly at the furthest extreme of private eccentricity are the tiny nonverbal marks that Nicolson made throughout the margins of the books he owned—a period here, two periods there, elsewhere a comma or double or triple commas, with or without flanking periods, with crosses for points of high excitement (Figure 35). Each of these marks is carefully placed alongside individual lines of text. At least one of these kinds of mark is merely mechanical: Nicolson adds " = " signs to indicate words broken across the line end by the printer (here again we see the annotator working effectively as a typesetter). What I have called his commas are more sophisticated: these are gnomic markers, usually used to signal commonplaces that float free of the text around them thanks to their sententiousness and broad applicability. Such symbols have recently been explored in detail by critics charting the rising status of literature in English in the late sixteenth and early seventeenth centuries.[76] But while many of his annotations do single out commonplace material, and seem to be following standard practice in making that material more "common," the variegation of the marks that Nicolson employed suggests that he is using public symbols to speak a more private language. He becomes, in effect, a literary seismograph, offering what looks like a highly personal, line-by-line response to the rising and falling interest levels of the text.

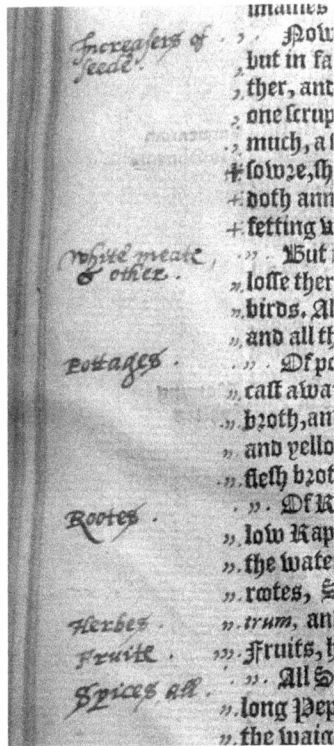

FIGURE 35. Marginalia in Robert Nicolson's copy of Christof Wirsung, *Praxis medicinae universalis* (1598), Washington, D.C., Folger Shakespeare Library, STC 25863, cs1292, T3v (p. 294).

The way in which Nicolson's annotations perplex our categories of private and public perhaps suggests the bluntness of those terms, and the need for some subtler category. Sherman's term "privy," denoting the selectively private, privileged space that you enter when you step into someone's closet and/or read someone's marginalia, might well prove fitter for purpose, especially given how well it fits the riddling, rabbit-out-of-a-hat games we earlier witnessed in the 1594 elegies.[77] Whatever term we choose, it will need also to cover the pasted-in armorials that are a common element in Nicolson's surviving books. A heraldic blazon looks like a public statement—"to blazon" meant "to depict or paint (armorial bearings) according to the rules of heraldry," but also "to proclaim, make public, 'trumpet'."[78] As Tara Hamling has recently emphasized, placing heraldry on walls and windows was an increasingly popular form of ostentation from the later sixteenth century onward.[79] Putting heraldry in books might seem to perform much the same function. But Nicolson also starts to play games with his pasted-in armorials. It is predictable that he should want to filch some in at the bottom of a page of his copy of the *Civitates orbis terrarum* that depicts the shields of the "Nobilis Hannoniae," the Dukes of Hainaut.[80] But in this volume he also does something stranger, pasting armorials into decorated initial letters seemingly without rhyme or reason. This practice becomes something of an art form in Nicolson's *Praxis medicinae universalis* (Figure 36), a hefty folio in which bits of heraldry are hidden on numerous pages; take, for example, an ounce (an argent, sable-spotted ounce, to be precise, thrust through the neck with a broken spear, or, headed gules), the Nicolson crest, hidden in a decorated letter "L."[81] Such paste-ins are often tiny: invisible until you start looking for them, and a bewildering presence when you find them. The strangeness continues in several decorated letters in the *Praxis* in which Nicolson writes names—"Thomas Holcroft miles" inside a letter "T," "Isabella Rutlandiae" inside an "I".[82] And then, to cap it all, there is a minute manuscript index stuck onto the rear pastedown, which turns out to be a finding aid to the various armorials and names that are scattered through the book.

The Exploded Book

To see his embellishments as instances of cutting helps us to connect them with other features of the books that Nicolson owned. For it seems likely that he was cutting and pasting on a larger scale than we have seen thus far, sometimes customizing his books and sometimes exploding them in order to radically transform their significance. A copy of Abraham Fleming's translation of Aelian, *A Registre of Hystories*, now at Illinois, offers an example of the former; it boasts a twelve-page manuscript index, signed "Ex industria Roberti Nicholsoni Londinensis 1590."[83] A book at Harvard better fits the latter category, the exploded book. This is a copy of the Latin and English versions of *A Dialogue betwene a Knyght and a Clerke*, probably printed around 1533.[84] The dialogue was originally written in the 1290s to defend the French crown against papal authority; condemned as heretical by Pope Boniface VIII, it later became a popular Wycliffite text, and in the 1530s it was republished for an entirely new antipapal context at the instigation of Thomas Cromwell.[85] Sixteenth-century commentators ascribed the *Dialogue* to the scholastic

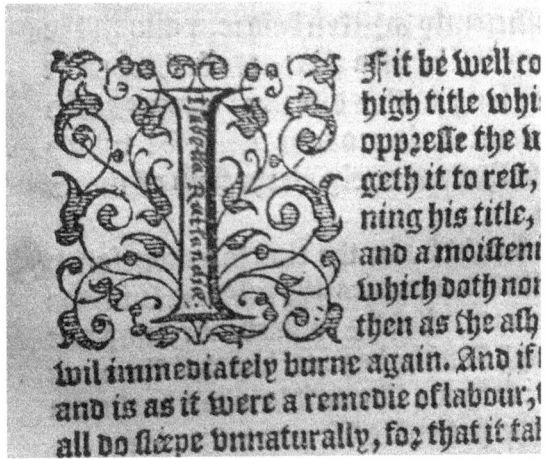

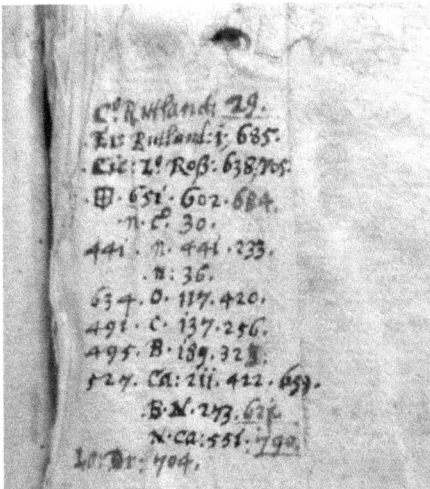

FIGURE 36. Pasted and manuscript additions to Christof Wirsung, *Praxis medicinae universalis* (1598); Folger STC 25863, cs1292, fols. 2D2v (p. 420), 2S1v (p. 642), and rear pastedown.

philosopher William of Ockham, presumably because it was felt to fit with his writings on papal power. Nicolson's volume is a Sammelband that combines copies of the English and the Latin texts of the work, with nine manuscript leaves as filling within the sandwich. Those leaves are devoted to the celebration of William of Ockham as one of the most illustrious sons of Surrey (the village of Ockham is northeast of Guildford). The interpolated encomium begins in prose, citing the judgments of Camden, Scaliger, Bale, Trithemius, and Foxe in praise of a great philosopher, "Subtilissimus omnium mortalium," "Nominalium parentem," "a worthy Divine, & of a right sincere judgment, as the times then would ether give or suffer"—and, inevitably therefore, a proto-Protestant. Nicolson then goes on to restate these commendations in what he calls "A breife Idilion of English epick verses." An "Idilion" is presumably something like an idyll, "A short poem, descriptive of some picturesque scene or incident, chiefly in rustic life," but the writing here is anything but idyllic; indeed, it could do with a sharp slash from Ockham's razor:

> O! would in Surrey mor such men were found;
> O! would mens vice, & sinn were sett a side;
> O! would that Ockams workes might be their guide;
> And to his good example them incline;
> who was a worthy & severe divine.

But for all the flat-footedness of the writing, Nicolson's manuscript interventions in the volume succeed in completely realigning the *Dialogue,* turning it from a piece of Protestant propaganda into a celebration of the intensely local. Pseudo-Ockham has been cut and regrafted onto a new stock. We might also want to see the badness of the poem as partly an effect of processes of material transfer. First Nicolson cites the prose sources in praise of Ockham; then he translates those prose sources into verse, which feels flatly prosaic as a result. This is an act of textual reconstitution akin to the shifting of letters in an anagram, or the play on the phoneme in a pun. This textual traffic goes hand in hand with the material reconstitution of the book.

Nicolson's most significant exploded book was also his magnum opus. This is a copy of *The First Part of the Diall of Days,* by Lodowick Lloyd, published and purchased in 1590 (Figure 37).[86] The *Diall* promised its readers a feast of ethnographic information: "*320. Romane triumphes, besides the triumphant Obelisks and Pyramydes of the Aegyptians, the Pillers, Arches, and Trophies triumphant, of the Græcians, and the Persians, with their Pompe and*

THE
Firſt part of the Diall
of ʼDaies,
Containing 320. Romane triumphes,
befides the triumphant Obelifks and ʼPyra-
*mydes of the Aegyptians,*the Pillers, Arches, and Trophies triumphant, of the Græcians, and the Perſians,with
their Pompe and Magnificence : Of feaſtes and Sacrifices both
*of the Iewes and of the Gentils,*with*the ſtately games and plaies*
*belonging to thefe Feaftes and Sacrifices,*with the birthes
and funeral ʼPomps of Kinges and Emperours, as
ɔ. you ſhall finde more at large in the 2.
part, wherein all kind of tri-
umphes are enlarged.

By Lodowick Lloid *Eſquire.*

Prou. 20.
Lucerna Domini fpiraculum hominis.

London
Printed for Roger Ward dwelling
at the figne of the Purfe in
the little old ʼBailie.
1590.

FIGURE 37. Lodowick Lloyd, *The First Part of the Diall of Days* (1590), title page. Oxford, Bodleian Library, 4° Rawl. 140 (1).

Magnificence: Of feastes and Sacrifices both of the Jewes and of the Gentils, with the stately games and plaies belonging to these Feastes and Sacrifices, with the birthes and funeral Pomps of Kinges and Emperours, as you shall finde more at large in the 2. part, wherein all kind of triumphes are enlarged." This is a comparative history focused on the powerful and on rituals of power. The book is arranged calendrically: Lloyd's "dial" (perhaps a sundial or a watch) gives us a page for every day of the year—although, since this is *The First Part of the Diall of Days*, Lloyd makes it only from January to June (the second part seems never to have been published). Each day we are treated to a ragbag of information: dates of battles or portents, scraps of astrology, and exercises in chronology, including notes on the precise dating of biblical events. For all its miscellaneity, the book would have helped its readers to ponder serious questions, such as the relationship between Christian and pagan history or the ways in which the stars influenced human affairs.

Lloyd's compilation as printed left no blank space for the addition of handwritten materials, unlike other day-by-day volumes published in the period, such as the *Ephemeris historica* of Michael Beuther.[87] Nicolson opened up Lloyd's text by having his copy of the *Diall* thickly interleaved. In the space thus created, he added vast amounts of new material, including entries for the missing half of the year, July to December. On Lloyd's title page he noted that the book has "divers Additions / By Robert Nicolsons industrie." He also created a new title page (placed at the beginning of July) in which he worried away at the question of what to call his creation: should it be "DIARIVM"; "DIVRNVM HISTORICVM"; "An historicall Journall. / or daybooke"; "EPHEMERIS HISTORICA," or perhaps "Heroica historia"; "Horologium historicum"; "The Compendious Historie"; "Polychronicon diarium"; or "Synopsis historiarum"?[88] What exactly was this thing that he was creating? The lengthy subtitle that Nicolson gave his work echoed Lloyd's, but promised in addition to cover the deeds of "Constant martyrs," "Reverend Bishops," and "valliant captaines," "with many other strange, rare, or admirable accidentes: by Lightening, thunder, earthquakes, extraordinarie fires; Inundations; prodigious births;. Navigations; Blasing starrs, Earth moveing. or removed," "from the creation of the world to this day." "This day" might by 1608 or it might be 1617—Nicolson was at work on the text over a long period. The title page also has a note presumably intended for the printer whose agency is explicitly invoked elsewhere: "Memorandum to place the histories of the Bible, & other theologicall histories: in the first place of every severall Day. /" The final organization of the material was to be made, not within the precincts of

DIARIVM
DIVRNVM HISTORICVM .199.

(scil:) An historicall Journall.
or daybooke

i. EPHEMERIS HISTORICA.

Besides the birth, Actions, & passion of Christ, & Apostles:
Wherin are perscribed the Nativities. Coronations.
Conquests Victories, Triumphes, marriages, Deathes, feastes, funeralls
and such like memorable Actes and Accidents: of many
sundry mightie Emperours, Romaine Bishops, renowned kinges, famous
queenes, & other noble, & notable Princes and
Potentates: wch haue dayly happened in seuerall
Empires, Kingdomes, cuntries, & Prouinces: of the world
the last six monethes of the yeare, vizt.
July, August, September, October, Nouember,
December, to the creation of the world to this day.
Gathered & written.

/ By ROBERT NICOLSON Gent /
Aᵒ Domini. 1608.

/. Necessarie for all estate / Varietie wth breuitie.
Pleasant, profitable & memorable.

Caius Iul: Cæsar the first Roman Emperoure
first of all other conformed the yeare, to the
course of the Sonne, & that there should be
365. dayes in the yeare; wth Dictio historius.

Note that Kalends was amongst the Romans, the
first day of euery moneth, or the very day of ye New Moone
wch commonly did concurr or fall out together in Greeke
Neomenia: But so called a Calando, because the priest
used then to call the people vnto the Court Curia
& there to pronounce vnto them, howe many daies
there were to the Nones, wch. / See this book, pag.

Md: to place the histories of the Bible, & other theologicall
histories: in the first place of euery seuerall Day. /
Varietie breedes delight;
Principibus placuisse viris non vltima laus est; /
Sim malus orator, dum bonus historicus. /

In all thinge varietie is very pleasing & nature
ioyeth in nothing more, then in diuersitie & change
But contrary wise a simple conformitie alwaies
one & the same is hurtfull & bringeth tediousnes wth
it incontinently. / & cf. /

Nicolson's interleaved book, but on the bed of the press—a bed on which the book never came to rest.

Eventually it seems that Nicolson settled for a single title, "DODECAM-ERON: A Book in 12 parts."[89] Had it been printed, the book would have absorbed Lloyd's text, presenting it in corrected form with new marginal notes. But it would also have contained lengthy additions, gathered from upward of 140 books—among them the 1589 and 1600 editions of Hakluyt, manuscripts such as Richard Robinson's account of the Armada victory, and a copy of Caxton's translation of the *Recuyell of the Histories of Troye*, the first book printed in English, which Nicolson dated to 1464.[90] He also drew on a variety of almanacs and pamphlets in what was a highly eclectic mix of sources. He documents his sources with characteristic precision, giving dates, formats, and page numbers for each citation; sometimes he specifies a printer and place of publication. This chimes with the strongly locative focus of the excerpts themselves, which are almost always focused around the particular times and places of this or that birth or death or marriage, or blazing star, or exploit of Sir Francis Drake. The project is underwritten by the desire to place the past, fixing it in time and space.

The *Dodecameron* certainly allows us to place Nicolson, since as well as being a would-be printed book, for general consumption, it is also a private journal, albeit a journal that has been shredded and collaged across the days of the year. A host of manuscript entries in the text are singled out as not to be printed, or "for my remembrance," or are just marked with Nicolson's initials in order to privatize them. From these entries we can reconstruct the course of Nicolson's early life, in particular his extensive travels as a merchant in the mid-1580s, which had taken him to Elsinore in Denmark, Königsberg in Prussia, and west along the Baltic through Heiligenbeil (modern Mamonovo), Braunsberg (Braniewo), Frauenberg (Frombork), and so on to Elbing, at the time "the sole Baltic entrepot for English goods," where he stayed for several months.[91] He made several visits to Gdansk, was present for the great fair at Torun, and made a five-hundred-mile detour to Emden, a center of trade for the Merchant Adventurers of London.[92] It was presumably during these travels that Nicolson met Sylvester, who was stationed in East Friesland on behalf of the Merchant Adventurers' Company in the mid-1580s.[93] But the highlight of the trip seems to have occurred on Friday, 22 September 1587, on the Vistula River a little way from Danzig, where he "plainly veiwed, & stedfastly beheld, Sigismundus .3. King of Poland, together with the Ladie Anna his Sister; and Prince Edward Fortunatus: aborde his royall

Shipp, lying then at anker." A manicule points out the crucial fact of the
encounter: "His majestie also then, & there, firmly fixed his royall eies on
me."[94] This intertwining of eye-beams of the English merchant with the
Polish monarch, with its emphasis on stasis, steadfastness, and fixity—and
the precisely located "then, & there"—perhaps defined Nicolson's relationship with adhesion ever after. He had been cut and pasted in to the European
aristocracy.

Much the same thing happens on a more local level. The *Dodecameron*
is full of the patronage and friendship connections we have already seen in
this chapter: thus we find, on 29 April 1594, the death of "Helen Nicolson
Ladie Branch," and, on 24 July 1588, the death of her husband, "at which
time, the vainly termed the invincible Spanish fleet, was on the coast of
England."[95] Here is the knighting of "the right honorable Cuthbert Buckle,
Lord Maior of London, (late my only Maister)" at Greenwich in May 1594,
and his death just over a month later.[96] But the volume also allows us to
understand Nicolson's relationships with the Thomas Holcrofts and Isabella
Rutlands whose names are filched into the *Praxis medicinae*. These people
are, he believes, his relations:

> The noble Ladie ELIZABETH Mannors (Baroness Ross) sole daughter &
> heire of the right honorable Lord Edward Mannors Earle of Rutland,
> Lord Ross of Hamlake, Belvoire, & Trusbut, Knight of the renowmed
> order of the Garter etc: By his honorable wife, ISABEL (daughter of Sir
> Thomas Holcroft, & his wife Julian Jennins:) was borne about the 14th
> of December. A°. D°. *1575. /.* Which said Countess Isabell & my Mother:
> were Cosen Germans once remoued; (By their mothers side.) For so the
> Ladie Julian Holcroft (mother of the said Countess & grandmother of
> the said Ladie Ross.) told to me, her selfe at her house in Tower streete,
> in London. A°. D°. 1588. /. Before the 10. october. /.[97]

On 30 March 1592, Nicolson reports, "I first sawe, kist, talkd & dyned with
the right honorable Ladie Isabell Countess Dowager of Rutland at her house
in Stepney; . . . which honorable Countess, & my mother, were Cosen Germans, once removed (by their mothers side)."[98] Elsewhere we learn of Isabel's
death at Stepney on 21 January 1605, and of the death of Baroness Ross on
12 April 1591, and her burial at Westminster, "wherof I was an eie-witness; to
my great greife, for the sayd Ladie Ross, her Mothers mother, & my mothers
mother were cosen germans, vizt brother and sisters children," so that "The

said Baroness Ross, & I: were cosen Germans twice removed."[99] (The said Baroness Ross had been married to William Cecil the younger, "nowe Lord Burghley," so this was no mean connection.)

There is a kind of manic precision to Nicolson's reiterated documentation of these relationships. The concern with genealogy seems to be shading into horary astrology, for which it might matter precisely where and when somebody told you that she or he was related to you. But these references help us to register the force of all those pasted-in armorials. Cutting—splicing the art of the herald with technology of the woodcut, and with the physical workings of knives or scissors and glue—is here part of a larger project of grafting, the grafting of an individual onto a family tree. We might think of Nicolson's marginalia as themselves a kind of cut, an opening out of the book to new purposes, or as a budding (the peculiar look of his italic hand, sprouting ornamental hairline strokes at every opportunity, contributes to this impression). And if we recall that the Latin words for book—*liber* and *codex*—both derive from bark, while the English word "book" derives from "beech" (as in the tree), then we may be some way to locating the life in dead wood.[100]

Following this paper trail from the notation of a payment for "a Booke in commendacion of the Ladye Branche" has taken us a long way from Stonley, into another life, another library, and another form of self-accounting, which intersperses the records of personal dealings into a historical record garnered from some very extensive reading. We have, to push a little harder on arboreal metaphors, truly gone out on a limb. We have no way of knowing whether Stonley was acquainted with his younger relative, or whether they were able to converse across the factional lines that seem to have divided their family. In Chapter 4 I explored how Stonley's books were networked outward to communities, via their inscriptions and their bindings; this chapter has also been all about the forging of connections through books, but it may be premised on a rupture, and the power of print to prevent meetings and occlude origins. That connective media such as books and newspapers can be locally disconnective is suggested by Leah Price, as she analyzes a plethora of nineteenth-century representations of unhappily married partners adopting the pretense of reading to avoid conversation.[101] Fast-forward to the early twenty-first century, and smartphones running social media apps do a similar job of abstracting us from people who are near at hand and connecting us with more dispersed communities. So, while cutting may allow for splicing and new growth, attachment in one site often means detachment from another. Arguably, what technologies such as the book or the smartphone afford us is simultaneous attachment and detachment; the funeral tears without the funeral, the friend status without the friendship. My next chapter, setting out from two innocuous-seeming books from Stonley's library, offers an even more extreme example of the power of print to divide people even as it links them.

Chapter 7

Meet the Chillesters

Fraud in Fox Fur

The events that led to Stonley's imprisonment for debt in 1597 were initiated by a man named Thomas Lichfield. Lichfield seems to have started his career as a singer in a group of court musicians that performed at the funeral of Henry VIII in 1547. Thereafter he became a groom of the Privy Chamber, and it is in this guise that he appears in the coronation list of Elizabeth I; one document refers to him as supervisor of the Queen's music.[1] Early in Elizabeth's reign he is noted as taking receipt of a number of her more musical New Year's gifts, including a song book from Thomas Kent, a "faire Lewte" from Thomas Browne, and a chest with three gitterns in it from John Roose.[2] Later he would himself become a participant in these exchanges, giving Elizabeth a lute inlaid with mother-of-pearl in 1579, a "Bandoro" in 1581, and "a spannysshe Gyttorne lute" in 1584.[3]

In the early 1560s, Lichfield was in financial trouble, partly thanks to his losses at gambling, which he attempted to recover by bringing a suit against several of his gaming companions in Star Chamber.[4] One was Gilbert Walker, who is known to literary history as the presumed author of a pamphlet entitled *A Manifest Detection of the Moste Vyle and Detestable Use of Diceplay, and Other Practises Lyke the Same* (1552?), one of the earliest examples of "rogue" or "coney-catching" literature in English.[5] Walker kept a dining house, or "ordinary," probably situated next to Fleet Bridge, at which Lichfield lost considerable sums of money. Another fellow dicer was a Lancashire man named Hamlet Harrington. Under interrogation, Harrington recalled how Lichfield once bewailed his fortunes to him, "saying that he was very sore in debt." Harrington had reassured him, saying "you are in place where you maye easely Recover the same" and offering to give him notice "of some thing whiche you maye obtayne at the Queenes Majesties handes." But when they met again, he reports, he taught Lichfield how to rub a dice against a stone to make it run high or low, so that he could repair his fortunes at the gaming table.

By the end of the decade, Lichfield had found an altogether better way to make money. In 1568 he received a patent that gave him "the moiety" (that is, half) of any sums of money that he could show had been embezzled from the Crown. The patent was supposed to last for five years, but it was extended until 1578, and Lichfield was still benefiting from it in 1585.[6] His investigations started close to home, with members of the Bassano family of court musicians, who (he said) had continued to draw Alessandro Bassano's annuity for fifteen years after his death. The Bassanos found themselves "troubled and seriously oppressed by Mr. Litchfield" but were eventually able to prove that they had not taken any money to which they were not entitled.[7] By 1573 Lichfield had turned to more distant quarries, pursuing Sir Valentine Browne, treasurer of Berwick, for irregularities in his accounts, including drawing a larger daily stipend than he was due during the siege of Leith, back in 1560. Pleading fifteen years of loyal service, Browne expressed deep concern about the accusations, which if taken seriously would strike at the root of his credit and make it impossible for him to recoup the personal expenses that he had incurred in office. Despite his protestations, he was imprisoned in the Fleet and removed from office as a result of Lichfield's investigation.[8]

The Exchequer, "easily the largest department" of central administration after the Royal Household, was at once Lichfield's main source of evidence for fraud and a goldmine of potentially fraudulent practice in itself, the more so since it was mired in a seemingly endless battle over precedence and a related controversy over the fees that it charged for its services.[9] Since at least the reign of Mary, the two chief officeholders in the Receipt (the "writer of the tallies" and the "clerk of the pells") had been raking over the ancient history of the Exchequer in an attempt to show that they were the embodiment of its authentic practices and so were due the lion's share of the fees. For a long period, between 1569 and 1593, the writer of the tallies was Robert Petre, brother of Sir William, so Stonley would have been close to the center of this dispute. Indeed, thanks to his longevity in office, Stonley was himself called upon to testify to the ancient ways of the Exchequer before a committee convened to end the civil war in 1580; his testimony buttressed Petre's case against his tireless adversary Chidiock Wardour, clerk of the pells.[10] In 1579, Thomas Lichfield put forward a bill in which he listed "Augmentacions of Fees" that he had found among the tellers' accounts. Among the officials called upon to explain their salary hikes were the auditors of the Exchequer, one of whom explained that increases in fees had been agreed as proper responses to rampant inflation: "in this later age the prices of all vendible thinges wherebie mannes lief is susteined ar universallie increaced and therfor more chargeablie to be mainteined." Another auditor, Stonley's Aldersgate neighbor William Fuller, went a step further in his explanation, putting price inflation down to "the dearth of all thinges" at this time.[11]

As a teller, Stonley was called upon to provide raw data for Lichfield's inquiries, some of which dated back to his early years in office. So, for example, on 10 June 1575 he made a declaration of sums he had paid out to Valentine Browne in the fifth and sixth years of Philip and Mary (1557–58) and in the second year of Elizabeth (1559–60). The second of these sums was £649, but the first was just £40.[12] It was almost certainly Lichfield's search for "concealments" that prompted Stonley to produce this document, now among the State Papers. Under the terms of Lichfield's patent, long-forgotten payments could be disinterred, long-moldering account books reopened. (Browne complained that he could not respond properly to Lichfield's assault because the clerks who had been under his charge and dealing with his accounts at the time were all dead.)[13] Stonley evidently counterattacked; from 1574, there survives a royal pardon clearing him of all offences committed in office since 1554. But it seems that this was not sufficient to defend his reputation from Lichfield's attacks.[14] Stonley also had other more direct dealings with the man who would eventually prove his nemesis. In 1581, he gave a reward of three shillings and four pence "To master Lichfeldes man for Bringing of two muscovia foxfurs."[15] Whether such furs would have been needed at the beginning of August is a moot point, but this detail suggests that the two men had the sort of relationship that could be oiled by gifts. Lichfield also seems to have contracted some substantial debts to Stonley, becoming bound by obligation for £200 on 7 June 1580, with one William Neale, and by a series of solo obligations in 1584 (8 February, 12 October, 17 October) to the tune of £500.[16]

We know about these debts only because of the list that Stonley was forced to draw up as a result of Lichfield's successful assault on his reputation. Lichfield was hot on the tellers' trail by 1576; a document compiled for his benefit in 1576, headed "A Briefe Note of the fower Tellers severall Chardges," stretching back to 1557, tots up the vast sums dealt with by each teller (£47,000 in one term, £29,000 the next) and concludes, ominously, that some of Stonley's figures don't add up.[17] More formal proceedings seem to have been initiated by a letter to Lord Burghley in August 1584. In this letter, Lichfield accused Stonley of multiple crimes. He had received money for "Fynes of Leases" (fees paid on the transfer or alteration of a tenancy), which he had noted down but "falsely Concealed . . . from hir highnes," and he had £1,000 of similar fines, of which he had not made a record. And there were serious irregularities in the payments of money "by specialle warraunte of tholde Lord Threasorer Sir Richard Sackeville and Sir Walter Mildmay" (of the three, only Mildmay was still alive; the old Lord Treasurer, William Paulet, had died in 1572, while Sackville had died in 1566).

Having confronted Stonley with "theese apparaunte deceiptes," Lichfield could report that he "standeth very obstinately in the denyalle therof and offereth to defende the same by lawe, which wilbe very tedious & Chardgeable unto me." So he handed the cross-investigation over to Cecil, "that with your Lordshippes good favour I may proceed in the opening of his notorious fraude to her highnes."[18] In a second, related document from 1584, entitled "Fynes of leases concealed by Richard Stoneley as by the severall receipt thereof may appeare under his owne hand," Lichfield lists £1,140 of fraudulent transactions. Stonley might have taken some consolation at this time from the knowledge that he was not alone. Several tellers had been accused of smaller frauds, and his near neighbor in Warwickshire Edward Fisher had been asked to repay £800 that his late father had allegedly taken in "arrerages of dead payes" (payments falsely made to people who were deceased).[19] Lichfield had even managed to detect a fraud of £175 per annum in "the great and superfluous allowance of waxe, yerely allowed to the Chafer for serving of the great Seale."[20]

Unsurprisingly, Lichfield made plenty of enemies as he followed the heady scent of cooked books, and this agent of suspicion rapidly became himself an object of suspicion. From (perhaps) 1574 there survives an anonymous, undated document entitled "A brief declaration of the commission that master Lichfield hath had out of the Queenes Majesties court of exchecker."[21] Initially the document seems sympathetic enough, itemizing the erroneous or fraudulent payments that Lichfield has discovered in the accounts of the Exchequer tellers, or of the county "receivers" who collected local land revenues. But then it becomes clear that this list is being compiled surreptitiously: its details "were secretlie taken out of a booke, which (For a bragging shew of service) master lichfeld had compild & collected together: But being better Remembrid, thinkeng hereby that he should have bewraied him selfe, durst not shew the saide booke."[22] The reason that Lichfield was "better Remembrid" was, it seems, because he did *not* wish to reveal the full extent of his discoveries to the Queen, and the reason for this was (so the document claims) that he had a nice line in "compounding"—making private arrangements to deal with instances of embezzlement without having to give a "moiety" of the money to the Crown. The book was somehow "conveied awaie" by Lichfield's man Philpot, and as a result of this, Philpot lost his job. But Lichfield knew all the details by heart, and he was careful to spirit away any evidence of malpractice after he had his money. "The most part of the certificates are now to seke: For some served his Cooke For his pastrie in the oven, some ad alia negocia magis obscoena gerenda [were put to other more obscene purposes], And some Remaine still lyeng in the dust." The document lists various people with whom Lichfield has made private deals, so that "the Queene had no part with ani of these," in number "to mani to be remembrid more tedious to be Recited."[23] We then move on to consider other aspects of the practices Lichfield engaged in, including his "deputations," or subcontracting of his patent to numerous local agents. Substantial sums could be involved in such arrangements, as when he farmed Yorkshire out to Richard Greene, late servant to the Earl of Warwick, in order to discharge a debt of £200, "being lost unto him at dice as I suppose."[24] Whoever wrote this document knew a thing or two about Lichfield's reputation.

Lichfield was killed by a servant in 1586. William Cecil wrote to Thomas Fanshawe and Peter Osborne at the Exchequer on 15 March, asking them to repair forthwith "to the howse or lodginges of Master Lichfield, whoe I understand is of late slaine by a lewde servant of his owne." They were to seize and seal up, Cecil instructed them, "all such Bookes, papers & writinges that you shall theare find," since many of them would concern the Queen. In a postscript he added: "I praie you advertise me of the manner of his deathe, and howe he died in his state of welthe, which I conceave was but poore."[25] This ignominious demise by no means brought an end to Stonley's tribulations. On 4 August 1586, Robert Petre wrote to Burghley that Stonley was unable to tie up his accounts to the tune of £16,000, so that the burden of payments was falling on the other three tellers, a situation that could not be borne for very long.

In February 1588, Stonley sent Burghley the first of several petitions attempting to explain his various misfortunes, claiming that £2,000 had been filched from him after the deaths of his clerks at times when he was keeping away from London for fear of plague; that £2,000 was stolen from his chest at

Westminster "when your honour measured the footsteps on my telling board"; and that he had lost £1,000 simply because he was overwhelmed by the vast sums he was receiving ("some years three hundred thousand pounds, and more"). Far from concealing anything, "I have charged myself with above forty thousand pounds more than any auditor can charge me withal."[26] By late December of the same year, Robert Petre had despaired of Stonley and his fellow teller Robert Tailor, decreeing that no money could pass through their hands "untill they shall gyve better answer with mony and not in words."

When Stonley realized that he was being circumvented, he complained that this would mean the death of his credit and would hugely impair his ability to pay his debt.[27] In 1593, we find Stonley compiling long lists of all the lands that he is trying to sell off.[28] Despite more than a decade of investigations, he seems still to have been handling Exchequer payments in the spring of 1596.[29] But the sound of patience finally ebbing away is clearly audible in a letter sent in May of the same year by Vincent Skinner, Petre's successor as writer of the tallies, lamenting "how falsely [Stonley] hath forsworn him self and how slyly he hath conveyed other money awaie which should have bene extant." By April 1597, Stonley was imprisoned, and the sale of his property was fully in train; his Exchequer office was filled in February 1598.[30] Two years later, he was dead.

The maneuvering of courtiers and officials fighting to stay afloat in a sea of debt, as documented by crumbling manuscripts buried deep in the archives, looks on the face of it to be worlds away from the public, official culture of the printed book. But, as this chapter shows, there are some compelling connections between the two spheres. My investigation sets out from a single, seemingly trivial coincidence, that Richard Stonley owned two books by authors with the same, very unusual surname, "Chillester." On 20 July 1582, he paid twenty pence for what he described as "the four bookes bounde up to gether in forrell called youthes wytte et alijs."[31] The 1597 inventory lists, in Stonley's bedchamber, a book entitled "Institution of Christian Princes," priced at four pence. The book Stonley bought in 1582 was a miscellany compiled by Henry Chillester; the book in the inventory was a translation ascribed to James Chillester. In neither the journal entry nor the inventory is the authorship noted; more than likely Stonley did not himself notice it. But to delve into the hinterland of these publications is to expose a network that connects this reader to these writers, even unwittingly. Behind the facade, we find a father-and-son duo who exploited the innocent appearance of the printed book for purposes that were not remotely innocent. This is a paper trail that leads, by crooked ways, into a murky world of spies and counterfeiters, of corrupt informers and renegade printers. Whether Stonley knew it or not, this was also his world. Tracing the network of attachments that produced a printed book for sale will allow us to feel some of the stickiness of the web he was caught up in.

James Chillester: *A Most Excellent Hystorie*

This paper trail starts with an innocuous quarto published in 1571 entitled *A Most Excellent Hystorie, of the Institution and Firste Beginning of Christian Princes, and the Originall of Kingdomes Wherunto is Annexed a Treatise of Peace and Warre, and Another of the Dignitie of Mariage. . . . First Written in Latin by Chelidonius Tigurinus, after Translated into French by Peter Bouaisteau of Naunts in Brittaine, and now Englished by James Chillester, Londoner* (Figure 39). This was a translation of a popular French work, Pierre Boiastuau's *L'histoire de Chelidonius Tigurinus*, which was first published in 1556, went through three editions in its first year of publication, and saw another twelve French editions by 1585.[32] The argument of the book is that monarchy is the best form of government, and that subjects are duty bound to obey their rulers, while kings are obliged to cultivate virtue, take advice from counsellors, and defend religion against the scourge of Islam. Rulers should promote peace, and they should also marry, since marriage is the best guard against "the abominable and filthie sinne of incontinencie."[33]

To a historian of ideas the argument of the *Hystorie* might appear to have its fair share of inconsistencies. Early on, for example, the text celebrates the bee as an insect that teaches us that monarchy is a natural way in which to organize a society; yet it then goes on to praise ants, which, although they "have no Prince, Gouernour, or Ruler," are exemplary in their orderliness and obedience (D3r). No comment is offered to assimilate this seeming counterexample.[34] Then, although the treatise cites St. Paul on the necessity of submission to higher powers, which are ordained of God, it sees no contradiction between this position and the admission that monarchy was, in its earliest stages, elective and ordained by men (E1r–2r). And for an apparently conservative book, it spends a lot of time focusing on the failings of rulers and the perils of tyranny, such that Boiastuau has to issue various disclaimers denying any seditious intent (C2v–3r, F4r). Such oddities are compounded

A most excellent Hystorie,

Of the Institution
and firste beginning of
Christian Princes, and the
Originall of Kingdomes:

Wherunto is annexed a trea-
tise of Peace and Warre, and another of
the dignitie of Mariage.

Very necessarie to be red, not only of all
Nobilitie and Gentlemen, but also
of euery publike persone.

First written in Latin by Chelidonius Tigurinus, after
translated into French by Peter Bouaistuau of
Naunts in Brittaine, and now englished
by Iames Chillester, Londoner.

Seen and allowed according to the
order appointed.

AT LONDON,
Printed by H. Bynneman
dwelling in Knightrider streat, at
the signe of the Marmayd.
ANNO. 1571.

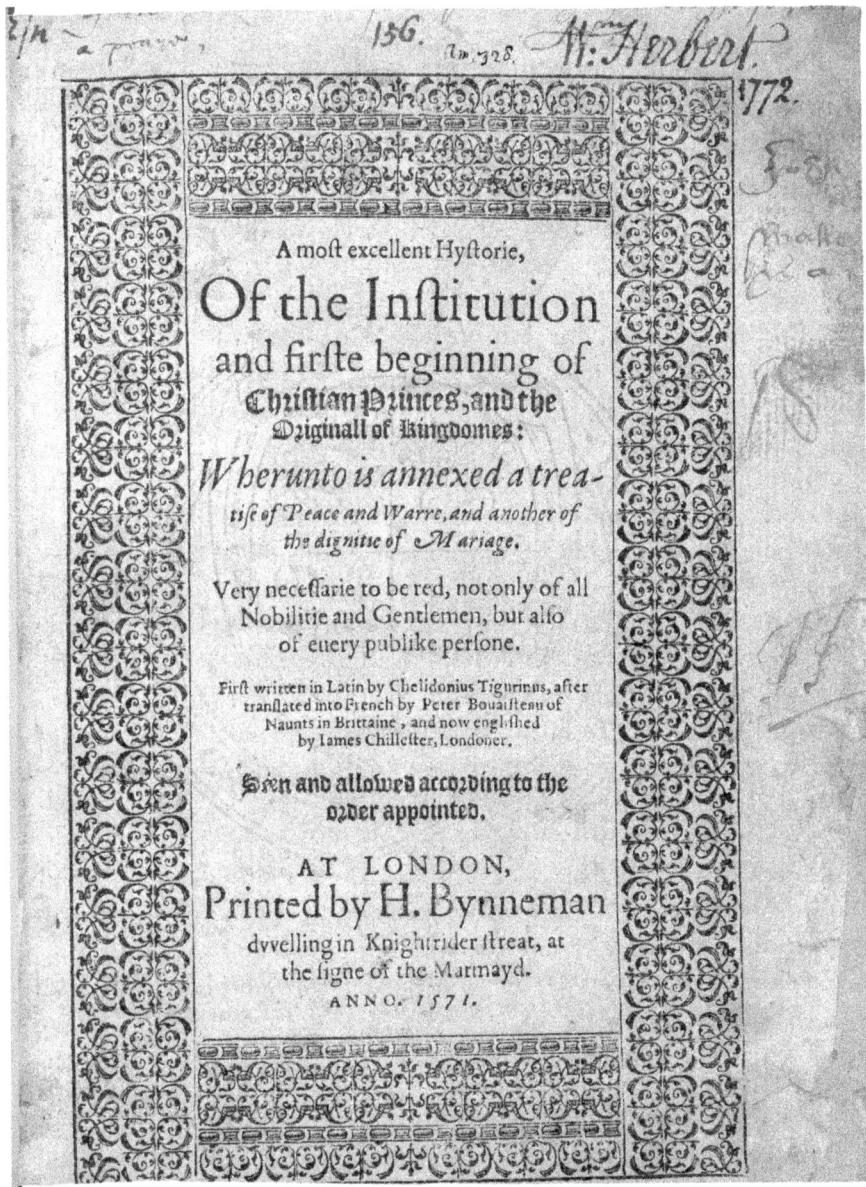

FIGURE 39. Chelidonius Tigurinus, *A Most Excellent Hystorie* (1571), title page.
Cambridge University Library, Syn.7.57.24.

in the English translation, which is dedicated not to the Duke of Nevers, as was the French original, but to the Queen of England.

Had Elizabeth troubled to glance at the volume, she might have been charmed to see the royal arms on the verso of the title page, along with verses asserting that "Whome God defendes and keepes, must flourishe stil and stand" (A1v). Perhaps she would have been reassured to hear (conventionally enough) that the book was not intended "to put your Majestie in remembrance of any thing that shoulde be wanting in your noble personage" but was instead offered as "a glasse for your highnesse, to see . . . the manyfolde benefites that God hath bestowed at all times, and in all ages on those that have loved and feared hym" (A4r). But what would she have made of the dedication's comments on the origins of rule, as it describes how "in the great world, by the wisdom of god and the universal consent of men, is elected and chosen one principal man (in nobleness and vertue surpassing the reste) to beare . . . rule and authoritie in the body of every common welth" (A2v)?[35] How might she have taken its emphasis on what happens to history's bad kings and princes, who "were (by the just judgment of God) shamefully overthrown and cast down from high estate and degree, to great wretchedness and miserie, to their great reproche and ignomie for ever" (A3r)? And would she have appreciated the *Hystorie*'s thoroughly patriarchal praise of marriage? Here Plato is cited to the effect that "man dothe rule and governe ouer the woman, as the shepheard over the sheepe," while Aristotle is wheeled out to reveal that "man by kinde, dooth know the aucthoritie and power that he hath over the woman." Similarly, in nature we observe that "the males do always commaund the females," and this goes for precious stones and plants as well as animals, "for amongs them suche as have any force, strengthe and power, we call alwayes the males, and the other more weake and inferiours, we call females" (2B4r–v). Of course, we cannot know what Elizabeth would have thought; probably she would have agreed, viewing herself as the exception that proved all rules. Looking on, however, we may sense a certain want of tact in this dedicatory gesture.

To date, nothing has been known about the man who made that gesture. The entry for James Chillester, "(*fl.* 1571), translator," in the *Oxford Dictionary of National Biography* comments that he "was (according to his title-page) a Londoner; nothing more seems known about his life." The remainder of the entry summarizes the contents of the *Hystorie* and concludes: "All this Chillester renders with vigour." But there is more to be said about this shadowy figure. Much of the relevant documentation was assembled by Christina

Garrett in her 1938 study of the Marian exiles. Garrett's entry for Chillester calls him a "man of doubtful status" who, when he was not translating Boaistuau's mirror for princes, "seems also to have spent a turbulent life as a counterfeiter and rebel."[36] Leafing through the *Calendar of State Papers, Foreign*, Garrett catches Chillester coining money in Oxford in order to finance the 1556 Dudley conspiracy to oust Philip and Mary and to replace them with Princess Elizabeth.[37] Fearing detection, Chillester next fled to France; a number of letters survive in which the ambassador to France, Nicholas Wotton, conveyed the exile's request that he be pardoned. He next resurfaced in the early 1570s, this time as a conspirator against Elizabeth, and was reported to Lord Burghley as "a dangerous fellow" but one "from whom much information may be gained if skilfully handled."

The story that Garrett begins to open up here is a fascinating one, with many more ramifications than she was able to pursue. (Chillester, as a lowly conspirator rather than a religious exile, was barely on her radar.) In particular, the later letters relating to Chillester, dating from March 1571/2, are far more detailed and interesting than Garrett's account suggests. Both are written by one William Herle, whose career as a double agent working in London's Marshalsea prison around the time of the Norfolk Rising has recently been explored in some detail by Robyn Adams.[38] Herle sent two letters relating to Chillester, who was at the time imprisoned in the Marshalsea.[39] The first sets out the case against him and requests that he be examined with great care; the second complains that he has pulled the wool over the eyes of his interrogators, with potentially serious consequences.[40] Taken together the letters offer a highly resonant poison-pen portrait of the counterfeiter and suggest that the *Hystorie* may be the latest in his long line of forgeries.

In Herle's account, Chillester's deceits begin with his strange surname: "Imprimis that James Chillister, was borne at saffron walldon, whose true name is James Davyd, butt alltred belike to avoyd som grett penallty, which declares the rest of his life to be according to his dooble name." Having established his fake identity, Herle moves on to Chillester's coining activities, which took place not at Oxford but at Otford, a royal palace in Kent of which Sir Henry Sidney had recently become Keeper. Herle asserts that Chillester, a servant of Sidney's, had "with one Harrison" "allured thither certayne of the monyers of the Towne, who conveying with them the stampes, dyd coyne together a grett masse of money of those vj peny peces of Phillip & Mary." But the plot was discovered, and the coiners "fled over the seas desgised as maryners, in the same ship wherin king Phillip was" (this would seem to date

the flight to November 1555).[41] Herle reports Chillester's delight in the fact
that the "pore workmen" were apprehended and executed for their crimes,
while the masterminds escaped.

Next, we learn, Chillester shaved off his beard and came back to England
to fetch a bag of money that he and Harrison had hidden. But Harrison beat
him to it, and Chillester accordingly "conspired how to kylle the sayd Harrison" (whether he succeeded is unclear).[42] All of this intersects somewhat
ironically with comments contained in the two letters sent to England by the
ambassador to France, Nicholas Wotton, late in 1556. In those letters, it is
reported that Chillester was seeking a pardon in order to satisfy his stricken
conscience. At the point when he realized he was about to be apprehended,
Wotton writes, Chillester had "buryed certayn coyning wedges or stampes yn
the grownde yn a secret playce. wherof no manne knowing but he him self
And then came awaye. And because yf the same wedges shild by eny chawnse
be fownd owte; they mighte happen yn to the handes of such as myght therby
committe the lyke offence: therfor he thought goode for the discharge of his
conscience" to plead that he might dig them up again.[43] The plea sounds
dubious enough in the original letter, but Herle's testimony invites us to read
it as a shocking ruse, in which "the discharge of his conscience" is a cover for
its complete abandonment.

Chillester was, in Herle's account, pardoned with the support of the Earl
of Pembroke following the capture of St. Quentin in 1557. Returning to
England and "having to this daye nothyng to lyve uppon," he went to Berwick, where he had dealings with two successive treasurers of the garrison
town. He became a servant of the first, Sir William Ingleby, whom he black-
mailed so successfully that now (Herle reports) "he caryes Ingelby in his
sleve," and he was "suborned . . . to be an accuser" of the second, Valentine
Browne (the nature of the accusation is not specified). Herle now turns to
the present, when Chillester is "a grett enemye to the Q. majestie a vehement
Papist in his religion (if he be of ani) desirows of innovatyon, & a reporter
of prophesyes to perswade men the better to rebellyon & to the desire of new
thinges." He is counted "a grett Cowncellor" among "all the Traytors &
Papists that wishe ylle to the state"; he had been "a grett favorere" of the
Duke of Norfolk and remains "wholly addicted to the scottish factyon."[44]
Moreover, he is something of a political theorist, "publisheng to those that
be of his leven how weke the governement is that now we have, as though it
were in his hed to frame a better polycye & to dele more wisely." Later Herle
records that "among other of his bookes that ar left in the sheriffes custody,

it appered [Chillester's] study was muche in Machiavell. De Principe./" This begins to sound like the man who translated Boaistuau's *Hystorie*.

But the truth, as Herle goes on to tell it, turns out to be rather more complex:

Item the sayd Chillester to joyn unto hym self some oppinion of lernyng, & to be thought of sownd religion towardes God, & of an honest dutye to his Prynce, hath dedicated a tretyse to the Q. majestie before christmas last, which was on[e] Goldwelles translatyon owt of frenche, that dwelled abowtt the strond, who being now dede, this Chillester hath sett furthe this worke in his own name, which worke he recoverd of Goldwelles wife, with whom he was & is more familier than honesty wold: As therin he makes small consycens, for that he abuseth mo[re] menes wives than on[e], yett having on[e] of his own, & in effect lyves so vicyowsly, as all his neighbors crye owtt uppon hym.

A marginal note specifies the book in question: "chelidomius Tigurinus worke in latten & traslated into french by on[e] Bowgsh [*sic*]. Of the instructyon of an christian prince, of the dignitye of mariaige, & of pece & warre."[45] Later, expressing his frustration at the ineffectual interrogation of Chillester, Herle repeated his claim: "to wyn some oppinion of duty & honesty, he fathers Goldwelles translatyon to be his, & hath dedicated yt to the Q. Majestie being more familier with the sayd Goldwelles wife, than was mete, wherby after her husbondes decesse he gatt the sayde worke./" Herle's distaste for this slippery enemy of the state leads him to mint a neologism not noted in the *OED*, as he brands Chillester "a Papiste & a versipeller"—a skin-turner.[46]

These two letters relating to James Chillester's activities, for all their venom and color, are somewhat isolated documents. There is no evidence that the authorities ever answered Herle's plea for a second interrogation, or that they shared his sense of the threat posed by this particular jailbird.[47] And of course we ought to treat Herle's testimony with great caution, coming as it does in the midst of an extended character assassination. Several elements in his testimony can, however, be corroborated. We get a fleeting glimpse of Chillester among the voluminous testimonies of the Dudley conspirators, when one John Dethicke, who had a reputation as an "alchemist" or coiner, recalls how he had bumped into Chillester, whom he had known in Boulogne before it fell to the French in 1550. Chillester, Dethicke relates, "told me that he hade the kepyng of Otford place And he warranttyd the house sure for the purpose but in fyne when the matter showld have byne browght to pas Chyllyster utterly refusyd yt And dyswadyd me there from yt/."[48] Herle's claim that Chillester was exiled in France in 1556 and was actively seeking a pardon for his coining is confirmed by Nicholas Wotton's letters. Furthermore, the pardon itself survives in a Patent Roll dated 26 August 1557, which records that "James Chellester late of Otteford, co. Kent, 'yoman'," had been indicted on 3 June 1556 for having "feloniously forged and counterfeited" silver coins at Otford, and that he was pardoned "of the said felony and treason, etc., so that he stand to right, etc." (The pardon at one point refers to "Chellester *alias* Davy," backing up Herle's claims about dual identity.)[49] Finally, Chillester's association with Henry Sidney, although it appears to leave no mark in Sidney's correspondence, was real and of long standing. In his letters to Burghley of March 1572, Herle complained of rumors that Chillester would soon be released from prison "amongest whom sir Harry Sydney had promised his ayd, so had master wilbraham, & he hoped likewise that the Erlle of Bedford wold joyne with them."[50]

What of Herle's claim that the *Most Excellent Hystorie* was a smokescreen, not translated by Chillester but instead stolen from one Goldwell "that dwelled abowtt the strond"? This is harder to corroborate. There are no printed books from the period, and no wills, that can provide a clear fix on a plausible candidate. Legal documents take us a little further. We learn from a jail delivery record that on 7 August 1565, "at the parish of St. Mary-le-Strande co. Midd[lesex][,] . . . Edith Sawnders late of London spynster stole a parcel-gilt goblett of sylver worth four marks, and six silver spoons worth forty shillings, of the goods and chattels of William Goldwell gentleman."[51] From 1567 there survives the record of a lawsuit relating to property in Whitecross Street, in the parish of St. Giles Without Cripplegate, the parties to which were Joyce and Richard Barlee, William Goldwell, and Alice, his wife.[52] And at some unknown date, probably in the 1560s, one Dunstan Avys launched a Chancery suit against Goldwell in relation to the "unconscyonable desire and gredye appetyte" he had displayed in dealings relating to a tenement in the parish of St. Mary le Strand.[53] Here we seem to have our man, although these documents tell us little about him, beyond a hint of wealth and an intermittent claim to gentry status.[54]

We get a more substantial glimpse into the translator's past thanks to a scuffle that took place in the first year of Elizabeth's reign, in London's Lombard Street. In the bill of complaint that he submitted to Star Chamber, a William Goldwell claimed that he had been lynched by three men: Robert

Holdyche, Robert Quicke, and Thomas Jenison.[55] They had assembled "with Swordes drawen, buklers and other weapons of malice prepensed" to beat and wound him, "whereuppon your said orator was in greate parell and danger of his life." Holdyche responded to Goldwell's bill by recalling a time "abowt three yeres past" when both men had served the vice-treasurer of Ireland, Sir Edmund Rous, "during whiche service the said Complainant used hym self towardes theire said Master in suche evell sort and maner both in dedes and words as is not seemly to be uttered in this honorable Court." After this time, Goldwell had returned to England, while Holdyche had stayed in Ireland in the service of Sir Henry Sidney, "now lord Justice of Ireland." Sent to London on business, Holdyche met by chance with Quicke and Jenison, "his old familiers and frendes unto the said Sir Henry Sydney knight," and went carousing with them in what he claimed was "a quyet and peacyble maner." Soon afterward they were set upon by Goldwell, he "most ungodly bering in mynd a contynuall grudge and hatred towardes the said holdich."

Goldwell's service to Rous is at issue in another lawsuit, this one brought in Chancery early in Elizabeth's reign. Here Rous, who was being pursued for more than £3,000 worth of debts incurred during his tenure as treasurer at war in Ireland, reported that he had deputed his duties to his clerk William Goldwell for a period lasting "two yeres nine monethes and xxj dayes" in the mid-1550s. During that time, Goldwell had systematically defrauded the Crown by various means, including the retrospective falsification of accounts that had already been signed off by the Earl of Sussex, then Lord Deputy.[56] Goldwell denied the accusations, asserting that all of his accounts had been properly checked by Rous in the presence of Valentine Browne, who was at that time Auditor of Ireland. (As usual we do not know the outcome of the case.) Although we have no firm evidence to prove that this is the right William Goldwell, it seems likely that it is, since his world feels so close to the spheres in which James Chillester operated. Both men were tangled in the administration of outlying bulwarks of the Elizabethan administration (Dublin, Berwick); both were attached to the treasurers; both were acquainted with the intimate relationship between money and violence. How Goldwell transformed himself into a gentleman whose parcel-gilt goblet and silver spoons could be stolen we do not know.

Goldwell's wife, Alice, who (according to Herle) handed the manuscript translation over to Chillester, is considerably more visible than her husband, especially after his death. She was one of at least eight children of Robert

Tomlinson of Boston in Lincolnshire, a Merchant of the Staple at Calais, and was mentioned last among his offspring in his will, proved in 1534.[57] She married Goldwell at St. Mary, Islington, on 5 February 1560.[58] Aside from Herle's references, the archives remain silent about her until some point in 1580–81, when she and her daughters endured a violent assault at the hands of a crowd of unmarried women. The damaged parchment on which the indictment is recorded reads: "True Bill that, on a certain day . . . Anne Lambe spinster, Margaret Ashe *alias* Cotton spinster servant of Humfrey Goslyn, . . . Daldersby spinster servant of John Smarte, Margaret Parsones spinster servant of James Gardener, and Elizabeth Burche spinster, all of the parish of the Stronde co. Midd., assembled riotously and assaulted Alice Goldewell widow, Sara Goldewell, Judeth Goldewell and Mary . . . , throwing them down and tearing and pulling out their hair."[59] Despite the gaps, it is clear that Alice, Sara, Judith, and Mary were subjected to a violent physical assault, "to their no small damage and harm." We do not know the motive for the attack, nor is it possible to say much about those involved, although some of the masters of these servingwomen were substantial enough to have their wills proved in the Prerogative Court of Canterbury; Humphrey Gosling was a vintner, James Gardener a tailor, by trade.[60] Was this a ritual act of shaming, punishing Alice for the sexual laxity ascribed to her by Herle?[61]

Alice surfaces again in a set of documents resulting from a Chancery suit brought against her at some point in the 1570s by one Richard Holderness.[62] He recalls how, "about three yeres nowe last past," he "was A suytor in the waie of marreaige unto one Alice Goldwell of the Strande . . . widowe." She came to live in his house, bringing with her "from her owne dwellinge howsse in the Strande" her children and "diverse ymplementes of howseholde plate and other moveables." Holderness invited her to have their match solemnized, but she "with muche fayer speache . . . did from tyme to tyme delaye the cawse." Meantime he spent upward of sixty pounds looking after her family and paying her debts. Finally he sent the Recorder of London, William Fleetwood, to talk to her, and she told Fleetwood that she was already contracted to another man, Nicholas Dorrington. Subsequently, she sent several of her allies—including "Master Doryngton Captayne Pulvertoppe Captayne Bowser and one master hyett of the ynner temple"—to the jilted Holderness to ask him to look after her property for a few weeks more, and to become bound by obligation for it.[63] He "beinge a younge man without skill" signed the document without appreciating the danger of its "generall wordes." Now he finds that Alice Goldwell is suing him for £400, threatening him with financial destruction. Alice's reply to this suit tells a very different story. In her account, Holderness tried to bounce her into marriage, pressing his suit "when she was syke in her bedde, and not able to styrre." Then he picked quarrels with her until she left his house, so that he could marry "the wife, that he is now married vnto." The dispute offers us another another clouded glimpse into the life of the woman "with whom [James Chillester] was & is more familier than honesty wold."[64]

At the end of our archival trail, Herle's account of the purloining of *A Most Excellent Hystorie* has scarcely been proven, but it has taken on a degree of plausibility. How does our sense of the work change as a result? The most striking thing now is how frequently Chillester lays claim to the work of translation. Unlike many self-effacing contemporaries, he puts his name and city squarely on the title page; he signs the dedicatory epistle "Your moste humble and obedient subiect / James Chillester"; and he even adds a declamatory "FINIS. *quoth* James Chillester" to the end of the book.[65] We might also read the modesty topoi that Chillester employs in the letter as, in reality, a triumph of effrontery: he refers to "this sayd authour (whiche I haue turned out of the frenche into our Englishe tong) though *not so eloquently as others could have doone*, yet (I trust) truly and according to the meaning of the sayde Authour."[66] Alert to its duplicities, the dedication as a whole, with its display of the royal arms and its verses in honor of Elizabeth, comes to seem implausibly effusive in its show of devotion: a case of the (non)translator protesting too much. And the edge of tactlessness remarked earlier now seems motivated, the work of a writer who conceals a knife in his cloak as he genuflects before his sovereign.

Due to a gap in the Stationers' Register, we do not know when the publisher Henry Bynneman entered the *Most Excellent Hystorie*; nor do we know in what month of 1571 it was published (Herle's "before christmas last" offers approximate evidence). But there is presumably a connection between the publication of the book and a pair of letters, dated 28 July 1571, that were sent from Sir Henry Sidney and Francis Russell, second Earl of Bedford, supporting Chillester as a candidate for the clerkship of the Merchant Taylors' Company. Bedford declares himself happy to throw his weight behind Chillester "forasmoche as I do knowe hym A man bothe honeste of Condicions, and one that hath bene ymployed in matters of charge for greate sommes of money, wherein he hathe shewed him self very carefulle, Aswelle for his owne dyscharge, As the securytie of those for whome he hathe dealte." Sidney tells the Merchant Taylors that he knows Chillester "to have bene of longe tyme exercysed in sondry causes of charge & otherwaies, wherein he hathe gotten good knowledge and experyens"; hence he thinks him "a veary mete and apte man to serve you in that place, and withalle nowe beinge growen into somme yeares, that he cannott so welle travelle abrode, as he hathe done, ys desyrous to stay him self (as he saiethe) in that quiett Rome, wherein I doubte not but that you shall finde hym bothe serviceable, and willinge to do, any thinge that shall apperteigne, to his dutie."[67] Although Chillester's bid failed, the letters back up Herle's claim that the purloining of the *Hystorie* was an attempt at impression management. Counterfeiting printed books rather than coins, Chillester sought "to joyn unto hym self some oppinion of lernyng, & to be thought of sownd religion towardes God, & of an honest dutye to his Prynce."[68]

Herle's character assassinations represent Chillester's most flagrant intrusion into the archive, but we can catch a few fleeting glimpses of this versipeller in the 1570s and 1580s. The parish registers of various London churches record the births and deaths of his children and waver somewhat comically on the subject of the father's profession. Chillester is variously referred to as "generosus" (a gentleman), "howsholder," "merchant," "a man of no trade," and "some tymes a clarke of the ordinance." (We also find an entry for his burial at St. Botolph Aldgate on 5 June 1586.)[69] But Chillester did find employment, and of a suitably seamy variety, in the last years of his life. On 2 February 1575/6, a despairing Elizabeth Goldyng sent a letter to Sir Walter Mildmay "Frome my poore howse in Salisbury Court."[70] Goldyng begged the Chancellor of the Exchequer to allow her more time "to answere master Lychefyld and Chyllyster demandes which trewly are moost rare and strange to me, To be calde too answere too Accounte for his Receptes that was never in any offyce of accountante/." The man whose account keeping she had to justify was her late husband, Sir Thomas (d. 1571), "of whose good Servyse I neede make no definicion." Since Sir Thomas had received all his money from the Crown by warrant, Elizabeth marvels "how he shuld receave a double paye as master Lychefylde subposethe," or how it could have taken so long for the Crown to notice the fact.

> But aboute Bartillmewtyde last past, James Chyllyster who dothe
> informe master Lychefylde was with me, and tolde me of this matter,
> and sayd no Lyveinge Creature coulde charge me but he / and therfore
> would have had somme monye of me to dyscharge me quyte therof /
> and so master Lychefylde shuld never haue had knoledge therof / But I

woulde be nomeanes deale so, forasmuche as yf yt were trew, the debte was to the Queenes Majestie whome I would not dysseve / But yf yt were trew I would rather be an umble pitissioner to her / And since my Commyng upp they haue bothe offeryd to agrye [i.e., agree] with me for the parte belonging to them / and would withdrawe yt so as the Queenes Majestie shuld have no parte thereof /.

The situation unfolding here is clear enough: after her husband's death, Elizabeth Goldyng is being asked to pay up for his alleged peculation in office. In response, she launches a counteraccusation that Lichfield has been attempting to compound with her and take all the recovered money for himself—precisely the charge leveled by the anonymous author of "A brief declaration of the commission," examined earlier. Into the midst of these unsavory transactions steps James Chillester, a man "who dothe informe master Lychefylde," informing the informer—but who has also offered to relieve the widow of her money without informing his master.

The "brief declaration of the commission" contains the only other reference I have thus far discovered to the association between Chillester and Lichfield. When listing the people with whom the latter has compounded, the document reads: "Of master Pelhams agreement, Bery master Lichfeldes man tolde Chillester that his master had CCth markes in hande, & must have another Cth markes at Christmasse."[71] The fact that Chillester was not identified as "master Lichfeldes man," and that he was passing information about Lichfield's shady dealings to the writer of the "brief declaration," suggests a degree of distance between the two, akin perhaps to the rivalry described in Elizabeth Goldyng's letter. But it also provides further evidence for their association. A more surreptitious connection may be inferred from the fact that Lichfield began in 1575 to pursue Sir Valentine Browne, treasurer of Berwick, for accounting errors that he had allegedly committed back in the first two years of Elizabeth's reign.[72] We might recall Herle's claim that Chillester had been "suborned . . . to be an accuser" of Browne, and suspect that he was pulling the strings in the effort to bring down this long-serving officeholder. As Chillester went into government service as a scourge of embezzlers, we see a poacher turning gamekeeper—or opting for some dangerous combination of the two roles.

The paper trail we have thus far unpicked has allowed us to unmask a single book from Stonley's library as an act of impression management that sugars over a history of illicit transactions stretching from Boulogne to Berwick. In buying the book, Stonley was (perhaps inadvertently) pasting himself into a network that extended to the outer reaches of the Elizabethan administration, on the Scottish borders and in Ireland, and in which every link was secured by fraud or the (possibly fraudulent) accusation of fraud. In the second half of this chapter, we shall see how this network was extended into the 1580s and came to implicate the popular prose fiction and poetry of the mid-Elizabethan era.

Henry Chillester: *The Witte of Grene Youthe*

Although there is no record of his birth, it appears that James Chillester had a son named Henry, probably named after Sir Henry Sidney, who may have been his godfather. That Henry was John's son can be known for sure only via records relating to a London Merchant Taylor named John God. God, who was probably born in the 1520s, has a bit part in Herle's letters sent from the Marshalsea prison in 1572.[73] There he is said to be Chillester's brother-in-law, a "grett Papiste, an extreme usurer, & an yll mynded man towards the Prynce," whose house ought to be searched "for wrytengs that may be there of thys Chillesters." We learn that God "(as he is a verey cruell fellow & a miserable) kylled with a rake a pore innocent chylde in a womans belly by betyng her uppon that bellye. xxti wekes past, wherby he scaped verey narrowly the danger of the Lawe."[74] God died in 1578, and in his will he left £6 13s. and 4d. to "Henry Chillester my nephewe."[75]

Before we move on to consider Henry, we should pause a moment on God, who may be a link figure in more ways than one. In 1570, Henry Bynneman (who would, in the following year, print Chillester's purloined Boaistuau) published a book entitled *A Discourse of the Great Crueltie of a Widowe towardes a Yong Gentleman, and by What Meanes He Requited the Same. Set Forth in English Verse by John God.*[76] The work was a translation into poulter's measure of a novella by Bandello that had already appeared in the story collections of Geoffrey Fenton and William Painter.[77] The sordid narrative involves a widow, Zilia, who is mourning her dead husband when one Philiberto, Lord of Virle, falls in love with her. She rejects him coldly but is finally persuaded to give him a single parting kiss, on condition that he will do anything she tells him to. She tells him not to speak for three years, a command so harsh that it turns all his love to hate and desire of revenge. Philiberto travels to France, where his vow of silence does not prevent him from engaging in military heroics that earn him the respect of King Charles VII. The king offers a reward of ten thousand francs for anyone who can cure his servant's dumbness, with the proviso that, should they fail, they will forfeit the same sum or their lives. Zilia hears the news and, filled with greed, comes to claim the prize. But although she repeatedly grants her servant all that he once desired, he refuses to speak, and delights to see her cast into prison in a near-suicidal state. Finally he relents, she repents, the pair are married, and they live happily ever after.

Although it seems appropriate that a "verey cruell fellow" should have translated this very cruel story, it is likely that the work was sent to the press not by God senior, who was by this time high up in the Merchant Taylors Company (he served as master from 1565 to 1566), but by his son of the same name, who was made free of the company in February 1561/2.[78] God junior was probably too old to have attended the Merchant Taylors' new school, but his younger brother Thomas is known to have studied there from 1570 to 1575.[79] The Latin acrostic verses on the name "IOANNES GODDVS" that preface *A Discourse* suggest literary aspirations, and the translation may have been intended as a conspicuous display of linguistic skill. Needless to say, we have no way of knowing whether "John God," whoever or whichever he was, made the translation himself.[80] This foray into Italianate prose fiction makes a suggestive bridge to the textual transactions of the younger Chillester.

Henry Chillester made his only intervention in print with a miscellany that survives in just one known copy, held by the British Library.[81] The work is characterized from the outset by its uncertainties. Like some of Shakespeare's plays, it comes with a choice of titles, but here there is also a choice of choices. On the title page, the book is called *Youthes Witte, or The Witte of Grene Youth* (Figure 40), with the ingratiating subtitle *Choose Gentlemen, and Mez-dames Which of Them Shall Best Lyke You.* At the beginning of the text, we are instead offered "Youthes Wit or the Wit of Grene Youth, with the Castell of Conceites, Choose Gentlemen & mes-Dames which of these two shall best like you." The promised *Castell of Conceites* never subsequently materializes, and the texts that do appear are a mixed bag. Without prior warning, the volume offers its readers four *novelle*, or short stories, followed by approximately 150 poems, the majority of which are love laments. No section division separates the prose from the verse; green youth was happy to be unpredictable. (For this reason, when the not-so-young Richard Stonley records that he has purchased "the four bookes bounde up to gether in forrell

›Youthes Witte,

OR

The VVitte of Grene Youth.

Choose Gentlemen, and Mez-dames which of them shall best lyke you.

Compiled and gathered together by HENRY
CHILLESTER.

*First view then reade, last iudge with regard :
geue th' Auctor good wordes he claimes no reward.*

VBIQVE   FLORESCIT.

LONDON

Imprinted by John Wolfe,

1581.

FIGURE 40. Henry Chillester, *Youthes Witte* (1581), title page. British Library, c.123.ff.3.

called youthes wytte et alijs," it is not quite clear whether he has bought just this compilation or has purchased some kind of Sammelband in which it is bound together with other items.)[82]

The presentation of the verse in the volume is also erratic. The titles of the poems regularly mislead; thus, a poem in which a dying man prays for salvation in the afterlife is entitled "After many misfortunes he craveth death as the ender of all calamities" (F3v), while a lament that rejects singing in favor of sighing is entitled "The lover being overcome, is compelled by necessitie to sing of sorrow" (G1r). Between these poems come six stanzas which have one heading, but which appear to be two different poems (F4v). One of the poems in the collection, "The tender budde that bravely ginnes to blow," is repeated twice (K4r–v, L1v–2r). Twenty-six of the poems are simply entitled "Another," but the subject of "Another" sometimes differs wildly from that of the preceding poem, as when an unusual poem in which a woman attacks a male adulterer follows a predictable poem about "the clogge of care that hangs on heavie harte" (P2r–v).

Youthes Witte is another book about which almost nothing has ever been written. The silence of the centuries was broken in 2006 when, having completed a first-line index of Elizabethan verse, Steven May explored the collection as a neglected source for "scores of unique poetic texts, some of which are quite good."[83] As well as containing poems by Arthur Gorges, Thomas Watson, Timothy Kendall, Nicholas Breton, Thomas Lord Vaux, and William Hunnis, *Youthes Witte* is also (May suggests) "the only Elizabethan poetic miscellany to which a woman (or women) contributed both commendatory and amatory verse."[84] May's sharp-eyed commentary represents an excellent preliminary survey, but I wish to question his working assumption that "Henry Chillester wrote many if not most of the poems in *Youthes Witte*." As with James Chillester's purloined Boaistuau, the question of authorship is vexed.[85]

The paratexts of *Youthes Witte* are contradictory in this matter, as in so much else. The book is described on the title page as "compiled and gathered together by Henry Chillester." While "compilation" can signify original composition in this period, the formulation notably avoids the more straightforward "*By* Henry Chillester."[86] An epigraph muddies the waters further:

First view then reade, last judge with regard:
geve th'Auctor good wordes he claimes no reward.

In the dedicatory letter, Chillester writes of "perfect[ing] this my *Youthes witte*," while the unsigned epistle to the reader that follows declares rather cryptically, "I have beene as much troubled in contriving these my conceites, as they that builde castles in SPAYNE (as the French Proverbe understandeth it) Or, as a Henne with two Chickens."[87] Here we seem to be approaching a claim that Chillester actually wrote the collection, contriving its conceits. But, as May notes, *Youthes Witte* was entered in the Stationers' Register, on 6 May 1581, not as the work of Chillester but rather as "by NICHOLAS ATKINSONNE." This is a disarmingly direct claim of authorship to set alongside the vacillations of the book itself.[88] Furthermore, as May goes on to observe, none of the commendatory poems refers to an H.C., but two of them are addressed to an "A.N.," which could well through the commonplace reversal of the letters refer to the same Nicholas Atkinson. Then, one poem in the collection itself (replying to a poem by Thomas Howell) is ascribed to an "A.N." (Q2r), and another poem celebrates the friendship between two women named Margaret Phillipson and Phebe Atkinson. Margaret Phillipson could conceivably be related to the "Mistres *Marie P.*" who writes a prefatory poem "*In commendation of her* servaunts worke" (A4r–v), and to the "P.M." who delivers a sharp retort to an insulting poem by "P.I." (M4r–v). All of this leads May to suggest that *Youthes Witte* "was not a one man show," though he assumes "for the sake of convenience" that Chillester is "the default author of all the unattributed works in the anthology."[89] But, armed as we are with more knowledge about Chillester family values, we might wonder whether Henry had much of a hand in it at all. Perhaps here we have another purloined publication, a work "borrowed" from a friend and taken to the printer for immediate economic gain. The prominence of Henry Chillester's name in the preliminary leaves of *Youthes Witte* looks suspiciously like his father's ostentation a decade earlier.[90]

Can we learn anything about Nicholas Atkinson? The most revealing poem in the collection, from the point of view of identifying its original milieu, is the acrostic "Upon two Gentlewomens names," which reads (from top to bottom) "Margarett Phillipsone Phebe Atkinsone Frends." We might guess that Phebe Atkinson was Nicholas's sister, and the parish registers prove us right. Nicholas was baptized on 24 March 1554 at St. Peter Cornhill in the City of London, one of at least seven children, including Phebe who was baptized on 3 May 1548.[91] He would therefore have been about twenty-seven at the time *Youthes Witte* appeared. Nicholas's father, Edward, was a Merchant Taylor and a tavern owner who held a court office as purveyor of the

Queen's wines. His drinking den in Cornhill was called the Sun; we know of a brawl that took place there in February 1554/5, in which Edward's apprentice Thomas Helys was killed by a cooper, the death blow being delivered with a cooper's adze.[92] Between 1577 and his death in 1579 Edward Atkinson was in serious financial difficulties, and the Privy Council intervened on his behalf on more than one occasion.[93] Although I have found no record of his marriage, Nicholas appears to have had at least two children, both daughters; the first, Cibill, was born on 11 November 1583 and christened at St. Peter; the second, Phebe (presumably named after his sister), was christened on 8 November 1584 at nearby St. Botolph, Bishopsgate. From the entry for Cibill's birth we learn Nicholas's profession: he is said to be a servingman.[94] (An obvious inference is that he served the Mistress Marie P. who supplies a poem to *Youthes Witte* "In commendation of her servaunts worke" [A4r–v].) The proximity of Cornhill and Bishopsgate makes it highly likely that another parish register entry roughly contemporary with these relates to Phebe senior's best friend: on 21 September 1582, a Margaret Phillipson was buried at St. Botolph.[95]

Meanwhile, there is one small but suggestive detail that links Nicholas Atkinson to a wider literary culture. At some point, probably in the late 1570s, his brother Edward married Mary Bryskett, the sister of Lodowick Bryskett, who had been a servant to Sir Henry Sidney in Ireland since the mid-1560s, who accompanied Philip Sidney on his European tour from 1572 to 1574, and whose friendship with Spenser is recorded in *A Discourse of Civill Life* (published in 1606 but probably written in the 1580s). Mary and Edward had a number of children whose births were registered at St. Peter Cornhill; a stillborn child born in 1579/80 was followed by Vincent (1580), Elizabeth (1585), and Jeames in 1587.[96] Although Lodowick was occupied in various Irish offices at this time, he frequently treated them as sinecures and left deputies in his stead, while he himself lived in England.[97] His own son Philip was baptized at St. Peter on 5 May 1580.[98] So in the period immediately prior to the publication of *Youthes Witte*, there was both a familial and a physical proximity between Nicholas Atkinson and a man who was a close friend of some of the most significant poets of the era, and who was moreover yet another client of Sir Henry Sidney.[99] This provides a possible line of transmission for a lyric beginning "Arise O noble Sidney now," which appears in the anthology (N4r–v) and which seems to derive from a farewell entertainment staged for Sidney by students at Shrewsbury School.[100]

Thus far we have focused on the rival author/compilers of *Youthes Witte*. We also need to factor in its publisher, John Wolfe (whom we earlier encountered as the publisher of John Eliot's 1593 *Survay of France*). Wolfe was at this time one of the most provocative names in English printing. In 1581, he had recently returned from the Continent, where he may have been employed by the Giunta family of booksellers in Florence; back in London, he became the bête noir of the Stationers' Company.[101] Having infringed other publishers' rights by printing lucrative titles that were already licensed, Wolfe was on several occasions hauled before the company authorities to explain himself. His plea was economic necessity: he and other renegade printers encroached upon textual property simply in order to make a living. But on one celebrated occasion he invoked a lofty role model for what he evidently saw as a crusade against the establishment: "Tush said he, Luther was but one man, and reformed alle the world for religion, and I am that one man, that must and will reforme the governement in this trade, meaning printing and bookeselling."[102]

Wolfe's opposition to the booktrade's practices led him to criticize the Queen, whose interests were at stake: "it was lawfulle for alle men to print all lawfulle bookes what commandment soever her Majestie gave to the contrary."[103] It was rumored that Wolfe and his renegade circle were stirring up careless talk in "Alehouses, tavernes and such like places" and inciting the common people to "dangerous, & undutifulle speaches of her Majesties most gracious government."[104] The Queen's Printer Christopher Barker remonstrated with him, "saying, Wolfe, leaue your Machevillian devices, & conceit of your forreine wit, which you have gained by gadding from countrey to countrey, & telle me plainely, if you meane to deale like an honest man, what you would have."[105] In late 1582, Thomas Norton complained about Wolfe to William Cecil, claiming that he had gone to the court, defying a plague-time proclamation, "under pretense that he is servant to master George Goring whome he stirreth to mainteine him in this case." Goring, one of Elizabeth's Gentleman Pensioners, had indeed written in defense of Wolfe, calling him "so well knowene unto me."[106] So it is telling that *Youthes Witte* should have been dedicated to Goring. The volume appears to be a three-way negotiation between Chillester, Wolfe, and Wolfe's patron. And it was printed by someone for whom stealing other men's copies was part of a quasi-religious crusade.[107]

The guiding hand of the printer might also be detected in the bifurcated nature of *Youthes Witte*, since the prose section occupies precisely five gatherings, A to E, and the poems begin at the start of quire F. The division between prose and verse, so messy from a literary point of view, is suspiciously neat in bibliographical terms. Whether or not we are right to be suspicious, there is more to be said about the prose works in the miscellany. All four stories turn out to be translations from foreign originals. The first, concerning a pair of star-crossed lovers who die when they finally get to consummate their passion, derives from Bandello's *Novelle* of 1554, albeit with some names changed.[108] The second and third tales come from a French work entitled *Les comptes du monde adventureux*, ascribed on the title page to A.D.S.D., who has been variously identified.[109] The second, set in Blois, is a version of the Titus and Gisippus story, featuring a prince and his servant who are besotted with the same beautiful woman. So firm is the prince's friendship that he sets up a bed trick that enables his pining servant to sleep with the lady, while he "satisfied himself with the maid" (C3v). The third tells of two lovers who run away together, forsaking the court of Hungary, only to be shipwrecked on a desert island, where they both starve to death. The fourth tale comes from Boccaccio's *Decameron*, where it is the second story of the fifth day. It follows two lovers from an island near Sicily who are separated by fortune and only reunited after long and improbable romance wanderings.

Once we have identified their sources, we can observe a curious feature that unites the first three translations. At a certain point in the action, the translator cracks the story open to make way for the singing of a lute song. In the first story, the lovelorn Hannibal, hearing that the object of his affections is in the next room, plucks up his courage and, "taking his lute in his hand," sings a song in which he begs for relief from the pangs of unrequited eros.[110] In the second, the servant whose relationship with a beautiful woman has been interrupted by his master withdraws into his chamber, "and taking his lute in hand," laments his situation, lambasting the "false dissembling dame / Whose luring lookes did lull [him] so asleepe." In the third tale, no sooner has the hero fallen in love than he is "enforced for the ease of his mind, to sing to his Lute" verses telling how he has learnt to revel in Cupid's yoke. These songs were presumably added to render the texts more fashionable and to align them with similarly intercut prose narratives by the likes of Gascoigne and Whetstone (the "Castell of Conceites" that fails to materialize in *Youthes Witte* may nod to the "Castle of Delight" that formed the first part of Whetstone's *Rocke of Regard*).[111] It would have been tidier had the fourth story also contained an inset song, but it does not.

It would also have been tidier had the poems been written specifically to fit into their particular narrative niches, but this seems unlikely. While the first ("Yeld me my heart, yeld me my libertie") is a generalized lament for unrequited love that works quite well in its context, the second ("Both love and death are now become my foes") mistakenly suggests that the servant has been searching for death, and it contains a renunciation of love that is strikingly inappropriate (the servant remains in love and, thanks to his master's generosity, will soon be in bed with the beautiful lady). The third song ("Like as the Steere that never felt the Yoake") is comparably irrelevant. Although the sense is hard to work out, it ends with some kind of accommodation between reason and desire, prompting the lover to cry "O happie yoake, O noble flame" (D1r). But the hero is at this point sighing bitterly and bewailing his misfortune for having fallen for a woman so far above his station. Perhaps the most telling detail is that this poem, alone of the three, has a title; it is headed "Another to the like effect" (D1r). As well as implying a relationship between the interpolated poems, and perhaps betraying a cavalier attitude to their subject matter (any old love lament will do), the heading also links the poems forward to the anthology, with its numerous poems headed "Another."

Although we ought not to look for modern editorial values in an Elizabethan miscellany, the impression of carelessness in *Youthes Witte* points to the lack of a single guiding hand. Many of the individual poems in the collection are demonstrably purloined from a range of writers and printed texts, as May shows, but the evidence that the whole thing is a literary forgery lies in the perceptible gap between writer/translator and editor. It is possible that Chillester wrote the poems and that Wolfe added the headings as he marked the manuscript up for printing; but the close proximity of Chillester, Wolfe, and Goring in the preliminaries makes this seem unlikely. Should we, then, ascribe the bulk of the authorship to Atkinson, who is a strong presence in the commendatory poems and the poetic section of the anthology? That too might be a mistake. For what those spliced-in lute songs are telling us is that there is something fundamentally iterable about all of the poems in the collection. Its seemingly innumerable love laments aim to provide a kind of generalized template for the expression of emotion. To search for authenticity in this poetry is radically inappropriate to what is essentially a poetics of ghostwriting.[112]

In a similar way, James Chillester's purloining of Boiastuau's *L'histoire de Chelidonius Tigurinus* appears curiously predictable, because the French work was already a forgery. The "Chelidonius Tigurinus" to whom the Latin "original" was ascribed, although he is solemnly listed as author in thousands of online library catalogues around the world, never existed, and seems to have been fabricated by Boaistuau for reasons that are now obscure.[113] To meet the Chillesters is thus in some sense to meet the early modern literary world, in which the quest for authenticity is doomed from the outset.

Stonley may not have known James and Henry Chillester, and may have been oblivious to the subterranean history that this exploration has unearthed. He did, however, come across John God, perhaps the John God that translated *A Discourse of the Great Crueltie of a Widowe,* since the journal for 1593 contains a payment "To master Hunt master Osburns clarke for the coppie of a Scire facias agenst John God for a house in Barkinge."[114] Stonley seems also to have been something of a connoisseur of the Italianate narratives that were peddled in *Youthes Witte.* He owned two of the landmark story collections of the 1560s, William Painter's *Palace of Pleasure* and Geoffrey Fenton's *Certain Tragicall Discourses,* and several key works in the same tradition from later decades. He probably knew Painter, who was a clerk of the ordnance at the Tower of London; we know that he was acquainted with Fenton, later principal secretary of state for Ireland, because on 17 December 1574 he loaned a little more than seventeen pounds to Geoffrey Fenton and George Hayes of London.[115] *Youthes Witte* was no incidental purchase, but was fully networked in to the London that our reader inhabited.

The nefarious "Machevillian" devices we have found behind the facades of the Chillester publications chime with the account given of Elizabethan "Italianate" prose fiction by R. W. Maslen. In his view, these texts were themselves slippery double agents, a fifth column smuggling in suspect foreign values, loosening allegiance to Queen and country, and teaching readers to delight in "the sometimes desperate gambles taken by the storyteller, the courtier, the chancer, the double-dealer, the spy."[116] Roger Ascham's tirade against "fonde bookes, of late translated out of *Italian* into English, sold in every shop in London, commended by honest titles the soner to corrupt honest maners: dedicated over boldlie to vertuous and honorable personages, the easielier to begile simple and honorable personages" responds to something fundamental in the literary culture of the period.[117] What Ascham's Manichaean vision fails to acknowledge is that many forms of deceit and imposture were licensed by authority. They were also (as the sheer obscurity of many of the figures I have been discussing suggests) the everyday shifts of Londoners struggling to survive and thrive in the city. Such shifts could turn even ordinary-seeming books into intricate webs of agents and interests. The web of his reading was also the web in which Stonley found himself bound up, and ready to be devoured.

Chapter 8

Reading in the Fleet

On 1 June 1597, just a few days after he had paid Francis Phillips for making the sale inventory of his books at Aldersgate Street, Stonley noted in journals a payment for books:

Bookes	To master Cottesford for muffettes	
	booke of the proverbes	xviijd
	To Johns the Prynter for the	
	Booke of Jacke of Newberrye alias	
	Wynchcum	iiijd

This is one of just two book purchases that Stonley records in the third volume of journals, penned during his incarceration in the Fleet.[1] As when he bought "the Survey of Fraunce with the Venus & Adhonay per Shakspere," here he acquired two publications that were starkly contrasting in terms of their content and their fates. The first, Peter Moffett's *Commentarie upon the Booke of the Proverbes of Salomon*, was a long-forgotten biblical commentary; it first appeared in 1592, with a revised second edition following in 1596. The latter, Thomas Deloney's *Pleasant History of John Winchcomb in his Younger Yeares called Jack of Newberie, the Famous and Worthy Clothier of England*, was a rags-to-riches tale so wildly popular that, although it was entered in the Stationers' Register on 7 March 1597, the earliest surviving edition (declaring itself the eighth edition on its title page) dates from 1619. In this chapter, I flesh out the journals' account of Stonley's life in the Fleet, as a prelude to an "indebted reading" of these two texts.

The Universe of Debt

Despite the paucity of references to book buying in the 1597–98 journal, it is clear that the prison was a site of considerable textual traffic. Stonley still spent almost every weekday "at my bookes" and his Sundays "reading the Scriptures," using formulae he had relied upon for many years. He also recorded payments for penknives, for wax books, and "For a Boxe with a lock to kepe the bondes & bills in thexchequer." His efforts to find some way out of debt forced him to write numerous letters, petitions, and schedules. And he kept the journal itself. We know that there was nothing furtive about his journal keeping, for it is here that (for the first time) other hands intrude into the personal record. The hands are those of the Fleet's deputy wardens, who sign their names to confirm receipt of payments for chamber rent, or for "libertie going abrode with my keper by master wardens Agrement."[2] They evidently knew that the books existed, and there is no sign that they did anything to stop Stonley from writing. Perhaps this was because he posed no political or religious threat, or perhaps it was because account keeping was deemed a necessary practice for debtors struggling to rebuild their decayed finances. Whatever the case, the result is a remarkable record of prison life.

For Stonley, imprisonment represented both a spectacular fall from grace and his conscription into a powerful cultural scenario, in which financial debt became the pretext for the confinement of the ultimate piece of personal property: the body itself.[3] The later sixteenth and early seventeenth centuries witnessed an "epidemic of debt," a credit crunch that was at once the cause and the consequence of a vast amount of litigation.[4] The sources of this ubiquitous indebtedness were multiple: severe inflation, a shortage of coin and concomitant reliance on credit, the pressure to consume conspicuously, and the ability of financial bonds—when backed up by sufficiently stiff penalty clauses—to get round the laws against usury.[5] The rise in defaulting fueled a huge increase in the prison population. Early seventeenth-century estimates set the number of "inslaved Christians" in England somewhere between five and ten thousand.[6] Stonley entered the Fleet at a time when its ancient buildings, long associated with the imprisonment of debtors, were being augmented by the creation of forty new lodgings.[7]

The early modern prison was radically unlike its modern descendants.[8] Rather than being exclusively a place to which criminals were consigned for punishment following a legal verdict of guilt, the prison was more often a provisional holding zone, a space of arrest.[9] For debtors, imprisonment offered some measure of protection from the predations of creditors, and hence an opportunity to set their financial affairs in order. High-status inmates might live in prison in a certain degree of luxury, importing servants, books, and furniture and venturing out at will. Meals could be taken at the communal table or in the privacy of one's chambers; foodstuffs might be supplied by the prison or sourced from outside. Visitors could be entertained, business transacted. Such openness was vital to debtors who needed access to legal and financial advice if they were to have any hope of release. None of this is to deny the vast range of carceral experiences. The public records of the period are full of petitions from prisoners (even in the supposedly liberal Fleet) who claimed to have been kept in close confinement, in crowded, life-threatening, and soul-destroying circumstances. Nonetheless, it seems that we can speak of a regime in which prisons were far more porous than they would subsequently become. Such porosity was a vital precondition for early modern prison writings, recently a growth area of scholarly interest. Those writings were so many and varied that one recent commentator urges us to see prisons as "a site of culture . . . to be considered alongside the court and the university as a place of significant textual, and literary, production."[10]

The evidence of Stonley's journal for 1597–98 does much to confirm our developing understanding of the early modern prison. It is clear that the bankrupt teller moved into the Fleet not as a solitary individual but as the center of a community. He rarely seems to have had fewer than three servants on hand at lunch or dinner, and the roster of servants was as prone to variation as were the menus, which may imply that they were moving between Aldersgate Street and the Fleet on a daily basis, or even more frequently. Stonley also seems to have had companions at dinner and supper in the Fleet quite as frequently as he did at home. On one occasion the "Strangers" present at supper were listed simply as "all my howsold," which seems to have included the cook from Aldersgate Street.[11] Family members, most prominently his brother Edward, his son-in-law William Heigham, and his grandson Harry Dawtrey, were frequent visitors. His wife, Anne, usually accompanied by a daughter or two, was much in evidence in April and May 1597; toward the end of May she fell ill at Doddinghurst, and she made no visits at all in June, perhaps because she was convalescing. A friend and associate named John Puxley, who seems to have been a solicitor in the ecclesiastical courts, dined with Stonley on at least fifteen occasions; another friend, a member of the Fishmongers' Company named Richard Newman, shared three meals with him.[12] A visitor who came just once was the author William Patten, who had been ejected from his post as teller of the Exchequer for embezzlement almost thirty years previously.[13] Stonley bought claret wine and canary sack from the Sun tavern in Fleet Street and received gifts of foods from relations, including "A gose & a dishe of Creme" from his daughter Anne Heigham.[14]

Stonley's long-standing association with the Fleet Street area is written into the material fabric of his prison journal, the parchment binding of which recycles a mortgage document from 1549 relating to his purchase of a tenement with "shoppe celler sellars chambres and garrettes therto belonging sett and being in Fletestreate in the parisse of seynt bryde in the suburbes of London." Like many a prisoner in the period, Stonley tried to make himself at home in his new locale.[15] This becomes clear when he records that he has been asked to give up his room to a fellow inmate, Sir Thomas Shirley, and to take "a far meaner" one for himself. Stonley refused to budge, "concidering I was ther settlyd & in good Eyre towardes the garden" (10r). The prison garden is mentioned at several points; he spent one day in April 1597 "at my bookes & abrode in the garden," and another in February 1598 "at my bookes & the garden walkes."[16] He also referred to taking "other exercise a brode in the fflet yarde" and to going out on several occasions "to se the Bowlers."[17] One of those occasions was a Sunday, and so can be taken as an anti-Puritan statement about the validity of engaging in sport on the sabbath.[18] But a certain spiritual anxiety emerges in the entry for Monday, 23 May 1597, when, Stonley records, "[I] bestowed the day at my Chamber & otherwise emonge the players at bowles I trust without offence."[19] He also journeyed out from the Fleet, making his first trip back to Aldersgate since his incarceration on 22 June 1597, and later paying a visit to his brother Edward, "being secke at [his] sisters at Pecham Rye."[20] In one entry he notes in neutral tones, "This day one Hilles a prisoner of the flete escaped from his keper being a brode in the Citie."[21]

Inside and outside the prison, Stonley was preoccupied by his financial affairs and the effort to pay off his crippling debt to the Queen. Particularly in the early part of the 1597–98 journal, he was engaged in constant discussions about the sale of his property, with Daniel Donne and William Heigham acting as his agents. We learn that Sir John Petre offered to buy his Essex lands for £4,800 and to rent a part of them back to Stonley for £60 a year; but this offer had to be rejected "by cause the land & grownd will not yeld so moch."[22] On 3 May 1597 Stonley went to Westminster with his keeper to plead his cause before the Lord Chief Baron of the Exchequer. His nemesis on this occasion was the attorney general, Edward Coke, "enve[igh]ing sore agenst & denying the Allowance of all my peticions." In one of his boldest queryings of authority, Stonley complained of Coke that "though he knew the Lawes yet in this matter he understande[s] not the course of thexchequer."[23] No sooner had he returned to the Fleet than he had to deal with two competitors for his lands, one William Smith and a Master Wroth, who were "so importune on me for grauntinge my good will . . . as when they cold [not] prevayle by fayre wordes they fell to thretinge." The next day he heard that the pair had gone straight from their meeting with him "to my wyf threteninge hir as though she had byn his kytchin may[d] to yeld hir good will" for the sale. "Which two," he adds bitterly, "the honest neighburs ther abowt cold be glade they dwelt further of[f]." Despite this, he subsequently consented to the sale on the advice of the Lord Treasurer.[24] Then he started to receive reports that his wife was "dangerously sick with a gref in hir side" at Doddinghurst, and he looked on glumly as his accumulated possessions were sold off. "This day a Commission was sat upon at Brent Wood for the deedinge of my goodes & landes in Essex and Likewise here in London, what will be done after god knowith."[25] He even had to pay ten shillings to Francis Phillips for pricing up his books.[26] On Saturday 4 June he wrote the most pious summary of his daily activities to be found in the surviving journals: "This day I walkyd in my vocacion & preyer with thankes to god at night."[27] Perhaps, newly divested of his goods, he had started to think of his chamber in the Fleet as a monastic cell.

As well as innumerable meetings with lawyers and potential purchasers of his lands, Stonley also documented his engagements with the prison community. The period of his most intense involvement with his fellow inmates was between Sunday 3 and Saturday 30 April 1597, when he gave up private dining and experimented with taking his meals at the communal table. (This was the "parlour commons," not the cheaper "hall commons," so his companions were the wealthier prisoners.)[28] On his first day of communal dining, Stonley listed "master fitzherbert master Lee master Phelips master Townsend master Witherington master Strowde master Smyth at our Table"; subsequently, he tends to note down just a few names and add "& al."[29] Ever alert to the unruly, Stonley's journal entries paint the Fleet parlor as an argumentative place. Dissatisfaction with the warden began to register on his third day there: "At this dyner was A lettre sent from one master Scudamore prisoner of the howse desiringe the gentleman of the howse to take some order with

the warden of his better usage of hym what they mean to do I know not."[30]
This was picked up eleven days later, when "some question rose bytwyxt Mr
Townsend & Mr Smyth towching the wardens Authorite in the howse so
farre as John Hore the wardens Clarke warned Smyth owt of Commons,"
ejecting him from the communal table.[31] A few days on, "at this bord was
some spech of one Drewes report a genst master Wentworth which sowndyd
somwhat Scandalous." Stonley distanced himself carefully from the scandal:
"what yt was certenly I knowe [not] nether like to deale in such causes."[32]
On 25 April, violence erupted: "this eveninge at Supper Master Strowde &
one Kyrton fell at such hote wordes as master Strowde called the other Pillery
knave[,] the other with that began to rise to goe to hym after yt was axed
what he wold have donne. Mary quod [he] in my fury I wold have kylled
him[.] But after ther fury was mitigated and folded up in the Table clothe."[33]
Their fury came back out of the tablecloth on 1 May, when Stonley was safely
back in his own quarters, but he heard about it nonetheless: "This day yt was
tolde me that Master Strowde syttinge at the Table, Kirtne, offred to sitt by
hym but he wold gyve no place wheruppon the other toke hym by the Arme &
flonke [i.e., flung] in the flore who toke wytnes of the gentlemen how he was
used[,] what will cum of yt I knowe not."[34]

     After this time, few references are made to other prisoners, although Ston-
ley does express interest in the high-profile dispute that broke out between
some of the prisoners and the warden (the dispute that had earlier seen Master
Smith banned from the dinner table), referring to it on three occasions.[35] The
prisoners had accused the warden, George Reynell, of extorting unlawful fees
on the basis of a document bearing forged signatures, "to theimpovreshinge of
the better sorte and to the lamentabell oppressinge of the poorer sorte."[36] The
visiting commissioners eventually found in Reynell's favor, but they spent some
time clarifying the rules to prevent future disputes. Stonley was probably interested in the issues at stake—as a debtor's prison that was run for the profit of
its warden, the Fleet was ripe with contradictions—but he was also interested
in the people sitting in judgment on the case.[37] Among them was his former
colleague Vincent Skinner, writer of the tallies and auditor in the Exchequer.
Stonley had sent him an expensive gilt bowl as a New Year's gift back in 1594,
but (as we have seen) this did not stop Skinner from later digging the knife in,
declaring in a letter to William Cecil's secretary "how falsely he hath forsworn
him self and how slyly he hath conveyed other money awaie."[38]

     In the circumstances, Stonley might have found himself rooting for the
prisoners, some of whom would have been known to him through the Petre

circle, with its patronage of recusant musicians. The troublesome "Master Smith" was Philip Smith, a Haberdasher who in 1567/8 had married Martha Byrd, sister of the musician William Byrd. He was in the Fleet for debt, and would die there in 1604.[39] Meanwhile the prisoners' "information" against Reynell had been exhibited in the Court of Exchequer by Robert Broughe, a Fletcher, who had married another of Byrd's sisters, Barbara, in 1555. Broughe was "a maker of organs, virginalls & other Instrumentes of Musicke" who in 1586 supplied "a payer of small virginalls" for John Petre's son and in 1589 furnished a new organ for Petre himself.[40] William Byrd was himself interrogated in relation to the accusations against Reynell.[41] Stonley's journal does not register any of these links, but it is hard to believe that they went unnoticed.

The records of the Fleet prison do not survive for this period, making it hard to pin down the precise identities of the people that Stonley named as fellow prisoners, especially since he usually omits first names. Fortunately for us, quite a few of them were notorious for the scale of their debts, so some degree of community reconstruction is possible, although this feels less like a community than a hall of mirrors, in which debtors repeatedly met their own images in scaled-up or scaled-down form. Some of the inmates were people that Stonley might have met at the Exchequer, when they came to claim money for prosecuting Elizabethan wars, and their mistakes resonate with the teller's own. One such was Sir Thomas Shirley, for whom Stonley refused to give up his room. Shirley was a member of the Sussex gentry who traveled with the Earl of Leicester to fight in the Low Countries in 1585, and who had been made a treasurer at war in 1586.[42] During his time in this post, it was estimated that £1,500,000 had passed through his hands, part of which he had diverted to his private use. When his habits of taking bribes and lending out Crown funds at interest were investigated, he said: "I ever took it that man may with honesty accept a gratuity given; if he may not also accept a gift proceeding in respect of a hazard, I must think it most wonderful and say, Lord have mercy on me!"[43] Shirley's debts to the Queen were finally estimated at more than £35,000. His inability to pay them off led to several spells of imprisonment and to the eventual sequestration of his estates. One summer Sunday in the Fleet, Stonley noted that "This day one Mr Jacobe at the request of Sir Thomas Shirley made a Lerned sermon in the Chapell."[44] Like Stonley, Shirley seems to have been concerned for the state of his soul.

Another Elizabethan veteran makes a still more pitiable appearance in the journal, when Stonley notes a piece of prison news: "This day master

Townsend told me that Capten Bellingam was departed of Surfet with over moche dringkinge Aqua composita & usqua Bath a quarte at [a?] mele god gyve us grace to advoyd it."[45] "Aqua composita" was a "strong water," a distillation of wine and herbs, while "usquebath" was the forerunner of whisky. The man who had killed himself with these concoctions was Henry Bellingham, a sea captain who had sailed alongside Drake in the 1587 raid on Cádiz and in the fleet assembled against the Armada in 1588.[46] We lack firm evidence that Bellingham was held in the Fleet—there are no other references to him in the journal, and the anecdote could refer to life outside the walls. But it is plausible that Bellingham was incarcerated, since his finances were deteriorating across the course of the 1590s. In 1596 he wrote a desperate letter to Robert Cecil, seeking his favor at a time, he said, when "my creditors call so on me for my debts as I must be enforced to sell my land outright to satisfy them; and when that is gone how I and my poor wife shall live God knoweth." Asserting that he had been "her Majesty's man in ordinary this three and twenty years," Bellingham made the familiar claim that he had spent far more than he gained in royal service. "Beg I neither can nor will, by God's grace."[47] It seems that he finally escaped his creditors by drinking himself to death. Stonley's "god gyve us grace to advoyd it" suggests that he understood the logic of Bellingham's demise all too well.

Along with Crown servants, the Fleet held members of the mercantile community. One of the more extravagant debtors incarcerated with Stonley was Gerard de Malynes, best known today as the author of numerous treatises on currency and exchange, the first of which appeared in 1601.[48] Born in Antwerp, Malynes was established from the mid-1580s as a London merchant with trading connections across Europe, and as a government informer. Lawrence Stone describes him as "a shrewd and unprincipled man of business, alternately affluent and bankrupt, imprisoned for debt and called to consultation by the Privy Council."[49] Pursued for around £18,000 by a Dutch business associate, Malynes took shelter in the Fleet, where he reputedly lived "in riotous sort" and continued both to pursue his business interests and to defer the payment of his debts by endless legal obfuscation.[50] Stonley lists Malynes as one of his companions at the communal table and notes on 14 July 1597 that "This day Alderman martin and others sat at the flet abowt garret moluns cause."[51]

Debt was also a political and a religious affliction. Some of Stonley's fellows would have been recusants broken by the crippling fines that the government imposed on those who refused to go to church. But at least one of Stonley's identifiable companions had attempted to turn the Elizabethan persecution of Catholics to his own benefit. Thomas Fitzherbert spent much of his life scheming to win the inheritances of his recusant relations.[52] Imprisoned for suspected involvement in the Babington Plot of 1586, he earned his freedom by betraying his father's hiding place. When his father died in prison, Thomas was left as the heir of his childless uncle, Sir Thomas Fitzherbert, who was himself imprisoned in the Tower. Sir Thomas did his best to disinherit his nephew, but that nephew outsmarted him, having his uncle's will posthumously overturned. But family money was not sufficient to prevent Fitzherbert from falling into debt. He stood as an M.P. in order to evade his creditors—apparently a standard strategy—but was arrested by a cousin on the morning of his election. Among those creditors was the notorious recusant hunter Richard Topcliffe, to whom Fitzherbert had offered to pay £5,000 for persecuting his father, his uncle, and his cousin to death (Topcliffe later claimed, and apparently received, the money). The journals record that Fitzherbert was a frequent companion during Stonley's stint at the communal table. On a number of occasions they converged there with "master Phelips," meaning Thomas Phelippes, the cryptographer and spy who had decoded the intercepted correspondence of the Babington Plotters with Mary Queen of Scots (and the brother of Francis, who inventoried Stonley's books).[53] We can only guess at what was said, or what went unsaid, at such gatherings.

Another striking presence in the Fleet hailed from the other side of the confessional divide. Listed among the "strangers" at dinner on 31 March 1597 was "master Johnson borne in Richmond in yorkshire banished with others in to a farre Cuntrey never to return."[54] This refers either to Francis Johnson or his younger brother George, born respectively in 1562 and 1563 in Richmond, the sons of a woolen draper, who by their thirties had both become religious separatists. Francis had been expelled from his fellowship at Christ's College, Cambridge, in 1590 for his Presbyterian views, and in September 1592 he was elected pastor of the new separatist church in London. He was arrested on 5 December of the same year and imprisoned in the Fleet for more than four years. George was a London schoolmaster who presided at separatist services after his brother's imprisonment. He was arrested in March 1593 and also spent four years in the Fleet, living in "the most dankish and unholesome roomes of the prison."[55] In March 1597 both brothers were released, with two other separatists, on condition that they sail for Newfoundland and never again return to England. The attempt to set up a colony seems to have met its end with the wrecking of one of the company's two ships on the rocks of what is now Nova Scotia.[56] But the relationship between the two Johnsons had fallen apart long before, thanks to Francis's decision (in 1594) to marry a woman named Thomasine Boyes, the widow of a separatist haberdasher. George objected violently to the match, urging the complete unsuitability of his brother's marriage to a woman noted for her ultrafashionable, gender-bending clothing and her habit of lying in bed until nine on the Lord's Day. This was the beginning of a feud which continued to fester when the brothers later moved to Amsterdam, and which was summarized in magnificent detail in George Johnson's *Discourse of some Troubles and Excommunications in the Banished English Church at Amsterdam,* published in 1603.[57]

One remarkable feature of the reference to "master Johnson" in his journals is that Stonley dined with this fiery separatist not at the communal table but in his private chamber. This suggests that he might have enjoyed a bizarre moment of intimacy with a man who had been "banished . . . in to a farre Countrey never to returne."[58] And if, as seems likely, Stonley knew the full story of the city wench, the pastor, and his brother, he might well have looked at that too with a certain intimacy, since he had himself been a customer of Thomasine's first husband, Edward Boyes, back in 1582. During a prolonged bout of sickness, when he had been "greved" with a cough, Stonley noted a payment of seven shillings and six pence "To Edward Boyes at Kinges hedde at Ludgat for a velvet night cape."[59] This luxurious purchase, made at Boyes's house a stone's throw from the Fleet, places him in the same city milieu that shaped Thomasine. If there was a jolt of recognition over dinner, it would have come with an appreciation of how the prison had compressed the networks that were dispersed in the city beyond the walls, creating a febrile microcosm out of the shared reality of debt.

Decayed Goods

For Alec Ryrie, early modern Protestantism was a religion for scholars: "It aspired to turn Christendom into a giant university, in which Christians would spend their time in private study or in attending the lectures and seminars which they called sermons, prophesyings, and conferences." Early modern Protestants were "insatiable readers," who read the Bible at fixed times every day, and who used a variety of commentaries and expositions to help them to internalize the text. A commentary, Ryrie stresses, was a "means of pressing the Word onto yourself," turning what might be rote reading into food for the soul. Stonley, with his habit of copying daily scriptural or moral excerpts into his journals, his fixed habits of morning and evening prayer and of sabbath scriptural reading, and his large library crammed with devotional and exegetical works, looks in many respects like an archetypal Protestant reader.[60] We have already seen hints of heightened religiosity in his prison journals: on one Sunday in July 1597 he even specifies, "after service in the Chappell I kept my Chamber reading the lamentacions of Jeremye."[61] Another eloquent entry is made on Sunday, 3 April, of the same year, when Stonley pays sixpence to an unspecified person "for mending the claspe of my byble."[62] We earlier encountered book clasps as part of the textile composition of the book (its system of internal and external attachments) and as the material furniture that worked to splice books in to a domestic sphere replete with chests and boxes. Here the entry for mending the clasp serves as a marker of Stonley's attachment to the text, which the deployment of a commentary aimed to intensify.

Who was the "Master Cottesford" who sold Stonley a copy of "muffettes booke of the proverbes"? There are more than twenty references to a "Mr Cottesford" at dinner and supper in the third volume of the journals. But once again, to complicate matters, there are two brothers who might fit the bill. John Cottesford was a goldsmith and citizen of London, and on one occasion Stonley actually specifies that it is John Cottesford who is visiting.[63] But his brother Samuel is in some ways the more likely candidate, since he had become a minister at Doddinghurst in 1582, and in that capacity he features several times in the first volume of the journals. There are some hints back then that Samuel was a controversial figure, a forward Protestant who inclined to criticize the Elizabethan religious settlement and to seek further reform of ecclesiastical institutions. Things begin well; Stonley makes approving references to Samuel's sermons on Genesis 18 and 24 in the summer and autumn of 1581, and takes notes on another ("harde . . . a sermon made by our minstre Master Cottesford as by my note boke of sermons may appere").[64] But we know that around this time, on 4 September, Samuel was hauled up before the Privy Council to answer charges made against him by John Walker, the archdeacon of Essex. Those charges were threefold: he had refused to wear the surplice, had failed to follow the Book of Common Prayer, and was excommunicate. Cottesford denied the first two accusations and claimed that his excommunication had been unjust and had already been overturned by Walker himself. (He also counterattacked, claiming that the archdeacon's court had failed to deal satisfactorily with the case of one Foster's wife, "suspected to be a harlot").[65] The nature of these accusations suggests that Stonley's entry for 1 September 1582, which does not name names, may also refer to Samuel Cottesford: "This morning after prayer I hard service at my parishe Church where our ministre begane service with the Surples on his backe rede the Psalmes of the day the xth ca. of the second of kinges the first lesson the third ca of St mathewes gospell for the second lesson[.] And after made his Sermon upon the iiijth ca of Hosea / and so ended the service at that tyme."[66] The anxieties expressed here, relating to clerical vestments and adherence to the prayer book, chime with those that Stonley had expressed in November of the previous year in relation to "master West our ministre," who had "refuz[ed] the Servise for the day According as yt is appoynted in the booke of Common preyer" and subsequently "made a Sermon without preyer at all for the quenes majestie & usinge for the week dayes no service at All."[67] Given Stonley's evident sensitivity to such hot-Protestant deviations from the established order, it is conceivable that he had himself reported Cottesford to the archdeacon.[68] Cottesford later moved from Doddinghurst via West Ham to Stepney, which may explain why there are no references to him in the second volume of the journals.[69]

The Cottesford brothers were closely associated; on one occasion John petitioned the Earl of Shrewsbury to offer a Yorkshire living to his clerical brother.[70] They were also associated in debt. A letter sent by the Privy Council on 14 March 1595 seeks intermediaries "to treate with the creditors of Samuell Cottesford, vicar of Stepney, and John Cottesforde of London, goldsmithe, being become indebted to divers persons by reason of suertishippe." "Suertishippe" means "suretyship": taking responsibility for the payment of a debt on behalf of another person. We do not know for whom the Cottesfords had stood surety, or for how much money, but they had clearly incurred serious sums of surrogate debt; the Privy Council urged that the brothers should have "some reasonable respitt, that they maie recover suche debtes as are due to them the better to enable them to give every man satisfaction, and in the meane while to perswade them to forbeare to ympeache them or their suerties of their liberty."[71]

From further Privy Council missives, we learn that John Cottesford was deep in debt to one Peter Beauvoir, who complains that Cottesford "doth owe him great sommes of money bothe for plate he had of the suppliant and for money he paied, beinge suerty for him."[72] To evade him, Beauvoir explains, Cottesford has gone into hiding, and so has been unable to exercise an official city role as a gauger of wines, oils, and liquors; Beauvoir petitions to be given the job himself so that he can recover his debts. The council seems initially to have supported Beauvoir, but it later switched sides, petitioning for Cottesford to keep his post so that he could pay off his debts and urging the city authorities to beware of anyone who "upon some sinester devise and prejudice against him" might suggest that Cottesford's "estate is much decayed."[73] On 2 January 1597, the council wrote again to the mayor on Cottesford's behalf: "wee heare good reporte of the man's honesty, having also divers wayes sustayned muche losse by suertyshippe and otherwyse."[74] Keeping his city post is "(as he informeth us) the only stay that he hathe left for himself, his wyfe and children." (The parish registers of St. Michael Bassishaw note the baptisms of eight of Cottesford's children between 1580 and 1594.) Cottesford evidently had friends in high places, but he was fighting to save his financial skin. All of this provides a context for the frequency with which "Mr Cottesford" appears as a guest at Stonley's table in 1597–98; it is more than likely that one or both brothers were his fellow inmates.

The bitter personal experience of debt underlies one of the two surviving works by Samuel Cottesford, a posthumously published sermon on 2 Kings 4–7 entitled *A Very Soveraigne Oyle to Restore Debtors.*[75] The oil in question was the miraculous oil that saved a widow struggling to satisfy rapacious creditors following her husband's death. In the sermon, the oil becomes a metaphor for the Christian fellow feeling and human sympathy that Cottesford finds to be wholly lacking in the lenders of his day. The preacher is passionate in his excoriation of the "hard, mercilesse, and unconscionable Creditor" who, refusing to allow his victim to work off a debt over time, "will have it presently, or else no way with him but one: all his Song is, To prison with him, I wil have my penni-worths of his carkeise, I will make dice of his bones." In his "blood-thirstie humour," the creditor would rather see the debtor "rot in prison, and wife and children starve all at home, then to accept of such beggarly payment."[76] This prompts Cottesford to recall "a certaine Jew, of whom wee reade, who having lent money to a Christian, the day being come, and the poore Christian not able to make payment, the Jew was contented, so he might have a pound of the Christians flesh, to loose the nine hundred crownes, for so much was the debt that the Christian ought him."[77] The preacher turns aside later in his discourse to attack the way that bankrupts are forced to sell off their goods at a knockdown price: "For it is commonly held, that those goods of the decayed, though as good as the Rich mans every way for value, and price, yet being in a ruinated, decayed and a poore broken mans hands, is worth some fourth part or lesse perhaps: This is the fashion of the World, whereunto every man fashioneth himselfe; that is, rather to keepe him downe, that is downe; or, if not downe, but going in the way, to beat him downe altogether, rather then to helpe to raise him up againe."[78] The vicar of Stepney acknowledges that in attacking these injustices, he might seem to be overstepping the mark: "againe it will be said, that I goe over-far in this point, medling with the Law, beyond my limits."[79] But he also makes it clear that he has a personal reason for loving the story of the widow's oil, calling it "this Scripture . . . whereof in the many dayes of my distractions, in the case which presently I doe here handle, I have made some use, and received some comfortable hope."[80] For our purposes, Cottesford offers a powerful analysis of the way that debt invades the body of the debtor, eating away flesh and bone and at the same time emptying things of their value. The "decay" of the debtor spreads to his goods; substance becomes less substantial when credit has flown.

Just as the prison was a hall of mirrors, so too was its reading matter. We do not know whether Stonley or Cottesford knew Peter Moffett, author of the *Commentarie upon the Booke of the Proverbes of Salomon*; his vicarage at Fobbing in Essex was not far from the Petre estates at West Horndon.[81] Some degree of private knowledge is suggested by the fact that he puts a name to the author, who is only identified by his initials on the two extant editions of the work. The work, which treats the Bible as a commonplace book to be expounded, expanded, and imprinted on the mind, was perfectly designed for readers seeking to intensify their attachment to scripture. The title page of the 1592 edition quotes Ecclesiastes 12: "The words of the wise are as goads, and as nailes fastened, they are the chiefe of choise, delivered by one shepheard."[82] That idea of fastening and binding is picked up in the dedication to the Earl of Bedford, which urges that "So many points of great importance and of singular frute, being comprehended in this one litle booke of Salomons Proverbes, you can not (most noble Earle) better bestow your labour, then in meditating therein both night and day, and in binding the sentences thereof, as it were in frontlets before your eyes." The allusion is to Exodus 13:16's phylacteries, boxes for physically attaching the scriptures to the human face.[83] The word "point"—as in "so many points of great importance"—seems particularly important to Moffett, who laments in the 1592 edition, "I am farre from handling of manie points exactly," and in the revised and extended 1596 edition complains that his absence from the press has left "escaps in the words or in the points and distinctions of any sentences."[84] The 1596 edition added an index, entitled "A Table of the chiefe poyntes contayned in the booke of Proverbes. The first number sheweth the chapter, and the second the verse, wherein each point is set downe."[85] The point of a point is its sharpness, and Moffett's *Commentarie* is full of references to inward piercing and engraving, as when he exclaims, "O that the pretious sentence of the Prophet David in the psalme, where he saith, that *the Lord is the Sunne, and a buckler,* were written not there onely, but in every one of our hearts, and graven not with a pen of iron, but by the spirit of God within our soules and consciences?"[86] To gloss the Bible is to dig divine precepts into the heart.

And one of the repeated points on which the text of the *Commentarie* hammers is that of suretiship. Proverbs 1–5 yields a lengthy comment about how "many by rash incurring of debt, do undo themselves and their families, so that not onely hereby it often commeth to passe, that their minds are much distracted, but that their bodies are imprisoned, and the things which they possesse, are taken away." Hence Solomon advises men "first, not to enter into suertyship, then (if peradventure this way he hath overshot himselfe) to use all good meanes of getting his word or bond released." Moffett admits that "charitie bindeth us sometimes to lend our goods to our neighbour: so also to become suertie for him." But none "should easilie or rashlie cast himselfe therinto," or rest in the trap of debt without employing "might and maine" to get out.[87] Proverbs 11:15 returns to this subject: "The danger of rash suertyship is herein laid open, which point hath before bin declared."[88] The theme recurs in 17:18 and 20:16 (where we are told that the foolish surety who "dissembleth and taketh on him the person of a rich man" "deserveth well to smart for such follie"), and 22:26–27 ("What reason hast thou to cast thy selfe into such extreem misery, as that thou shalt be put to give or sell the bed whereon thou lyest[?]").[89] Such reflections on the dangers of a social order founded on credit would doubtless have stuck in the heart of our reader. Just as, in the Fleet, the bankrupt man met other debtors, large and small, around every corner, so his books were liable to fall open at a page that spoke of debt.

From Riches to Rags

What are we to make of "the Booke of Jacke of Newberrye alias Wynchcum" that Stonley acquired from "Johns the Prynter" for four pence? His purchase of *Jack of Newberie* was, like that of *Venus and Adonis*, conspicuously up to the minute; the work had been entered in the Stationers' Register less than three months previously. Stonley also appears to be extending booktrade connections from within the Fleet. "Johns the Prynter" was Richard Jones, almost certainly a Welshman; in the latter part of his long career his gillyflower device bore the motto "Heb Ddieu heb ddim" ("Without God without anything").[90] Jones's printing and bookselling operations seem to have moved around a narrowly defined area of London, never very far from the Fleet. Between 1565 and 1576 his colophons mostly place Jones in St. Paul's Churchyard, but on the title page of Isabella Whitney's 1567(?) *Copy of a Letter* he is described as "dwelling in the upper end of Fleetlane: at the Signe of the spred Egle," as he was in R.C.'s 1574 *Blasing of Bawdrie*.[91] By 1576 he had moved a few steps north, to a shop "over-agaynst S. Sepulchers Church without Newgate," and from 1581 his title pages place him a little further west, "at the signe of the Rose and Crowne, neer to Saint Andrewes church in Holborne."[92] His publications included works by Nicholas Breton, Angel Day, Christopher Marlowe (the 1590 *Tamburlaine*, which Jones purged of "some fond and frivolous Jestures" that he considered ill suited to tragedy), George Peele, Philip Stubbes, and George Whetstone.[93] Kirk Melnikoff identifies Jones as a distinctly literary publisher who had a tendency to emphasize the elite and neo-chivalric associations of his publications. At the same time, his staple was ballads.[94] It was presumably this commitment that made him a natural publisher for Thomas Deloney, "the Balleting Silk-weaver" renowned for turning British history, current events, and scandalous sensations into popular songs, when the balladeer started writing prose fiction in the later 1590s.[95]

The story of John Winchcomb, the Berkshire clothier whose virtuous labors and determination to transform the plight of the poor lead him to wealth and royal favor, is set somewhere around the time of Stonley's birth, in an unreformed Henrician age when the likes of Cardinal Wolsey and Catherine of Aragon stalked the earth. Winchcomb does not quite rise from rags to riches; he starts out as a lowly weaver whose "singular vertue" wins him the hand of his widowed mistress and the headship of the firm.[96] But from the outset this is a morality tale about the possibility of transforming your lot through a combination of merriment and hard graft. The point is driven home when we are taken to see the "15. faire Pictures" that Winchcomb had hanging in his "faire large Parlour" (G4r). The portraits depict kings, emperors, and captains who came from nowhere, with fathers who were potters, cobblers, weavers, or, in the case of the emperor Diocletian, bookbinders. As someone who had risen from obscure origins to a height of fortune, Stonley might well have identified with Winchcomb. At one point Jack is even "chosen against the Parliament a Burgesse," as was Stonley when he sat for Newton in Lancashire in 1571.[97]

Whether the bourgeois milieu of *Jack of Newberie* would have resonated with our imprisoned reader is a moot point. Although it is set in Berkshire, Deloney's narrative might be said to inhabit the mercantile world that Stonley had known firsthand in London. But perhaps these are not quite the same worlds, since Winchcomb is emphatically a producer rather than a merchant. At the heart of the story is his extraordinary factory (to use a word that seems to have been coming into being in this period).[98] Describing this powerhouse, the text slips from prose to verse, to offer a heart-warming celebration of capitalist enterprise:

> Within one roome being large and long,
> There stood two hundred Loomes full strong:
> Two hundred men, the truth is so,
> Wrought in theese Loomes, all in a rowe.
> By every one a pretty boy,
> Sate making quils with mickle joie.
> And in another place hard by,
> A hundred women merrily,
> Were carding hard with joyfull cheere,
> Who singing sate with voices cleare.
> And in a chamber close beside,
> Two hundred maidens did abide. . . . (D2r–v)

The loom was traditionally imagined as a site for the singing of godly songs. Here the songs are not explicitly religious; rather, their job is to make a vital connection between work and pleasure. The paradox of "carding hard with joyfull cheere" resolves itself in song. Deloney's celebration of the sheer scale of Winchcomb's operation continues as his description moves on to the subject of child labor:

> Then to another roome came they,
> Where children were in poor aray:
> And every one sate picking wooll,

The finest from the coarse to cull:
The number was seaven score and ten,
The children of poore silly men:
And these, their labours to requite,
Had every one a penny at night:
Beside their meate and drink all day,
Which was to them a wondrous stay. (D2v)

When the King and Queen visit, they are struck by the beauty of the children, and by the time they and the assembled nobility had finished turning them into gentlemen "not one was left to picke wooll . . . and God so blessed them, that each of them came to be men of great account and authority in the land" (G2v). Success is contagious, spreading from things to people: just as the wool will be purged of its coarseness and turned into fine cloth, so every wool-picking child is a miniature Jack of Newbury, destined for greatness.

The meat and drink that the children enjoy signifies not just as food but also for its value as symbolic capital. The verses go on to tell us that Jack gets through "ten good fat Oxen" a week, and that he employs a butcher, a brewer, a baker, and five cooks in order to keep his household running (D2v–3r). The crucial point is that Jack's household rivals those of the gentry and nobility. The narrative repeatedly provides opportunities for Jack, "scant Marquesse of a mole hill" as he calls himself, to trump the established elites and to win the monarch's favor thanks to the sheer scale of his resources (E1r). It is not just that his establishment has its own almost infallible source of income; what matters is that it produces cloth, which is the very stuff of status. When war with the Scots threatened, Jack "came home in all haste, and cut out a whole broadcloth for horsemens coats, and so much more as would make up coates for the number of a hundred men"; envious onlookers comment that "the best Nobleman in the Countrie would scarce have done so much" (D4r–v). And when Henry VIII paid a visit to his factory, the floor was "covered with broadcloathes in stead of greene rushes: these were choice peeces of the finest wool, of an Azure colour, valued at an hundred pound a cloath, which afterward was given to his Majestie" (F1r). Jack does not merely own the means of production; he owns the means for producing the social order.[99]

Jack of Newberie is, as we might expect, very attentive to stuff. When the widow of Winchcomb's master attempts to seduce him, she tells him to "take a cushion and sit downe by mee." "Dame quoth hee I thanke you, but there is no reason I should sit on a cushion till I have deserved it" (A4v). When the King comes visiting, the text notes that the sumptuous banquet is "served all in glasse" (F1r). Winchcomb's portrait collection is housed not just in "a faire large Parlour" but in "a faire large Parlour which was wainscotted about," and we learn that the paintings are "covered with curtaines of green silke, fringed with gold" (G4r). Jack's wife has a minor life crisis when she contemplates how, thanks to her husband's wealth, she will have to wear a French hood and silk gown: "Alas . . . having never been used to such attyre, I shall not know where I am, nor how to behave my selfe in it: and beside, my complexion is so blacke, that I shall carry but an ill favoured countenance under a hood" (K1r). Deloney, by contrast, is unfazed by a world in which status is created through display. In the last chapter of the book, an unscrupulous knight takes advantage of one of Winchcomb's working girls, gets her pregnant, then disowns her completely. Winchcomb disguises the girl as a wealthy widow, dressed in the obligatory gown and French hood, and dupes the knight into marrying her.

Stonley, fresh from paying to have his goods inventoried for sale, must have looked somewhat ruefully on this stark account of the relationship between the social order and the order of things. But the most tormenting section of Deloney's text for our imprisoned reader would have been the chapter devoted to a draper named Randoll Pert who owed Winchcomb five hundred pounds. "In the end" this draper "fell greatly to decay, in so much that hee was cast into prison, and his wife with her poore children turned out of doores." His creditors were merciless—all except Jack, who judged that "if he be not able to pay me when hee is at libertie, hee will never be able to pay me in prison" (K3r).

Randoll Pert lies long in jail, and his wife "which before for dayntinesse would not foule her fingers" is forced "to goe about and wash buckes [dirty clothes] at the Thames side, and to be a chare-Woman in rich mens houses" (K3r–v). When he is eventually released from prison, Pert becomes "a Porter to carry burthens from one place to another." His disgrace is inevitably inscribed in his clothing, "an old ragged doublet, and a torne payre of breeches, with his hose out at the heeles, and a paire of olde, broken slip shooes on his feet, a rope about his middle instead of a girdle, and on his head an old, greasie cap" (K3v). When he meets Winchcomb he at first attempts to run away, fearing that he will be thrown into the debtors' prison once again. But Winchcomb, after some brief moralizing, takes Pert off to the scrivener's to make a merry bond quite unlike Shylock's, thanks to which he will be paid when his debtor is sheriff of London. Then he buys Pert "a faire sute of apparell, Marchantlike, with a faire blacke cloake, and all other thinges fit to the same," and sets him up in business. Pert rapidly grows "into great credite," is elected sheriff, and gladly pays back the five hundred pounds (K4v). Credit breeds credit; this is the utopian logic that Stonley and his ilk experienced via its negation, as distrust bred more distrust and led on to social annihilation.

One last detail of the narrative that might have cut Stonley to the quick: as well as being a draper, like the Branches, Pert sold his wares in "*Canweeke streete*"—Candlewick Street, in the parish of St. Mary Abchurch (K4v). The reference is unsurprising; as John Stow explained in *The Survey of London*, the street may have taken its name from candlemakers, but "of olde time" it was occupied by "divers Weavers of woollen clothes" brought from Flanders and Brabant by Edward III. "These weavers . . . being in short time worne out," "their place is now possessed by rich Drapers sellers of woollen cloth, & c."[100] But such an overlaying of fact and fiction might have been a final turn of the screw for this particular reader.

"It Is Mete, That His Body Suffre for It"

Jack of Newberie creates the rosy fantasy of a creditor who wishes his debtor "cleare of all other mens debts, so that I gave him mine to begin the world again" (K3r). But for Stonley there was to be no beginning the world again. Age and debt were unflinchingly allied, and they pointed in one direction: an ignominious grave. Books offered no escape: even the most rose-tinted of narratives could be a reminder of the inescapability of debt. As it happens, it is possible to gauge the extent of his personal investment in his reading by paying close attention to the extracts that Stonley transcribed every day from Richard Taverner's collections of Erasmian commonplaces. Whereas in the 1593–94 volume of the journals he was quite careful in his transcriptions, he was notably less patient in 1597–98, frequently abbreviating materials; he may have been partly incited to this by the unwieldy length of some of the anecdotes contained in the first volume he was copying from, *The Garden of Wysdome*. But there is at least one case where an omission was motivated by the subject matter of the book rather than by mere convenience. This is in the tales relating to Alfonsus, King of Aragon, which appear early in the second book of the *Garden*.

The first story begins: "A Certayne knyght had ryotously & prodigally wasted al his patrimony & landes which were very greate, and moreover had indebted hym selfe excedyngly moche. His frendes in the courte were sutors to the kynge for hym, that at least hys bodye myght not be imprisoned for hys debtes." The King is unflinching, saying: "Yf he had bestowed this so great ryches eyther in the service of me hys prynce or upon the commune weale of hys countrey, or in relevynge of hys kynsfolkes, I coulde heare your sute. Now syth he hath spent so great substaunce upon hys body, it is mete, that his body suffre for it." Taverner points the moral: "Let thys be a lesson to all prodigalities chyldren to plucke backe theyr fete betymes ere all be wasted, leaste yf they do not, they happen to be served as this wyse gentylman was."[101] Stonley leaves out the entire narrative, and his omission cannot result from eye-skip or carelessness, since he transcribes the stories relating to Alfonsus that follow after this particular episode without a break. The tale of the prodigal knight was simply too close to the bone for the imprisoned teller. He could have contested the detail; he was no knight, he had not inherited wealth only in order to waste it, and he had not spent all of his money on goods of the body (witness the book that he was transcribing, with its freight of spiritual wisdom). But the logic of the narrative—bodily suffering for self-interested, bodily expenditure—can only have been painful. This is another moment where a silence in the journals creates a small chink in the facade, an index to a life that was coming unstuck.

Conclusion

Richard Stonley's wife, Anne, outlived him by more than a decade, dying in 1613. Unlike her husband she left a will, which offers us a rare opportunity to catch a hint of her voice.[1] Drawn up on 22 May 1607, and reconfirmed on 12 July 1611, the will makes it clear that she was still a resident of St. Botolph's, Aldersgate. She begins tersely, declaring that she is "in perfect remembrance thankes be unto god" and bequeathing her soul "into the handes of Almighty god my maker and Redeemer." Neither she nor the scribe insisted on a lengthy formula, harping on the efficacy of Christ's redeeming grace or expressing the testator's hopes of joining the company of the angels. Anne was curt, too, on the matter of her marriages; she asked to be buried "in the parish church of St Buttolph aforesaid where my husband lyes," neglecting to mention the fact that she had two husbands buried in the church. That fact can be gleaned from her funeral monument, which was transcribed in the 1633 edition of Stow's *Survey of London*:

> Here lyeth the body of *Anne*, daughter of
> *John Branche*, Citizen and Draper of
> *London*, by *Joane* his wife, daughter
> and heire of *John Wilkinson*, sometime
> Alderman of this Citie. She was marri-
> ed first to *Robert Dunne*, and (after his
> death) to *Richard Stoneley*, Esquire.
> By *Dunne* she had three sonnes; Sir Da-
> niel Dunne, Knight, and Doctor of Law,
> her eldest; *Samuel Dunne*, and *Wil-*
> *liam Dunne*, the yongest, Doctor of Phy-
> sicke. And by *Stoneley* she had divers
> children, whereof two lived to be marri-
> ed; *Dorothie*, to *William Da[u]trey*

of *Sussex*; Anne, to *William Hig-*
ham of *Essex,* Esquire. Her life was
vertuous and godly, and so dyed the ele-
venth day of January, *An. Dom.* 1611.
being of the age of fourscore and six yeers,
having seene her childrens children, to the
fourth generation: and lyes buried
betweene her husbands, and among some
other of her children, according to her desire.[2]

This is a powerful statement. Despite the calamity of her husband's professional disgrace and bankruptcy, Anne and her executors were clearly determined to emphasize her own illustriousness. As far as she was concerned, her
house was firmly grounded.

Anne's will plays to the four generations in an appended "schedule" of
gifts of gold and silver. Sir Daniel Donne, by this time president of the High
Court of Admiralty, was to be her executor and chief heir. His wife received
£20, his four sons and two married daughters £10 each. Dorothy Dawtrey
was to have "a neast of bowles silver and double guilt with a Cover," Anne
Heigham "a salte of Silver and double guilte with a Cover and two new white
silver bowles." Dawtrey's son Henry and daughter Anne both got £10 in
gold; for Henry there was also "a standinge Cupp silver and double guilte,"
for Anne "a tankard of silver double guilte and a dozen of silver spoones with
the maiden heads on the endes." (Such "maidenhead spoons" survive in large
numbers from the period and represent a Catholic holdover in domestic
material culture, since the "maiden" would before the Reformation have been
identified as the Virgin.)[3] Her Heigham grandson Richard received £10 and
her granddaughter (unnamed) £5, as did *her* elder child (again unnamed) and
younger daughter, Dorothy.

The legacies go on through Anne's cousins, to household servants,
including Roger Batte, a presence through all three volumes of Stonley's
journals, and to the poor of Aldersgate, of Doddinghurst, and of Garnish
Hall (the Branche family estate in Essex). Finally, "to the children of the
hospitall"—presumably nearby St. Bartholomew's—"five pownd." But the
most moving bequests in the will are those that are not fully specified in its
text. "My chaine, & Ringes and other Jewells you shall finde in a box in
papers all their names written uppon the papers to whome I give them."

Similarly, she writes that her linen is in "an yron bonde cheste that standeth in my maides chamber," and is to be given "to them whose names are there written and the writinges pinned on the clothes." Such an act of labeling was of course practical, forestalling the need for detailed description of every item in the will. But it is hard not to read into it a certain intimacy, as some of the most precious items escape from the legal formulae and materialize as a box of gifts that needs to be tracked down and unpacked.

In a published discussion, Peter N. Miller asks Natalie Zemon Davis to address some of the challenges of reconstructing the past from documents such as inventories.[4] In this case, the inventory in question is that of Margrieta van Varick, a Dutch immigrant to Brooklyn in the seventeenth century, who was the subject of an exhibition at the Bard Graduate Center in New York in 2009–10. Davis is invited to ruminate on how a historian can use a list of objects to learn something about their (otherwise thinly documented) owner. She begins by suggesting that you can make use of parallel cases, people you do know about who would have had experiences similar to those of your subject. But if you want to get at emotional life, Davis continues, it helps to have books. "If only I knew what was in the packet of books that the estimators did not open because they were all in Dutch and other foreign tongues; if only I had those books and saw some interesting seventeenth-century novels, or some Dutch poetry." Perhaps one could speculate about Margrieta's library—"my guess would be that this was not a very big bookshelf, with perhaps twenty books on it." Davis is also interested in Margrieta's patterns of gift giving. Well, her will, Miller says, "is focused on the children. And there are gifts, but mostly they are money, silver coins; there is even a gold Arabian ducat . . . and they are all wrapped up in napkins." At this detail, Davis is suddenly excited: "I think it is lovely that you can know that. I have done hundreds and hundreds of wills in my time, . . . and I very rarely find anything about how things are presented." Later she speculates about whether this had to do with Margrieta's "special memories about the gifts that she bought from India, the East Indian trade, and the Japanese trade."

Davis's excitement about wrapping shines out in a conversation about how we might unwrap an early modern life, seizing on the scant information in the records and using it to unfold the possibilities of the period. It also resonates in the context of a new cultural history that is ever more attentive to things that would once have been considered superficial, overturning a model of knowledge that assumes that what is immediately presented is obvious, and that the truth lies deep within. Anne Stonley may not have had memories of Indian or Japanese wrapped gifts, but she would have had her own set of associations relating to boxes and chests: her wedding trousseau; her chests of linen in upstairs rooms; the numerous cases of letters, prints, and money with which her domestic spaces had once been stuffed. And, of course, the books; her husband's books, her own books, their shared books.

In her study of the invention of modern shopping, Rachel Bowlby proposes that the book is a consumer good well ahead of its time. The rise of the self-service supermarket in the twentieth century led to the invention of packaging, the wrapping that simultaneously protects, standardizes and advertises the substances within. But the book, Bowlby writes, is "an ancient precursor of the modern package, a product that comes with its 'outer cover' built into it as part and parcel of the whole."[5] Before the advent of decorative publishers' bindings in the nineteenth century, this claim might appear to be less forceful, but books have always had many layers of wrapping (blank leaves, title pages, prefaces, dedications) that literary critics now know as paratexts.[6] As we have seen, there are powerful grounds for thinking about early modern, bespoke bindings as a clothing of the book that ligatures it to its owner(s) and to the wider world. In the sixteenth and seventeenth centuries it was not yet proverbial that "you can't judge a book by its cover," although it was easy enough to find a moralist to remind you that "the Book is not the better for its Clasps."[7] These are the simultaneously true-and-false ideas that typify our relationship to materiality more generally. Publishers lavish considerable care on dust jackets, but "serious" readers ignore them or throw them away. Writers, meanwhile, can be seriously spooked by the jacket designs that are imposed upon them, seeing in them a version of the death of the author that Roland Barthes hailed as the birth of the reader.[8]

Shakespeare's First Reader has attempted to refuse the disavowal of things and to attend to the book as an adhesive rather than an autonomous object. We have seen books that stick to each other in unexpected combinations— the *Survay of France* and *Venus and Adonis*, bought on a single day in 1593; a biblical commentary and *Jack of Newberie* bought on another day in 1597. We have seen books that adhere to the household: maps and moral images that are at once between two covers and on the wall, treasuries of knowledge that are simultaneously books and chests of money. We have explored the book as a site of sociability, in networks that stretch from London to Moscow, and as a sticky web in which its reader might be caught. By refusing to distinguish between those attachments of a book that are material (part of its physical design), interpersonal (part of the social network that produced, distributed, and consumed it), and environmental (part of its situatedness as an object among other objects), *Shakespeare's First Reader* has evolved a methodology for thinking about the book in the inventory or the account book, the book that is owned but that may never have been read, or unwrapped in full, or annotated with pen in hand. You do not need to open a book in order to engage with its more dispersed and sometimes intangible outer wrappings: the title, the name of the author, the book's reputation, its meanings for a culture. We need to expand our definition of reading to encompass all of the things that readers do with books—all of the ways in which books stick to us and we to them.

Notes

The following abbreviations appear in the notes:

Arber   Edward Arber, ed., *A Transcript of the Registers of the Company of Stationers of London, 1554–1640 A.D.*, 5 vols. (London: Privately printed, 1875–1894)
BL   British Library, London
CUL   Cambridge University Library
ERO   Essex Record Office, Chelmsford
GUL   Glasgow University Library
HMC   Historical Manuscripts Commission
HMCS   HMC. *Calendar of the Manuscripts of the Most Hon. the Marquis of Salisbury*, 24 vols. (London: HMSO, 1883–1976)
HoP   *History of Parliament* (http://www.historyofparliamentonline.org)
LMA   London Metropolitan Archives
ODNB   *Oxford Dictionary of National Biography*
OED   *Oxford English Dictionary*
PCC   Prerogative Court of Canterbury
PLRE   *Private Libraries in Renaissance England* (http://plre.folger.edu)
STC   A. W. Pollard et al., eds, *A Short-Title Catalogue of Books Printed in England, Scotland, and Ireland, and of English Books Printed Abroad, 1475–1640*, 2nd ed., 3 vols. (London: Bibliographical Society, 1976–91)
TNA   National Archives, Kew, London

PREFACE

1. Kaufmann, *Arcimboldo*, 61, 96, 259n21.
2. Elhard, "Reopening the Book," 120.
3. Sherman, *Used Books*; Orgel, *Reader in the Book*; Price, *How to Do Things*.
4. See for example Miller, *Stuff*; Gell, *Art and Agency*.
5. Genette, *Paratexts*.
6. Stallybrass, "Books and Scrolls."

INTRODUCTION

1. Eliot, *Mill on the Floss*, I:236.
2. Larkin, *Complete Poems*, 51.

3. Proust, "On Reading," 99.

4. Ibid., 99–100.

5. Joyce, *Dubliners*, 21.

6. Dojc and Krausova, *Last Folio*, 14–17.

7. For the use of calendrical Books of Hours as "livres de raison," repositories of family history, see Reinburg, *French Books of Hours*, 62–71.

8. Eliot, *Mill on the Floss*, II:238.

9. Milton, *Areopagitica*, A3v.

10. Bennett, *Vibrant Matter*.

11. Müller, *White Magic*, 180–89.

12. Ingold, *Being Alive*, 19–32.

13. Grafton and Jardine, "'Studied for Action,'" 30–78.

14. On reading's mise-en-scène, see Stewart, *Look of Reading*. On furniture, physical and mental, see Knight, "'Furnished for Action.'"

15. McGann, *Critique*; McGann, *Textual Condition*; McKenzie, *Bibliography and the Sociology of Texts*, 4; see also Pearson, *Books as History*.

16. Scarry, *Dreaming by the Book*, 5. For another meditation on this theme, see Mendelsund, *What We See When We Read*.

17. Rayner, *Psychology of Reading*; Juhasz and Pollatsek, "Lexical Influences."

18. McLeod [Cloud], "From Tranceformations," 61.

19. See Brown, "Thing Theory," 4, on breakage and the perception of thingness; and on book technology, Saenger, *Space Between Words*; Sherman, *Used Books*, 48; Wolf, *Proust and the Squid*.

20. Miller, *Stuff*, 51.

21. Spicksley, ed., *Business and Household Accounts*, 71.

22. Ago, *Gusto for Things*, 213–14; Ago, *Il gusto delle cose*, 57, 119.

23. Sidney, *Countesse of Pembrokes Arcadia*, A3r–v.

24. Harington, *Epigrams*, 130; Heywood, *An Hundred Epigrammes*, C6r–v.

25. Kinnaston, *Corona Minervae*, C4v–D1r.

26. Ibid., C3r. See further the essays collected in Scott-Warren and Zurcher, eds., *Text, Food*.

27. Price, *How to Do Things*, 27.

28. Ibid., 27.

29. Ibid., 20.

30. Ibid., 22–23.

31. Bruster, *Shakespeare*, ch. 8 ("The New Materialism in Renaissance Studies"); Harris, "Shakespeare's Hair"; Harris, *Untimely Matter*.

32. Fleming, *Graffiti*; Jones and Stallybrass, *Renaissance Clothing*.

33. Ibid., 7–11.

34. Miller, *Stuff*, 70.

35. Sidney, *Sir P.S. his Astrophel and Stella*, A2r; Sidney, *Defence*, E4v.

36. Gell, *Art and Agency*, 114.

37. Thorpe, "The Love of Stuff."

38. *ODNB*, "Stonley, Richard (1520/21–1600)." See also *HoP*, "Stoneley, Richard (c. 1520–1600)."

39. Library of Birmingham, RL 432719 (Itchington manor court roll); I am grateful to Penelope Upton for this reference. On the rural economy of Warwickshire in this period, see Alcock, ed., *Warwickshire Grazier*.

40. Upton, "Change and Decay," 144–72.
41. Emmison, *Tudor Secretary*, 8–21.
42. Ibid., 22–25.
43. ERO D/DP/A4 (unpaginated), 18 November 1549.
44. *ODNB*, "Dun [Donne], Sir Daniel (1544/5–1617)"; "Dunn, William," in Pelling and White, *Physicians*.
45. BL, Add. MS 16940, fol. 28b; TNA, C78/50/20.
46. *HoP*, "Stoneley, Richard (c.1520–1600)"; *Calendar of Patent Rolls: Elizabeth* 6 (1572–5), 327.
47. For the institutional context of Stonley's financial activities, see Coleman, "Artifice or Accident?" and Gray, "Exchequer Officials."
48. Selwyn and Selwyn, "'Profession of a Gentleman,'" 502–3; Wilson-Lee, *Catalogue*.
49. Compare for example the library of John, Lord Lumley, which was less than 7 percent English; Jayne and Johnson, eds., *Lumley Library*, 11; or that of Thomas Knyvett, in which 9 percent of the books were in English in 1618; McKitterick, ed., *Library of Thomas Knyvett*, 26. It is possible that formal library catalogues underreport English books, particularly ephemera.
50. See Hotson, "Library of Elizabeth's Embezzling Teller," and the modern edition of the booklist at http://plre.folger.edu.
51. TNA, SP 12/181/16.
52. See for example Jardine, *Erasmus, Man of Letters*; Jardine, *Temptation in the Archives*.
53. Felski, *The Limits of Critique*, ch. 5; Latour, *Reassembling the Social*. See also Smith, *Grossly Material Things*; Smith, "'Rare Poems Ask Rare Friends.'"
54. For "flat ontology," see Harman, "Demodernizing the Humanities."
55. A good example of the simultaneously loose and deep attachment between people and things is found in Rachel Bowlby's description (*Carried Away*, 2) of being stuck in an IKEA line when the cash registers have stopped working: "We just can't leave now. These carts bear the tangible results of an afternoon's hard work. . . . And we are attached to these things already. The big brown box contains what a joyous, newly verbal two-year-old, still trailing clouds of consumerly innocence, is already proudly calling 'my IKEA bed.'"

CHAPTER 1

1. 460/9r ("dimidium" means "a half").
2. Shakespeare, *Shakespeare's Poems*, 15.
3. Ibid., 514.
4. Meres, *Palladis Tamia*, 2O1v–2r.
5. On the authorial presentation manuscript, see Woudhuysen, *Sir Philip Sidney*, 88–103.
6. For publishers as readers, see Lesser, *Renaissance Drama*; on Field, see Hooks, *Selling Shakespeare*, 35–65.
7. Duncan-Jones, "Much Ado with Red and White."
8. Fish, *Is There a Text in This Class?*
9. Folger Shakespeare Library, MS C.b.10, no. 66. Malone used the "ancient MS. Diary, which some time since was in the hands of an acquaintance of Mr. Steevens," to confirm his suspicion that *Venus* had first appeared in 1593; *Inquiry into the Authenticity*, p. 67. The entry was also cited as "a manuscript diary that lately passed through the hands of Francis Douce, Esq." in Shakespeare, *Plays*, ed. Johnson and Steevens, II:152.

10. On the relationship between Shakespeare, chronology and biography in this period, see de Grazia, *Shakespeare Verbatim*.

11. Bodleian MS Douce d.44, fols. 69–104. Douce seems to have received the volumes somewhat discontinuously, as he writes: "A third Vol. of Stoneley's Journal afterwards fell into my hands which is intitled "Recepts and payment from the XIIIIth of May 1593 Anno regni Rne Elizabeth xxxvto" (91r). A folded sheet containing Douce's transcription of the first page and a half of the second volume is currently stored as a loose leaf in Folger MS V.a.460.

12. Bodleian, Arch G.e.31; *Venus* is here bound together with Fletcher, *Licia*, and the price of £25 was for both books; Bodleian MS Malone 26, fol. 79v (Malone to the bishop of Dromore, 6 August 1805). On Ford, see Lister, "William Ford"; Scragg, "William Ford." Lister states that *Venus* and *Licia* were separated by Ford and sold, respectively, to Malone and Richard Heber, and were only reunited at the Bodleian in 1833 (p. 347).

13. Doyle, *Complete Sherlock Holmes*, 238.

14. Shakespeare, *Othello*, 3.3.325–27.

15. Shakespeare, *Winter's Tale*, 4.3.25–26; 4.4.246–49.

16. *OED*, "trifle, n."

17. Kearney, *Incarnate Text*, 180–91; Walsham, "The Pope's Merchandise."

18. Anon., *Discovery of the Jesuits Trumpery*.

19. Kearney, *Incarnate Text*, 187.

20. *OED*, "tawdry-lace, n." For what may be a gift of tawdry lace ("a power tokyn of St Awdrye") from the bishop of Ely to Thomas Cromwell in 1533, see Heal, *Power of Gifts*, 34–35.

21. Patten, *Expedicion into Scotlande*, B8r, C4v.

22. Miller, *Stuff*, 51.

23. On the relationship between idle wares and unprofitable poems in this period, see Hutson, *Thomas Nashe*, 20–37.

24. Felski, *Limits of Critique*, 146, 173, 184–85.

25. Bale, *A Comedy Concernynge Thre Lawes*, B4v.

26. See, for example, Botero, *Relations*, Q3v, on the Low Countries, where "Each Faction cals it selfe a Church; and every new-fangled giddie *Enthusiasticall* Button-maker, is able enough to make a Faction."

27. Epstein and Safro, *Buttons*, 14.

28. Fink and Ditzler, *Buttons*, 10; Tom Wolfe, "Preface," in Epstein and Safro, *Buttons*, 12; Jones and Stallybrass, *Renaissance Clothing*, 282–83. See also Welch, "Scented Buttons."

29. Dekker, *Batchelers Banquet*, B4r. "Codlings" are a variety of apple.

30. British Library, MS Egerton 2806, 7v; TNA PROB 11/79/451; Arnold, ed., *Queen Elizabeth's Wardrobe Unlock'd*, 106. Ludwell, who had been Stoneley's tailor in the 1580s (see 459/13r, 25r, 41r), died in 1592, and so cannot have been the vendor of his Scottish buttons.

31. ERO, D/DP/A20, quoted in Edwards, *John Petre*, 112; Yeandle, ed., "Sir Edward Dering," 184.

32. Smith, ed., *Calendar*, 171.

33. For the importing of Scottish buttons into Ireland in 1575, see Flavin, *Consumption and Culture*, 106.

34. Jones and Stallybrass, *Renaissance Clothing*, 23.

35. Ibid., 23.

36. Ibid., 24–26; Welch, "New, Old and Second-Hand Culture."

37. Shakespeare, *Merchant of Venice*, 1.2.70–73.

38. Kelly, "What Are 'Canions'?"

39. *OED*, "canion/cannion/canon, *n.*"

40. Stubbes, *The Anatomie of Abuses*, E2v–3r.

41. Margues, *Description du Monde Desguisé*, B2r. My thanks to Geoff Wall and Nick Hammond for help with this excerpt.

42. Ibid, B3r.

43. Estienne, *Deux dialogues*, M3r–v; Estienne, *Deux dialogues*, ed. P.-M. Smith, 186.

44. "Quelle mousche a piqué les cousturiers (que vous appelez tailleurs) d'emprunter les noms des instruments de guerre?"; Estienne, *Deux dialogues*, M4r.

45. "Il vous faut estre resolu que pour parler bon langage courtisan, vostre premiere maxime doit estre de ne cercher [*sic*] ni ryme ni raison en iceluy"; ibid., M4r.

46. "Monsieur, cest accoustrement vous arme bien"; ibid., M4v–M5r.

47. BL, MS Egerton 2806, fols. 84v, 106r.

48. Rublack, *Dressing Up*, 16–21, 17. See also Frugoni, *Books, Banks, Buttons*, 103–5.

49. See the *OED* blog at http://public.oed.com/aspects-of-english/shapers-of-english/material-world-the-language-of-textiles/.

50. 459/5v.

51. 459/77v–78v.

52. 459/46v.

53. Smith, " 'This One Poore Blacke Gowne' "; Walsham, "Jewels for Gentlewomen."

54. Rabelais, *Complete Works*, 149.

55. Hearn, ed., *Dynasties*, 199; TNA, PROB 10/7367/7; Bearman et al., eds., *Fine and Historic Bindings*, 139. On the clothing/binding of Milton's presentation volumes, see Poole, *Milton*, 80–81.

56. https://www.royalcollection.org.uk/collection/1080417/eikon-basilike-the-portraicture -of-his-sacred-majestie-in-his-solitudes-and. I am grateful to Lucy Razzall for this reference. Compare the description in the *Catalogue of the Valuable Collection of the Late George Nassau, Esq* (London: W. Nicol, 1824), p. 114, lot 2424, of a large-paper copy of Slater, *New-Yeeres Gift*, "*said to be bound in a piece of Charles the First's waistcoat, with the blue ribbon.*" See further Scott-Warren, "Ligatures."

57. Magdalene College, Cambridge, Ferrar Papers, vol. 141, 20r, 21v. For further juxtapositions of books with buttons in Stonley's journals, see 459/62v and 459/63v. In the latter entry, Stonley specifies that he is buying his buttons from John Nelson, a leather seller who was his near neighbor in Aldersgate (see his will of 1591, TNA, PROB 11/77/39). For an excellent recent analysis of early modern "paratextiles," see Canavan, "Reading Materials."

58. 459/10r, 15r, 41r, 46v.

59. Hunnis, *Seven Sobs*, Ad4.397.

60. Meurier, *Nosegay.*

61. The Stationers' Register entry dates from 1 July 1581: "Richard Jones Lycenced unto him under the handes of the wardens, *A Dolefull Discourse of a Dutche gentlewoman distraughte of hir wittes*, To the which is added *the harde Happe of Twoo Norfolke gentlewoman* vj d"; Arber, II:395.

62. Gillespie, *Print Culture and the Medieval Author*; Knight, *Bound to Read.*

63. Pratt, "Stab-Stitching"; Knight, "Needles and Pens."

64. The 1593 edition collates A^2 B–G^4 H^1; presumably there was a final blank leaf, missing in the Bodleian copy, as in the 1594 edition.

65. Bodleian Library, Arch.G.e.31 (1–2); Morgan, "Frances Wolfreston" (esp. 214, 218).

66. The book is Folger Shakespeare Library, STC 22356. A. S. W. Rosenbach's note to this effect is penned on the inside of the vellum cover.

67. Folger Shakespeare Library, shelf mark STC 22341.8. The volume, discussed in Knight, *Bound to Read*, 70–72, is bound in contemporary limp vellum with gilt initials "G.O." on upper and lower covers. The copy of *The Passionate Pilgrim* is a composite of the first and second editions, and the date is conjectural; see further Shakespeare, *Shakespeare's Poems*, 489–94.

68. Huntington Library, shelf mark 59000–59002, discussed in Knight, *Bound to Read*, 73–75; Edmonds, *Annotated Catalogue*; Hallam, "Lamport Hall Revisited."

69. Parker, "Preposterous Events."

70. Eliot, *Survay of France*. The only exception to this statement is a facsimile edition (Amsterdam: Theatrum Orbis Terrarum, 1979).

71. For quantitative analysis of this dependency, see Demetriou and Tomlinson, " 'Abroad in Mens Hands.' "

72. Arber, II:287b, 29 April 1592. The book was entered as "*a treatise conteyninge a survey of the Realme of Ffraunce by the parliamentes thereof. &c.*"

73. Cambridge University Library, Syn.6.59.11. It may be significant that Puckering wrote to Stonley on 30 April 1593, requiring him to visit him the next day "to understand such matter, as then shall be imparted unto yow," and signing off "Your loving frend"; ERO, D/DFa 04, item 11. There is currently no biography of John Eliot, who is not in *ODNB*. For a speculative account of his literary relationships, see Yates, *John Florio*, 147–83; Lever, "Shakespeare's French Fruits." We might entertain the possibility of relating the *Survay* and *Venus and Adonis* via the Warwickshire connections of Shakespeare, Eliot, Stonley, and Shakespeare's publisher Richard Field; but for a skeptical analysis of the Shakespeare/Field connection, see Hooks, *Selling Shakespeare*, 35–65.

74. For Wolfe's news publishing, see Parmelee, *Good Newes from Fraunce*, 33–35, 55. On the prominence of publisher-commissioned translations in this period, see Boutcher, "From Cultural Translation to Cultures of Translation?" 31–34.

75. Eliot, *Survay*, G2r–v.

76. De Belleforest, *Cosmographie*.

77. Conley, *Self-Made Map*, 202–43 (p. 237). See also Peters, *Mapping Discord*, 48–55, which situates Bouguereau in a broader transition from verbal to visual mapping in this period.

78. De Belleforest, *Cosmographie*, vol. 1, 2L1r–2r (pp. 367–69).

79. Bouguereau, *Theatre Francois*, facsimile edition intro. F. de Dainville, S.J. (Amsterdam: Theatrvm Orbis Terrarum, 1966), section II ("Du Pays de Picardie").

80. *Survay*, D2v.

81. *OED*, "survey, *n.*" The usage is anticipated in 1572 by Periegetes, *Surveye of the World*. On the efflorescence of cartography in this period, see Cormack, *Charting an Empire*.

82. Luborsky and Ingram, *Guide to English Illustrated Books*, 352.

83. 459/63v.

84. 459/95v.

85. Bodleian, 4°.F.2.Art. BS.

86. Tankard, "Reading Lists," 339–40.

87. Ibid., 344.

88. Eco, *Infinity of Lists*, 113.

89. Belknap, *The List*, xii–xiii.

90. Stallybrass, "Books and Scrolls."

91. Brayman Hackel, *Reading Material*; Sherman, *Used Books*. For one indexing reader of fiction, see Schurink, "'Like a Hand in the Margine of a Booke.'"

92. Crane, *Framing Authority*; Moss, *Printed Commonplace-Books*.

93. Smyth, "'Shreds of Holinesse'"; Fleming, "Renaissance Collage."

94. Roberts, *Reading Shakespeare's Poems*, 83–101 (p. 84).

95. On the table book, see Stallybrass et al., "Hamlet's Tables."

96. 459/46v.

97. On the "parcels" of a reckoning, see Parker, "Cassio, Cash, and the 'Infidel o,'" 233–34.

98. Stallybrass et al., "Hamlet's Tables," 411–12. On Stonley's diet, see Hudson, "Food, Dining." On digestion, see the essays in Scott-Warren and Zurcher, eds., *Text, Food*.

99. Vine, "Commercial Commonplacing," 203; Yeo, *Notebooks*, 18–20.

100. Vine, "Commercial Commonplacing," 203.

101. Ibid., 209.

102. Ibid., 210.

103. Hobbes, *Leviathan*, II:58. For commentary, see Pettit, *Made with Words*, 42–54.

104. Hobbes, *Leviathan*, II:64.

105. See further Connor, *Women, Accounting, and Narrative*.

106. Smith, *Shakespeare and Masculinity*, 71–82.

107. 460/49v.

108. McMillin and MacLean, *Queen's Men*.

109. Helgerson, *Elizabethan Prodigals*.

110. Marotti, "'Love Is Not Love.'"

111. For the Inns, see Archer, Goldring, and Knight, eds., *Intellectual and Cultural*, esp. part III ("Literature and Drama"); for apprentices, Whitney, "'Usually in the Werking Daies.'"

112. BL, Add. MS 42518, fol. 422v; for the dating of the annotations see Demetriou, "Tendre cropps."

113. Duncan-Jones, *Ungentle Shakespeare*, 63–64.

114. 460/10v; Foulface, *Bacchus Bountie*.

115. Belknap, *The List*, 5.

CHAPTER 2

1. Dawson, "Histories and Texts," 416–17.

2. Rublack and Hayward, eds., *First Book of Fashion*; Groebner, "Inside Out"; Rublack, *Dressing Up*, 33–79.

3. Yamey, *Art and Accounting*, 128.

4. Osborn, ed., *Autobiography of Thomas Whythorne*, 143 (orthography modernized).

5. Botonaki, *Seventeenth-Century English Women's Autobiographical Writings*, 49.

6. Shakespeare, *Sonnets*, 91.

7. Sidney, *Major Works*, 159 (*Astrophil and Stella*, Sonnet 18).

8. Taylor, *Sources of the Self*.

9. For recent editions and studies, see Merry and Richardson, eds., *Household Account Book of Sir Thomas Puckering*; Spicksley, ed., *Business and Household Accounts*; Dyer, *A Country Merchant*.

10. Smyth, *Autobiography*.

11. Ibid., pp. 10–11, 13–14, 54.

12. Osborn, ed., *Autobiography of Thomas Whythorne*, 13–18. On the role of individualism in Whythorne's self-writing, see Mousley, "Early Modern Autobiography."

13. De Grazia, "Shakespeare in Quotation Marks"; Fleming, *Graffiti*, 41–42.

14. These include *The Garden of Wysdom* (London: John Harvye, 1539), *Proverbes or Adagies with newe addicions gathered out of the Chiliades of Erasmus* (London: Richard Bankes, 1539), and *Catonis disticha moralia ex castigatione D. Erasmi Roterodami* (London: Richard Taverner, 1540). On Taverner's promulgation of Erasmus, see McConica, *English Humanists*, 117–18, 183.

15. For versions of this formula, see, for example, 459/5v ("making up my bokes of Accompt"), 6r ("I kept home abowt my Bookes of Accompte"), 60v ("about thengrosinge of my Bookes"); 91r ("my self kept home at my Bookes of Accompt").

16. 459/10v has "at my bookes in reading of the Scriptures." On the temporality of print reading, with particular attention to Sunday reading, see Lupton, "Immersing the Network in Time."

17. 459/61v; cf. 461/62v.

18. Hotson, "Library," 52.

19. Horne, *Life and Minor Works of George Peele*, 4–20; Woodbridge, ed., *Money*, 8, 10–11.

20. Peele, *Maner and Fourme*, A4r–v.

21. Peele, *Maner and Fourme*, sample entries for 24 May 1554.

22. Peele, *Pathe Waye to Perfectnes*.

23. Howe, "Authority of Presence," lists eleven English titles printed between 1501 and 1570 bearing author portraits.

24. Oldcastle, *Here Ensueth a Profitable Treatyce*.

25. Mellis, *A Briefe Instruction*, A2v. On the relationship between these publications see Yamey, "Oldcastle, Peele and Mellis." The appraisal of Stonley's book at two shillings in 1597 may shed light on this question. Whereas Peele's works were both published in folio, Mellis's was an octavo; and since Mellis expands on Oldcastle by adding specimen pages, it seems unlikely that the lost 1543 text employed a large format.

26. Gleeson-White, *Double Entry*; Soll, *The Reckoning*.

27. Aho, *Confession and Bookkeeping*, 69. See also Poovey, *A History of the Modern Fact*, 29–65, and Sullivan, *Rhetoric of Credit*, 23–43.

28. Aho, *Confession and Bookkeeping*, 72–78.

29. Pacioli, *Double-Entry Book-Keeping*, 13.

30. Aho, *Confession and Bookkeeping*, 66–69; Smyth, *Autobiography*, 67; Soll, *Reckoning*, 20–28.

31. Peele, *Pathe Waye to Perfectnes*, *4v. On the authorship of these lines, see Tomlin, "A New Poem by Arthur Golding?"

32. Peele, *Pathe Waye to Perfectnes*, A1v.

33. Colinson, *Idea Rationaria*, A1r; cited in Smyth, *Autobiography*, 71.

34. Mellis, *Briefe Instruction*, B3r.

35. Groebner, "Inside Out," 114.

36. Boys, "Samuel Pepys's Personal Accounts," 310, 316–17.

37. Peele, *Pathe Waye to Perfectnes*, *3r (my emphases).

38. Gleeson-White, *Double-Entry*, 22–23; see also Frugoni, *Books, Banks, Buttons*, 1–25.

39. Smyth, *Autobiography*, 122; see also pp. 83–85, 100.

40. Rublack, *Dressing Up*, 51, 60, and see also pp. 64 and 72 for references to Schwarz's exactitude.

41. Smyth, *Autobiography*, 60.

42. Muldrew, *Economy of Obligation*, 60–69.

43. Baxter, "Early Accounting."

44. Smyth, *Autobiography*, 70–71, 82; see also 87–88.

45. See *OED*, "emption, *n*. 1," where it is glossed as "the action of buying."

46. The deletions begin on 459/48v.

47. Mellis, *Briefe Instruction*, C4r, E3r.

48. Aho, *Confession and Bookkeeping*, 72; Connor, *Women, Accounting, and Narrative*, 47.

49. Sullivan, *Rhetoric of Credit*, 32. The most striking exception to the general rule of legible deletion is found at 461/12v, where Stonley deletes part of an entry for a sizable purchase of books.

50. Sullivan, *Rhetoric of Credit*, 31. On the material form of Stonley's journals, see further Preston, "Moving Lines," 72–88. I am grateful to Andrew Preston for sharing his work with me.

51. Here I dissent from Felicity Heal, who in her *ODNB* entry for Stonley asserts that "in the second surviving diary, in contrast to the first, he used the pre-Tridentine Catholic calendar to date entries, suggesting an attachment to saints and feasts rejected by the protestant church." On the survival of saints' days, see further Cressy, "Protestant Calendar"; Lawrence-Mathers, "Domesticating the Calendar."

52. Oxford, Trinity College, K.10.3. For another English source that continued to list Catholic feasts, see Grafton, *A Litle Treatise*, A3–8v.

53. 459/36r. Compare on 460/43r the purchase of "7 brod allmanakes of Master Buckmaster & 3 others" for 12d., on 27 November 1593. "Brod" may indicate that these were in broadsheet rather than codex format. For Thomas Buckminster (1531/2–1599), see *ODNB*.

54. 459/10r; 460/78v; see Stallybrass et al., "Hamlet's Tables," 401–2.

55. 459/31r.

56. 459/12v.

57. 459/68v–69r. Compare the major reorganization that goes on in August through October 1582, as Stonley decides to amalgamate several tailors' bills (73r, 75r) and servants wages (77r) into a single large record (78v–79r), with "square" braces, akin to those used in formal Exchequer accounts.

58. This section begins on 18 February 1581/2 (midway down 459/48r) and continues into the first few days of March 1581/2 (459/49v).

59. On the mediated nature of Pepys's diary and other life-writings from the period, see Smyth, *Autobiography*, 209–12.

60. 459/39v–99r.

61. 460/49v, 51r–v. A "pye" was "an alphabetical index to rolls and records"; *OED*, "pie, *n. 3*," sense 2. Conceivably such indexes were an archival twist on the church books known as "pies," or pie books (perhaps thanks to their pied, black-and-white appearance), that enabled their users to determine the dates of movable and immovable feasts.

62. For the early modern book as cognate with other textual receptacles, see Knight, "'Furnished' for Action," and Razzall, "Containers and Containment." For another analysis of Stonley's journals in terms of their textual compartments, see Stewart, "Materiality."

63. Stallybrass, "Ephemeral Matter"; Colenbrander, "The Sitter in Jan Gossaert's 'Portrait of a Merchant.'"

64. See, for example, 460/3r–22r.

65. Canfield, *Rule of Perfection*, C1r.

66. Chillingworth, *Religion of Protestants*, 2Y3r.

67. British Museum 912,0208.1; Gerbino and Johnston, *Compass and Rule*, 60–61; see also pp. 50–53 on the increasing sophistication of carpenters' rules in the period.

68. TNA, E159/412/435 (unpaginated).

69. On the glamour of the study and its writing implements in this period, see Thornton, *Scholar in His Study*.

70. See on 459/8v a payment of sixty shillings "To John Williamson Cloksmyth for the new Clocke at Duddingherst and settinge up the same with the old Cloke to Bote," of 33s. 4d. "To the same for a new Turnbroch set up at Estham [East Ham]," and of 2s. "To the same for one yeres wages keping the Turnebroche at London ending at mydsummer last" (this annual payment is repeated on fol. 88r). On 459/68v Stonley pays ten shillings "To the Cloksmyth in full of his Bargen made with Thomas Cook [and settinge up the newe] for the old Clokes turnbroches and settinge up the new at Duddingherst." 459/66v records a payment of 10s. "To the Clockman for a dyall," and 460/55v a payment of 12d. "for a Stringe to my gold watch."

71. Howell, *Londinopolis*, 2I3r (p. 369).

72. 459/10v, 21r; cf. 30r.

73. Sherman, *Telling Time*, 35.

74. I am grateful to Dunstan Roberts for compiling these figures.

CHAPTER 3

1. Shakespeare, *Cymbeline*, 2.2.12–13. Subsequent references are supplied parenthetically.

2. On "movables" and their significance in Shakespeare, see Maus, *Being and Having*, 43–44.

3. Stallybrass, "Value of Culture," 275–77.

4. Donne, *Sermons*, 8.

5. Anon., *Welch Mans Inventory*. The broadside seems to have been part of a spate of "Welch-mans" titles, including Anon., *The Welch-mans Life, Teath and Periall*.

6. For these titles, see Spufford, *Small Books*, 146, 227–29.

7. For "her" as an equivalent of "him" in representations of Welsh, see OED, "her, *pron.2* and *n.2*." sense 4.

8. Scott-Warren, *Sir John Harington*, 121–29.

9. Riello, "'Things Seen and Unseen,'" 131–32.

10. Orlin, "Fictions"; Riello, "'Things Seen and Unseen.'"

11. Will of John Allinson (1597), TNA PROB 11/90/239. For an inventory that was made by a testator and is clearly partial in its valuations, see the 1626 will of Henry Darrell, PROB 11/149/416.

12. Leedham-Green, *Books in Cambridge Inventories*; Clark, "Ownership of Books."

13. On the ubiquity of these kinds of difficulty, see Walsby, "Book Lists."

14. On the role of books in *Cymbeline*, with detailed attention to intertextuality and processes of "noting" in this scene, see Scott, *Shakespeare and the Book*, 42–56.

15. Howell, *Londinopolis*, 2F1v.

16. ERO, D/DFa 04, item 4 (Richard Stonley to William Paulet, Lord Treasurer, 3 March 1570).

17. LMA, CLA/008/EM/02/01/001/175v.

18. *HoP*, "Jones, Edward (d. *c.* 1609) of Gray's Inn, London."

19. *HMCS*, XIV 141.

20. Nashe, *Pierce Penilesse*, D4v.

21. 460/35v, 57r, 82v.

22. Erler, ed., *Records of Early English Drama*, xlii–xliii; 459/59r.

23. Baldwin, *Beware the Cat*, A5v–6v; Evenden and Freeman, *Religion and the Book*, 64–65, 128.

24. Smith, *Thomas East*, 52–53.

25. The inventory exists in two forms; a fair copy included as part of Stonley's indictment in an (unpaginated) Exchequer Memoranda Roll, TNA, E159/412/435, and an earlier draft that is part of a massive accumulation of materials relating to Stonley's property, TNA E178/2980. The lists are identical, save that the former omits one red leather standish (inkwell), worth 2s. 6d., in the gallery next to Stonley's bedchamber. My citations in this chapter are drawn from the fair copy.

26. LMA, Parish Register of St. Andrew Undershaft; will of William Phillip of London, TNA, PROB 11/17/101; will of Johane Philipp alias Philipps alias Phelipps, Widow of London, PROB 11/121/293.

27. Howard and Chester, eds., *Visitation of London,* I:161; see also the family letters in Norfolk Record Office, MC 254.

28. TNA, LR 9/131 (Francis Phelippes to Robert Phelippes at Southwalsham in Norfolk, 15 October 1596).

29. *ODNB*, "Phelippes, Thomas (*c.* 1556–1625x7), cryptographer and intelligence gatherer"; see Chapter 8 below.

30. TNA, PROB 11/77/101.

31. For an appraiser's eye-view of the process of inventorying, see Wrightson, *Ralph Tailor's Summer*, 112–30.

32. 460/20v, 61r; cf. 82r, 83v.

33. TNA, E178/2980.

34. Other books that have gone missing from Stonley's library include the collection that he gave to his godson Harry Browne; see 459/50r and Chapter 4 below.

35. *OED*, "mill," *n.* 2.

36. Holinshed, *Chronicles*, Ad4.1; Foxe, *Actes and Monumentes,* Ad4.29.

37. Musculus, *Common Places*, Ad4.42; Alley, *Ptochomuseion*, Ad4.41.

38. Schedel, *Liber chronicarum*, Ad4.61.

39. The first two-volume edition of this work, initiated in 1551, was Turner, *Herbal,* Ad4.40.

40. Ad4.76; Brant, *Shyppe of Fooles*, Ad4.39; Ad4.109; Heliodorus, *Aethiopian Historie,* Ad4.99; Painter, *Palace of Pleasure*, Ad4.96; Gascoigne, *Hundreth Sundrie Flowres*, Ad4.126; Gascoigne, *Posies*, Ad4.134.

41. Anon., *Le tresor des livres d'Amadis*, Ad4.165.

42. West, "An Architectural Typology," 449, lists the bedchamber-library as one of three key types found in the period. See also Hackel, *Reading Material*, 35–42; Cambers, *Godly Reading,* 54–71.

43. On the development of the gallery in the later sixteenth century, see Girouard, *Elizabethan Architecture*, 69–71.

44. Braun and Hogenburg, *Civitates orbis terrarum* (Cologne: T. Graminaeus, 1572–1618), Ad4.319; Saxton, *[Atlas,]* A4.320.

45. Tortorel and Perissin, *Tableaux*, Ad4.321; Benedict, *Graphic History*. The wording of the inventory corresponds to the epistle "Au lecteur" from the first, shorter version of the print series (Benedict, *Graphic History*, pp. 30–31).

46. See the discussion in Chapter 4.

47. Gesner, *Icones avium omnium*, Ad4.307.

48. Udall, *Floures for Latine Spekynge*, Ad4.357; Rainolde, *Foundacion of Rhetorike*, Ad4.349; Whittington, *De octo partibus orationis*, Ad4.366.

49. Boccaccio, *Thirtene Most Plesant and Delectable Questions*, Ad4.371; Hurtado de Mendoza, *Lazarillo de Tormes* (the running headline of this edition was "The Spaniardes life"), Ad4.372; De Rojas, *Celestine*, Ad4.369.

50. Anon., *Joyeuses adventures*, Ad4.373–74; Domenichi, *Facetie, motti, et burle*, Ad4.370. Harvey's 1571 Domenichi is now Folger Shakespeare Library, H.a.2.

51. Blague, *Schole of Wise Conceytes*, Ad4.368; Hulsbusch, *Sylva*, Ad4.354.

52. Holyband, *Arnalt & Lucenda*, Ad4.356.

53. Holyband, *French Littelton*, Ad4.346.

54. See 459/12r (3 August 1581): "for an Isops fables & master Nowelles Catachisme for Richard Stanton" (16d.), and 459/50r (5 March 1582), where Stonley gives books to his godson Harry Browne.

55. In 1562/3, Giles Godet entered a woodcut entitled "The Creation of the World" in the Stationers' Register; for commentary, see Watt, *Cheap Print*, 183–85.

56. The "Gostwike" in question was presumably a descendant of John Gostwick (by 1493–1545), of Willington, Bedfordshire, who became treasurer and receiver-general of first fruits and tenths under Henry VIII. Gostwick's son John (d. 1541) had married Sir William Petre's daughter Elizabeth. In 1562 Stonley acquired lands in Bedfordshire from the Gostwicks (Page, ed., *Victoria County History of Bedford*, III:209–14), and the first entry in Stonley's surviving journals is a payment "To Thomas Fysher for ridinge Charges to Master Gostwikes"; 459/3r.

57. The Old Testament images illustrate the refusal of Shadrach, Meshach, and Abednego to worship the golden idol of King Nebuchadnezzar, in Daniel 3, and the triumph of the Jews over a powerful adversary in Esther 6. For the popularity of this kind of image, see Hamling, *Decorating the Godly Household*, and esp. pp. 249–50 for the depiction of the fiery furnace from Daniel 3 in a plasterwork overmantel dating from 1603–25 at Stockton House in Wiltshire. For an illustrated Bible that may have supplied the source for the representation of Haman and Mordecai, see Wells-Cole, *Art and Decoration*, 250–51.

58. For the informality of the Elizabethan parlor, see Girouard, *Elizabethan Architecture*, 62, 68.

59. A payment in the journals "To Maior the Brickleyer for mending the halpas in my parler" (459/97r) may relate to this room (a halpas, or haut-pas, was a raised dais).

60. For the storage of books in studies, see Cambers, *Godly Reading*, 71–79.

61. Bull, *Christian Prayers*, Ad4.393; Hunnis, *Seven Sobs*, Ad4.397; Rogers, *A Golden Chaine*, A4.399.

62. Pennell, " 'Pots and Pans History.' "

63. *OED*, "jack," *n.* 1, II.7.

64. Wall, *Recipes for Thought*, 145–58 (p. 158).

65. Ibid., 151.

66. See Syson and Thornton, *Objects of Virtue*; and for moral inscriptions in the kitchen Morrall, "Inscriptional Wisdom."

67. Stonley also had "an olde picture of the late lord Treasurer" (William Paulet, first Marquess of Winchester, who had died in 1572) in his parlor.

68. Burke, "Representations of the Self," 26.

69. Foister, "Paintings," 275, comments that "frames are mentioned quite frequently in [inventories made in] the second half of the sixteenth century, but are rarely described in detail, so that it is difficult to know if picture frames proper or stretchers are meant." For the popularity of setting maps alongside paintings in a long gallery, see ibid., 277.

70. Cooper, "Enchantment of the Familiar Face," 173.

71. Jones, Print, 39–41 (see esp. p. 39 for the Stationers' Register entry of 1567/8 for "A Dyscription of vij principall vices with ye Devyces of the same").

72. On anti-Catholic satire, see Jones, Print, 133–59 (for friars, usually shown whipping nuns, pp. 146–55); Pierce, Unseemly Pictures, 35–67.

73. Girouard, Elizabethan Architecture, 71.

74. Boissard, Habitus variarum orbis gentium. On the appeal of lavishly illustrated books to members of the Elizabethan elite, see Evenden and Freeman, Religion and the Book, 221–26.

75. Jones, Print, ix; see also Foister, 277–78.

76. Rouillé, Promptuaire des medalles; Du Verdier, Prosopographie; see Chapter 6 below.

77. Du Verdier, Prosopographie, *4r.

78. Cebes, Table, Ad4.302. References to this text are supplied parenthetically. On Poyntz and the Table, see Brigden, Thomas Wyatt, 46–47, 248–50.

79. Gell, Art and Agency, 81–86.

80. Torrentinus et al., Elucidarius, Ad4.83, O2r.

81. Batman, Golden Booke, D1r–v.

82. On the (non)circulation of Venetian paintings in Elizabethan England, see Goldring, "A Portrait," 554, and the subsequent letter by Mark Evans (Burlington Magazine 154 [2012], 712), which notes that there is a copy of Titian's St. Mary Magdalene in Penitence in the 1590 Lumley inventory. Barron, "The Subject Pictures," 71–73, suggests that a painting of Ariosto by "Lucios" in Lumley's collection "may have derived from Ariosto's portrait by Titian, published in 1532 as a woodcut in the third edition of Orlando Furioso" (p. 73). I would contend that "Lucios" is a misreading, and that the entry (on fol. 40v) reads "The Picture of Lodovicus Orioustus the Poete done by tucioun the paynter /"—making this a second Elizabethan Titian.

83. Foister, "Paintings," 277, notes two inventories with images of Jerome, the first of Sir Ralph Waren (1554), the second of an unnamed merchant (1562). Both kept the images in their parlors.

84. Jardine, Erasmus, Man of Letters, 55–82.

85. On the material culture of writing and its depiction in portraiture, see Thornton, Scholar in His Study.

86. Tudor-Craig et al., "Old St Paul's," 18–26.

87. Foister, "Edward Alleyn's Collection"; Tudor-Craig et al., "Old St Paul's," 21.

88. Tudor-Craig et al., "Old St Paul's," 8–18, 26–31.

89. Ibid., 30.

90. Ibid., 18–19; Blayney, Stationers' Company, 656–57.

91. The earliest parish records to note the presence of the family in Shoreditch date from the early seventeenth century. A Jacob Gipkine of Hoxton was buried at St. Leonard's, Shoreditch, on 17 November 1603, and Judith Gipkyn, wife of John, was buried there on 9 July 1614. See the transcriptions of the parish registers published by Alan Nelson at http://socrates.berkeley.edu/~ahnelson/PARISH/Leonard.html.

92. *HMCS*, XVI:238. It is possible that the father was the "John Gibkin" who died in 1596 and was buried at St. Botolph, Bishopsgate (LMA, Parish Register of St. Botolph's).

93. Jones, *Print*, 27–32.

94. Wrightson, *Ralph Tailor's Summer*, 123.

95. TNA, E159/357/5. See further Roberts and Scott-Warren, "Armagil Waad."

96. Ago, *Gusto for Things*, 55–59.

97. Hutchins, *Davids Sling*, Ad4.293; Strigelius, *Harmony of King Davids Harp*, Ad4.244; Mexía, *Foreste*, Ad4.16; Batman, *Batman uppon Bartholome*, Ad4.6; Bilson, *Perpetual Governement*, Ad4.227; Bancroft, *Survay*, Ad4.8; Hooker, *Lawes*, Ad4.259.

98. The one occasion on which it might be possible to attempt a similar comparison for other kinds of objects relates to the entry on 459/24v (12 October 1581), when Stonley buys a number of items, including a "pere of Tables with a set of Table men" for six shillings and eight pence. The "set of Chessmen and a Chessboard with Foxe & geese" in Stonley's gallery was assessed at ten shillings. On early modern English book pricing, see McKitterick, " 'Ovid with a Littleton.' "

99. Anon., *Thordynary of Crysten Men*, Ad4.9.

100. Bible, *New Testamen* [*sic*], Ad4.52; Hardyng, *Chronicle*, Ad4.55.

101. Watson, *Twoo Notable Sermons*, Ad4.175; Standish, *Discourse*, Ad4.183.

102. Tyndale, *Exposicion*, Ad4.283; Cranmer, *Confutation*, Ad4.391.

103. Nowell, *A Catechisme*, 459/12r; De Chauliac, *Guidos Questions*, 459/65r.

104. Jeninges, *Discovery of the Damages*, 460/79r; Becon, *Governans of Vertue*, 460/73v.

105. Webster, *White Divel*, A2r; see further Saenger, *Commodification*, 68.

106. Lesser and Farmer, "Popularity of Playbooks Revisited," 14; Cummings, "Print, Popularity," 136. On the relationship between reading and news in the 1590s, see Scott-Warren, "News, Sociability and Bookbuying."

107. Maunsell, *The First Part of the Catalogue*, Ad4.212.

108. Ibid., π4r.

109. Ibid., π3r, π2r. The biblical reference is to Acts 19:19.

110. Razzall, "Containers," 3–20.

111. Meriton, *Nomenclatura clericalis*, Rıv–2. My thanks to Lucy Razzall for this reference.

112. Westminster Archives, Commissary Court of the Dean and Chapter of Westminster wills, Camden 27. See further Scott-Warren, "In Search of 850 Lost Books."

113. TNA, PROB 11/149/416. For Peele, see above, chapter 2.

114. Penny, "Toothpicks and Green Hangings," 589.

115. 459/27r.

116. 459/91v. *OED*'s first citation for "chest, *v.*" dates from 1616.

117. Clanchy, *From Memory to Written Record*, 162–64.

118. TNA, E192/3.

119. Scott-Warren, *Sir John Harington*, 104, 133; Pearson, "English Private Library," 385–86; Leong, " 'Herbals she peruseth,' " 563. For the use of fragrant and preservative plants in book chests, see Knight, *Of Books and Botany*, 9.

120. Cardano, *Cardanus Comforte*, Ad4.235, A3r.

121. Calfhill, *Aunswere*, Ad4.100, 2M2v. On phylacteries, see Kearney, *Incarnate Text*, 105–8.

122. MacLeod et al., *The Lost Prince*, 132–33.

123. Marnix, *Bee Hive*, D6r.

124. Kent Records Centre, Maidstone, U350 C2/34; Edward Dering to his wife at Surrenden Dering, 10 January 1632.

125. Knight, "'Furnished' for Action."

126. Donne, *John Donne*, 3.

127. On the transition from wood to pasteboard in this period, see Pearson, *English Bookbinding Styles*, 22–23; for the relationship between wood and clasps, ibid., 27. On the place of wood in the material culture and economy of early modern England, see Nardizzi, *Wooden Os*, 5–15.

128. In the category of *sylvae*, Stonley owned Cousin, *Sylva narrationum*, Ad4.294; Hulsbusch, *Sylua*, Ad4.354; and Mexía, *Foreste*, Ad4.16. For the dominance of compendious books in Roman inventories, see Ago, *Gusto for Things*, 191–93, 197–202. On Renaissance encyclopedism, see Kenny, *Palace of Secrets* and Rhodes, "Shakespeare's Encyclopaedias"; for the book as treasury, Carruthers, *Book of Memory*, 40–51, 323; Razzall, "Containers," 28–29.

129. Maslen, *Elizabethan Fictions*, 4.

130. Vicary, *Englishemans Treasure*, Ad4.245; Gesner, *Treasure of Evonymus*, Ad4.125; Gesner, *Newe Jewell of Health*, Ad4.95.

131. Cooper, *Thesaurus*, Ad4.192; Marlorat, *Totius diuinae ac canonicae Scripturae, thesaurus*, Ad4.45.

132. Blagrave, *Mathematical Jewel*, Ad4.258.

133. Batman, *A Christall Glasse of Christian Reformation*, Ad4.15; Whetstone, *Rocke of Regard*, Ad4.139; Painter, *Palace of Pleasure*, Ad4.96; Cogan, *Haven of Health*, Ad4.410.

134. Conway, *Meditations and Praiers* (running title: "The Posye of Flowred Prayers"), Ad4.196; Hunnis, *Seven Sobs*, Ad4.397; Fleming, *Diamond of Devotion*, 459/36r.

135. Gascoigne, *Hundreth Sundrie Flowres*, Ad4.126 (and see Ad4.134); Spenser, *Shepheardes Calender*, Ad4.60, 261. It is possible that the entries in Stonley's inventory relate to a book in the tradition of Anon., *Kalender of Shepherdes*, rather than to Spenser's poem.

136. Rabelais, *Complete Works*, 153–58.

137. Bowen, *Enter Rabelais, Laughing*, 95–100.

138. On this phenomenon, see also Saenger, *Commodification*, 40–41, 95–98.

139. Arnold, *Names of ye Baylifs Custos Mairs and Sherefs*; Benese, *Measurynge of all Maner of Lande*. On the development of the title page from manuscript incipits and colophons, see Smith, *The Title-Page*.

140. Grendler, *Critics*.

141. Ibid., 10–11.

142. Ibid., *Critics*, 11. See more recently Gjerpe, "The Italian *Utopia*," and for another polygraph writer/editor see Terpening, *Lodovico Dolce*.

143. Grendler, *Critics*, 12; cf. Nelson, "Utopia Through Italian Eyes."

144. On Munday, see Hamilton, *Anthony Munday*; Hill, *Anthony Munday*.

145. Munday, *Mirrour of Mutabilitie*; Munday, *Banquet of Daintie Conceits*; De Guevara, *Archontorologion*.

146. Fleming, *Panoplie of Epistles*; Fleming, *Diamond of Devotion*; Fleming, *Conduit of Comfort*; Fleming, *Foote-Path to Felicitie*.

147. See *ODNB*, "Norden, John (*c.* 1547–1625), cartographer," "Lloyd, Lodowick [Ludovic] (*fl.* 1573–1607), writer and courtier," "Phillips [Phillip], John (*d.* 1594x1617), author."

148. Grendler, *Critics*, 11.

149. Jayne and Johnson, eds., *Lumley Library*.

150. Loveman, *Samuel Pepys*, 42–47; Fehrenbach and Leedham-Green, eds., *Private Libraries*, 137–269.

151. My formulation is adapted from a modern account of the power of reading, Spufford, *Child That Books Built*.

CHAPTER 4

1. For a list of the surviving books (currently around two dozen, including all of the individual titles in *Sammelbände*), see the items labeled "[Reconstruction]" in the booklist in *Private Libraries in Renaissance England* (http://plre.folger.edu/books.php). See also Nelson, "Shakespeare and the Bibliophiles."

2. Donne's annotational style is most clearly displayed in his copy of Bodin, *De magorum dæmonomania*, Middle Temple Library, Bay L530.

3. Sherman, "Social Life of Books," 164–65.

4. For an exploration of books as tokens of value in late Henrician Oxford and London, see Lazarus, "Lucius Florus."

5. 459/43r, 46v.

6. 459/17r, 30r, 66v.

7. 459/24v, 5r.

8. 459/81r.

9. 459/60v, 7r.

10. Bible, *The. Holie. Bible,* Oxford, Trinity College, K.10.3.

11. Bible, *Psalmes of David and others,* Bodleian Library, Oxford, Broxb.29.2; Nixon, "Elizabethan Gold-Tooled Bindings," 256. On this binder, see further Foot, *Henry Davis Gift,* I:35–49.

12. Du Verdier, *Imagines deorum,* CUL, Rel. C.58.3.

13. Scott-Warren, "Ligatures."

14. Hosius, *Confessio,* St. Andrews University Library, TypNAn.B59SD. Stonley recorded the purchase price of two shillings on the title page. The book was assessed at sixpence in the 1597 inventory.

15. LMA, X019/015/147r.

16. Sutton, *Disce vivere*; Bodleian, Vet. A2.f.329, notes inside vellum front cover and two front flyleaf rectos.

17. Anon., *Preces privatae*; CUL, Pet. F.3.12; reproduced in Scott-Warren, "Reading Graffiti," 374.

18. Bodleian, Wood 54; Kiessling, *Library Catalogue of Anthony Wood,* cat. 4447.

19. St. John's College, Cambridge, Dd.17.5; Keynes, "More Books from the Library of John Donne."

20. Sandys, *A Relation of a Journey*; CUL, Syn.4.61.5; Scott-Warren, "Reading Graffiti," 379.

21. TNA, PROB 11/421/391.

22. Colynet, *True History,* Bodleian Library, Wood 475, G1r.

23. On the relationship between book annotation and the internalization of political and religious authority, see Saunders, "Marked Books," ch. 1.

24. Erasmus, *Paraphrases,* Pierpont Morgan E3 098 C. The second volume of the *Paraphrases* is listed in the 1597 inventory, but Stonley's ownership is noted only in the first volume (4G8v) of this copy.

25. Thucydides, *The Hystory,* Middle Temple Library, L(D), 2P3v.

26. *ODNB,* "Cawood, John (1513/14–1572), printer." Blayney, *Stationers' Company,* 753, 766, claims that there is no evidence of Cawood's printing and publishing before 1553, and expresses surprise at Cawood's appointment as Queen's Printer. But he himself cites a document from 1551 referring to "Caywood a printer dwelling at the signe of the holy goste" (p. 754), so it may be that Cawood's earliest editions have not survived.

27. LMA, Parish Register of St. Gregory by St. Paul's; TNA C1/1184/44–46; TNA, PROB 11/47/274 (will of William Hill).

28. Blayney, *Stationers' Company,* 1004.

29. Huntington Library, 60100 (this copy was bought by one Robart Beys). The price notation in Stonley's copy is on 2P4v.

30. *ODNB,* "Howlet [Huloet], Richard (*fl.* 1552), lexicographer." Huloet, *Abcedarium,* Houghton Library, Harvard, STC 13940, 2N4r.; Anglicus, *Promptorium puerorum,* Ad4.101.

31. Houghton Library, Harvard, STC 13940, 2N4v.

32. Blayney, *Stationers' Company,* 999–1001.

33. Huloet, *Abcedarium,* π2r; Binns, "STC Latin Books," 347.

34. 459/25r, 43r, 46v, 58r, 62v, 95r.

35. Guildhall Library, MS 5370; Steer, ed., *Scriveners' Company Common Paper.* I am grateful to Will Poole for suggesting this connection to me, and to Amy Bowles for sharing her photographs of the manuscript.

36. Heywood, *Woorkes,* Beinecke Library, Yale, If H51 a562. The copy was first noted by Cameron, "John Heywood and Richard Stonley."

37. Flynn, *John Donne,* 62.

38. TNA, SP 12/172, fol. 166 (27 August 1584). A line linking the names makes clear that "bothe thes" refers to Dawtrey and Bassett. William Dawtrey's servant William Hill was questioned on 31 August 1584, but "No matter [was] found in this man and therefore dismissed"; he was formerly the servant of "master Robert Worseley of lancashire"; TNA, SP 12/172, fol. 177. For an anthology of English recusant booklists, many of them resulting from raids, see Walsham and Havens, eds., "Catholic Libraries."

39. Pepys and Godman, *Church of St Dunstan, Stepney,* 31–32.

40. Manning, "Catholics and Local Office Holding," 56–57; Fisher, "Privy Council Coercion," 311, 318. Stonley might have associated with Margaret's father, William Roper, as a fellow governor of Lewisham School from 1574; see *Calendar of Patent Rolls: Elizabeth I 6 (1572–5),* 327.

41. On Heywood, More, and the More family see Johnson, *John Heywood,* 17–18, 23–24, 67–68; Flynn, *John Donne,* 25–35, 60–79.

42. TNA, PROB 11/54/149 (19 April 1572); *HoP,* "Bassett, James (c. 1526–58), of Umberleigh, Devon and London."

43. A "partlet" was "an item of clothing worn over the neck and upper part of the chest, esp. by women to cover a low décolletage" (*OED,* "partlet," *n.* 2).

44. BL, Lansdowne MS 75, fol. 142; see also MS 46, fols. 32, 34, 51, 55; MS 51, fols. 161, 163; MS 55, fol. 194; MS 58, fol. 68; MS 59, fol. 18; MS 72, fols. 160, 178, 205, 207; vol. 75, 109; vol. 78, fol. 60. For his legal wranglings see, e.g., TNA, C2/Eliz/W3/53, C2/Eliz/P9/25.

45. BL, Lansdowne MS 80, fol. 41.

46. TNA E192/3, part 3.

47. 459/94r.

48. For Verney, who married Margaret Greville, daughter of Sir Fulke Greville of Beauchamp's Court, Alcester, Warwickshire, see *HoP*, "Verney, Sir Richard (1564–1630), of Compton Verney, Warws."

49. For interactions between Stonley and the Grevilles, see 459/43v; 461/5v, 11r, and TNA E192/3, part 3.

50. SP 12/248, fol. 79.

51. SP 12/248, fol. 80. "Why do I use my paper, ink, and pen?" was a poem on Campion's martyrdom, part of which was set to music by William Byrd.

52. SP 12/248, fol. 81. The first book was probably the Jesus Psalter, a very popular recusant devotional work attributed to the Brigittine monk Richard Whitford; the second, a poem by Robert Southwell, first printed in 1595. For Bolt, who ended his life as chaplain to the Augustinian canonesses of Louvain, see Edwards, *John Petre*, 24, 30–31, 73; Harley, *William Byrd*, 97–98, 141.

53. Warwickshire Record Office, CR 1908/73/3. Edward Fisher was the heir of Thomas Fisher, who before his death in 1577 had united the manors of Itchington and Tachbrook under the name "Fisher's Itchington"; Salzman, ed., *Victoria History*, VI:121.

54. Here I am identifying an entry for "The Lyves of Adam and others" as Jacopo de Voragine, *The Lyfe of Adam* (London: Julyan Notarye, 1504), an English edition of the *Golden Legend*; PLRE (Ad4.309) currently leaves this title unidentified. Anon., *Thordynary of Crysten Men*, Ad4.9; More, *Baravelli opus elegans*, Ad4.25.

55. Watson, *Twoo Notable Sermons*, Ad4.175; Peryn, *Spirituall Exercyses*, Ad4.304; Wizeman, "Marian Counter-Reformation in Print," 162.

56. Standish, *Discourse*, Ad4.183; Allen, *Apologie*, Ad4.199.

57. Church of England, *Articles*, Ad4.285; Doré, *L'Image de vertu*, Ad4.299.

58. Canisius, *Authoritatum sacrae scripturae*, Ad4.54; De Sainctes, *Liturgiae*, Ad4.81.

59. See Walsham and Havens, "Catholic Libraries," 248, for evidence that ownership inscriptions and details of provenance could form part of the evidence against the owners of Catholic books.

60. Bible, *Newe Testamen* [*sic*], Ad4.52. For the Bishops' Bible, see above, pp. 116-17. Stonley also owned two French testaments (Ad4.104, 210) and "An olde Frenche bible" (Ad4.377).

61. Cranmer, *Confutation*, Ad4.391.

62. Crowley, *Setting Open*, Ad4.133; cf. the copy of T.C., *A Spirituall Purgation*, Ad4.184; but note also Ad4.148, which PLRE identifies tentatively as de Valsergues, *Les six livres du sacrement de l'autel*.

63. Among these, besides Foxe's "Book of Martyrs," we find Foxe, ed., *Whole Workes*, Ad4.46; Calvin, *Commentaries*, Ad4.223; Luther, *An Exposition of Salomons Booke, called Ecclesiastes*, Ad4.280.

64. For anti-Catholicism, see Kirchmeyer, *Popish Kingdome*, Ad4.141; Batman, *Christall Glasse of Christian Reformation*, Ad4.15. Among the establishment apologetics are Jewel, *Defence*, Ad4.153 (cf. Ad4.43); Bridges, *Defence*, Ad4.7; Rogers, *English Creede*, Ad4.260; Hooker, *Lawes*, Ad4.259.

65. 459/55r.; Nowell, *Confutation*, Ad4.98, Ad4.143.

66. These include Bilson, *Perpetual Governement*, Ad4.227; Sutcliffe, *Answere*, Ad4.229; Whitgift, *Defense*, Ad4.50; Bancroft, *Survay*, Ad.4.8.

67. 460/43r, 53v; Daniel Donne's copy of this book is Folger Shakespeare Library, STC 1352 copy 3.

68. Wiburn, *Checke or Reproofe*, Ad4.231; Bunny, *Truth and Falshood*, Ad4.226.

69. Green, *Print and Protestantism*, 305–11; Milton, "Qualified Intolerance"; Walsham, "The Spider and the Bee." For Protestant books in the collection of a devout French Catholic who was Stonley's close contemporary, see Walsby, "Library," 132–33.

70. Felicity Heal, in her *ODNB* article on Stonley, notes a letter sent to him by a recusant named Francis Blount (BL, Add MS 81277, item J). Writing from Deptford on 26 January 1594, Blount complains that he cannot "procure meat to putte in my mothe soche is my discredite throw the means of that poorsiuantes vissitation of me." For a possible identification, see *HoP*, "Blount, Francis (*b.* c. 1535), of Broke, Wilts." See also 460/19r., which shows a Francis Blount dining at Doddinghurst on two successive days in July 1593.

71. Green, *Print and Protestantism*, 305–8; Ryrie, *Being Protestant*, 287–88. Stonley's inventory (Ad4.182) lists à Kempis as "A Tretise of the followinge of Christe," and *PLRE* comments that "the translation cannot be determined." The word "imitation" comes to dominate in later versions of the title, however, and the word "Treatise" is present only in editions of the translation by William Atkinson, printed between 1504 and 1528 (STC 23954.7 et seq.), so Stonley's may well have been an early edition.

72. Parsons, *Christian Exercise*. Editions of Bunny's version appeared from 1584. Green, *Print and Protestantism*, 309; Ryrie, *Being Protestant*, 290–92.

73. De Estella, *Methode unto Mortification*, A4r., Ad4.290.

74. Among the prayer books are Conway, *Meditations and Praiers*, Ad4.196; Augustine, *Certaine Select Prayers*, Ad4.197; "The golden booke of prayers" (unidentified), Ad4.203; and two copies of Fisher, *Psalmi*, Ad4.305 and Ad4.394.

75. 459/12v, 25r, 60r; Whitaker, *Ad rationes decem*; Anon., *Particular Declaration*. For other references to Campion, see 459/10v, 30v, 31r–v, 33v.

76. 459/33v. Kilroy, *Edmund Campion*, 336, notes that Stonley "records encountering the procession in Cheapside, as if by chance," but adds that the profusion of his diary entries about Campion and his confederates "make chance the least likely explanation."

77. 459/50v.

78. See further Kilroy, *Edmund Campion*, 343–44. For the use of the word "almesfolke" as a synonym for "Catholics," see Flynn, *John Donne*, 60.

79. This count assumes that Stonley was buying his books close to their time of publication, an assumption which (as suggested earlier) is broadly borne out by the surviving journals, but which cannot be relied upon.

80. Buchanan, *Rerum Scoticarum historia*, St. Andrews University Library, Buch DA775.B8B83.

81. 460/43r, 53v.

82. 459/43r, 95v; 460/43r.

83. 459/50r; see further the will of Roger Browne, TNA PROB 11/100/293.

84. 459/12r. Richard Stanton may have been a descendant of the Richard Stanton, gentleman, of West Ham, who died in 1564; TNA, PROB 11/47/362. Stonley also had a John Stanton among his servants in the early 1580s. 459/52r, 75r, 95v.

85. 459/9r, 11r; see also 95v.

86. Ferrarius, *Good Orderynge*, Ad4.420, St. Andrews University Library, TypBl.B59KF, 2R3v–4r.

87. Ad4.177, 190.

88. Aesop, *Fabulous Tales*, ¶2r. On Smith's printing career see Thomas, "Foreign to the Company."

89. Johnson, "The Stationers Versus the Drapers."

90. Aesop, *Fabulous Tales*, ¶3r.

91. On Aesop's importance to early modern print culture, see Lerer, *Children's Literature*, 51–56.

92. Blayney, *Stationers' Company*, 198–99.

93. Plomer, *Robert Wyer*, 11.

94. Laroche, *Medical Authority*.

95. Elyot, *Castell of Helth*, Glasgow University Library, Hunterian Au.4.11(a).

96. Moulton, *Glasse of Helth*, GUL Au.4.11(b), I4r.

97. Ibid., A1r, D3v.

98. Plutarch, *Governau[n]ce of Good Helthe*, GUL Au.4.11(d).

99. Da Vigo, *Lytell Practyce*, GUL Au.4.11(i), A8r–v.

100. Bacon, *All of the Beste Waters Artyfycialles*, GUL Au.4.11(k), A2r.

101. Avicenna, *Prognosticacion*, GUL Au.4.11(e).

102. Hippocrates, *Boke of Knowledge*, GUL Au.4.11(g), A2r., A4r.

103. Aristotle, *Nature, and Dysposycyon* [*sic*], Au.4.11(j), B3r.

104. Askham, *Litell Treatyse*, GUL Au.4.11(h); *ODNB*, "Askham [Ascham], Anthony (c. 1517–1559), writer on astronomy and almanac maker."

105. Askham, *Litell Treatyse*, A6v.

106. Proclus, *Descripcion of the Sphere*, Au.4.11(c), A3v.

107. Cressy, *Literacy and the Social Order*.

108. Elyot, *Castel of Helth*, C3r.–4r.

109. 461/25v.

110. See, for example, Philip Benedict's verdict on the politics of Tortorel and Perrissin's graphic history of the French Wars of Religion (also in Stonley's collection, Ad4.32I): "The work's Protestant origin may be discerned, but the *Wars, Massacres and Troubles* was ultimately less tendentious than virtually any other Protestant history of this period" (*Graphic History*, 167). Compare also the religious diversity of Holinshed, *Chronicles*, Ad4.1, as explored by Kewes, Archer, and Heal, eds., *Oxford Handbook of Holinshed's Chronicles*.

CHAPTER 5

1. Bacon, *Advancement of Learning*, M1v–2r.

2. 459/16r, 28v.

3. 459/47v; *ODNB*, "Palavicino, Sir Horatio (c. 1540–1600), merchant and diplomat."

4. TNA, SP 15/12, fol. 26; *ODNB*, "Anes, Dunstan [*formerly* Gonsalvo Anes; *alias* Gonzalo Jorge] (c. 1520–1594), merchant."

5. Kirk and Kirk, eds., *Returns of Aliens*, III:359. The will of Dominic Buscier, proved in 1591, is TNA, PROB 11/85/151.

6. TNA, SP 70/30, fol. 21.

7. TNA, SP 70/42, fol. 183.

8. TNA, SP 70/47, fol. 78.

9. TNA, PROB 11/57.

10. Morgan and Coote, eds., *Early Voyages*, II:202–3.

11. Ibid., II:215.

12. TNA, C78/80/1.

13. Morgan and Coote, eds., *Early Voyages*, II:275; Willan, *Early History*, 92.

14. Dmitrieva and Murdoch, *Treasures of the Royal Courts*, 14–15.

15. Willan, *Early History*, 128.

16. On Glover see ibid., esp. pp. 96–97.

17. Morgan and Coote, eds., *Early Voyages*, II:337.

18. Ibid., II:337; Willan, *Early History*, 130–31.

19. TNA, C78/80/1.

20. Hakluyt, *Principall Navigations*, 2V4v–5r.

21. Ibid., 2V5r.

22. Ibid., 2Y5v–6r. On the geopolitical significance of English Old World exploration in this period, see MacLean, "East by North-East."

23. Latour, "Visualisation and Cognition." See also Vitkus, "Indicating Commodities."

24. Braun and Hogenburg, *Civitates orbis terrarum*.

25. TNA, C78/80/1.

26. Morgan and Coote, eds., *Early Voyages*, II:206.

27. Fletcher, *Russe Common Wealth*, Ad4.273. References to this text will be supplied parenthetically.

28. For an extended analysis of Fletcher's account, see Stout, *Exploring Russia*, 117–88.

29. See further ibid., 147–88.

30. On Fletcher's involvement in the torture of seminary priests, ibid., 68.

31. On this battle over styles, see ibid., 25; and on Anglo-Russian diplomatic protocol in the period, see Dmitrieva and Murdoch, eds., *Treasures of the Royal Courts*, 13–29.

32. Quoted in Willan, *Early History*, 116–17. On the clash between Elizabethan mercantile and Russian political imperatives, see Stout, *Exploring Russia*, 24–31, 78–80.

33. Ibid., 193.

34. Ibid., 189–98; Cambridge, Trinity College, VI 7 50, A1r.

35. De Crenne, *Torments*, 91; De Crenne, *Angoysses*, 257: "souffroit La Neptunus naviguer ses undes salées."

36. *Torments*, 128, 142; *Angoysses*, 336: "un tres belle cité, qui lors estois nommée Eliveba"; 369: "homme si anticque, debile et cassé."

37. *Torments*, 145; *Angoysses*, 375: "gens pervers et inicques, lesquelz ne vouloyent obeyr ne avoir de superieur."

38. *Torments*, 144; *Angoysses*, 374: "accompaigné du desir, qui continuellement me stimuloit."

39. *Torments*, 186; *Angoysses*, 471: "la clemence divine a esté de nous piteuse, puis qu'elle n'a voulu permettre, que le peché d'adultaire eust esté par nous commis."

40. De Crenne, *Les oeuvres*. On the circulation of the work in sixteenth-century France, see Wood, *Hélisenne de Crenne*, 27–49.

41. De Crenne, *Torments*, 8; De Crenne, *Angoysses*, 99: "il m'estoit si tres aggreable."

42. *Torments*, 10; *Angoysses*, 103: "moymesmes miserablement, je fuz prise."

43. *Torments*, 24; *Angoysses*, 128–29: "l'impetuosité d'Amours avoit rompu en moy les laqz de temperance et moderation, qui me faisoit exceder toute audace fœminine . . . j'estoye toute embrasée du feu Venerien."

44. *Torments*, 30; *Angoysses*, 139: "me donna si grand coup qu'au cheoir je me rompiz deux dentz, dont de l'extreme douleur, je fuz longue espace sans monstrer signe d'esperit vital."

45. *Torments*, 51; *Angoysses*, 179: "j'useroys de cruelle vindication en luy faisant tres griefz et innumerables tourmens: puis apres que mon appetit seroyt rassasié de le travailler, je te feroye

present de son corps tout desrompu et laceré: et à l'heure t'enfermeroys en une tour, ou par force et contraincte je te feroye coucher avecq luy."

46. *Torments*, 69; *Angoysses*, 213: "Helisenne fut enclose en une tour et eut en sa compaignie seulement deux damoyselles."

47. Boccaccio, *Elegy of Lady Fiametta*, xvii–xxii; Wood, *Hélisenne de Crenne*, 26.

48. De Crenne, *Torments*, 34; De Crenne, *Angoysses*, 146: "parquoy ne me semble que flye de le divulguer à ce vieillart, qui est du tout refroidy, impotent, et inutile aux effectz de nature, il me reprimera, et blasmera ce que aultresfois luy a esté plaisant. . . . Il ne me peult contraindre d'user de son conseil, et si prendray plaisir à parler de celluy que j'ayme plus ardemment, que jamais amoureux fut aymé de sa dame."

49. *Torments*, 36; *Angoysses*, 151: "je croy qu'elle ne scauroit estre en lieux si penibles que en mon miserable corps. . . . Et moy paovre malheureuse qui suis tourmentée en corps et ame de la flamme d'amours."

50. *Torments*, 7; *Angoysses*, 96–97: "L'epistre dedicative de Dame Helisenne à toutes honnestes dames, leur donnant humble salut. Et les enhorte par icelle à bien et honnestement aymer, en evitant toute vaine et impudicque amour"; "vous pourrez eviter les dangereulx laqs d'amours."

51. *Torments*, 157; *Angoysses*, 397, "Composées par Dame Helisenne. . . . Comprenant la mort de ladicte Dame"; https://en.wikipedia.org/wiki/Category:Fiction_narrated_by_a_dead_person.

52. See Bromilow, "Fictions of Authority," 139–44.

53. On the geography of the *Angoysses*, see Wood, *Hélisenne de Crenne*, 60–61.

54. De Crenne, *Torments*, 194; De Crenne, *Angoysses*, 489: "il apperceut aupres du corps d'Helisenne ung petit pacquet couvert de soye blanche, lequel en grand promptitude il leva . . . laquelle singulierement aux lectures se delectoit."

55. *Torments*, 198–99; *Angoysses*, 501–3: "estant fort curieuse de veoir choses nouvelles," "affin de manifester au monde les peines, travaulx, et angoysses douloureuses, qui procedent à la occasion d'amours." Neal and Rendall, *Torments*, 199, note that Jupiter effectively christens the book with this command.

56. De Crenne, *Torments*, 199; De Crenne, *Angoysses*, 503: "Jupiter feist response, que pour ce faire n'y avoit lieu plus convenable que la tres inclite et populeuse cité de Paris."

57. *Torments*, 199; *Angoysses*, 503–4: "je vous supplye de vous enquerir aux nobles Orateurs, poetes et hystoriographes, s'il n'y a rien de nouvellement composé."

58. Webster, *White Divel*, A2r.

59. De Crenne, *Torments*, 8; De Crenne, *Angoysses*, 100: "j'estoye de forme elegante, et de tout si bien proportionée, que j'excedoye toutes aultres femmes en beaulté de visage, je m'eusse hardiment osé nommer des plus belles de France."

60. Pérez Fernández, "Translation, *Sermo Communis*, and the Book Trade."

61. "Traicte des deceptions de servitures envers leur Maisters," Ad4.369, referring to a French edition entitled *Le Celestine, en laquelle est traicte des deceptions des serviteurs envers leurs maistres* (USTC reports editions with this title between 1527 and 1542); "The Spaniards liefe," Ad4.372, referring to Rowland, trans., *Pleasaunt Historie*; the running title of this book is "The Spaniardes life"; the first, lost edition appeared in 1576. On the circulation of the *Celestina* in England, see Mabbe, *Spanish Bawd*, 44–66.

62. De Rojas, *Celestina: A Novel in Dialogue*, 17; De Rojas, *Celestina: A Critical Edition*, 39: "lingiere, perfumiere, maistresse de faire le fard, et de refaire pucellages, macquerelle et ung peu sorciere."

63. Rowland, trans., *Pleasaunt Historie*, A2r–v. For Rowland see Rowland, trans., *Life of Lazarillo*, 30–32; *ODNB*, "Rowland, David (*fl.* 1568–1576), author and translator."

64. On the significance of international currents of bookselling and translation in early modern Europe, see Coldiron, *Printers Without Borders*.

65. For a forceful statement of this argument, see Boutcher, "Beyond English."

CHAPTER 6

1. 460/82v.

2. 460/75v.

3. Corporation of London Archives, DL/C/213/394. The individual depositions are unnumbered.

4. Katherine was one of the deponents in the case; she called Grace "a verye malicious and uncharitable person," "an unquiet woman," "especially noted for her evell tongue."

5. On the relationship between Communion and community relations, see Bossy, *Peace in the Post-Reformation*.

6. Hyde was a neighbor in Abchurch parish; LMA, Parish Register of St. Mary Abchurch, lists his marriage to Margarett Griffen on 11 May 1573.

7. The will of Anthony Crane, proved 20 December 1585, bequeaths "my gret signet ring" to "Mother Davys on the banckside" (TNA, PROB 11/68/710).

8. 459/34v.

9. TNA, PROB 11/120/96.

10. TNA, PROB 11/49/114.

11. ERO, D/DP A6, entry for 18 September 1555.

12. Panek, "Why Did Widows Remarry?"

13. TNA, PROB 11/72/725.

14. For a violent altercation in 1576 between John Branche and Sir Thomas Lodge, father of the author, see Sisson, *Thomas Lodge*, 36.

15. TNA, PROB 11/83/291.

16. S.P., *An Epitaph*, A3r.

17. Ibid., A3v.

18. *ODNB*, "Phillips [Phillip], John (*d.* 1594x1617), author."

19. Phillips, *Commemoration*, A2r.

20. Ibid., A2r.

21. Ibid., A3r.

22. Ibid., A4v.

23. Chambers, *William Shakespeare*, II: 190–91. Chambers notes (ibid., II: 190) that a William Harvey was a juror on the inquisition post mortem for Sir John Branche but judges that "this is probably a coincidence."

24. Hervey, *Epicedium*, A2r. On the date of composition of *Cornelia*, see Erne, *Beyond The Spanish Tragedy*, 211.

25. Arber II:644, 648. None of the elegies appears to have been entered in the register. The *Epicedium* and its putative author are discussed in Scoufos, "Harvey."

26. Hervey, *Epicedium*, A2r.

27. Ibid., A3r.

28. Ibid., A3v–4r.

29. *ODNB*, "Sylvester, Josuah (1562/3–1618), poet and translator."

30. Sylvester, *Monodia*, A2r.

31. Ibid., A3v.

32. Ibid., A4v.

33. Ibid., A4r.

34. Huntington Library ## 81089–81090; British Library C.40.e.67; TNA, PROB 11/ 83/291.

35. Phillips, *Commemoration* (Huntington Library # 81089), A2v–3r.

36. Corns, "Early Modern Search Engine."

37. Hervey, *Epicedium*, A3v, A4v.

38. Fleming, "Renaissance Collage," 453–54.

39. IGI (accessed via http://www.familysearch.org). The fullest account of Nicolson to date is Williams, "Minor Maecenas."

40. The date of the marriage is established by Williams, "Bear Facts," 92. For earlier generations of this substantial family, see *HoP*, "Caryll (Carrell), John (c. 1505–66), of Warnham, Suss."

41. TNA, PROB 11/95/103.

42. Norden, *Pensive Mans Practise*, A2r, A3r.

43. See, for example, Sylvester, trans., *Bartas*, B7r; Williams, "Minor Maecenas," 11.

44. Sylvester's poem was entered in the Stationers' Register on 25 May 1594; Arber II:650.

45. Sylvester, trans., *Du Bartas* (1633), 3K2v–3r (epistle IX).

46. Sylvester, trans., *Du Bartas* (1621), 3H5r.

47. For the epithalamium see Sylvester, *Wood-mans Bear*, C5r-7r., and for commentary Williams, "Bear Facts." The device and the canzone are in Sylvester, trans., *Du Bartas* (1633), 3K3r–4v. Williams, "Minor Maecenas," 13, identifies Martha's brother Simon Carrell of the Inner Temple as the author of another of the prefatory verses in the 1605 *Devine Weekes*.

48. For the castle, see Sylvester, *Du Bartas* (1633), 2Q6r; for the spectacles, 3F4v–6v.

49. Ahl, "Ars est caelare artem," 27.

50. Sylvester, *Bartas*, 2A8v–2B1r, B6r.

51. Sylvester, *Du Bartas* (1633), 3H4v–5r.

52. Mynors's will left £10 to St. Bartholomew's and £20 to St. Thomas's; £30 for the release of poor debtors imprisoned in the city; £20 for the "poorest of the schollers" in the two universities; and two shillings each to the hundred poorest freemen of the Drapers' Company.

53. S.P., *Epitaph*, A3v.

54. Phillips, *Commemoration*, A3v–4r.

55. Sylvester, *Monodia*, A4v.

56. The inscriptions on Dame Helen's funeral monument, together with an itemization of her charitable provisions, made their way into Anthony Munday's revised edition of John Stow's *Survey of London* (London: Nicholas Bourn, 1633), X4r–v.

57. Phillips, *Commemoration*, A4r.

58. TNA, PROB 11/84/123. Buckle also bequeathed "forty shillinges and a Cloke" to George Nicolson, presumably Robert's brother. Helen Branche had left Buckle "one white silver playghted cupp which was Master doctor Cromers," hoping he would forward the execution of her will.

59. Du Verdier, *Prosopographie*, Fitzwilliam Museum, Cambridge (no shelf mark); Rouillé, *Promptuaire des medalles*, Oxford, Merton College, 17.A.9. The latter bears the signature of "Franchois Carpreau, 1586," possibly the Francis Carpreau named in the will of his brother

John Carpreau (apparently a native of Flanders or Brabant), proved in 1586; TNA, PROB 11/69/163. On the development of portrait collections based on ancient coins and medals, see Mortimer, "The Author's Image," 36–37.

60. Anon., *Danse macabre*, British Library IA 40884. Some sections of the printed text of the *Danse* are missing and have been supplied in manuscript by a previous owner (or conceivably by a bookseller). Mela, *De totius orbis descriptione*, John Carter Brown Library, A507.M517P (and see Anon., "The John Carter Brown Library," *Times Literary Supplement*, 1921, 720). Nanni, *Berosus Babilonicus*, Princeton University Library, shelf mark 2613.1510. A copy of Curtius Rufus, *De gestis Alexandri Magni*, signed by Nicolson in 1591, was sold at Sotheby's, *Catalogue of Valuable Printed Books from the Broxbourne Library* (second portion, 8–9 May 1978).

61. Bible, *The. Holie. Bible.*, Chetham's Library, Manchester, A.7.18. Bible, *Gospels of the Fower Evangelistes*; ODNB, sub "Parker, Matthew (1504–1575)." The *Gospels*, inscribed by Nicolson in 1591, were sold by Sokol books in 2010.

62. Higden, *Polycronycon.* The volume is referred to in Ames et al., *Typographical Antiquities*, III:41; Stewart, *A Catalogue*, 223; *The Library of the Late Sir John Arthur Brooke, Bt.* (Sotheby's, 1921), lot 775; *Times Literary Supplement*, 1921, 734; Ellis's *Catalogue of Rare Books* 216 (1923), lot 138; Quaritch Catalogue 641 (1946), lot 433, and Catalogue 676 (1950), lot 216. The map was removed and acquired by the British Library in 1928; it is now Maps C.2.cc.3 and is dated to 1610 (Heawood, *English County Maps*, 10). I am grateful to Dunstan Roberts for these references.

63. Braun and Hogenburg, *Civitates orbis terrarum* (Cologne: Gottfried von Kempen, 1581–82); New York Public Library, *KB + 1581. De Nicolay, *Navigations*; Huntington Library, 15396 (copy viewable on *EEBO*); Hakluyt, *Principall Navigations*; New York Public Library, I(Q70), with "Ex Roberti Nicolsoni Londinensis Libris. 1590. 9/2.o." on the title page.

64. Wirsung, *Praxis medicinae universalis*; Folger Shakespeare Library STC 25863, cs1292.

65. Sherman, *John Dee*, ch. 4.

66. Hakluyt, *Principall Navigations*, B5r.

67. Nicolay, *Navigations*, B8v.

68. Ibid., X7v.

69. Ibid., H8r.

70. Hakluyt, *Principall Navigations*, New York Public Library, I(Q70), 2P4v. I am grateful to Matthew Day for sharing with me his initial transcriptions of the marginalia in this volume.

71. Ibid., H5r.

72. Ibid., *4r, 2E6v; for comparable annotations see 2O3r, 3B2v, 3F3v, 3G6r, 3P2r.

73. Ibid., 2Q4v.

74. Ibid., 2E6v.

75. Willan, *Muscovy Merchants*, 28.

76. Stallybrass and Lesser, "First Literary *Hamlet*."

77. Sherman, *John Dee*, 50.

78. *OED*, "blazon, *v.*," 1, 6a.

79. Hamling, "'Wanting Arms.'"

80. Braun and Hogenburg, *Civitates orbis terrarum*, New York Public Library, *KB + 1581, 3/23.

81. Wirsung, *Praxis medicinae universalis*, 2D2v (p. 420).

82. Ibid., 2S1v (p. 642), 2Q5v (p. 618).

83. Aelianus, *Registre of Hystories*, University of Illinois, IUA00084.

84. Anon., *Dialogue betwene a Knyght and a Clerke*; Houghton Library, Harvard, STC 12511; bound with Anon., *Disputatio inter clericum et militem*; Hougton Library, Harvard, STC 12510. The Houghton catalogue entry explains that the English edition represented here is not a perfect fit with either STC 12511 or STC 12511a.

85. Warner, *Henry VIII's Divorce*, 36.

86. Lloyd, *Diall*; Bodleian 4° Rawl. 140 (1). My references are to the signatures of the printed work and the pagination of the interleaved manuscript sections, as appropriate. The copy is bound with another work by Lloyd, *Triplicitie*.

87. Beuther, *Ephemeris historica*. For the Montaigne family copy (CUL Montaigne 1.7.6), annotated from the sixteenth to the eighteenth century, see Marchand, ed., *Livre de raison*; compare the Lambarde family copy, annotated from the sixteenth to the twentieth century, Drapers' Hall, London, H./Add.14.

88. Lloyd, *Diall*; Bodleian 4° Rawl. 140 (1), 199.

89. Ibid., B1r.

90. Ibid., 40.m.; 198.g., 205; 40.t., 140.y., 140.a.a.

91. Zins, *England and the Baltic*, 67.

92. Baumann, *Merchant Adventurers*, 13–15. For the travels of Nicolson's uncle Henry Parvish to the Frankfurt fair in the 1570s, see ibid., 172.

93. These travels are recalled in Sylvester, *Wood-mans Bear*.

94. Lloyd, *Diall*; Bodleian 4° Rawl. 140 (1), 164–65, 171.

95. Ibid., Q3r, 207.

96. Ibid., 166.h.

97. Ibid., 369.

98. Ibid., 140.e.

99. Ibid., 40.f., 140.o.

100. See further Stallybrass and Farrell, "Book-Tree-Leaf-Body."

101. Price, *How to Do Things*, 45–71.

CHAPTER 7

1. Ashbee and Lasocki, eds., *Biographical Dictionary*, II:722.

2. Lawson, ed., *Elizabethan New Year's Gift Exchanges*, 43–44.

3. Ibid., 256, 278, 337.

4. TNA, STAC 5/L7/7; cf. STAC 5/L7/1.

5. Walker, *Manifest Detection*.

6. *HoP*, "Lichfield, Thomas (d. 1586)."

7. Ashbee and Lasocki, *Biographical Dictionary*, 723; *HMCS*, I:576.

8. *HoP*, "Browne, Sir Valentine (d. 1589)"; TNA, SP 59/19, fol. 40; *Calendar of State Papers, Foreign*, XI:175.

9. Elton, "Elizabethan Exchequer," 355.

10. TNA, E407/71/96; Elton, "Elizabethan Exchequer," 371.

11. BL, Lansdowne MS 28, fol. 2; MS 35, fols. 10, 30, 73, and fol. 23 for Fuller (mentioned in Stonley's accounts at 459/82r. and 94r). For Lichfield's response to the auditors, see Lansdowne MS 35, fol. 32.

12. TNA, SP 59/93, fol. 83.

13. TNA, SP 59/2, fol. 205.

14. TNA, C66/1116, m.37. For the various statutes relating to the debts of tellers to the Queen, see England and Wales, *Statutes*, II:2P4r–6r (pp. 451–55).

15. 459/12r.

16. TNA, E192/3, part 3.

17. TNA, E407/71/48.

18. BL, Lansdowne MS 40, fol. 86.

19. BL, Lansdowne MS 44, fol. 16v; MS 46, fol. 38r; MS 47, fols. 134, 139. See also *ODNB*, "Patten, William (d. in or after 1598), author"; Elton, "Elizabethan Exchequer," 375–76.

20. BL, Lansdowne MS 44, fol. 17v.

21. BL, Lansdowne MS 19, fol. 114r.

22. Ibid., fol. 115v.

23. Ibid.

24. Ibid.

25. TNA, SP 46/34, fol. 40r.

26. *HMCS*, III 310.

27. *HMCS*, XXIII:4; *HMCS*, III:377.

28. *HMCS*, IV:401.

29. Neal and Leighton, eds., *Calendar*, 111.

30. E407/71/88; SP 46/40, fols. 192, 192d; Smith, ed., *Calendar*.

31. 459/10r.

32. Tigurinus, *L'histoire*; Doukas, "Pierre Boaistuau," 75. Doukas's discussion of the *Histoire* (pp. 195–227) represents the first critical treatment of the text.

33. Tigurinus, *Most Excellent Hystorie*, A3v. Subsequent references to this work will be supplied parenthetically.

34. On this subject, see Burke, "Fables of the Bees."

35. Wood, "Identity and Gender," 185–87, finds a thinly veiled "cheekiness" in the dedication.

36. Garrett, *Marian Exiles*, 119–20.

37. On the Dudley conspiracy, see *ODNB*, "Sutton [Dudley], Henry (d. 1564?), conspirator," and Loades, *Two Tudor Conspiracies*, 151–75.

38. Adams, " 'The service I am Here for' "; see also Adams, "A Spy on the Payroll?" For an analysis of the intelligence roles that Herle played as revealed in his letters relating to Chillester, see Adams, " 'Both Diligent and Secret,' " 198–201.

39. A letter sent from Thomas Waye, Keeper of the Marshalsea, to William Cecil states that Chillester was imprisoned at Cecil's commandment, describing him as "a very power man" who "dothe morne very pytyusly"; TNA, SP 52/22, fol. 53.

40. The letters, respectively BL, MS Lansdowne 13, fols. 162r–164v (19 March 1571/2) and TNA, SP 12/86/1, fols. 2r–6v (1 April 1572), have been edited as part of the "Letters of William Herle" edition, produced by the Centre for Editing Lives and Letters (http://www.livesandletters.ac.uk/herle/index.html).

41. *ODNB*, "Philip [Philip II of Spain, Felipe II] (1527–1598)."

42. It is possible that Harrison lived and continued to ply his trade in Ireland. In Collins, ed., *Letters and Memorials*, I:96, a letter sent from Henry Sidney to the council from Limerick in 1575 mentions two Englishmen counterfeiting Spanish coins in Cork; one is "a Gentleman (as he sayeth) and is called *Harrison*, and moche delighted (as he confesseth) a long Tyme in

Alcumistical Practizes." For the association of coining and alchemy, see Deng, *Coinage and State Formation*, 105.

43. TNA, SP 69/10, fol. 12.

44. For an account of the Ridolfi plot of 1571, the aftershocks from which provide the broader context for Herle's letters at this time, see *ODNB*, "Howard, Thomas, fourth duke of Norfolk (1538–1572), nobleman and courtier."

45. British Library, MS Lansdowne 13, fols. 162r–64v (163r).

46. TNA, SP 12/86/1, fols. 2r–6v (fols. 5r, 4v); See, however, *OED*, "versipellous, *adj.*," for which the earliest citation is 1650.

47. In his letter of March 1572 Thomas Waye, Keeper of the Marshalsea, writes to Burghley that "of lat [he] was a poynted by my L of lester & your lordshype for the fettyng of one Chylester out of Essex / the whiche ys a very power man & dothe ly by your honers comandyment yn the Marshalse." He states that Chillester "most umbly be secheth to be exsamyned." TNA, SP 52/22, fol. 53.

48. TNA, SP 11/8, fol. 113 ("Further deposition of Dethicke; with an account of his life"). Dethicke claimed that he had been acquainted with Chillester in Boulogne during its English years (1544–50).

49. *Calendar of Patent Rolls: Philip and Mary*, IV:267. Chillester's accomplice is named in the pardon as John Sachefeld, also of Otford.

50. TNA, SP 12/86/1, fol. 2v.

51. LMA, MJ/SR/0135/4; translation in Jeaffreson, ed., *Middlesex County Records*, I:52–56.

52. Hardy and Page, eds., *Calendar to the Feet of Fines*, II:145. The will of Richard Barley, baker of St. Giles Without Cripplegate, was proved on 12 May 1596 (PCC, PROB 11/87/399).

53. TNA, C 3/4/42. Avys may be identifiable with Dunstan Anes, father-in-law of Roderigo Lopez (see *ODNB*, "Dunstan Anes [c. 1520–1594]" and above, p. 144). I am grateful to Alan Stewart for this suggestion.

54. There are also some potentially relevant records in London Metropolitan Archives (LMA), parish registers of St. Giles, Cripplegate. A Prudence Goldwell was buried on 3 April 1561, and a Marion Goldwell was buried on 19 April 1561; their father's name was William.

55. TNA, STAC 5/G45/36. For Thomas Jenison (c. 1525–1587), who according to one account "lived like a hog and died like a dog," see *ODNB*.

56. TNA, C3/156/90; C4/20/40. For Rous (by 1521–1569 or later), see *HoP*; for his debts, as assessed in 1556, TNA SP 62/1 f.61.

57. PCC, PROB 11/25/101. Among her relatives was the prolific translator Thomas Paynell; see *ODNB*, "Paynell, Thomas (d. 1564?)," and Moore, "Gathering Fruit."

58. LMA, parish registers of St. Mary, Islington.

59. LMA, MJ/SR/0230/45, translation from the Latin original in Jeaffreson, ed., *Middlesex County Records*, I:125.

60. TNA, PROB 11/69, will of Humfrey Goslen of the White Hart, Strand, Middlesex (23 July 1586); PROB 11/90, will of James Gardiner, tailor of Savoy, Middlesex (9 June 1597). For Gosling, see also Foster, ed., *London Marriage Licences*, 138.

61. Laura Gowing hazards that this may be "an attack on (supposed) immorality, perhaps sponsored by the servants' mistresses, or perhaps a trading dispute, or overcharging for goods" (personal communication).

62. TNA, C 3/97/88.

63. "Captain Pulvertoppe" is probably William Pulvertoft, gentleman, of Boston, Lincolnshire; Clement Hyett was an overseer and witness of his will (TNA, PROB 11/60/120),

proved on 8 February 1578. Alice's father's will, previously cited, refers to "my cousin Agnes Pulvertoft." The will of Thomas Robertson (PROB 11/24/105, 19 September 1531), another Lincolnshire Calais merchant who was related to the Tomlinsons, contains references to land transactions involving John and Richard Pulvertoft.

64. An Alice Goldwell, living in Tower Ward, was assessed at £8 in the 1581 subsidy. This may be the same Alice Goldwell for whom letters of administration were granted in 1582; she died in the parish of St. Lawrence Pountney; see *Prerogative Court of Canterbury Administrations*, 3, *1581–1595* (London: British Record Society, 1954).

65. Tigurinus, *Most Excellent Hystorie*, 2D4r.

66. Ibid., A4r. (my emphasis). It is of course conceivable that Chillester merely adapted a preexisting dedicatory letter written by Goldwell.

67. Guildhall Library, MS 34010/1, p. 536. Herle reports from the Marshalsea that a friend of Chillester's named Overton had boasted to him that "his fryndes wold sue for the sayd Chillesters enlargement, seing he was comitted for suche trifelles, amongest whom sir Harry Sydney had promised his ayd, so had master wilbraham, & [*deleted:* they] he hoped likewise that the Erlle of Bedford wold joyne with them."

68. Compare Ralph Robynson's translation of More's *Utopia* as *A Frutefull Pleasaunt, [and] Wittie Worke, of the Best State of a Publique Weale* (London: Abraham Vele, 1556), which he probably published as part of an early, unsuccessful bid to gain the clerkship of the Goldsmiths' Company. See Bishop, "Clerk's Tale."

69. There are two potentially relevant marriage records for men named James Chillester; one is to Christiana Hudson, of the parish of St. Alphage, London Wall, on 17 September 1546 (Armytage, ed., *Allegations for Marriage Licenses*, 8), the other to Jone Hunte in St. Margaret's, Westminster, in July 1574 (Burke, ed., *Memorials of St. Margaret's Church*, 288). The records of christenings and burials are for a James Chilister (christened 11 May 1574, St. Mary Magdalen, Old Fish Street); Brigett Chelester (christened 10 February 1575, St. Mary Abchurch [hereafter "St. M."], buried 19 May 1592 St. Botolph, Aldgate [hereafter "St. B."]); Martin "the sonne of Jeames Gillister gener[osus]" (baptized 14 February 1577/8, St. M.); "Aells chillister [*sic*]" (baptized 9 July 1583, St. B.), probably the same as Alyce Chillister (buried 8 June 1586, St. B.); Rose Chilister (christened 27 December 1585, St. B., buried 10 May 1588, St. B., at the age of two, cause of death "pyning," and said to be daughter of "the late deceassed James chellester merchant" or elsewhere of "Jeames Chillester a man of no trade dwellinge in master whytes Renttes in hownsditche"); James Chelister "howseholder" (buried 5 June 1586, St. B.); Bridget Chilester, daughter of "Jeames Chillester some tymes a clarke of the ordinance . . . dwelling with her mother being a widowe in the howse of Mrs Fredrick also a widow being in the libertie of Eastsmithfield" (buried 19 May 1592, St. B.). The St. B. registers also note the burial of Martin Chillester, "servant to Thomas Lycorice a shoomaker," on 16 October 1590 and a collection for "One Mistris Chillister being a parishioner visseted with sicknes" on 27 August 1587.

70. TNA, SP 46/30, fol. 119 (22 November 1585).

71. BL, MS Lansdowne 19, fol. 115r.

72. TNA, SP 59/93, fol. 83; SP 59/19 f. 87.

73. God's age can only be estimated from the fact that he married his wife, Elizabeth Broke, in 1544 (*London Marriage Licenses 1521–1869*, accessed via Ancestry [http://www.ancestry.co.uk]). She outlived him, remarried, and died in 1606 (will of Elizabeth Culpeper of Wilmington, Sussex, TNA, PROB 11/108/38 [28 July 1606]).

74. BL, MS Lansdowne 13, fol. 163v.

75. TNA, PROB 11/60/312 (4 June 1578).

76. Bandello, *Discourse*.

77. The story is Novella XXVII in Bandello, *Prima parte*; see also Painter, *Palace of Pleasure*, II:3X4r–4D4r.; Fenton, *Certaine Tragicall Discourses*, 2F2v–2I2v.

78. Guildhall Library, MS 7090/2 (Merchant Taylors' court minutes), fol. 5r. The minutes provide abundant evidence of the fractiousness of the younger John God; he was regularly in trouble for "opprobrious words" (fol. 75r) and for disobeying company ordinances (e.g., fols. 65v, 185r, and MS 7090/3, fol. 47v).

79. Hart, *Merchant Taylors' School Register*; Guildhall Library, MS 7090/2, fol. 69v. God junior was mentioned in his father's will, where he was described as married to one "Johan" and as "alreadie by me fully advaunced." His place seems not to have been secure, however, since the testator adds: "And for that I see good likelihood of husbandry in my saide John God, and for that he is like to have maynie Children, I giue and bequeath unto [him] Twoo hundred poundes in money which I will shall remaine in the handes of Elizabeth my wief untill the same maye be bestowed for the obtayning of somme good thinge towardes his better staye of lyvinge."

80. The *Discourse* seems not to have sold well. When Bynneman died in 1583, his postmortem inventory listed six hundred copies of the book, which were assessed at roughly three for a penny; Eccles, "Bynneman's Books," 84, 86, 91. Only two copies, one a fragment, survive today.

81. Chillester, *Youths Witte*; BL, C.123.ff.3; see *British Library Journal* (1977), 77–78. Subsequent page references to this work are supplied parenthetically.

82. 459/10r.

83. May, "*Youthes Witte*"; May and Ringler, *Elizabethan Poetry*.

84. May, "*Youthes Witte*," 3–8. It is possible that a poem beginning "Two things there are that much torment my mind" (N2v–3r) constitutes an unrecognized source for Shakespeare's Sonnet 144.

85. Ibid., 8.

86. *OED*, "compile, *v.*," 3: "To compose as original work (esp. a work of definite form or structure, *e.g.* a sonnet)." For early modern authorship as compilation, see Knight, *Bound to Read*.

87. "Bâtir des châteaux en Espagne" is a French proverb for wishful activity, equivalent to the English "castles in the air" (Addis, "Castles in the Air"). A hen with two chicks was proverbially busy.

88. Arber, II:179b.

89. May, "*Youthes Witte*," 3.

90. My suspicions about the nature of Chillester's involvement in this miscellany also make me sceptical about May's suggestion ("*Youthes Witte*," 8–10) that Chillester was the "H.C." who published another collection, *The Forrest of Fancy*.

91. There is a record of a Nicholas Atkinson at St. Alban Hall, Oxford, c. 1572; Clark, ed., *Register*, vol. 2, part 2, p. 41.

92. *Calendar of Patent Rolls: Philip and Mary*, I:278–79.

93. Dasent, ed., *Acts of the Privy Council* X:235–36; XI:27–28. The latter entry refers to Edward Atkinson as a vintner and is dated 22 January 1578/9; he was buried at St. Peter on 5 February 1578/9. His eldest son, Edward, succeeded him both as merchant tailor (Guildhall MS 34010/1, p. 509) and as purveyor of the Queen's wines (see LMA, Parish Register of St. Peter, entries for 15 December 1580 and 22 September 1583).

94. LMA, register of St. Botolph, Bishopsgate. It is possible that Nicholas was also the father of a Nicholas Atkinson, christened at St. Dunstan in the East on 17 September 1581.

95. Nicholas Atkinson was still thought to be alive on 4 April 1587 when Robert Thrower, wax chandler of London, made his will (TNA, PROB 11/73/384, proved 3 March 1589). A Nicholas Atkinson was buried on 13 January 1588/9 at St. Lawrence Pountney, and another at St. Botolph Bishopgate on 19 March 1623/4; in neither entry are any further details specified.

96. Jones, "Bryskett," 274; *ODNB,* "Bryskett, Lodowick [Lewis] (*c.* 1546–1609x12)."

97. Jones, "Bryskett," 255.

98. Ibid., 258. Philip's date of birth, incorrectly transcribed in Jones, was 29 April 1580.

99. The prominence of Cornhill and Bishopsgate in Atkinson's biography might also provide a geographical link to Thomas Watson, the possible author of one of the commendatory poems in *Youthes Witte* (May, "*Youthes Witte,*" 5–6). According to *ODNB* ("Watson, Thomas [1555/6–1592]"), Watson was born in the parish of St. Helen, Bishopsgate, and returned there in 1581.

100. May, "*Youthes Witte,*" 7–8.

101. On Wolfe, see *ODNB*; Loewenstein, "John Wolfe's Reformation"; Gadd, "Hunting Down John Wolfe," 193–201.

102. TNA, SP 12/15, fol. 60r.

103. Ibid.

104. TNA, SP 12/15, fol. 60v.

105. TNA, SP 12/15, fol. 61r.

106. BL, Lansdowne MS 48, ff.185–6.

107. Gadd, "Hunting Down John Wolfe," 197. Whether Henry Chillester was, like his father, angling for patronage through print is impossible to determine. It is possible that he was the "Chillister" who in November 1585 carried a message from Thomas Digges at Flushing to Francis Walsingham in London (*Calendar of State Papers, Foreign,* XX:176–77). A letter survives from a Henry Chillester to Robert Cecil, dated 5 November 1598, requesting that munitions be sent to Munster; TNA, SP 63/202/3, fol. 319.

108. Bandello, *Novelle,* fols. F8v–G3v; Novella XXVII ("Due amanti si trovano una notte insieme, & il giouane di gioia si muore, e la fanciulla di dolor s'accora"). The story had previously been translated, via the greatly expanded French version of Belleforest (no. 22), by Fenton in *Certaine Tragicall Discourses,* fols. E7r–H4v. The version in *Youthes Witte* is translated directly from the Italian, although it omits Bandello's headnote, which points out that the satisfaction of desire can lead to sudden death: "nessuno . . . può chiamarsi felice in questo mondo."

109. A.D.S.D., *Comptes du Monde,* fols. A1r–7v, L4r–7v; Tomita, *Bibliographical Catalogue,* 130.

110. Bandello at this point has his Livio tell his griefs through the wall: "Era medesimamente Livio solo, il perche fatto buon'animo, e preso più d'ardire del solito, per il tavolato che era in mezo cominciò per si fata maniera con singhiozzi, lagrime, e sospiri, à narrar le sue amorose e mortali passioni à Camilla, & humilmente à supplicarla che di lui volesse haver pietà" (fol. G2r).

111. Whetstone, *The Rocke of Regard,* B8v–C1r.

112. On the iterability of early modern lyric, see Zarnowiecki, *Fair Copies,* esp. pp. 22–46.

113. Much of the work is in fact a translation of Clichtove's *De regis officio opusculum* (1519); see Tudor, "*L'institution des princes chrestiens.*"

114. 460/65v. A *scire facias* was commonly a writ "to require a person to show cause to the court why the execution of a judgment passed should not be made"; Dean, *Law-Making*, 59.

115. *ODNB*, "Painter, William (1540?–1595), translator and administrator"; "Fenton, Sir Geoffrey (*c.* 1539–1608), translator and administrator in Ireland"; TNA, E192/3, part 3. Hayes was a receiver of land revenues for Essex, Hertford, London, and Middlesex; for his debts to the Queen, see the letter of September 1578 in *HMCS*, XIII:162.

116. Maslen, *Elizabethan Fictions*, 19.

117. Ascham, *Scholemaster*, Iiv. This story can also be linked back to its roots in the testimony of the spy William Herle, for Herle has recently been revealed as a reader of Boccaccio; see Scott-Warren, "Portrait of the Spy."

CHAPTER 8

1. The second reference (461/12v), a revised and partially deleted entry for a purchase on 20 April 1597 of "Bookes" worth 6s. 8d. (unrevised) and 27s. and 7d. (revised) is intriguing, but it has frustrated all of my attempts to make sense of it, so it is not discussed here.

2. 461/19r, 4v, 23r, 68r. Toward the end of the volume Thomas Phillips writes out full receipts for chamber rent, rather than just signing; see, for example, 461/75v.

3. For a powerful meditation on this dispensation, see Bailey, *Of Bondage*.

4. Murray, "Measured Sentences," 154.

5. Bailey, *Of Bondage*, 10–11.

6. Ibid., 118.

7. Brown, *History of the Fleet Prison*, 4, 7.

8. The account that follows is indebted to Ahnert, *Rise of Prison Literature*, 8–28, and to the essays collected in *Huntington Library Quarterly* 72 (2009), "Prison Writings in Early Modern England," ed. Sherman and Sheils. For other contemporaneous carceral regimes, see Spierenburg, *Prison Experience*; Griffiths, *Lost Londons*.

9. Murray, "Measured Sentences," 150–51.

10. Ibid., 150. For a countervailing emphasis on the difficulties (for some) of writing in prison, see Freeman, "The Rise of Prison Literature." For a collection of booklists relating to imprisoned Catholics, see Walsham and Havens, eds., "Catholic Libraries."

11. 461/17r.

12. For Puxley, who appears frequently in the second and third volumes of the journals, see his will of 1599, TNA PROB 11/94/397, which records debts to Stonley, and the depositions in Corporation of London Archives, DL/C/213/493–95. For Newman, whose name appears in all three journals, see his 1619 will, TNA, PROB 11/134/185, and LMA CLA/008/EM/01/01/001, 175r (a document relating to property in Trinity Lane).

13. 461/32r; *ODNB*, "Patten, William (*d.* in or after 1598), author." Patten's *Calendar of Scripture* is listed in Stonley's inventory, Ad4.107.

14. 461/4r, 35r, 30r.

15. See 461/7r for an explicit reference to dining in the prison chamber as dining "At home."

16. 461/7v, 65v.

17. 461/22r.

18. 461/7r.

19. 461/24r.

20. 461/33v: "being the fyrst tyme I came there since my commytment"; 461/68v.

21. 461/53r (13 November 1597).

22. 461/6r.

23. 461/17v.

24. 461/18r–v. Smith's accounts, which document the rents that he received for these estates, are now Folger Shakespeare Library, MS V.b.246.

25. 461/25r–v.

26. 461/25r.

27. 461/28r.

28. See 461/7r (3 April 1597): "This day after service in the Chappell I entre[d] Comons in the parler"; cf. Bodleian, Rawl. MS 1123, fol. 28r. for the price differentials.

29. It is striking that Stonley often includes "my self" in the list of strangers in this section of the journal; see, for example, 461/10r.

30. 461/7v (5 April 1597).

31. 461/11v (16 April 1597).

32. 461/12v (20 April 1597).

33. 461/15r.

34. 461/17r. The reading here is uncertain; "in the flore" probably means "on the floor" (see *OED*, "in, *prep*.," 2a), but the verb is conjectural. For a comparable usage, see Marcellinus, *Roman Historie*, M1v: "he could not endure either to read or subscribe, but flung it in the floore."

35. 461/36v, 39r, 40r.

36. Harley, *William Byrd*, 121. For reflections on this case, see Brown, *History of the Fleet Prison*, 10, and for related Fleet petitions in 1597, see Murray, "Measured Sentences," 159.

37. 461/39r. On the implications of the decentralized, for-profit status of early modern prisons, see Ahnert, *Rise of Prison Literature*, 17–22.

38. *HoP*, "Skinner, Vincent (d. 1616)"; 460/53v; TNA, E407/71/88 (28 May 1596).

39. Harley, *World of William Byrd*, 93–94.

40. Harley, *William Byrd*, 96–97; Harley, *World of William Byrd*, 95–97.

41. Harley, *World of William Byrd*; Harley, *William Byrd*, 122–23.

42. *ODNB*, "Sherley [Shirley], Sir Thomas (*c*. 1542–1612)."

43. *HMCS*, VII:363 (24 August 1597); Stone, *An Elizabethan*, 200.

44. The identity of Jacob is unclear; for a possible candidate, see *ODNB*, "Jacob, Henry (1562/3–1624)."

45. 461/22v (19 May 1597).

46. Hakluyt, *Principal Navigations*, 3L1r; Laughton, ed., *State Papers*, II:119n.

47. *HMCS*, VI:242 (3 July 1596).

48. *ODNB*, "Malynes [Malines, de Malines], Gerard [Garrett, Gerald] (*fl.* 1585–1641)."

49. Stone, *An Elizabethan*, 225.

50. Ibid., 225–27.

51. 461/14r, 15r, 38v.

52. *HoP*, "Fitzherbert, Thomas (c. 1550–1600), of Norbury, Derbys."

53. 461/7r–v; *ODNB*, "Phelippes, Thomas (*c*. 1556–1625x7)." Phelippes had contracted at least £10,000 of debt to the Queen, partly thanks to the costs of running an overseas intelligence network after the death of Sir Francis Walsingham.

54. 461/5v.

55. *ODNB*, quoting Lansdowne MS 77, fol. 66r.

56. For further details see Quinn, "Johnson, George."

57. Johnson, *A Discourse of Some Troubles*; for commentary, see Finch, "'Fashions of Worldly Dames.'"

58. 461/5v.

59. 459/51v.

60. Ryrie, *Being Protestant*, 273, observing that Stonley switches in the 1581 volume (at 459/32v) from quoting individual verses to quoting chapter headings, writes that "he seems to have read the Geneva Bible's chapter-summaries more carefully than the text itself." Although the change might suggest a desire to save labor, it could just as easily indicate the expansion of Stonley's daily reading. Among the commentaries in Stonley's library were Peter Martyr, Calvin, and Hemmingsen on the Pauline epistles (Ad4.27, 47, 316); Calvin, Erasmus, Flaminio, and Aepinus on the Psalms (Ad4.78, 86, 191, 167); Rudolph Walther on Acts (Ad4.310); Augustine Marlorat on Matthew and Revelations (Ad4.311, 262); Babington on the Commandments (Ad4.276); and Luther on Ecclesiastes (Ad4.280).

61. 461/39r.

62. 461/7r; the entry coincides with another "for glewinge my dagger chepe," which cost one penny.

63. 461/3v.

64. 459/62r, 70r, 79v.

65. *HMCS*, XIII:206; *ODNB*, "Walker, John (d. 1588), Church of England clergyman." See also Emmison, *Elizabethan Life*, 77.

66. 459/74v.

67. 459/30r, 21r.

68. See Haigh's characterization of Stonley as anti-Puritan in "The Character of an Anti-Puritan," 686.

69. The dedication to Cottesford, *Treatise Against Traitors*, is signed from "Woodgrange in West-ham in Essex, the 6. of November. 1591" (¶8v). See also LMA, DL/C/214/104–5 for Cottesford's testimony in a case from 1591 relating to tithes at West Ham.

70. Lambeth Palace Library, Shrewsbury Papers, fol. 141. In 1597 John and Samuel were witnesses to the will of the godly preacher Thomas Crooke (c. 1545–98); see the transcription in Usher, "Fortunes of English Puritanism," 112.

71. Dasent, ed., *Acts of the Privy Council*, XXV:290.

72. Ibid., XXVI:58. Abraham Beauvoir, goldsmith of London, makes his loving brother Peter his executor in his will of 1618, TNA, PROB 11/131/475.

73. Dasent, ed., *Acts of the Privy Council*, XXVI:260.

74. Ibid., XXVI:408.

75. Cottesford, *Soveraigne Oyle* (London: George Hodges, 1622).

76. Ibid., E4v–F1v.

77. The figure of nine hundred crowns suggests that Cottesford's source is not *The Merchant of Venice* but Le Sylvain, *Orator*, 2D3r. For a reading of Shakespeare's play in the light of discourses of surety, see Lim, "Surety and Spiritual Commercialism." For the suggestion that the play explores the implications of desperate debt for the body of the debtor, see Bailey, *Of Bondage*, 51–74.

78. Cottesford, *Soveraigne Oyle*, I3r–v.

79. Ibid., F2v.

80. Ibid., M3r.

81. Venn and Venn, eds., *Alumni Cantabrigienses*, "Muffett, Peter." When Stonley was preparing to sell off land in East Ham in 1588, one of the parcels was called "Moffett's"; *HMCS*, III:310.

82. Moffett, *Commentarie* (1592), A1r.

83. Ibid., A4v.

84. Ibid., A5r; Moffett, *Commentarie* (1596), A3v.

85. Ibid. 2I3r.

86. Ibid., C6r.

87. Ibid., F3v–4v.

88. Ibid., K2v.

89. Ibid., P3v, S3v, X3r–v.

90. Jones, "Wales and the Stationers' Company," 188; see also p. 185 for Jones's printing of Nowell's *Least Catechism* in Welsh.

91. Whitney, *Copy of a Letter*; R.C., *A New Booke*. See *STC*, III:92–93.

92. Twyne, *Schoolemaster*; Smythe, *Certen Instructions*.

93. Marlowe, *Tamburlaine*, A2r.

94. Melnikoff, "Jones's Pen," 195; *ODNB*, "Jones, Richard (*fl.* 1564–1613)."

95. *ODNB*, "Deloney, Thomas (*d.* in or before 1600)."

96. Deloney, *Jack of Newberie*, A4r.

97. Ibid., K3v; http://www.historyofparliamentonline.org/volume/1558-1603/constituencies/newton.

98. *OED*, "factory, *n.*," 4a. The earliest citation in this sense is a reference to "a Factory for Books" from 1618.

99. For a contextualization of *Jack of Newberie*'s fantasy in relation to the decline of the English cloth trade in the later sixteenth century, see Hentschell, *Culture of Cloth*, ch. 2.

100. Stow, *Survay*, M6r.

101. Taverner, *Second Booke of the Garden of Wysedome*, A3v–4r.

CONCLUSION

1. LMA, Consistory Court of London wills, X019/015/147r, proved 4 March 1613. Anne had perhaps been living on her jointure, for disputes over which see Brownlow, *Reports*, Y2r, and TNA, CP40/1881.

2. Stow, *Survey of London*, 2F5v.

3. Woolgar, *Culture of Food*, 190.

4. Krohn and Miller, eds., *Dutch New York*, 117–29.

5. Bowlby, *Carried Away*, 106–7.

6. See further Smith and Wilson, eds., *Renaissance Paratexts*; Saenger, *Commodification*.

7. Anon., *Advice of a Father*, C5v.

8. For a modern author's troubled meditation on the book cover, see Lahiri, *The Clothing of Books*.

Bibliography

MANUSCRIPT SOURCES

Library of Birmingham
    RL 432719 (Manor court roll for Bishop's Itchington)
Cambridge, Magdalene College
    Ferrar Papers, vol. 141
Essex Record Office
    D/DP/A4, A20 (Petre family account books)
    D/DFa 04 (Letters and documents relating to Stonley's work in the Exchequer)
London, British Library
    Lansdowne MSS 19, 28, 35, 40, 44, 46–47, 51, 55, 58, 59, 72, 75, 78, 80
    Egerton MS 2806 (Wardrobe Accounts of Elizabeth I)
    Add. MS 16940 (Grants of Arms, Elizabethan)
    Add. MS 42518 (Gabriel Harvey's copy of Chaucer, *Workes* [1598])
    Add. MS 81277, item J (Letter to Stonley from Francis Blount, 1594)
London, Corporation of London Archives
    DL/C/213/394 (Consistory Court of London depositions)
London, Guildhall Library
    MS 5370 (Scriveners' Company Common Paper)
London, London Metropolitan Archives
    X019/015 (Consistory Court of London wills)
    CLA/008/EM/01–02 (City Land Grants)
    MJ/SR/0135/4 (Middlesex Sessions Roll)
London, National Archives
    C1/1184/44–46 (Court of Chancery, William Sparke vs. Henry Byrde)
    C2/Eliz/W3/53 (Court of Chancery, Walter Watton vs. Philip Bassett, 1589)
    C2/Eliz/P9/25 (Court of Chancery, John Preston vs. Philip Bassett, 1596)
    C3/4/42 (Court of Chancery, Dunstan Avys vs. William Goldwell, 1560s?)
    C3/97/88 (Court of Chancery, Richard Holderness vs. Alice Goldwell)
    C3/156/90 (Court of Chancery, Sir Edward Rous vs. William Goldwell)
    C4/20/40 (Court of Chancery, Sir Edward Rous vs. William Goldwell)
    C66/1116, m.37 (Court of Chancery, Patent Rolls, Pardon for Richard Stonley, 1574)
    C78/50/20 (Court of Chancery, Francis and Jane Michell vs. John Branche, 1579)
    C78/80/1 (Court of Chancery, Richard Stonley and John Branche vs. Muscovy Company,
        1578)

CP40/1881 (Court of Common Pleas, Thomas Glascock vs. Anne Stonley and John Williams, 1611)
E159/357/5 (Exchequer, King's Remembrancer, Memoranda Roll)
E159/412/435 (Exchequer, King's Remembrancer, Memoranda Roll)
E178/2980 (Special Commission of the Court of Exchequer)
E192/3 (Exchequer papers; bonds and bills assigned by Stonley to the Crown)
E407/71 (Papers relating to fees and duties in the Exchequer of Receipt)
LR 9/131 (Memoranda of Auditors of Land Revenue)
PROB 10–11 (Prerogative Court of Canterbury wills)
SP 11–12 (State Papers Domestic, Mary I and Elizabeth I)
SP 15 (State Papers Domestic, Edward VI-James I, Addenda)
SP 46 (State Papers Domestic, Supplementary)
SP 52 (State Papers Scotland, Elizabeth I)
SP 59 (State Papers Scotland: Border Papers)
SP 62–63 (State Papers Ireland, Mary I to George III)
SP 69–70 (State Papers Foreign, Mary I and Elizabeth I)
STAC 5/G45/36 (Star Chamber, William Goldwell vs. Robert Holdyche and Thomas Jennison, 1559)
STAC 5/L7/1 (Star Chamber, Thomas Lichfield vs. Robert Newman, 1564–65)
STAC 5/L7/7 (Star Chamber, Thomas Lichfield vs. Hamlet Harrington, 1564–65)
Maidstone, Kent Records Centre
U350 C2/34 (letters of Edward Dering)
Norfolk Record Office
MC 254 (letters of Sawer and Phillips families of Norfolk)
Oxford, Bodleian Library
MS Douce d.44 (Francis Douce's notes on Stonley's journals)
MS Malone 26 (letters of Edmund Malone)
Rawl. MS 1123 (records relating to Fleet Prison, 1598)
4° Rawl. 140 (1) (Robert Nicolson's "Ephemeris historica")
Warwick, Warwickshire Record Office
CR 1908/73/3 (mortgage of the Manor of Tachbrook)
Washington, DC, Folger Shakespeare Library
MS V.b.246 (Account book of William Smith)
MS C.b.10, no. 66 (Letter from Francis Douce to George Steevens, 1794)
MS V.a.459–61 (Journals of Richard Stonley)

PRINTED SOURCES

Adams, Robyn. "'Both Diligent and Secret': The Intelligence Letters of William Herle." Unpublished doctoral dissertation, Queen Mary, University of London, 2004.
———. "'The service I am here for': William Herle in the Marshalsea Prison, 1571." *Huntington Library Quarterly* 72 (2009): 217–38.
———. "A Spy on the Payroll? William Herle and the Mid Elizabethan Polity." *Historical Research* 83 (2010): 266–80.
Addis, John. "Castles in the Air." *Notes and Queries*, 4th ser., IV (1869): 184.
Aelianus, Claudius. *A Registre of Hystories*. London: Thomas Woodcock, 1576.

Aesop. *The Fabulous Tales of Esope the Phrygian.* London: Richard Smith, 1577.

Ago, Renata. *Gusto for Things: A History of Objects in Seventeenth-Century Rome,* trans. Bradford Bouley and Corey Tazzara, intro. Paula Findlen. Chicago: University of Chicago Press, 2013.

———. *Il gusto delle cose: Una storia degli oggetti nella Roma del Seicento.* Rome: Donzelli, 2006.

Ahl, Frederick. "Ars est caelare artem: Art in Puns and Anagrams Engraved." In Jonathan Culler, ed., *On Puns: The Foundation of Letters,* 17–43. Oxford: Basil Blackwell, 1988.

Ahnert, Ruth. *The Rise of Prison Literature in the Sixteenth Century.* Cambridge: Cambridge University Press, 2013.

Aho, James. *Confession and Bookkeeping: The Religious, Moral, and Rhetorical Roots of Modern Accounting.* New York: State University of New York Press, 2005.

Alcock, N. W., ed. *Warwickshire Grazier and London Skinner, 1532–1555: The Account Book of Peter Temple and Thomas Heritage.* London: British Academy, 1981.

Allen, William. *An Apologie and True Declaration of the Institution of the Two English Colleges.* Rheims: Mounts in Henault [i.e., J. Foigny?], 1581.

Alley, William. *Ptochomuseion: The Poore Mans Librarie.* London: John Day, 1565.

Ames, Joseph, et al. *Typographical Antiquities.* 4 vols. London: William Miller, 1810–19.

Anglicus, Galfridus. *Promptorium puerorum, sive Medulla grammaticae.* [London:] Fredericus de Egmondt and Petrus, 1499.

Anon. *Advice of a Father.* London: For the author, 1664.

———. *Danse macabre.* Paris: Jean Tréperel, 1500.

———. *A Dialogue betwene a Knyght and a Clerke.* London: Thomas Berthelet, 1533?

———. *A Discovery of the Jesuits Trumpery, Newly Packed Out of England.* London: Henry Gosson [1641].

———. *Disputatio inter clericum et militem.* London: Thomas Berthelet, 1531.

———. *The Kalender of Shepherdes.* London: Richard Pynson, 1506.

———. *Les joyeuses adventures et plaisant facetieux deviz.* Lyon: N.p., 1555.

———. *Le tresor des livres d'Amadis de Gaule.* Paris: Robert le Mangnier, 1564.

———. *A Particular Declaration or Testimony, of the Undutifull and Traiterous Affection Borne against her Majestie by Edmond Campion Jesuite.* London: Christopher Barker, 1582.

———. *Preces privatae.* London: William Seres, 1573.

———. *Thordynary of Crysten Men.* London: Wynkyn de Worde, 1502.

———. *The Welch Mans Inventory.* London: Thomas Lambert, 1641.

———. *The Welch-mans Life, Teath and Periall.* London: Thomas Lambert, 1641.

Arber, Edward, ed. *A Transcript of the Registers of the Company of Stationers of London, 1554–1640 A.D.* 5 vols. London: Privately printed, 1875–94.

Archer, Jayne Elisabeth, Elizabeth Goldring, and Sarah Knight, eds. *The Intellectual and Cultural World of the Early Modern Inns of Court.* Manchester: Manchester University Press, 2011.

Aristotle. *Here Begynneth the Nature, and Dysposycyon [sic] of the Dayes in the Weke.* London: Robert Wyer, 1535?

Armytage, G. J., ed. *Allegations for Marriage Licenses Issued from the Faculty Office of the Archbishop of Canterbury at London, 1543–1869.* London: Harleian Society, 1886.

Arnold, Janet, ed. *Queen Elizabeth's Wardrobe Unlock'd.* Leeds: Maney, 2014.

Arnold, Richard. *In this Booke is Conteyned the Names of ye Baylifs Custos Mairs and Sherefs of the Cite of Londo[n].* Antwerp: A. van Berghen, 1503?

Ascham, Roger. *The Scholemaster.* London: John Day, 1570.

Ashbee, Andrew, and David Lasocki, eds. *A Biographical Dictionary of English Court Musicians 1485–1714.* 2 vols. Aldershot: Ashgate, 1998.

Askham, Antony. *A Litell Treatyse of Astrouomy [sic]: Very Necessary for Physyke and Surgerye.* London: Wyllyam Powell, 1550.

Augustine, St. *Certaine Select Prayers Gathered out of S. Augustines Meditations.* London: John Day, 1574.

Avicenna. *Prognosticacion, Drawen out of the Bookes of Ipocras, Avicen, and other Notable Auctours of Physycke.* London: Robert Wyer, 1530?

Bacon, Francis. *Of the Proficience and Advancement of Learning, Divine and Humane.* London: Henry Tomes, 1605.

Bacon, Roger. *This Boke doth Treate All of the Beste Waters Artyfycialles.* London: Robert Wyer, 1530?

Bailey, Amanda. *Of Bondage: Debt, Property, and Personhood in Early Modern England.* Philadelphia: University of Pennsylvania Press, 2013.

Baldwin, William. *A Marvelous Hystory Intitulede, Beware the Cat.* London: Wylliam Gryffyth, 1570.

Bale, John. *A Comedy Concernynge Thre Lawes.* Wesel: Dirik van der Straten, 1548?

Bancroft, Richard. *A Survay of the Pretended Holy Discipline.* London: J. Wolfe, 1593.

Bandello, Matteo. *A Discourse of the Great Cruelty of a Widow*, trans. John God. London: Henry Bynneman, 1570.

———. *La prima parte de le novelle.* Lucca: Vincenzo Busdraghi, 1554.

———. *Novelle.* Milan: Meda, 1560.

Barron, Kathryn. "The Subject Pictures." In Mark Evans, ed., *Art Collecting and Lineage in the Elizabethan Age: The Lumley Inventory and Pedigree*, 71–73. N.p.: Roxburghe Club, 2010.

Batman, Stephen. *Batman uppon Bartholome his Booke De proprietatibus rerum.* London: Thomas East, 1582.

———. *A Christall Glasse of Christian Reformation.* London: John Day, 1569.

———. *The Golden Booke of the Leaden Goddes.* London: Thomas Marsh, 1577.

Baumann, Wolf-Rüdiger. *The Merchant Adventurers and the Continental Cloth-Trade (1560s–1620s).* Berlin: De Gruyter, 1990.

Baxter, W. T. "Early Accounting: The Tally and the Checker-Board." In R. H. Parker and B. S. Yamey, eds., *Accounting History: Some British Contributions*, 197–235. Oxford: Clarendon Press, 1994.

Bearman, Frederick, et al., eds. *Fine and Historic Bindings from the Folger Shakespeare Library.* Washington DC: Folger, 1992.

Becon, Thomas. *The Governans of Vertue.* London: James Nicholson, 1544?

Belknap, Robert E. *The List: The Uses and Pleasures of Cataloguing.* New Haven: Yale University Press, 2004.

Benedict, Philip. *Graphic History: The "Wars, Massacres and Troubles" of Tortorel and Perrissin.* Geneva: Droz, 2007.

Benese, Richard. *This Boke Sheweth the Maner of Measurynge of all Maner of Lande.* Southwark: James Nicolson, 1537?

Bennett, Jane. *Vibrant Matter: A Political Ecology of Things.* Durham: Duke University Press, 2010.

Beuther, Michael. *Ephemeris historica.* Paris: Michael Fezandat and Robert Granjon, 1551.

Bible. *The Gospels of the Fower Evangelistes Translated in the Olde Saxons Tyme.* London: John Day, 1571.

———. *The. Holie. Bible.* London: Richard Jugge, 1568.

———. *The New Testamen* [*sic*] *Both in Latin and English After the Vulgare Texte*, trans. Miles Coverdale. London: Richard Grafton and Edward Whitchurch, 1538.

———. *The Psalmes of David and Others.* London: Lucas Harison and George Byshop, 1571.

Bilson, Thomas. *The Perpetual Governement of Christes Church.* London: C. Barker, 1593.

Binns, James. "STC Latin Books: Further Evidence for Printing House Practice." *Library*, 6th ser., I (1979): 347–54

Bishop, Jennifer. "The Clerk's Tale: Civic Writing in Sixteenth-Century London." In Liesbeth Corens, Kate Peters, and Alexandra Walsham, eds., *The Social History of the Archive: Record Keeping in Early Modern Europe*, 112–30. Oxford: Oxford University Press, 2016.

Blagrave, John. *The Mathematical Jewel Shewing the Making, and Most Excellent Use of a Singuler Instrument So Called.* London: Walter Venge, 1585.

Blague, Thomas. *A Schole of Wise Conceytes.* London: Henry Binneman, 1569.

Blayney, Peter W. M. *The Stationers' Company and the Printers of London, 1501–1557.* Cambridge: Cambridge University Press, 2013.

Boccaccio, Giovanni. *The Elegy of Lady Fiametta*, trans. Mariangela Causa-Steindler and Thomas Mauch. Chicago: University of Chicago Press, 1990.

———. *Thirtene Most Plesant and Delectable Questions*, trans. H. G. London: Richard Smyth, 1571.

Bodin, Jean. *De magorum dæmonomania.* Basel: Thomas Guarinus, 1581.

Boissard, Jean Jacques. *Habitus variarum orbis gentium.* Köln: Kaspar Rutz, 1581.

Bossy, John. *Peace in the Post-Reformation.* Cambridge: Cambridge University Press, 1998.

Botero, Giovanni. *Relations of the Most Famous Kingdomes and Common-wealths thorowout the World.* London: John Haviland, 1630.

Botonaki, Effie. *Seventeenth-Century English Women's Autobiographical Writings: Disclosing Enclosures.* Lewiston, NY: Edwin Mellen Press, 2004.

Bouguereau, Maurice. *Le theatre Francois.* Amsterdam: Theatrvm Orbis Terrarum, 1966.

———. *Le theatre Francois ou sont comprises les chartes generales et particulieres de la France.* Tours: Maurice Bouguereau, 1594.

Boutcher, Warren. "Beyond English: Going Back into (Literary) Europe." Lecture delivered at Queen Mary, University of London, 16 March 2017.

———. "From Cultural Translation to Cultures of Translation? Early Modern Readers, Sellers and Patrons." In Demetriou and Tomlinson, eds., *Culture of Translation*, 22–40.

Bowen, Barbara. *Enter Rabelais, Laughing.* Nashville: Vanderbilt University Press, 1998.

Bowlby, Rachel. *Carried Away: The Invention of Modern Shopping.* London: Faber, 2000.

Boys, Peter G. "Samuel Pepys's Personal Accounts." *Accounting, Business and Financial History* 5 (1995): 308–20.

Brant, Sebastian. *The Shyppe of Fooles.* London: Wynkyn de Worde, 1509.

Braun, Georg, and Frans Hogenburg. *Civitates orbis terrarum.* Cologne: T. Graminaeus, 1572–1618.

———. *Civitates orbis terrarum.* Cologne: Gottfried von Kempen, 1581–82.

Bridges, John. *A Defence of the Government Established in the Church of Englande.* London: T. Chard, 1587.

Brigden, Susan. *Thomas Wyatt: The Heart's Forest.* London: Faber and Faber, 2012.

Bromilow, Pollie. "Fictions of Authority: Hélisenne de Crenne and the *Angoysses douloureuses qui procedent d'amours* (1538)." In Pollie Bromilow, ed., *Authority in European Book Culture*, 137–51 . Farnham: Ashgate, 2013.

Brown, Bill. "Thing Theory." *Critical Inquiry* 28 (2001): 1–22.

Brown, Roger Lee. *A History of the Fleet Prison, London: The Anatomy of the Fleet.* Lewiston: Edward Mellon Press, 1996.

Brownlow, Richard. *Reports of Diverse Choice Cases.* London: Matthew Walbancke, 1651.

Bruster, Douglas. *Shakespeare and the Question of Culture.* Basingstoke: Palgrave, 2003.

Buchanan, George. *Rerum Scoticarum historia.* Edinburgh: Alexander Arbuthnot, 1583.

Bull, Henry. *Christian Prayers and Holy Meditations.* London: Henry Middleton, 1568.

Bunny, Francis. *Truth and Falshood, or, A Comparison Betweene the Truth Now Taught in England, and the Doctrine of the Romish Church.* London: Raph Lacson, 1595.

Burke, A. M., ed. *Memorials of St. Margaret's Church, Westminster.* London: Eyre and Spottiswode, 1914.

Burke, Peter. "Fables of the Bees: A Case-Study in Views of Nature and Society." In Mikuláš Teich, Roy Porter, and Bo Gustafsson, eds., *Nature and Society in Historical Context*, 112–23. Cambridge: Cambridge University Press, 1997.

———. "Representations of the Self from Petrarch to Descartes." In Roy Porter, ed., *Rewriting the Self: Histories from the Renaissance to the Present*, 17–28. London: Routledge, 1997.

C., H. *The Forrest of Fancy.* London: Thomas Purfoote, 1579.

C., R. *A New Booke Intituled the Blasinge of Bawdrie.* London: Richard Jhones, 1574.

C., T. *A Spirituall Purgation Sent unto Al Them that Laboure of Luthers Errour.* London: Hugh Syngelton, 1548.

Calendar of Patent Rolls: Elizabeth I. London: HMSO, 1939–.

Calendar of Patent Rolls: Philip and Mary. 4 vols. London: HMSO, 1936–39.

Calendar of State Papers, Foreign Series, for the Reign of Elizabeth. 23 vols. London: Longman, Green, 1863–1950.

Calfhill, James. *An Aunswere to the Treatise of the Crosse.* London: Lucas Harryson, 1565.

Calvin, Jean. *Commentaries . . . upon the Prophet Daniell*, trans. Anthony Gilby. London: John Daye, 1570.

Cambers, Andrew. *Godly Reading: Print, Manuscript and Puritanism in England, 1580–1720.* Cambridge: Cambridge University Press, 2011.

Cameron, K. "John Heywood and Richard Stonley." *Shakespeare Association Bulletin* 14 (1939): 55.

Canavan, Claire. "Reading Materials: Textile Surfaces and Early Modern Books." *Journal of the Northern Renaissance* 8 (2017). https://www.northernrenaissance.org/reading-materials -textile-surfaces-and-early-modern-books/.

Canfield, Benet [Benoît de Canfield]. *The Rule of Perfection.* Roan: Cardin Hamillion, 1609.

Canisius, Peter. *Authoritatum sacrae scripturae et sanctorum patrum.* Cologne: G. Calenium et al., 1570.

Cardano, Girolamo. *Cardanus Comforte Translated into Englishe. And Published by Commaundement of the Right Honourable the Earle of Oxenford.* London: Thomas Marshe, 1573.

Carruthers, Mary. *The Book of Memory: A Study of Memory in Medieval Culture.* Cambridge: Cambridge University Press, 2008.

Cebes. *The Table of Cebes*, trans. Francis Poyntz. London: T. Berthelet, 1531?

Chambers, E. K. *William Shakespeare: A Survey of Facts and Problems.* 2 vols. Oxford: Clarendon Press, 1930.

Chillester, Henry. *Youths Witte, or the Witte of Grene Youth.* London: John Wolfe, 1581.

Chillingworth, William. *The Religion of Protestants.* Oxford: Leonard Lichfield, 1638.

Church of England. *Articles to be Enquired of in the Generall Visitation of Edmonde Bisshoppe of London.* London: John Cawood, 1554.

Clanchy, Michael. *From Memory to Written Record: England 1066–1307.* 2nd ed. Oxford: Blackwell, 1993.

Clark, Andrew, ed. *Register of the University of Oxford.* 4 vols. Oxford: Oxford Historical Society, 1887–89.

Clark, Peter. "The Ownership of Books in England, 1560–1640: The Example of Some Kentish Townsfolk." In Lawrence Stone, ed., *Schooling and Society*, 95–111. Baltimore: Johns Hopkins University Press, 1976.

Cogan, Thomas. *The Haven of Health.* London: William Norton, 1584.

Coldiron, A. E. B. *Printers Without Borders: Translation and Textuality in the Renaissance.* Cambridge: Cambridge University Press, 2015.

Coleman, Christopher. "Artifice or Accident? The Reorganization of the Exchequer of Receipt c. 1554–1572." In Christopher Coleman and David Starkey, eds., *Revolution Reassessed: Revisions in the History of Tudor Government and Administration*, 163–98. Oxford: Clarendon Press, 1986.

Colenbrander, Herman Th. "The Sitter in Jan Gossaert's 'Portrait of a Merchant' in the National Gallery of Art, Washington: Jan Snoeck, c. 1510–85." *Burlington Magazine* 152 (2010): 82–85.

Colinson, Robert. *Idea Rationaria, or the Perfect Accomptant.* Edinburgh: David Lindsay et al., 1683.

Collins, Arthur, ed. *Letters and Memorials of State.* 2 vols. London: T. Osborne, 1746.

Colynet, Anthony. *The True History of the Civill Warres of France.* London: T. Woodcock, 1591.

Conley, Tom. *The Self-Made Map: Cartographic Writing in Early Modern France.* Minneapolis: University of Minnesota Press, 1996.

Connor, Rebecca Elisabeth. *Women, Accounting, and Narrative: Keeping Books in Eighteenth-Century England.* London: Routledge, 2004.

Conway, Sir John. *Meditations and Praiers Gathered out of the Sacred Letters and Vertuous Writers.* London: William How, 1571.

Cooper, Tarnya. "The Enchantment of the Familiar Face: Portraits as Domestic Objects in Elizabethan and Jacobean England." In Tara Hamling and Catherine Richardson, eds., *Everyday Objects: Medieval and Early Modern Material Culture and Its Meanings*, 157–77. Farnham: Ashgate, 2010.

Cooper, Thomas. *Thesaurus linguae Romanae et Britannicae.* London: H. Wykes, 1565.

Cormack, Lesley B. *Charting an Empire: Geography at the English Universities, 1580–1620.* Chicago: University of Chicago Press, 1997.

Corns, Thomas N. "The Early Modern Search Engine: Indices, Title Pages, Marginalia and Contents." In Neil Rhodes and Jonathan Sawday, eds., *The Renaissance Computer: Knowledge Technology in the First Age of Print*, 95–105. London: Routledge, 2000.

Cottesford, Samuel. *A Treatise against Traitors.* London: William Home, 1591.

———. *A Very Soveraigne Oyle to Restore Debtors.* London: George Hodges, 1622.

Cousin, Gilbert. *Sylva narrationum.* Lyon: Jean Frellon, 1548.

Crane, Mary Thomas. *Framing Authority: Sayings, Self, and Society in Sixteenth-Century England.* Princeton: Princeton University Press, 1993.

Cranmer, Thomas. *A Confutation of Unwritten Verities*, trans. E. P. Wesel?: [J. Lambrecht,] 1556?

Cressy, David. *Literacy and the Social Order: Reading and Writing in Tudor and Stuart England*. Cambridge: Cambridge University Press, 1980.

———. "The Protestant Calendar and the Vocabulary of Celebration in Early Modern England." *Journal of British Studies* 29 (1990): 31–51.

Crowley, Robert. *A Setting Open of the Subtyle Sophistrie of Thomas Watson Doctor of Divinitie*. London: Henry Denham, 1569.

Cummings, Brian. "Print, Popularity, and the Book of Common Prayer." In Andy Kesson and Emma Smith, eds., *The Elizabethan Top Ten: Defining Print Popularity in Early Modern England*, 135–44. Farnham: Ashgate, 2013.

Curtius Rufus, Quintus. *De gestis Alexandri Magni*. Paris: Ponset le Preux, 1508.

D., A.D.S. *Les comptes du monde adventureux*. Paris: Estienne Groulleau, 1555.

Dasent, J. R., ed. *Acts of the Privy Council of England*. 46 vols. London: HMSO, 1890–1940.

Da Vigo, Giovanni. *This Lytell Practyce of Joha[n]nes de Vigo in Medycyne*. London: Robert Wyer, 1552?

Dawson, Mark. "Histories and Texts: Refiguring the Diary of Samuel Pepys." *Historical Journal* 43 (2000): 407–31.

Dean, David. *Law-Making and Society in Elizabethan England: The Parliament of England, 1584–1601*. Cambridge: Cambridge University Press, 1996.

De Belleforest, François. *La cosmographie universelle de tout le monde*. 3 vols. Paris: Michel Sonnius, 1575.

De Chauliac, Guy. *Guidos Questions Newly Corrected*. London: Thomas East, 1579.

De Crenne, Hélisenne. *Les Angoysses douloureuses qui procedent d'amours*, ed. Christine de Buzon. Paris: Honoré Champion, 1997.

———. *Les oeuvres de ma dame Helisenne*. Paris: Charles Langelier, 1543.

———. *The Torments of Love*, trans. Lisa Neal and Steven Rendall. Minneapolis: University of Minnesota Press, 1996.

De Estella, Diego. *A Methode unto Mortification*, ed. Thomas Rogers. London: John Windet, 1586.

De Grazia, Margreta. "Shakespeare in Quotation Marks." In Jean I. Marsden, ed., *The Appropriation of Shakespeare: Post-Renaissance Reconstructions of the Works and the Myth*, 57–71. New York: St. Martin's, 1991.

———. *Shakespeare Verbatim: The Reproduction of Authenticity and the 1790 Apparatus*. Oxford: Oxford University Press, 1991.

De Guevara, Antonio. *Archontorologion, or the Diall of Princes*, ed. Anthony Munday. London: Bernard Alsop, 1619.

Dekker, Thomas. *The Batchelers Banquet*. London: Thomas Pavier, 1604.

Deloney, Thomas. *The Pleasant History of John Winchcomb in his Younger Yeares Called Jack of Newberie*. London: Humfrey Lownes, 1619.

Demetriou, Tania. "Tendre cropps and Flourishing Metricians: Gabriel Harvey's Chaucer." Unpublished research paper.

Demetriou, Tania, and Rowan Tomlinson, "'Abroad in Mens Hands': The Culture of Translation in Early Modern England and France." In Tania Demetriou and Rowan Tomlinson, eds., *The Culture of Translation in Early Modern England and France, 1500–1660*, 1–21. Basingstoke: Palgrave Macmillan, 2015.

Deng, Stephen. *Coinage and State Formation in Early Modern English Literature.* Basingstoke: Palgrave Macmillan, 2011.

De Nicolay, Nicolas. *The Navigations, Perigrinations and Voyages, Made into Turkie.* London: John Stell, 1585.

De Rojas, Fernando. *The Celestina: A Novel in Dialogue,* trans. Lesley Byrd Simpson. Berkeley: University of California Press, 1955.

———. *Celestine: A Critical Edition of the First French Translation (1527) of the Spanish Classic "La Celestina,"* ed. Gerard J. Brault. Detroit: Wayne State University Press, 1963.

———. *Celestine en laquelle est traicte des deceptions des seruiteurs enuers leurs maistres.* Paris: Galliot du Pré, 1527.

De Sainctes, Claude. *Liturgiae, siue missae sanctorum patrum.* Antwerp: Christopher Plantin, 1560.

De Valsergues, Jean d'Albin. *Les six livres du sacrement de l'autel pour la confirmation du peuple francoys.* Paris: Guillaume Chaudière, 1562.

De Voragine, Jacopo. *The Lyfe of Adam.* London: Julyan Notarye, 1504.

Dmitrieva, Olga, and Tessa Murdoch. *Treasures of the Royal Courts: Tudors, Stuarts and the Russian Tsars.* London: V&A, 2013.

Dojc, Yuri, and Katya Krausova. *Last Folio: A Photographic Memory.* Munich: Prestel, 2015.

Domenichi, Lodovico. *Facetie, motti, et burle, di diversi signori.* Florence: Giunta, 1564.

Donne, John. *John Donne,* ed. Janel Mueller. Oxford: Oxford University Press, 2015.

———. *Sermons Preached at the Jacobean Courts, 1615–1619,* ed. Peter McCullough. Oxford: Oxford University Press, 2015.

Doré, Pierre. *L'Image de vertu demonstrant la perfection de la vierge Marie.* Paris: Estienne Groulleau, 1559.

Doukas, Georgios. "Pierre Boaistuau (c. 1517–1566) and the Employment of Humanism in Mid-Sixteenth-Century France." Unpublished doctoral dissertation, University of Birmingham, 2012.

Doyle, Arthur Conan. *The Complete Sherlock Holmes.* New York: Doubleday, 1930.

Duncan-Jones, Katherine. "Much Ado with Red and White: The Earliest Readers of Shakespeare's *Venus and Adonis* (1593)." *Review of English Studies,* n.s. 44, 176 (1993): 479–501.

———. *Ungentle Shakespeare: Scenes from his Life.* London: Thomson, 2001.

Du Verdier, Antoine. *Imagines deorum.* Lyon: Barthélemy Honorat, 1581.

———. *La prosopographie, ou, description des personnes insignes.* Lyon: Antoine Gryphius, 1573.

Dyer, Christopher. *A Country Merchant, 1495–1520: Trading and Farming at the End of the Middle Ages.* Oxford: Oxford University Press, 2012.

Eccles, Mark. "Bynneman's Books." *Library,* 5th ser., 12 (1957): 81–92.

Eco, Umberto. *The Infinity of Lists,* trans. Alastair McEwen. London: MacLehose, 2009.

Edmonds, Charles. *An Annotated Catalogue of the Library at Lamport Hall, Northamptonshire.* Privately printed, 1880.

Edwards, A. C. *John Petre: Essays on the Life and Background of John, 1st Lord Petre, 1549–1613.* London: Regency Press, 1975.

Elhard, K. C. "Reopening the Book on Arcimboldo's *Librarian.*" *Libraries and Culture* 40 (2005): 115–27.

Eliot, George. *The Mill on the Floss.* 3 vols. London: Ward, Lock, 1860.

Eliot, John. *The Survay of France.* London: John Wolfe, 1592.

Elton, G. R. "The Elizabethan Exchequer: War in the Receipt." In S. T. Bindoff et al., eds., *Elizabethan Government and Society: Essays Presented to Sir John Neale,* 355–88. London: Athlone Press, 1961.

Elyot, Thomas. *The Castell of Helth.* London: Thomas Berthelet, 1541.

Emmison, F. G. *Elizabethan Life: Morals and the Church Courts.* Chelmsford: Essex County Council, 1973.

———. *Tudor Secretary: Sir William Petre at Court and Home.* London: Longmans, Green, 1961.

England and Wales. *The Statutes at Large.* 2 vols. London: Bonham Norton and John Bill, 1618.

Epstein, Diane, and Millicent Safro. *Buttons.* London: Thames and Hudson, 1991.

Erasmus, Desiderius. *The Paraphrase of Erasmus upon the Newe Testamente.* 2 vols. London: Edward Whitchurch, 1548.

Erler, Mary, ed. *Records of Early English Drama: Ecclesiastical London.* London: British Library, 2008.

Erne, Lukas. *Beyond* The Spanish Tragedy*: A Study of the Works of Thomas Kyd.* Manchester: Manchester University Press, 2001.

Estienne, Henri. *Deux dialogues du nouveau langage François.* Antwerp: Guillaume Niergue, 1579; ed. P.-M. Smith. Geneva: Slatkine, 1980.

Evenden, Elizabeth, and Thomas S. Freeman. *Religion and the Book in Early Modern England: The Making of Foxe's "Book of Martyrs."* Cambridge: Cambridge University Press, 2011.

Fehrenbach, R. J., and E. S. Leedham-Green, eds. *Private Libraries in Renaissance England,* I. Binghamton: Medieval and Renaissance Texts and Studies, 1992.

Felski, Rita. *The Limits of Critique.* Chicago: University of Chicago Press, 2015.

Fenton, Geoffrey. *Certaine Tragicall Discourses.* London: Thomas Marsh, 1567.

Ferrarius, Joannes. *A Woorke . . . Touchynge the Good Orderynge of a Common Weale.* London: Jhon Wight, 1559.

Finch, Martha L. " 'Fashions of Worldly Dames': Separatist Discourses of Dress in Early Modern London, Amsterdam, and Plymouth Colony." *Church History* 74 (2005): 494–533.

Fink, Nancy, and Maryalice Ditzler. *Buttons: The Collector's Guide to Selecting, Restoring and Enjoying New and Vintage Buttons.* London: Apple, 1993.

Fish, Stanley. *Is There a Text in This Class? The Authority of Interpretative Communities.* Cambridge, MA: Harvard University Press, 1980.

Fisher, John. *Psalmi seu precationes.* London: Thomas Berthelet, 1544.

Fisher, R. M. "Privy Council Coercion and Religious Conformity at the Inns of Court." *Recusant History* 15 (1979–81): 305–24.

Flavin, Susan. *Consumption and Culture in Sixteenth-Century Ireland: Saffron, Stockings and Silk.* Woodbridge: Boydell, 2014.

Fleming, Abraham. *The Conduit of Comfort.* London: William Seres, 1579.

———. *The Diamond of Devotion.* London: Henry Denham, 1581.

———. *The Foote-Path to Felicitie.* London: Stationers' Company, 1608.

———. *A Panoplie of Epistles or a Looking-Glass for the Unlearned.* London: Ralph Newberie, 1576.

Fleming, Juliet. *Graffiti and the Writing Arts of Early Modern England.* London: Reaktion, 2001.

———. "The Renaissance Collage: Signcutting and Signsewing." *Journal of Medieval and Early Modern Studies* 45 (2015): 443–56.

Fletcher, Giles. *Of the Russe Common Wealth.* London: Thomas Charde, 1591.

Flynn, Dennis. *John Donne and the Ancient Catholic Nobility.* Bloomington: Indiana University Press, 1995.

Foister, Susan. "Paintings and Other Works of Art in Sixteenth-Century English Inventories." *Burlington Magazine* 123 (1981): 273–82.

Foot, Mirjam M. *The Henry Davis Gift: A Collection of Bookbindings*. 3 vols. London: British Library, 1978.

Foster, Joseph, ed. *London Marriage Licences, 1521–1869*. London: B. Quaritch, 1887.

Foulface, Philip. *Bacchus Bountie Describing the Debonaire Dietie of his Bountifull Godhead*. London: Henry Kyrkham, 1593.

Foxe, John. *The Ecclesiasticall History Contaynyng the Actes and Monumentes*. London: John Day, 1570.

———, ed. *The Whole Workes of W. Tyndall, John Frith, and Doct. Barnes*. London: John Daye, 1573.

Freeman, Thomas S. "The Rise of Prison Literature." *Huntington Library Quarterly* 72 (2009): 133–46.

Frugoni, Chiara. *Books, Banks, Buttons: And Other Inventions from the Middle Ages*, trans. William McCuaig. New York: Columbia University Press, 2003.

Gadd, Ian. "Hunting Down John Wolfe for the New *DNB*." In R. Myers, M. Harris, and G. Mandelbrote, eds., *Lives in Print: Biography and the Book Trade from the Middle Ages to the 21st Century*, 193–201. London: British Library, 2002.

Garrett, Christina Hallowell. *The Marian Exiles: A Study in the Origins of Elizabethan Protestantism*. Cambridge: Cambridge University Press, 1938; repr. 1966.

Gascoigne, George. *A Hundreth Sundrie Flowres Bounde up in One Small Poesie*. London: R. Smith, 1573.

———. *The Posies of George Gascoigne Esquire*. London: R. Smith, 1575.

Gell, Alfred. *Art and Agency: An Anthropological Theory*. Oxford: Clarendon Press, 1998.

Genette, Gérard. *Paratexts: Thresholds of Interpretation*, trans. Jane E. Lewin. Cambridge: Cambridge University Press, 1997.

Gerbino, Anthony, and Stephen Johnston. *Compass and Rule: Architecture as Mathematical Practice in England, 1500–1750*. New Haven: Yale University Press, 2009.

Gesner, Conrad. *Icones avium omnium, quae in historia avium Conradi Gesner describuntur*. Zurich: Christopher Froschouer, 1555.

———. *The Newe Jewell of Health*, trans. George Baker. London: Henry Denham, 1576.

———. *Treasure of Evonymus, Conteyninge the Secretes of Nature, to Destyl Medicines*, trans. Peter Morwyng. London: John Day, 1559.

Gillespie, Alexandra. *Print Culture and the Medieval Author: Chaucer, Lydgate, and Their Books, 1473–1557*. Oxford: Oxford University Press, 2006.

Girouard, Mark. *Elizabethan Architecture: Its Rise and Fall, 1540–1640*. New Haven: Yale University Press, 2009.

Gjerpe, Kristin. "The Italian *Utopia* of Lando, Doni and Sansovino: Paradox and Politics." In Terence Cave, ed., *Thomas More's* Utopia *in Early Modern Europe: Paratexts and Contexts*, 47–66. Manchester: Manchester University Press, 2008.

Gleeson-White, Jane. *Double Entry: How the Merchants of Venice Created Modern Finance*. London: Allen and Unwin, 2011.

Goldring, Elizabeth. "A Portrait of Sir Philip Sidney by Veronese at Leicester House, London." *Burlington Magazine* 154 (2012): 548–54.

Grafton, Anthony, and Lisa Jardine. "'Studied for Action': How Gabriel Harvey Read His Livy." *Past and Present* 129 (1990): 30–78.

Grafton, Richard. *A Litle Treatise, Conteyning Many Proper Tables*. London: Richard Tottel, 1571.

Gray, Madeleine. "Exchequer Officials and Crown Property." In R. W. Hoyle, ed., *The Estates of the English Crown*, 112–36. Cambridge: Cambridge University Press, 1992.

Green, Ian. *Print and Protestantism in Early Modern England.* Oxford: Oxford University Press, 2000.

Grendler, Paul. *Critics of the Italian World, 1530–1560: Anton Francesco Doni, Nicolò Franco and Ortensio Lando.* Madison: University of Wisconsin Press, 1969.

Griffiths, Paul. *Lost Londons: Change, Crime, and Control in the Capital City, 1550–1660.* Cambridge: Cambridge University Press, 2008.

Groebner, Valentin. "Inside Out: Clothes, Dissimulation, and the Arts of Accounting in the Autobiography of Matthäus Schwarz, 1496–1574." *Representations* 66 (1999): 100–121.

Hackel, Heidi Brayman. *Reading Material in Early Modern England: Print, Gender and Literacy.* Cambridge: Cambridge University Press, 2005.

Haigh, Christopher. "The Character of an Anti-Puritan." *Sixteenth Century Journal* 35 (2004): 671–88.

Hakluyt, Richard. *Principal Navigations.* London: George Bishop et al., 1599.

———. *The Principall Navigations, Voiages and Discoveries.* London: Christopher Barker, 1589.

Hallam, H. A. N. "Lamport Hall Revisited." *Book Collector* 16 (1967): 439–49.

Hamilton, Donna B. *Anthony Munday and the Catholics, 1560–1633.* Aldershot: Ashgate, 2005.

Hamling, Tara. *Decorating the Godly Household: Religious Art in Post-Reformation Britain.* New Haven: Yale University Press, 2010.

———. "'Wanting Arms': Heraldic Decoration in Lesser Houses." In Nigel Ramsay, ed., *Heralds and Heraldry in Shakespeare's England*, 205–19. Donington: Shaun Tyas, 2014.

Hardy, W. J., and W. Page, eds. *A Calendar to the Feet of Fines for London and Middlesex.* 2 vols. London: For the authors, 1892–93.

Hardyng, John. *The Chronicle of Jhon Hardyng in Metre.* London: Richard Grafton, 1543.

Harington, Sir John. *The Epigrams of Sir John Harington*, ed. Gerard Kilroy. Farnham: Ashgate, 2009.

Harley, John. *William Byrd: Gentleman of the Chapel Royal.* Abingdon: Routledge, 1999.

———. *The World of William Byrd: Musicians, Merchants and Magnates.* Farnham: Ashgate, 2010.

Harman, Graham. "Demodernizing the Humanities with Latour." *New Literary History* 47 (2016): 249–74.

Harris, Jonathan Gil. "Shakespeare's Hair: Staging the Object of Material Culture." *Shakespeare Quarterly* 52 (2001): 479–91.

———. *Untimely Matter in the Time of Shakespeare.* Philadelphia: University of Pennsylvania Press, 2008.

Hart, E. P. *Merchant Taylors' School Register.* 2 vols. London: Eastern Press, 1936.

Heal, Felicity. *The Power of Gifts: Gift Exchange in Early Modern England.* Oxford: Oxford University Press, 2014.

Hearn, Karen, ed. *Dynasties: Painting in Tudor and Jacobean England, 1530–1630.* London: Tate, 1995.

Heawood, Edward. *English County Maps in the Collection of the Royal Geographical Society.* London: Royal Geographical Society, 1932.

Helgerson, Richard. *The Elizabethan Prodigals.* Berkeley: University of California Press, 1983.

Heliodorus. *An Aethiopian Historie*, trans. Thomas Underdoune. London: Fraunces Coldocke, 1569.

Hentschell, Roze. *The Culture of Cloth in Early Modern England: Textual Constructions of a National Identity*. Aldershot: Ashgate, 2008.

Hervey, William. *Epicedium, A Funerall Song, upon the Vertuous Life, and Godly Death, of the Right Worshipfull the Lady Helen Branch*. London: Thomas Creede, 1594.

Heywood, John. *An Hundred Epigrammes*. London: Thomas Berthelet, 1550.

———. *Woorkes*. London: Thomas Powell, 1562.

Higden, Ranulph. *Polycronycon*. Southwark: Peter Treveris, 1527.

Hill, Tracey. *Anthony Munday and Civic Culture: Theatre, History and Power in Early Modern London, 1580–1633*. Manchester: Manchester University Press, 2004.

Hippocrates. *The Boke of Knowledge: Whether a Sycke Person Beynge in Peryll Shall Lyve, or Dye. &c*. London: Robert Wyer, 1548?

Hobbes, Thomas. *Leviathan*, ed. Noel Malcolm. 3 vols. Oxford: Clarendon Press, 2012.

Holinshed, Raphael. *The First and Second Volumes of Chronicles*. London: John Harison et al., 1587.

Holyband, Claudius. *The French Littelton*. London: Thomas Vautrollier, 1576.

———. *The Pretie and Wittie Historie of Arnalt & Lucenda with Certen Rules and Dialogues Set Foorth for the Learner of th'Italian Tong*. London: Thomas Purfoote, 1575.

Hooker, Richard. *Of the Lawes of Ecclesiasticall Politie*. London: John Windet, 1593.

Hooks, Adam. *Selling Shakespeare: Biography, Bibliography, and the Book Trade*. Cambridge: Cambridge University Press, 2016.

Horne, David. *The Life and Minor Works of George Peele*. New Haven: Yale University Press, 1952.

Hosius, Stanislaus. *Confessio catholicæ fidei christiana*. Antwerp: Joannes Steelsius, 1559.

Hotson, Leslie. "The Library of Elizabeth's Embezzling Teller." *Studies in Bibliography* 2 (1949–50): 49–61.

Howard, J. J., and Joseph Lemuel Chester, eds. *The Visitation of London: Anno Domini 1633, 1634, and 1635*. 2 vols. London: Harleian Society, 1880–83.

Howe, Sarah. "The Authority of Presence: The Development of the English Author Portrait, 1500–1640." *Papers of the Bibliographical Society of America* 102 (2008): 464–99.

Howell, James. *Londinopolis; An Historicall Discourse or Perlustration of the City of London*. London: Henry Twiford et al., 1657.

Hudson, Zoe. "Food, Dining and the Everyday Life of Richard Stonley." Unpublished M.Res. dissertation, University of Kent, 2014.

Huloet, Richard. *Abcedarium Anglico Latinum*. London: William Riddell, 1552.

Hulsbusch, Joannes. *Sylva sermonum iucundissimorum*. Basel: Samuel Apiarius, 1568.

Hunnis, William. *Seven Sobs of a Sorrowfull Soule for Sinne*. London: Henry Denham, 1583.

Hurtado de Mendoza, Diego. *The Pleasaunt Historie of Lazarillo de Tormes*. London: Abel Jeffes, 1586.

Hutchins, Edward. *Davids Sling against Great Goliah: Conteining Divers Treatises*. London: Henry Denham, 1581.

Hutson, Lorna. *Thomas Nashe in Context*. Oxford: Clarendon Press, 1989.

Ingold, Tim. *Being Alive: Essays on Movement, Knowledge and Description*. London: Routledge, 2011.

Jardine, Lisa. *Erasmus, Man of Letters: The Construction of Charisma in Print*. Princeton: Princeton University Press, 1993.

———. *Temptation in the Archives: Essays in Golden Age Dutch Culture*. London: UCL Press, 2015.

Jayne, Sears, and Francis R. Johnson, eds. *The Lumley Library: The Catalogue of 1609.* London: British Museum, 1956.

Jeaffreson, J. C., ed. *Middlesex County Records.* 4 vols. London: Middlesex County Records Society, 1886–92.

Jeninges, Edward. *A Briefe Discovery of the Damages that Happen to this Realme by Disordered and Unlawfull Diet.* London: Roger Ward, 1590.

Jewel, John. *A Defence of the Apologie of the Churche of Englande.* London: H. Wykes, 1567.

Johnson, George. *A Discourse of Some Troubles and Excommunications in the Banished English Church at Amsterdam.* Amsterdam: N.p., 1603.

Johnson, Gerald D. "The Stationers Versus the Drapers: Control of the Press in the Late Sixteenth Century." *Library*, 6th ser., 10 (1988): 1–17.

Johnson, Robert Carl. *John Heywood.* New York: Twayne, 1970.

Jones, Ann Rosalind, and Peter Stallybrass. *Renaissance Clothing and the Materials of Memory.* Cambridge: Cambridge University Press, 2000.

Jones, Deborah. "Lodowick Bryskett and His Family." In Charles J. Sisson, ed., *Thomas Lodge and Other Elizabethans*, 243–362. Cambridge, MA: Harvard University Press, 1932.

Jones, Malcolm. *The Print in Early Modern England: An Historical Oversight.* New Haven: Yale University Press, 2010.

Jones, Philip Henry. "Wales and the Stationers' Company." In Robin Myers and Michael Harris, eds., *The Stationers' Company and the Book Trade*, 185–202. Winchester: St. Paul's Bibliographies, 1997.

Joyce, James. *Dubliners*, ed. Hans Walter Gabler with Walter Hettche. New York: Vintage, 1993.

Juhasz, Barbara J., and Alexander Pollatsek. "Lexical Influences on Eye Movements in Reading." In Simon Liversedge et al., eds., *The Oxford Handbook of Eye Movements*, 873–93. Oxford: Oxford University Press, 2011.

Kaufmann, Thomas DaCosta. *Arcimboldo: Visual Jokes, Natural History, and Still-Life Painting.* Chicago: University of Chicago Press, 2009.

Kearney, James. *The Incarnate Text: Imagining the Book in Reformation England.* Philadelphia: University of Pennsylvania Press, 2009.

Kelly, F. M. "What Are 'Canions'?" *Burlington Magazine* 32, 180 (1918): 102–9.

Kenny, Neil. *The Palace of Secrets: Béroalde de Verville and Renaissance Conceptions of Knowledge.* Oxford: Clarendon Press, 1991.

Kewes, Paulina, Ian W. Archer, and Felicity Heal, eds. *The Oxford Handbook of Holinshed's Chronicles.* Oxford: Oxford University Press, 2013.

Keynes, Geoffrey. "More Books from the Library of John Donne." *Book Collector* 26 (1977): 29–35.

Kiessling, Nicolas K. *The Library Catalogue of Anthony Wood.* Oxford: Oxford Bibliographical Society, 2002.

Kilroy, Gerard. *Edmund Campion: A Scholarly Life.* Farnham: Ashgate, 2015.

Kinnaston, Sir Francis. *Corona Minervae.* London: William Sheares, 1635.

Kirchmeyer, Thomas. *The Popish Kingdome, or Reigne of Antichrist*, trans. Barnaby Googe. London: R. Watkins, 1570.

Kirk, R. E. G. and E. F. Kirk, eds. *Returns of Aliens Dwelling in the City and Suburbs of London from the Reign of Henry VIII to That of James I.* 4 vols. Aberdeen: Huguenot Society of London, 1900–1908.

Knight, Jeffrey Todd. *Bound to Read: Compilations, Collections, and the Making of Renaissance Literature.* Philadelphia: University of Pennsylvania Press, 2013.

———. "'Furnished for Action': Renaissance Books as Furniture." *Book History* 12 (2009): 37–73.

———. "Needles and Pens: Sewing in Early English Books." *Journal of Medieval and Early Modern Studies* 45 (2015): 523–42.

Knight, Leah. *Of Books and Botany in Early Modern England: Sixteenth-Century Plants and Print Culture.* Farnham: Ashgate, 2009.

Krohn, Deborah L., and Peter N. Miller, eds. *Dutch New York between East and West: The World of Margrieta van Varick.* New Haven: Yale University Press, 2010.

Lahiri, Jhumpa. *The Clothing of Books.* London: Bloomsbury, 2017.

Larkin, Philip. *Complete Poems,* ed. Archie Burnett. London: Faber, 2012.

Laroche, Rebecca. *Medical Authority and Englishwomen's Herbal Texts, 1550–1650.* Farnham: Ashgate, 2009.

Latour, Bruno. *Reassembling the Social: An Introduction to Actor-Network-Theory.* Oxford: Oxford University Press, 2005.

———. "Visualisation and Cognition: Drawing Things Together." In H. Kuklick, ed., *Knowledge and Society: Studies in the Sociology of Culture Past and Present,* 1–40. Greenwich, CT: JAI Press, 1986.

Laughton, John Knox, ed. *State Papers Relating to the Defeat of the Spanish Armada.* 2nd ed. 2 vols. in 1. London: Navy Records Society, 1987.

Lawson, Jane A., ed. *The Elizabethan New Year's Gift Exchanges, 1559–1603.* Oxford: British Academy, 2013.

Lawrence-Mathers, Anne. "Domesticating the Calendar: The Hours and the Almanac in Tudor England." In Anne Lawrence-Mathers and Phillipa Harman, eds., *Women and Writing, c. 1340–c. 1650: The Domestication of Print Culture,* 34–61. York: York Medieval Press, 2010.

Lazarus, Micha. "Lucius Florus and a Pownde of Prunes: What Was a Book in Tudor Oxford?" Unpublished research paper.

Leedham-Green, Elisabeth. *Books in Cambridge Inventories: Book-Lists from the Vice-Chancellor's Court Probate Inventories in the Tudor and Stuart Periods.* 2 vols. Cambridge: Cambridge University Press, 1986.

Leong, Elaine. "'Herbals she peruseth': Reading Medicine in Early Modern England." *Renaissance Studies* 28 (2014): 556–78.

Lerer, Seth. *Children's Literature: A Reader's History, from Aesop to Harry Potter.* Chicago: University of Chicago Press, 2008.

Lesser, Zachary. *Renaissance Drama and the Politics of Publication: Readings in the English Book Trade.* Cambridge: Cambridge University Press, 2004.

Lesser, Zachary, and Alan B. Farmer. "The Popularity of Playbooks Revisited." *Shakespeare Quarterly* 56 (2005): 1–32.

Le Sylvain. *The Orator Handling a Hundred Severall Discourses, in Forme of Declamations.* London: Adam Islip, 1596.

Lever, J. W. "Shakespeare's French Fruits." *Shakespeare Survey* 6 (1953): 79–90.

Lim, Walter S. H. "Surety and Spiritual Commercialism in *The Merchant of Venice.*" *Studies in English Literature, 1500–1900* 50 (2010): 355–81.

Lister, Anthony. "William Ford (1771–1832): 'The Universal Bookseller.'" *Book Collector* 38 (1989): 343–71.

Lloyd, Lodowick. *The First Part of the Diall of Daies.* London: Roger Ward, 1590.

————. *The Triplicitie of Triumphes*. London: R. Jhones, 1591.

Loades, D. M. *Two Tudor Conspiracies*. Cambridge: Cambridge University Press, 1965.

Loewenstein, Joseph. "For a History of Literary Property: John Wolfe's Reformation." *English Literary Renaissance* 18 (1988): 389–412.

Loveman, Kate. *Samuel Pepys and His Books: Reading, Newsgathering, and Sociability, 1660–1703*. Oxford: Oxford University Press, 2015.

Luborsky, Ruth Samson, and Elizabeth Morley Ingram. *A Guide to English Illustrated Books*. Tempe, AZ: Medieval and Renaissance Texts and Studies, 1998.

Lupton, Christina. "Immersing the Network in Time: From the Where to the When of Print Reading." *ELH* 83 (2016): 299–317

Luther, Martin. *An Exposition of Salomons Booke, called Ecclesiastes*. London: John Daye, 1573.

Mabbe, James. *The Spanish Bawd*, ed. José María Pérez Fernández. London: Modern Humanities Research Association, 2013.

McConica, James Kelsey. *English Humanists and Reformation Politics Under Henry VIII and Edward VI*. Oxford: Clarendon Press, 1965.

McGann, Jerome. *A Critique of Modern Textual Criticism*. Chicago: University of Chicago Press, 1983.

————. *The Textual Condition*. Princeton: Princeton University Press, 1991.

McKenzie, D. F. *Bibliography and the Sociology of Texts*. London: British Library, 1986.

McKitterick, David, ed. *The Library of Thomas Knyvett of Ashwellthorpe, c. 1539–1618*. Cambridge: Cambridge University Library, 1978.

————. "'Ovid with a Littleton': The Cost of English Books in the Early Seventeenth Century." *Transactions of the Cambridge Bibliographical Society* XI (1997): 183–234.

MacLean, Gerald. "East by North-East: The English Among the Russians, 1553–1603." In Jyotsna G. Singh, ed., *A Companion to the Global Renaissance: English Literature and Culture in the Era of Expansion*, 163–77. Oxford: Wiley-Blackwell, 2009.

MacLeod, Catherine, et al. *The Lost Prince: The Life and Death of Henry Stuart*. London: National Portrait Gallery, 2012.

McLeod, Randall [as Random Cloud]. "From Tranceformations in the Text of Orlando Furioso." *Library Chronicle of the University of Texas at Austin* 20 (1990): 60–85.

McMillin, Scott, and Sally-Beth MacLean. *The Queen's Men and Their Plays*. Cambridge: Cambridge University Press, 1998.

Malone, Edmund. *An Inquiry into the Authenticity of Certain Miscellaneous Papers and Legal Instruments*. London: T. Cadell and W. Davies, 1796.

Manning, Roger B. "Catholics and Local Office Holding in Elizabethan Sussex." *Historical Research* 35 (1962): 47–61.

Marcellinus, Ammianus. *The Roman Historie*, trans. Philemon Holland. London: Adam Islip, 1609.

Marchand, J., ed. *Le livre de raison de Montaigne sur l'Ephemeris historica de Beuther*. Paris: Compagnie Française des Arts Graphiques, 1948.

Margues, Nicolas. *Description du monde desguisé*. Paris: Thomas Richard, 1563.

Marlorat, Augustin. *Propheticae, et apostolicae, id est, totius diuinae ac canonicae Scripturae, thesaurus*. London: Thomas Vautrollier, 1574.

Marlowe, Christopher. *Tamburlaine the Great*. London: Richard Jhones, 1590.

Marnix, Philips van. *The Bee Hive of the Romishe Church*. London: Thomas Dawson, 1579.

Marotti, Arthur F. "'Love is not love': Elizabethan Sonnet Sequences and the Social Order." *ELH* 49 (1982): 396–428.

Maslen, R. W. *Elizabethan Fictions: Espionage, Counter-Espionage, and the Duplicity of Fiction in Early Elizabethan Prose Narratives.* Oxford: Oxford University Press, 1997.

Maunsell, Andrew. *The First Part of the Catalogue of English Printed Bookes: Which Concerneth Divinitie.* London: Andrew Maunsell, 1595.

Maus, Katharine Eisaman. *Being and Having in Shakespeare.* Oxford: Oxford University Press, 2013.

May, Steven W. "*Youthes Witte*: An Unstudied Elizabethan Anthology of Printed Verse and Prose Fiction." *Renaissance Papers* (2006): 1–12.

May, Steven W., and William A. Ringler Jr. *Elizabethan Poetry: A Bibliography and First-Line Index of English Verse, 1559–1603.* 3 vols. London: Thoemmes Continuum, 2004.

Mela, Pomponius. *De totius orbis descriptione.* Paris: Gilles de Gourmont, 1507.

Mellis, John. *A Briefe Instruction and Maner How to Keepe Bookes of Accompts.* London: Hugh Singleton, 1588.

Melnikoff, Kirk. "Jones's Pen and Marlowe's Socks: Richard Jones, Print Culture, and the Beginnings of English Dramatic Literature." *Studies in Philology* 102 (2005): 184–209.

Mendelsund, Peter. *What We See When We Read.* New York: Vintage, 2014.

Meres, Francis. *Palladis Tamia.* London: Cuthbert Burbie, 1598.

Meriton, George. *Nomenclatura clericalis, or, The Young Clerk's Vocabulary in English and Latine.* London: Richard Lambert, 1685.

Merry, Mark, and Catherine Richardson, eds. *The Household Account Book of Sir Thomas Puckering of Warwick, 1521: Living in London and the Midlands.* Stratford-upon-Avon: Dugdale Society, 2012.

Meurier, Gabriel. *The Nosegay of Morall Philosophie,* trans. Thomas Crewe. London: Thomas Dawson, 1580.

Mexía, Pedro. *The Foreste or Collection of Histories,* trans. Thomas Fortescue. London: William Jones, 1571.

Miller, Daniel. *Stuff.* Cambridge: Polity Press, 2010.

Milton, Anthony. "A Qualified Intolerance: The Limits and Ambiguities of Early Stuart Anti-Catholicism." In Arthur F. Marotti, ed., *Catholicism and Anti-Catholicism in Early Modern English Texts,* 85–115. Basingstoke: Macmillan, 1999.

Milton, John. *Areopagitica.* London: N.p., 1644.

Moffett, Peter. *A Commentarie upon the Booke of the Proverbes of Salomon.* London: Robert Dexter, 1592.

———. *A Commentarie upon the Whole Booke of the Proverbs of Salomon.* London: Robert Dexter, 1596.

Moore, Helen. "Gathering Fruit: The 'Profitable' Translations of Thomas Paynell." In Fred Schurink, ed., *Tudor Translation,* 39–57. Basingstoke: Palgrave Macmillan, 2011.

More, Thomas. *Eruditissimi viri Ferdinandi Baravelli opus elegans, quo refellit Lutheri calumnias.* London: R. Pynson, 1523.

———. *A Frutefull Pleasaunt, [and] Wittie Worke, of the Best State of a Publique Weale,* trans. Ralph Robynson. London: Abraham Vele, 1556.

Morgan, E. Delmar, and C. H. Coote, eds. *Early Voyages and Travels to Russia and Persia.* 2 vols. London: Hakluyt Society, 1886.

Morgan, Paul. "Frances Wolfreston and 'Hor Bouks': A Seventeenth-Century Woman Book-Collector." *Library,* 6th ser., XI (1989): 197–219.

Morrall, Andrew. "Inscriptional Wisdom and the Domestic Arts in Early Modern Northern Europe." In Natalia Filatkina et al., eds., *Konstruktion, Manifestation und Dynamik der Formelhaftigkeit in Text und Bild,* 121–38. Trier: Universität Trier, 2012.

Mortimer, Ruth. "The Author's Image: Italian Sixteenth-Century Printed Portraits." *Harvard Library Bulletin*, n.s., 7 (1996): 7–87.

Moss, Ann. *Printed Commonplace-Books and the Structuring of Renaissance Thought.* Oxford: Clarendon Press, 1996.

Moulton, Thomas. *This is the Glasse of Helth.* London: Robert Wyer, 1547?

Mousley, Andy. "Early Modern Autobiography, History and Human Testimony: The Autobiography of Thomas Whythorne." *Textual Practice* 23 (2009): 267–87.

Muldrew, Craig. *The Economy of Obligation: The Culture of Credit and Social Relations in Early Modern England.* Basingstoke: Palgrave Macmillan, 1998.

Müller, Lothar. *White Magic: The Age of Paper.* Cambridge: Polity, 2014.

Munday, Anthony. *A Banquet of Daintie Conceits.* London: Edward White, 1588.

———. *The Mirrour of Mutabilitie.* London: Richard Ballard, 1579.

Murray, Molly. "Measured Sentences: Forming Literature in the Early Modern Prison." *Huntington Library Quarterly* 72 (2009): 147–67.

Musculus, Wolfgang. *Common Places of Christian Religion.* London: Reginalde Wolfe, 1563.

Nanni, Giovanni. *Berosus Babilonicus de his quae praecesserunt inundationem terrarum.* Paris: Apud Collegium Plessiacum, 1510.

Nardizzi, Vin. *Wooden Os: Shakespeares Theatres and England's Trees.* Toronto: University of Toronto Press, 2013.

Nashe, Thomas. *Pierce Penilesse his Supplication to the Divell.* London: John Busby, 1592.

Neal, Simon R., and Christine Leighton. *Calendar of Patent Rolls 38 Elizabeth I (1595–1596) C66/1443–1457.* Kew: List and Index Society, 2007.

Nelson, Alan. "Shakespeare and the Bibliophiles: From the Earliest Years to 1616." In *Owners, Annotators, and the Signs of Reading,* ed. Robin Myers et al., 49–73. London: British Library, 2005.

Nelson, Eric. "Utopia Through Italian Eyes: Thomas More and the Critics of Civic Humanism." *Renaissance Quarterly* 59 (2006): 1029–57.

Nixon, Howard M. "Elizabethan Gold-Tooled Bindings." In Dennis Rhodes, ed., *Essays in Honour of Victor Scholderer,* 219–70. Mainz: Karl Pressler, 1970.

Norden, John. *The Pensive Mans Practise: The Second Part.* London: John Oxenbridge, 1599.

Nowell, Alexander. *A Catechisme, or First Instruction and Learning of Christian Religion.* London: John Day, 1570.

———. *A Confutation, As Wel of M. Dormans Last Boke As Also of D. Sander.* London: Henry Bynneman, 1567.

Oldcastle, Hugh. *Here Ensueth a Profitable Treatyce.* London: John Gough, 1543.

Orgel, Stephen. *The Reader in the Book: A Study of Spaces and Traces.* Oxford: Oxford University Press, 2015.

Orlin, Lena Cowen. "Fictions of the Early Modern English Probate Inventory." In Henry S. Turner, ed., *The Culture of Capital: Property, Cities and Knowledge in Early Modern England,* 51–83. New York: Routledge, 2002.

Osborn, James M., ed. *The Autobiography of Thomas Whythorne.* Oxford: Clarendon Press, 1961.

P., S. *An Epitaph of the Vertuous Life and Death of the Right Worshipfull Ladie, Dame Helen Branch of London Widow.* London: Thomas Creede, 1594.

Pacioli, Luca. *Double-Entry Book-Keeping,* trans. Pietro Crivelli. London: Institute of Book-Keepers, 1924.

Page, William, ed. *Victoria County History of the County of Bedford.* 4 vols. Folkestone: Institute of Historical Research, 1904–14.

Painter, William. *Palace of Pleasure.* 2 vols. London: Richard Tottell et al., 1566–67.

Panek, Jennifer. "Why Did Widows Remarry? Remarriage, Male Authority, and Feminist Criticism." In Dympna Callaghan, ed., *The Impact of Feminism in English Renaissance Studies,* 281–98. Basingstoke: Palgrave Macmillan, 2007.

Parker, Patricia. "Cassio, Cash, and the 'Infidel o': Arithmetic, Double-Entry Bookkeeping, and *Othello*'s Unfaithful Accounts." In Jyotsna G. Singh, ed., *A Companion to the Global Renaissance: English Literature and Culture in the Era of Expansion,* 223–41. Oxford: Wiley-Blackwell, 2009.

———. "Preposterous Events." *Shakespeare Quarterly* 43 (1992): 186–213.

Parmelee, Lisa Ferraro. *Good Newes from Fraunce: French Anti-League Propaganda in Late Elizabethan England.* Rochester, NY: University of Rochester Press, 1996.

Parsons, Robert. *The First Booke of the Christian Exercise Appertayning to Resolution.* Rouen: Robert Parsons, 1582.

Patten, William. *The Expedicion into Scotlande of the Most Woorthely Fortunate Prince Edward.* London: Richard Grafton, 1548.

Pearson, David. *Books as History: The Importance of Books Beyond Their Texts.* London: British Library and Oak Knoll Press, 2008.

———. *English Bookbinding Styles, 1451–1800.* London: British Library, 2005.

———. "The English Private Library in the Seventeenth Century." *Library* 13 (2012): 379–99.

Peele, James. *The Maner and Fourme How to Kepe a Perfecte Reconyng.* London: Richard Grafton, 1554?

———. *The Pathe Waye to Perfectnes, in th'Accomptes of Debitour, and Creditour.* London: Thomas Purfoote, 1569.

Pelling, Margaret, and Frances White. *Physicians and Irregular Medical Practitioners in London 1550–1640 Database.* http://www.british-history.ac.uk/no-series/london-physicians/1550–1640.

Pennell, Sara. "'Pots and Pans History': The Material Culture of the Kitchen in Early Modern England." *Journal of Design History* 11 (1998): 201–16.

Penny, Nicholas. "Toothpicks and Green Hangings." *Renaissance Studies* 19 (2005): 581–90.

Pepys, Walter C., and Ernest Godman. *The Church of St Dunstan, Stepney.* London: Committee for the Survey of the Memorials of Greater London, 1905.

Pérez Fernández, José María. "Translation, *Sermo Communis*, and the Book Trade." In José María Pérez Fernández and Edward Wilson-Lee, eds., *Translation and the Book Trade in Early Modern Europe,* 40–60. Cambridge: Cambridge University Press, 2014.

Periegetes, Dionysius. *The Surveye of the World, or Situation of the Earth, So Muche as is Inhabited.* London: Henry Bynneman, 1572.

Peryn, William. *Spirituall Exercyses and Goostly Meditacions.* London: John Waley, 1557.

Peters, Jeffrey N. *Mapping Discord: Allegorical Cartography in Early Modern French Writing.* Newark: University of Delaware Press, 2004.

Pettit, Philip. *Made with Words: Hobbes on Language, Mind, and Politics.* Princeton: Princeton University Press, 2008.

Phillips, John. *A Commemoration of the Life and Death of the Right Worshipfull and Vertuous Ladie; Dame Helen Branch.* London: John Danter, 1594.

Pierce, Helen. *Unseemly Pictures: Graphic Satire and Politics in Early Modern England.* New Haven: Yale University Press, 2008.

Plomer, Henry R. *Robert Wyer, Printer and Bookseller*. London: Bibliographical Society, 1897.

Plutarch. *The Governau[n]ce of Good Helthe*. London: Robert Wyer, 1549?

Poole, William. *Milton and the Making of "Paradise Lost."* Cambridge, MA: Harvard University Press, 2017.

Poovey, Mary. *A History of the Modern Fact: Problems of Knowledge in the Sciences of Wealth and Society*. Chicago: University of Chicago Press, 1998.

Pratt, Aaron T. "Stab-Stitching and the Status of Early English Playbooks as Literature." *Library*, 7th ser., 16 (2015): 304–28.

Prerogative Court of Canterbury Administrations, 3, 1581–1595. London: British Record Society, 1954.

Preston, Andrew. "Moving Lines: The Anthropology of a Manuscript in Tudor London." Unpublished M.A. dissertation, University of Akron, 2014.

Price, Leah. *How to Do Things with Books in Victorian Britain*. Princeton: Princeton University Press, 2012.

Proclus. *The Descripcion of the Sphere or the Frame of the Worlde*. London: Robert Wyer, 1550.

Proust, Marcel. "On Reading." In Marcel Proust, *On Reading Ruskin*, ed. and trans. Jean Autret et al. New Haven: Yale University Press, 1987.

Quinn, David B. "Johnson, George." In *Dictionary of Canadian Biography*, http://www.bio graphi.ca/en/bio/johnson_george_1E.html.

Rabelais, François. *Complete Works*, trans. Donald M. Frame. Berkeley: University of California Press, 1991.

Rainolde, Richard. *A Booke Called the Foundacion of Rhetorike*. London: John Kingston, 1563.

Rayner, Keith. *Psychology of Reading*. 2nd ed. New York: Psychology Press, 2012.

Razzall, Lucy. "Containers and Containment in Early Modern Literature." Unpublished doctoral dissertation. University of Cambridge, 2013.

Reed, Aileen, and Robert Maniura. *Edward Alleyn: Elizabethan Actor, Jacobean Gentleman*. London: Dulwich Picture Gallery, 1994.

Reinburg, Victoria. *French Books of Hours: Making an Archive of Prayer, c. 1400–1600*. Cambridge: Cambridge University Press, 2012.

Rhodes, Dennis, ed. *Essays in Honour of Victor Scholderer*. Mainz: Karl Pressler, 1970.

Rhodes, Neil. "Shakespeare's Encyclopaedias." In Jason König and Greg Woolf, eds., *Encyclopaedism from Antiquity to the Renaissance*, 444–60. Cambridge: Cambridge University Press, 2013.

Riello, Giorgio. " 'Things Seen and Unseen': The Material Culture of Early Modern Inventories and Their Representation of Domestic Interiors." In Paula Findlen, ed., *Early Modern Things: Objects and Their Histories, 1500–1800*, 125–50. London: Routledge, 2013.

Roberts, Dunstan, and Jason Scott-Warren. "Armagil Waad." In R. J. Fehrenbach and Joseph L. Black, eds., *Private Libraries in Renaissance England*, IX:1–35. Tempe: Arizona Center for Medieval and Renaissance Studies, 2017.

Roberts, Sasha. *Reading Shakespeare's Poems in Early Modern England*. Basingstoke: Palgrave Macmillan, 2003.

Rogers, Thomas. *The English Creede*. London: Andrew Maunsell, 1585.

———. *A Golden Chaine, Taken out of the Psalmes of King David*. London: Henry Denham, 1579.

Rouillé, Guillaume. *La premiere partie du promptuaire des medalles des plus renommees personnes*. Lyon: Guillaume Rouillé, 1553.

Rowland, David, *The Life of Lazarillo de Tormes*, ed. Keith Whitlock. Warminster: Aris and Phillips, 2000.

———, trans. *The Pleasaunt Historie of Lazarillo de Tormes*. London: Abell Jeffes, 1586.

Rublack, Ulinka. *Dressing Up: Cultural Identity in Renaissance Europe*. Oxford: Oxford University Press, 2010.

Rublack, Ulinka, and Maria Hayward, eds. *The First Book of Fashion: The Books of Clothes of Matthäus and Veit Konrad Schwarz of Augsburg*. London: Bloomsbury Academic, 2015.

Ryrie, Alec. *Being Protestant in Reformation Britain*. Oxford: Oxford University Press, 2013.

Saenger, Michael. *The Commodification of Textual Engagements in the English Renaissance*. Aldershot: Ashgate, 2006.

Saenger, Paul. *Space Between Words: The Origins of Silent Reading*. Stanford, CA: Stanford University Press, 1997.

Salzman, L. F., ed. *The Victoria History of the County of Warwick*, vol. 6, *Knightlow Hundred*. London: Institute of Historical Research, 1951.

Sandys, George. *A Relation of a Journey Begun An. Dom. 1610*. London: W. Barrett, 1615.

Saunders, Austen. "Marked Books in Early Modern English Society, c. 1550–1700." Unpublished doctoral dissertation, University of Cambridge, 2013.

Saxton, Christopher. [*Atlas of the counties of England and Wales.*] London: N.p., 1579.

Scarry, Elaine. *Dreaming by the Book*. Princeton: Princeton University Press, 1999.

Schedel, Hartmann. *Liber chronicarum*. Nuremberg: Sebald Schreyer and Sebastian Kamermaister, 1493.

Schurink, Fred. "'Like a Hand in the Margine of a Booke': William Blount's Marginalia and the Politics of Sidney's *Arcadia*." *Review of English Studies* 59 (2008): 1–24.

Scott, Charlotte. *Shakespeare and the Book*. Oxford: Oxford University Press, 2007.

Scott-Warren, Jason. "In Search of 850 Lost Books." http://www.english.cam.ac.uk/cmt/?p = 3716.

———. "Ligatures of the Early Modern Book." In *Book 2.0* 7 (2017): 33–44.

———. "News, Sociability and Bookbuying in Early Modern England: The Letters of Sir Thomas Cornwallis." *Library*, 7th ser., 1 (2000): 377–98.

———. "Portrait of the Spy as a Young Man." http://www.english.cam.ac.uk/cmt/?s = herle.

———. "Reading Graffiti in the Early Modern Book." *Huntington Library Quarterly* 73 (2010): 363–81.

———. *Sir John Harington and the Book as Gift*. Oxford: Oxford University Press, 2001.

Scott-Warren, Jason, and Andrew Zurcher, eds. *Text, Food, and the Early Modern Reader: Eating Words*. London: Routledge, 2019.

Scoufos, Alice Lyle. "Harvey: A Name-Change in *Henry IV*." *ELH* 36 (1969): 297–318.

Scragg, Brenda J. "William Ford, Manchester Bookseller." In Peter Isaac and Barry McKay, eds., *The Human Face of the Book Trade*, 155–70. Winchester: St. Paul's Bibliographies, 1999).

Selwyn, Pamela, and David Selwyn. "'The Profession of a Gentleman': Books for the Gentry and the Nobility (c. 1560 to 1640)." In Elisabeth Leedham-Green and Theresa Webber, eds., *The Cambridge History of Libraries in Britain and Ireland*, I:489–519. Cambridge: Cambridge University Press, 2006.

Shakespeare, William. *Cymbeline*, ed. Martin Butler. Cambridge: Cambridge University Press, 2005.

———. *The Merchant of Venice*, ed. Jay L. Halio. Oxford: Clarendon Press, 1993.

———. *Othello*, ed. E. A. J. Honigmann. Walton-on-Thames: Thomas Nelson, 1997.

―――. *The Plays of William Shakespeare*, ed. Samuel Johnson and George Steevens, rev. Isaac Reed. 21 vols. London: J. Johnson et al., 1803.

―――. *Shakespeare's Poems*, ed. Katherine Duncan-Jones and Henry Woudhuysen. London: Thomson, 2007.

―――. *The Sonnets and A Lover's Complaint*, ed. John Kerrigan. Harmondsworth: Penguin, 1986.

―――. *The Winter's Tale*, ed. Jonathan Bate and Eric Rasmussen. Basingstoke: Macmillan, 2009.

Sherman, William H. *John Dee: The Politics of Reading and Writing in the English Renaissance*. Amherst: University of Massachusetts Press, 1995.

―――. "The Social Life of Books." In Joad Raymond, ed., *The Oxford History of Popular Print Culture*, I:164–71. Oxford: Oxford University Press, 2011.

―――. *Used Books: Marking Readers in Renaissance England*. Philadelphia: University of Pennsylvania Press, 2008.

Sherman, William H., and William J. Sheils, eds. "Prison Writings in Early Modern England." Special issue of the *Huntington Library Quarterly* 72 (2009).

Sherman, Stuart. *Telling Time: Clocks, Diaries and English Diurnal Form, 1660–1785*. Chicago: University of Chicago Press, 1996.

Sidney, Sir Philip. *The Countesse of Pembrokes Arcadia*. London: William Ponsonby, 1590.

―――. *A Critical Edition of the Major Works*, ed. Katharine Duncan-Jones. Oxford: Oxford University Press, 1989.

―――. *The Defence of Poesie*. London: William Ponsonby, 1595.

―――. *Sir P.S. his Astrophel and Stella*. London: Thomas Newman, 1591.

Sisson, C. J., ed. *Thomas Lodge and Other Elizabethans*. Cambridge, MA: Harvard University Press, 1933.

Slater, Master. *The New-Yeeres Gift: Presented at Court, from the Lady Parvula to the Lord Minimus*. London: N. and I. Okes, 1636.

Smith, Bruce R. *Shakespeare and Masculinity*. Oxford: Oxford University Press, 2000.

Smith, C. L., ed. *Calendar of Patent Rolls, 40 Elizabeth I (1597–1598): C66/11477–1492*. Kew: List and Index Society, 2009.

Smith, Helen. *Grossly Material Things: Women and Book Production in Early Modern England*. Oxford: Oxford University Press, 2012.

―――. " 'This One Poore Blacke Gowne Lined with White': The Clothing of the Sixteenth-Century Book." In Catherine Richardson, ed., *Clothing Culture: 1350–1650*, 194–208. Aldershot: Ashgate, 2004.

―――. " 'Rare Poems Ask Rare Friends': Popularity and Collecting in Elizabethan England." In Andy Kesson and Emma Smith, eds., *The Elizabethan Top Ten: Defining Print Popularity in Early Modern England*, 79–99. Farnham: Ashgate, 2013.

Smith, Helen, and Louise Wilson, eds. *Renaissance Paratexts*. Cambridge: Cambridge University Press, 2011.

Smith, Jeremy L. *Thomas East and Music Publishing in Renaissance England*. Oxford: Oxford University Press, 2003.

Smith, Margaret M., *The Title-Page: Its Early Development, 1460–1510*. London: British Library, 2000.

Smyth, Adam. *Autobiography in Early Modern England*. Cambridge: Cambridge University Press, 2010.

———. "'Shreds of Holinesse': George Herbert, Little Gidding, and Cutting Up Texts in Early Modern England." *English Literary Renaissance* 42 (2012): 452–81.

Smythe, Sir John. *Certen Instructions, Observations and Orders Militarie.* London: Richard Johnes, 1594.

Soll, Jacob. *The Reckoning: Financial Accountability and the Making and Breaking of Nations.* London: Allen Lane, 2014.

Spenser, Edmund. *The Shepheardes Calender.* London: Hugh Singleton, 1579.

Spicksley, Judith M., ed. *The Business and Household Accounts of Joyce Jeffreys Spinster of Hereford, 1638–1648.* Oxford: Oxford University Press for the British Academy, 2012.

Spierenburg, Pieter. *The Prison Experience: Disciplinary Institutions and Their Inmates in Early Modern Europe.* New Brunswick, NJ: Rutgers, 1991.

Spufford, Francis. *The Child That Books Built.* London: Faber and Faber, 2002.

Spufford, Margaret. *Small Books and Pleasant Histories: Popular Fiction and Its Readership in Seventeenth-Century England.* London: Methuen, 1981.

Stallybrass, Peter. "Books and Scrolls: Navigating the Bible." In Jennifer Anderson and Elizabeth Sauer, eds., *Books and Readers in Early Modern England,* 42–79. Philadelphia: University of Pennsylvania Press, 2002.

———. "Ephemeral Matter." Unpublished paper presented at the conference "Ephemerality and Durability in Early-Modern Visual and Material Culture," University of Cambridge, 24–25 May 2013.

———. "The Value of Culture and the Disavowal of Things." In Henry S. Turner, ed., *The Culture of Capital: Property, Cities and Knowledge in Early Modern England,* 275–92. New York: Routledge, 2002.

Stallybrass, Peter, and Joe Farrell. "Book-Tree-Leaf-Body." Unpublished e-mail conversation.

Stallybrass, Peter, and Zachary Lesser. "The First Literary *Hamlet* and the Commonplacing of Professional Plays." *Shakespeare Quarterly* 59 (2008): 371–420.

Stallybrass, Peter, et al. "Hamlet's Tables and the Technologies of Writing in Renaissance England." *Shakespeare Quarterly* 55 (2004): 379–419.

Standish, John. *A Discourse Wherin is Debated Whether the Scripture Should be in English.* London: R. Caly, 1554–55.

Steer, Francis W., ed. *Scriveners' Company Common Paper, 1357–1628, with a Continuation to 1678.* London: Company of Scriveners, 1968.

Stewart, Alan. "The Materiality of Early Modern Life Writing: The Case of Richard Stonley." In Zachary Leader, ed., *On Life-Writing,* 161–79. Oxford: Oxford University Press, 2015.

Stewart, C. J. *A Catalogue of the Library Collected by Miss Richardson Currer, at Eshton Hall, Craven, Yorkshire.* London: J. Moyes, 1833.

Stewart, Garrett. *The Look of Reading: Book, Painting, Text.* Chicago: Chicago University Press, 2006.

Stone, Lawrence. *An Elizabethan: Sir Horatio Palavicino.* Oxford: Clarendon Press, 1956.

Stout, Felicity Jane. *Exploring Russia in the Elizabethan Commonwealth: The Muscovy Company and Giles Fletcher, the Elder, 1546–1611.* Manchester: Manchester University Press, 2015.

Stow, John. *A Survay of London.* London: John Wolfe, 1598.

———. *A Survay of the Cities of London and Westminster,* rev. John Strype. London: A. Churchill et al., 1720.

———. *A Survay of London.* London: Nicholas Bourn, 1633.

Strigelius, Victorinus. *Part of the Harmony of King Davids Harp,* trans. Richard Robinson. London: John Wolfe, 1582.

Stubbes, Philip. *The Anatomie of Abuses*. London: Richard Jones, 1583.

Sullivan, Ceri. *The Rhetoric of Credit: Merchants in Early Modern Writing*. London: Associated University Presses, 2002.

Sutcliffe, Matthew. *An Answere to a Certaine Libel Supplicatorie*. London: Christopher Barker, 1592.

Sutton, Christopher. *Disce vivere. Learne to Live. A Brief Treatise of Learning to Live*. London: Elizabeth Burby, 1608.

Sylvester, Josuah. *Monodia*. London: Peter Short, 1594.

————. *The Wood-mans Bear*. London: Thomas Jones and Laurence Chapman, 1620.

————, trans. *Bartas: His Devine Weekes and Workes*, trans. Josuah Sylvester. London: Humfrey Lownes, 1605.

————, trans. *Du Bartas his Divine Weekes, and Workes: with a Compleate Collectio[n] of all the other most Delight-full Workes Translated . . . by . . . Josuah Sylvester Gent*. London: Humphray Lownes, 1621.

————, trans. *Du Bartas his Divine Weekes, and Workes: with a Compleate Collectio[n] of all the other most Delight-full Workes Translated . . . by . . . Josuah Sylvester Gent*. London: Robert Young, 1633.

Syson, Luke, and Dora Thornton. *Objects of Virtue: Art in Renaissance Italy*. London: British Museum, 2001.

Tankard, Paul. "Reading Lists." *Prose Studies* 28 (2006): 337–60.

Taverner, Richard. *The Second Booke of the Garden of Wysedome*. London: Richard Bankes, 1539.

Taylor, Charles. *Sources of the Self: The Making of Modern Identity*. Cambridge: Cambridge University Press, 1989.

Terpening, Ronnie H. *Lodovico Dolce, Renaissance Man of Letters*. Toronto: University of Toronto Press, 1997.

Thomas, Sidney. "Foreign to the Company." *Library*, 5th ser., 3 (1948): 186–92.

Thornton, Dora. *The Scholar in His Study*. New Haven: Yale University Press, 1997.

Thorpe, Nick. "The Love of Stuff." https://aeon.co/essays/we-should-love-material-things -more-than-we-do-now-not-less.

Thucydides. *The Hystory Writtone by Thucidides the Athenyan*. London: William Tylle, 1550.

Tigurinus, Chelidonius [pseud.]. *L'histoire de Chelidonius Tigurinus sur l'institution des princes chrestiens, & origine des royaumes*, trans. Pierre Boaistuau. Paris: V. Sartenas, 1559.

————. *A Most Excellent Hystorie, of the Institution and Firste Beginning of Christian Princes*. London: Henry Bynneman, 1571.

Tomita, Soko. *A Bibliographical Catalogue of Italian Books Printed in England, 1558–1603*. Farnham: Ashgate, 2009.

Tomlin, Rebecca. "A New Poem by Arthur Golding?" *Notes and Queries* 59 (2012): 501–5.

Torrentinus, Hermannus, et al. *Elucidarius poeticus*. Basel: Nicolaus Brylinger, 1544.

Tortorel, Jean, and Jacques Perissin. *Tableaux ou histoires diverses*. Geneva: Nicolas Castellin and Pierre Le Vignon, 1570.

Tudor, H. "*L'institution des princes chrestiens*: A Note on Boaistuau and Clichtove." *Bibliothèque d'Humanisme et Renaissance* 45 (1983): 103–6.

Tudor-Craig, Pamela, et al. *"Old St Paul's": The Society of Antiquaries' Diptych, 1616*. London: London Topographical Society, 2004.

Turner, William. *The First and Seconde Partes of the Herbal of William Turner Doctor in Phisick*. Cologne: Heirs of Arnold Birckman, 1568.

Twyne, Thomas. *The Schoolemaster*. London: Richard Jones, 1576.

Tyndale, William. *An Exposicion uppon the v. vi. vii. Chapters of Mathew.* Antwerp?: J. Grapheus?, 1533?

Udall, Nicholas. *Floures for Latine Spekynge Selected and Gathered oute of Terence.* London: Thomas Berthelet, 1534.

Upton, Penelope. "Change and Decay: The Warwickshire Manors of the Bishop of Coventry and Lichfield from the Late Thirteenth to the Late Sixteenth Centuries." Unpublished doctoral thesis, University of Leicester, 2002.

Usher, Brett. "The Fortunes of English Puritanism: An Elizabethan Perspective." In Kenneth Fincham and Peter Lake, eds., *Religious Politics in Post-Reformation England: Essays in Honour of Nicholas Tyacke,* 98–112. Woodbridge: Boydell, 2006.

Venn, John, and J. A. Venn, eds. *Alumni Cantabrigienses.* Cambridge: Cambridge University Press, 1924.

Vicary, Thomas. *The Englishemans Treasure, or Treasor for Englishmen with the True Anatomye of Mans Body.* London: John Perin, 1586.

Vine, Angus. "Commercial Commonplacing: Francis Bacon, the Waste-Book, and the Ledger." *English Manuscript Studies, 1100–1700* 16 (2011): 197–218.

Vitkus, Daniel. "Indicating Commodities in Early English Discovery Narratives." In Heidi Brayman, Jesse M. Lander, and Zachary Lesser, eds., *The Book in History, the Book as History: New Intersections of the Material Text,* 185–205. New Haven: Yale University Press, 2016.

Walker, Gilbert. *A Manifest Detection of . . . Diceplay.* London: Abraham Vele, 1555?

Wall, Wendy. *Recipes for Thought: Knowledge and Taste in the Early Modern English Kitchen.* Philadelphia: University of Pennsylvania Press, 2015.

Walsby, Malcolm. "Book Lists and Their Meaning." In Malcolm Walsby and Natasha Constantinidou, eds., *Documenting the Early Modern Book World: Inventories and Catalogues in Manuscript and Print,* 1–24. Leiden: Brill, 2013.

———. "The Library of the Breton Jurist and Historian Bernard D'Argentré in 1582." In Malcolm Walsby and Natasha Constantinidou, eds., *Documenting the Early Modern Book World,* 117–40. Leiden: Brill, 2013.

Walsham, Alexandra. "Jewels for Gentlewomen: Religious Books as Artefacts in Late Medieval and Early Modern England." In R. N. Swanson, ed., *The Church and the Book,* 123–42. Woodbridge: Boydell, 2004.

———. "The Pope's Merchandise and the Jesuits' Trumpery: Catholic Relics and Protestant Polemic in Post-Reformation England." In Jennifer Spinks and Dagmar Eichberger, eds., *Religion, the Supernatural and Visual Culture in Early Modern Europe,* 370–409. Leiden: Brill, 2015.

———. "The Spider and the Bee: The Perils of Printing for Refutation in Tudor England." In John N. King, ed., *Tudor Books and Readers: Materiality and the Construction of Meaning,* 163–90. Cambridge: Cambridge University Press, 2010.

Walsham, Alexandra, and Earle Havens, eds. "Catholic Libraries: An Introduction." In R. J. Fehrenbach et al., eds., *Private Libraries in Renaissance England: A Collection and Catalogue of Tudor and Early Stuart Book-Lists,* VIII:129–261. Tempe: Arizona Center for Medieval and Renaissance Studies, 2014.

Warner, J. Christopher. *Henry VIII's Divorce: Literature and the Politics of the Printing Press.* Woodbridge: Boydell, 1998.

Watson, Thomas. *Twoo Notable Sermons, Made . . . Before the Quenes Highnes, Concernynge the Reall Presence.* London: John Cawood, 1554.

Watt, Tessa. *Cheap Print and Popular Piety, 1550–1640.* Cambridge: Cambridge University Press, 1991.

Webster, John. *The White Divel.* London: Thomas Archer, 1612.

Welch, Evelyn. "New, Old and Second-Hand Culture: The Case of the Renaissance Sleeve." In Gabriele Neher and Rupert Shepherd, eds., *Revaluing Renaissance Art,* 101–19. Aldershot: Ashgate, 2000.

———. "Scented Buttons and Perfumed Gloves: Smelling Things in Renaissance Italy." In Bella Mirabella, ed., *Ornamentalism: The Art of Renaissance Accessories,* 13–39. Ann Arbor: University of Michigan Press, 2011.

Wells-Cole, Anthony. *Art and Decoration in Elizabethan and Jacobean England.* New Haven: Yale University Press, 1997.

West, Susie. "An Architectural Typology for the Early Modern Country House Library, 1660–1720." *Library,* 7th ser., 14 (2013): 441–64.

Whetstone, George. *The Rocke of Regard.* London: Robert Waley, 1576.

Whitaker, William. *Ad rationes decem Edmundi Campiani Iesuitae.* London: Thomas Chard, 1581.

Whitgift, John. *The Defense of the Aunswere to the Admonition against the Replie of T.C.* London: Humfrey Toye, 1574.

Whitney, Charles. " 'Usually in the Werking Daies': Playgoing Journeymen, Apprentices, and Servants in Guild Records, 1582–92." *Shakespeare Quarterly* 50 (1999): 433–58.

Whitney, Isabella. *The Copy of a Letter, Lately Written in Meeter, by a Yonge Gentilwoman: to her Unconstant Lover.* London: Richard Jhones, 1567?

Whittington, Robert. *De octo partibus orationis.* London: Wynkyn de Worde, 1514?

Wiburn, Perceval. *A Checke or Reproofe of M. Howlets Untimely Shreeching* [sic] *in her Majesties Eares.* London: Toby Smyth, 1581.

Willan, T. S. *The Muscovy Merchants of 1555.* Manchester: Manchester University Press, 1953.

———. *The Early History of the Russia Company, 1553–1603.* Manchester: Manchester University Press, 1956.

Williams, Franklin B. "The Bear Facts About Josuah Sylvester, the Woodman." *English Language Notes* (December 1971): 90–98.

———. "Robert Nicholson, A Minor Maecenas." *Notes and Queries,* n.s., 1 (1954): 11–13.

Wilson-Lee, Edward. *The Catalogue of Shipwrecked Books: Young Columbus and the Quest for a Universal Library.* London: William Collins, 2018.

Wirsung, Christof. *Praxis medicinae universalis, or, A Generall Practise of Physicke.* London: George Bishop, 1598.

Wizeman, William, S.J. "The Marian Counter-Reformation in Print." In Elizabeth Evenden and Vivienne Westbrook, eds., *Catholic Renewal and Protestant Resistance in Marian England,* 143–64. Abingdon: Routledge, 2016.

Wolf, Maryanne. *Proust and the Squid: The Story and Science of the Reading Brain.* Cambridge: Icon Books, 2008.

Wood, Diane S. *Hélisenne de Crenne: At the Crossroads of Renaissance Humanism and Feminism.* Madison, NJ: Fairleigh Dickinson University Press, 2000.

Wood, Tara Sue. " 'To the Most Godlye, Virtuos, and Mightye Princes Elizabeth': Identity and Gender in the Dedications to Elizabeth I." Unpublished doctoral dissertation, University of Arizona, 2008.

Woodbridge, Linda, ed. *Money and the Age of Shakespeare: Essays in New Economic Criticism.* Basingstoke: Palgrave Macmillan, 2003.

Woolgar, C. M. *The Culture of Food in England, 1200–1500*. New Haven: Yale University Press, 2016.

Woudhuysen, Henry. *Sir Philip Sidney and the Circulation of Manuscripts, 1558–1640*. Oxford: Oxford University Press, 1996.

Wrightson, Keith. *Ralph Tailor's Summer: A Scrivener, His City and the Plague*. New Haven: Yale University Press, 2011.

Yamey, Basil S. *Art and Accounting*. New Haven: Yale University Press, 1989.

———. "Oldcastle, Peele and Mellis: A Case of Plagiarism in the Sixteenth Century." *Accounting and Business Research* 35 (1979): 209–16.

Yates, Frances A. *John Florio: The Life of an Italian in Shakespeare's England*. Cambridge: Cambridge University Press, 1934.

Yeandle, Laetitia, ed. "Sir Edward Dering, 1st Bart., of Surrenden Dering and His 'Booke of Expences,' 1617–1628." www.kentarchaeology.ac/authors/020.pdf.

Yeo, Richard. *Notebooks, English Virtuosi, and Early Modern Science*. Chicago: University of Chicago Press, 2014.

Zarnowiecki, Matthew. *Fair Copies: Reproducing the English Lyric from Tottel to Shakespeare*. Toronto: University of Toronto Press, 2014.

Zins, Henryk. *England and the Baltic in the Elizabethan Era*, trans. H. C. Stevens. Manchester: Manchester University Press, 1972.

Index

Botolph Aldgate, 214; St. Botolph–
without– Bishopsgate, 221; St. Giles Without Cripplegate, 210; St. Gregory by St.
Paul's, 125; St. Katherine Colman, 144; St.
Mary Abchurch, 12, 162–66, 172, 175, 180–
81, 245; St. Mary le Strande, 210; St. Mary
Spital, 134; St. Michael Bassishaw, 238; St.
Paul's Cathedral, 99, 125; St. Peter Corn-
hill, 220–21; St. Sepulchres without New-
gate, 241; St. Thomas's, 276n52; Strand,
209, 212; Thames (river), 152; Tower, 225;
Tower Street, 195; Trinity Hall, 82; White-
cross Street, 210; Wood Street, 83
Loyola, Ignatius, 133
Ludwell, Thomas, 28, 256n30
Lumley, John, 1st Baron Lumley, 113, 255n49,
265n82
Luther, Martin, 133–34, 222
Lyly, John, 8, 10–11, 45

Mabb, John, 131
MacDurnan Gospels Binder, 116, 119
Machiavelli, Niccolò, 209, 222, 225
Malone, Edmund, 23–24, 255n9, 256n12
Manners, Edward, 3rd Earl of Rutland, 195
Manners, Elizabeth, 15th Baroness de Ros,
195–96
maps, 40, 90, 92–94, 178, 277n62
Margaret Roding (Essex), 12
Margery (servant), 43
Margues, Nicolas, 30
Marlorat, Augustine, 111, 134
Marlowe, Christopher, 37, 45, 241
Martin, Sir Richard, 233
Martyr, Peter, 85–86, 110, 134
Mary I (queen of England), 124, 127, 129, 131,
133, 199–200, 207
Mary I (queen of Scotland), 234
Maslen, R.W., 110, 225
Matal, Jean, 150
materiality, 5–11, 51, 91, 108, 180, 250
Maunsell, Andrew, 104–5, 108
May, Steven, 219–20, 224
Mazzuello, Antony, 144
McGann, Jerome, 7
McKenzie, D.F., 7
McLeod, Randall, 7
Mela, Pomponius, 183
Mellis, John, 56–57, 260n25
Melnikoff, Kirk, 241
Mercator, Gerhard, 94, 150

Merchant Taylors' Company, 213–14, 216–17,
220
Meres, John, 130
Meurier, Gabriel, 35
Mexía, Pedro, 102–3
Middleton, Thomas, 37, 99
Mildmay, Sir Walter, 93, 101, 201, 214
Miller, Daniel, 7, 26–27
Miller, Peter N., 249
Milton, John, 4
Moffett, Peter, 226, 239–40
Monarcho (jester), 28
Montaigne, Michel de, 51, 278n87
More, Sir Thomas, 35, 46, 103, 130–31, 133
Moss, Ann, 42
Moulton, Thomas, 139
Munday, Anthony, 99, 113, 276n56
Munster, Sebastian, 39
Muscovy Company, 146–51, 154–55, 165, 186
Musculus, Wolfgang, 86, 110, 134
Museum Minervae, 9
Mynors, John, 165–67, 170, 180
Mytham, James, 144

napery, 72, 84, 90, 101, 231
Nashe, Thomas, 47, 82
Neale, William, 200
Neile, Richard, 106
Neile, William, 106
Nelson, John, 257n57
Nevers, Duke of, 206
Newell, Charles, 106
Newfoundland, 234–35
Newman, Richard, 228, 284n12
news, 5–6, 19, 38, 53, 103, 113, 196, 232–33,
258n74, 266n106
Newsham, Bartholomew, 70–71
Newton (Lancs.), 12, 242
Nicholas of Lyra, 85
Nicolson, Benjamin, 175, 178
Nicolson, George, 276n58
Nicolson, Margaret, 165
Nicolson, Martha Carrell, 175, 178–80
Nicolson, Robert, 17, 173–*Dodecameron*,
190–96
Nicolson, William, 165
Norden, John, 113, 178–79
Norton, Thomas, 222
Nowell, Alexander, 103, 134, 137
Nuremberg Chronicle, 86–87, 102, 110

Acknowledgments

This book has been a long time in the making, and I end it with a weight of debt that could easily land me in the Fleet prison. It would be impossible to list all those who have provided help, encouragement, references, and advice along the way. You know who you are, and I am profoundly grateful to you all.

Special thanks are due to the Cambridge Humanities Research Grant Scheme, which gave me funding to employ two research assistants to develop the project at an early stage. Dunstan Roberts did some excellent detailed analysis of the journals and tracked down innumerable documents in the labyrinthine recesses of the National Archives. Harriet Phillips explored the material culture of the Aldersgate Street inventory and greatly expanded my understanding of Stonley's domestic spaces. Conversations shared and conferences convened with Lucy Razzall had a powerful influence on my sense of how matter matters. John Paul Ghobrial's zeal for microhistory kept me going during my more microscopic moments, and Andrew Zurcher's unflagging encouragement was hugely important to me. My colleagues and students on the "Material Renaissance" paper in Cambridge have done much to shape the thinking in this book, as have the graduate students with whom I discussed materiality on the Renaissance M.Phil. Seminar and conference audiences in Cambridge, Edinburgh, Leeds, London, Oxford, Montpellier, Venice, and York, together with several meetings of the Renaissance Society of America, forced me to get my arguments into some sort of shape and to see where the biggest holes lay.

I would never have completed this project without the help of Alan Nelson, who generously shared his transcription of the Stonley journals; I am also grateful to the editors of the wonderful *Private Libraries in Renaissance England* website for identifying so many items in his collections and providing a referencing system for the library. Elisabeth Leedham-Green shared with me an early transcription of the Stonley booklist and devoted a memorable morning to the effort to crack some tough legal documents. Penelope Upton supplied early archival references to the Stonleys in Warwickshire over lunch in Bishop's Itchington. Angela McShane very generously workshopped the 1597 inventory with her MA students at the V&A, teaching me a great deal in the process. Heartfelt thanks are also due to the library staff, who tolerated my innumerable request slips with such good humor, and in particular to the staff of the Cambridge University Library Rare Books Room, who bore the brunt. Renae Satterley at the Middle Temple, Robert MacLean at Glasgow, and Heather Wolfe at the Folger are just a few of many librarians whose assistance went well beyond the call of duty.

Finally, I would like to express my thanks to my children, Daniel and Benjamin, for their benign bemusement; and to Mary, for everything.